TRANSFORMING CRIMINAL JUSTICE

D1563320

Transforming Criminal Justice

An Evidence-Based Agenda for Reform

Edited by

Jon B. Gould *and* Pamela R. Metzger

NEW YORK UNIVERSITY PRESS
New York

NEW YORK UNIVERSITY PRESS
New York
www.nyupress.org

References to Internet websites (URLs) were accurate at the time of writing. Neither the author nor New York University Press is responsible for URLs that may have expired or changed since the manuscript was prepared.

Library of Congress Cataloging-in-Publication Data
Names: Gould, Jon B., editor. | Metzger, Pamela R., editor.
Title: Transforming criminal justice : an evidence-based agenda for reform / edited by Jon B. Gould and Pamela R. Metzger.
Description: New York : New York University Press, [2022] | Includes bibliographical references and index.
Identifiers: LCCN 2022001989 | ISBN 9781479818808 (hardback) | ISBN 9781479818815 (paperback) | ISBN 9781479818822 (ebook) | ISBN 9781479818839 (ebook other)
Subjects: LCSH: Criminal justice, Administration of—United States—History—21st century. | Criminal courts—United States. | Courts of special jurisdiction—United States.
Classification: LCC HV9950 .T668 2022 | DDC 364.60973—dc23/eng/20220526
LC record available at https://lccn.loc.gov/2022001989

New York University Press books are printed on acid-free paper, and their binding materials are chosen for strength and durability. We strive to use environmentally responsible suppliers and materials to the greatest extent possible in publishing our books.

Manufactured in the United States of America

10 9 8 7 6 5 4 3 2 1

Also available as an ebook

For Ann, Michael and Emily; Cole, Joe and Phoebe; and in honor of the many dedicated individuals and organizations working to reform a justice system that for too long has been subject to the whims of anecdote and polemic.

CONTENTS

Introduction

JON B. GOULD AND PAMELA R. METZGER

On August 26, 2020, two days after police had shot and paralyzed a Black man in Kenosha, Wisconsin, and a day after a white teenager carrying a semiautomatic rifle had killed two protestors decrying police actions there, the NBA's Milwaukee Bucks refused to take the basketball court in protest. "We are calling for justice," the Bucks' players said in a collective statement, urging Wisconsin lawmakers to reconvene and "take up meaningful measures to address issues of police accountability, brutality and criminal justice reform."[1]

The Bucks' message generated mass support across the league as arenas went dark for three days during the NBA playoffs. When play resumed on August 29, it was accompanied by a joint statement from the league and the players union. Together, they announced a "social justice coalition . . . of representatives from players, coaches and governors . . . focused on a broad range of issues." Among these was "meaningful police and criminal justice reform."[2]

Police shootings and the Black Lives Matters protests certainly galvanized popular attention to the problems of the criminal justice system, but in many ways criminal justice reform was already "having a moment in U.S. politics."[3] As *Politico* magazine explained:

Until recent years, candidates usually competed to look tough on crime and paint their opponents as soft. But 2020 [was] different. Throughout the primary, Democratic candidates, including the nominee Joe Biden, devoted significant space on their platforms to their ideas for fixing the criminal justice system. And the Republican incumbent, Donald Trump, [ran] as a reformer too, touting a key legislative justice-reform achievement on his watch, the First Step Act.[4]

To anyone who lived through the 1980s and 1990s and the "Get Tough" period in American criminal justice policy,[5] the move to reform the justice system may appear as nothing less than miraculous. But this was not a change that occurred overnight. A combination of political organizing, lower crime rates, and popular frustration at inequitable treatment in the justice system moved the pendulum on justice policy.[6] At the center of this shift was also a rise in empirical research on the criminal justice system—a movement to understand "what works"[7] in practice and a desire for "evidence-based" solutions.[8]

Evidence-based practice (EBP) is hardly a new concept. Employed initially in medicine, "EBP is the objective, balanced, and responsible use of current research and the best available data to guide policy and practice decisions."[9] Put another way, rather than relying on anecdotes, collective assumptions, or even a sense of "the way things have always been," EBP bases criminal justice policy on the results of social scientific research. If studies indicate that crime is situated at particular "hot spots," such as outside convenience stores or shopping malls and at a particular time of day, then law enforcement will be both more effective and efficient if officers deploy to those areas and times rather than patrolling across town.[10] If imprisonment alone fails to address drug addiction and even feeds further crime, then alternative interventions are necessary.[11] And, if public defense attorneys are unable to provide effective representation because their caseloads are too high or they cannot obtain investigative assistance, then additional resources are needed to protect the constitutional guarantee of due process.[12]

This is a remarkable turn in justice policy, and the opportunity for reform has only grown as more political and justice leaders espouse support, media coverage draws attention, and public protest keeps up the pressure. At such a moment, it is important that reform be guided by research and not impulse. New measures should reflect what works rather than reinforce anecdotes or advance assumptions.

This is true regardless of ideology. One may believe strongly in retribution, convinced that the justice system should enforce "an eye for an eye." However, if mass incarceration makes the United States an outlier among other nations with little advantage to public safety, it is difficult to see what the advantages are to taxpayers, public safety, and the general welfare. By the same token, the call to decriminalize drug use is appealing to many. But before doing so, it is essential to understand which substances, if any, serve as a gateway to serious addiction as well as theft or other crime to support that habit. For years, "law and order" and "getting tough on crime" have become throwaway lines in political campaigns to scare voters into acting on emotion rather than reason. With the country now in a period of criminal justice realism—the public and policy makers seemingly willing to examine the workings of the justice system with a clear eye—it is all the more important that research light the way forward to reform.

Purpose of the Book

This book provides a road map for those who want to change the face of American criminal justice. It addresses pressing problems facing the criminal justice system and offers a blueprint of initiatives for reform. Using lessons gleaned from empirical research, the book provides policy makers, practitioners, academics, and interested lay people a plan for how and why to reform the criminal justice system.

The book brings together many of the nation's top criminologists, legal researchers, and practitioners to explore and address essential issues of concern to reform the United States criminal justice system. Some topics—such as prosecutorial discretion and defense inadequacies—will likely be familiar. Others, including the victimization of marginalized people, rural justice, and sentinel events initiatives, may surprise readers, since these issues do not garner as much media attention. In each case, the topics and recommendations are informed by reliable research.

This collection is not simply a compendium of "what smart researchers think about the justice system"; neither is it a rumination on the potential contours of the criminal justice system. Broad theorizing is important, and we are admirers of those scholars who explore the theoretical underpinnings of the criminal justice system.[13] But if they prescribe remedies for the justice process, their arguments are often normative rather than based in research. The same can be true for the policy prescriptions of politicians,[14] who sometimes seek a solution for a perceived crisis without understanding the source of the problem or the ramifications of the proposed remedy.

This book, then, is for the reader looking to fill the gap between highly theoretical works that examine the criminal justice system from the 30,000-foot level and prescriptive policy proposals that offer a series of reforms without providing context or explaining the basis for reform. Assembled here is an empirically grounded account of what is broken in the criminal justice system as well as a blueprint for how it can and should be addressed. Part translation of scholarly research, part account of the justice system's workings and failings, and part agenda for action, the book aims to educate and move readers to effect change.

Overview of the Book

The collection addresses thirteen significant issues in justice reform, starting from a suspect's first interaction with the police and continuing to sentinel events review, in which justice practitioners can learn from mistakes that may occur in cases. For each issue, we address topics in which there is research to guide reform. We do not claim that these issues are exclusive or that reformers should fail to look to other proposals for action. Indeed, as we write this book, calls to "defund the police" have gained traction. Such proposals may be worthy of consideration, but as of yet there is little research to explain what happens when municipalities limit the reach of their police forces or transfer law enforcement functions to other agencies.[15] We recognize there is a bit of a chicken-and-egg conundrum here. How can one recommend an initiative without the willingness first to test and then evaluate an intervention? But among the proposals advanced for criminal justice reform, we aim to focus attention on those already established by research. The ideas in this book have been proven to work. There is little additional field testing to be done, theories to be explored, or trial balloons to be floated. The ideas offered here can—and should—be implemented.

That is not to say that the path to reform is straightforward. As the contributors here explain, evidence-based reform is an iterative process. One takes initial research on the criminal justice system and applies it to novel circumstances or in broader contexts. Those results are then assessed, and analysis from the first wave of intervention forms the basis for new initiatives. Along the way, proposals that initially seemed promising may prove to be unsuccessful, or the unforeseen costs of an intervention may be too great. Moreover, research findings may bump up against assumptions or anecdotal understandings, some built up over years.

This can occur at the highest levels of government. When Jeff Sessions took over as United States Attorney General in 2017, he sought to revive the DARE program, an antidrug curriculum begun in the 1980s, even though the National Criminal Justice Reference Service had told Congress in 1998 "the program did not reduce substance abuse."[16] Perhaps Sessions, a product of the years when First Lady Nancy Reagan famously urged youth to "Just Say No" to drugs, simply wished DARE to work. As he told a conference of counselors, "In recent years, people have not paid much attention to that message, but they are ready to hear it again."[17]

Evidence-based reform, then, is not easy; neither are the recommendations contained in the following chapters a cure-all. Rather, these measures represent a sound starting point. They help clear away options that are unlikely to work and will focus policy makers and practitioners on options for which there is evidence of success. Almost as important, they seek to set a standard in which criminal justice policy-making is based on, or at least informed by, evidence and research. The consequences of criminal justice interventions and the costs of error are too high to premise policy-making on hunches, assumptions, or even whims. Instead, justice officials should look to research, evidence, and sober analysis to guide their behavior.

As the contributors to this book take up their respective topics, they aim to follow a similar structure. Authors describe a problem or a series of problems that confront the criminal justice system. They explain the significance of those problems, discuss the research that clarifies the issues, and offer measures to address the problems. The chapters are both educational and prescriptive, helping readers to understand *what* is plaguing the criminal justice, *why* it is a problem, *how* it can be addressed, and *who* should do it.

Although confronting multiple issues, the authors also converge on common themes. Foremost is the conclusion that the American criminal justice system is riddled with weaknesses that cause harm and require greater accountability. Whether these problems are the unintended consequences of a fair-functioning process or the essential quality of a carceral state finds different perspectives among the contributors, as does the scope of reforms recommended. To some authors, the solution is to eliminate entire processes, such as cash bail, that have been central to the justice system. To others, the response is new technologies—such as police body-worn cameras—or post hoc review of known errors. Even as the prescriptions in this book are based on empirical evidence, the reader is left to consider the scope of response required.

Race, Class, Research, and Reform

The contributors also examine racial, ethnic, and economic inequities, which permeate the entire criminal justice system. These issues are woven into each chapter in the book. They may be as distinct as disparities in sentencing patterns or as subtle as the implicit biases that judges bring to postconviction appeals. These are insidious problems that require attention, and many of the proposals offered in the ensuing chapters seek to address these inequities in the criminal justice system while also reforming other problems. For example, prohibiting prosecutors from considering a suspects' prior record in charging not only relegates criminal history to the sentencing phase of a case where it belongs but also may reduce the likelihood that minority defendants, who themselves may have been subject to disproportionate policing in the past, are not further penalized. The issues are intertwined in charging, just as race, ethnicity, and poverty intersect with so many areas of criminal justice policy. Reform of the criminal justice system must keep these concerns at the forefront of consideration.

We recognize two interrelated critiques of our approach. The first involves arguments that the criminal justice system is so stained by inequities rooted in race and economic status that the solution must be to tear it down, not offer reforms. Those arguments often take the form of calls to defund police or abolish the criminal justice system entirely. At the same time, even many abolitionists concede that people who are subject to police overreach still seek the protection of the justice system;[18] know from experience that building alternative ways to prevent harm and promote safety is a large and long-term challenge; and remain open in the interim to "non-reformist reforms," or improvements to the criminal justice system that can gradually reduce reliance on that system.[19]

We further acknowledge critiques that describe research on the justice system as "normative," influenced by "institutional biases [of] who studies, what gets studied, how it gets studied, and how results are interpreted."[20] We cannot depend on even empirical research for change, these critics charge, as the results only reinforce existing power structures in which the "rich get richer and the poor get prison."[21] We hardly disagree that the criminal justice system is inequitable; indeed, reams of research—much of it offered in this book—underscore that point. We also agree that social science research is not purely "objective"—a point established by the postmodernists decades ago. Among other constraints, research on the criminal justice system is subject to the types of topics and researchers that receive funding. But those sources and researchers have become increasingly diverse since the 1980s, to the point where we are now treated to a range of studies that incorporate a variety of perspectives and experiences into analyses of multiple aspects of the criminal justice system.[22] We strongly believe that components of this growing body of research are sufficiently reliable to guide policy and that the desire for perfection should not blind us to the important lessons this research offers.

The Chapters

The chapters aim to follow the path of a case through the criminal justice system, starting with research to improve police practices, following to prosecutor behavior, criminal defense, bail, sentencing, and corrections. From there, the book takes the reader to a series of issues that are central to the goal of improving the justice system. Authors address the needs of victims, the threat of firearm violence, the difficulties of reentry, the varying priorities of rural and urban justice systems, the interplay between the civil and criminal justice systems, the scourge of wrongful convictions, and the rise of sentinel events review.

Chapter 1: Policing and Body-Worn Cameras

The book begins with a chapter on policing and body-worn cameras (BWCs), authored by Professors Michael White of Arizona State University and Aili Malm of California State University, Long Beach. As

White and Malm explain, the use of police body-worn cameras (BWCs) expanded rapidly during the 2010s in response to allegations of police misbehavior and excessive use of force. Early research associated the cameras with many positive effects, including reductions in the use of force and citizen complaints, quicker prosecutions, and increased perceptions of procedural justice among citizens. However, more recent research demonstrates that BWCs do not guarantee positive outcomes. There has also been strong resistance to BWCs in some jurisdictions, and the costs of a BWC program are significant both in the short and long terms.

The mixed story on BWCs raises questions about their future in twenty-first-century policing. Should police departments start a new BWC program? Should departments that already have a BWC program continue to use the cameras? White and Malm argue forcefully that BWCs should become a routine feature of policing today. The coauthors review a range of outcomes to demonstrate the multifaceted value of cameras for police departments and explain why BWCs work in some contexts and not in others. They conclude with a clear, evidence-based recommendation that police should adopt body-worn cameras.

Chapter 2: Prosecutors and Charging

If police are the first step in the criminal justice system, the next step in case processing involves prosecutors, who are perhaps the most powerful and least understood actors in the criminal justice system. Of prosecutors' work, charging has been the least studied and yet crucially important stage. In this chapter, Professors Jon Gould of the University of California, Irvine and Belén Lowrey-Kinberg of St. Francis College, in collaboration with Rachel Bowman of Arizona State University, open a window on prosecutors' charging decisions. Discussing their own research, the authors explain how prosecutors approach new cases and describe the factors—some appropriate, others extralegal such as the background of suspects—that prosecutors employ in deciding whether to pursue cases and which charges to file. In the end, the coauthors offer three proposals and lessons for reform. Charging should be conducted by a specialized unit staffed by experienced prosecutors; training and supervision are essential to prevent disparate results based on prosecutors' backgrounds; and lasting reform requires cultural change in which career prosecutors, not necessarily self-styled "reformers," are the linchpins of success.

Chapter 3: Participatory Defense

The vast majority of defendants in criminal courts are represented by public defenders or assigned counsel, yet public defense is terribly underfunded and public defenders are overloaded. Defense lawyers meet their clients for the first time just minutes ahead of court proceedings. Caseloads are enormous, limiting attorneys' opportunities to prepare, and case processing encourages defendants to plead guilty rather than challenge the state's evidence. Many policy prescriptions have been offered to increase funding and reduce caseloads, but those measures focus on courts and lawyers as the locus of power and change.

This chapter discusses participatory defense, a community-organizing model for defendants, their families, and communities. Drawing on their own experiences creating a participatory defense hub and their research of client assessments, Raj Jayadev, a MacArthur "Genius" award winner, and Professor Janet Moore of the University of Cincinnati describe the advantages and challenges of participatory defense. As they explain, the initiative is part policy initiative and part movement, designed to improve public defense, rebalance power disparities that disproportionately harm low-income defendants and defendants of color, and reduce the footprint of the US criminal justice system that incarcerates a higher percentage of its citizens than do other industrialized nations. In the end, the authors argue that participatory defense will not only reform the criminal justice system but also empower citizens and communities to reduce reliance on that system as a solution to social problems.

Chapter 4: Abolishing Bail

Part of America's mass incarceration problem is driven by pretrial detention, as defendants—many of them persons of color—wait in jail because they cannot afford bail. Critics of the bail system in the United States have called for abolishing money bail and replacing it with an approach that actuarially assesses a person's risk. Under this measure, low-risk defendants would be released on their own recognizance, whereas most medium-risk and select high-risk defendants would be released ahead of trial with minimal conditions. Only the highest risk defendants would be detained pretrial. However, given the shortcomings of most pretrial assessment tools, a risk-based bail system would not meaningfully reform the current bail system, in which the poor are detained prior to adjudication, whereas people with means are able to buy their freedom pending trial.

Drawing on research conducted by themselves and others, Professors Christine Scott-Hayward of California State University, Long Beach and Henry Fradella of Arizona State University call for a right to unconditional bail in nearly all criminal offenses. Under this approach, courts could impose a narrow range of pretrial release conditions solely to ensure the accused's participation in subsequent court proceedings and mitigate substantial possibilities of harm to either the victim(s) or the public. Only a small minority of criminal defendants—those charged with serious crimes such as murder and sexual assault—would be eligible for pretrial detention. As provocative as this proposal may sound, the last round of reform to bail has not worked. Empirical research supports these new measures. Policy makers, prosecutors, defenders, and judges should follow the evidence.

Chapter 5: Revisiting Sentencing Reform

If bail reform will help reduce the jail population, then sentencing reform will do even more for prisons. Since the 1980s, the United States has been in the midst of an "imprisonment binge," as the prison population increased from about 300,000 to just over 1.6 million.[23] These dramatic increases were not due to increases in serious crime rates; in fact, the crime rate in the United States has declined steadily for decades.[24]

Most criminologists and legal scholars contend that changes in sentencing policies and practices fueled the growing use of imprisonment in the United States. Whether we are talking about mandatory minimum sentences, three-strikes sentencing provisions, or truth-in-sentencing statutes, the explosion in the prison population can be attributed primarily to past sentencing policies designed to increase the length and certainty of punishment.

A new wave of research casts doubt on the previous "get tough" period in American criminal justice and overly punitive sentencing policies that disproportionately affect racial and ethnic minorities. In their chapter, Professor Cassia Spohn, Megan Verhagen, and Jason Walker of Arizona State University critique twentieth-century sentencing policy and its impact on mass incarceration. The coauthors discuss the factors that motivated prior changes and the goals they were designed to achieve. Contending that past policy has produced inequitable and unjust sentencing outcomes, the three propose a series of sentencing reforms designed to undo the damage inflicted by the earlier changes and better align sentencing to the goals and needs of American criminal justice policy.

Chapter 6: Corrections and Recidivism

The evidence-based movement in criminal justice has also reached jails and prisons, where the theory and practice of corrections are now advanced through science. Policies and programs that work are given prominence, whereas those shown to be ineffective are discarded. However, when "what works" for corrections means "what works to reduce recidivism," policies and programs that do not directly reduce recidivism are discarded and thus any other benefits they could provide are lost.

There are multiple other criteria to measure correctional success, including the ways that programming affects inmates' behavior in prison, their physical and mental health, and their relations with correctional staff, among others. These alternative measures also center attention on the correctional setting, where more immediate interventions can be entertained and where improving the quality of inmates' lives and behavior also provides a means to reduce recidivism. Professor Kevin Wright, Stephanie Morse, and Madison Sutton of Arizona State University highlight the advances of the evidence-based corrections movement and discuss the shortcomings of recidivism as the sole measure of correctional success. Instead, they advocate a shared approach between prisons, nonprofit groups, industry, and the inmates themselves to improve lives and reduce crime through better correctional programming, employment opportunities, affordable housing, and a focus on physical and mental health.

Chapter 7: Reentry

If Wright, Morse, and Sutton offer a broad overview of correctional success, Kelly Orians and Troy Rhodes focus more discretely on the path back from prison to society. The majority of prisoners will eventually return to their communities. Otherwise known as "reentry," this process comes with multiple structural barriers and policy missteps, unwelcoming communities, and poor decisions that unfortunately make reentry a revolving door that sends up to three-quarters of the released back to prison within five years. Failed reentry affects more than individuals leaving incarceration—their children and families suffer. Their communities are not improved, and all US residents bear the tremendous financial and social burdens of individuals who are unable to reach their full potential as contributing community members while they cycle back and forth from incarceration. It is impossible to solve the problem of mass incarceration without addressing failed reentry and the racially and economically biased policies that fuel these disparities.

In this chapter, Orians, a law professor who has been the codirector of The First 72+, an organization that assists former prisoners with reentry, and Rhodes, a counselor with The First 72+ and himself a beneficiary of the program, propose a different approach to facilitate reentry. Rather than leave returning offenders to fend for themselves, Orians and Rhodes argue for community-engaged support that will assist returnees and their families and reduce the likelihood of reoffending. More specifically, the pair offer two bold proposals based on research and experience. First, they say, states should repeal policies that prevent returning prisoners from associating with former offenders and instead invest in community-based reentry services that are led by the formerly incarcerated. Second, they advocate for the creation of a tax-funded temporary guaranteed income (TIP) for the formerly incarcerated that would be available immediately upon release and administered by community-led nonprofits and local governments that are attuned to the needs and challenges facing those undergoing reentry. In perhaps the most provocative idea in this book, Orians and Rhodes provide evidence that TIP will improve the lives of former inmates and their families, facilitate long-term self-sufficiency, and reduce costs spent on prison.

Chapter 8: Invisible Victims

Crime, by definition, involves a victim, but some victims are more readily recognized and understood than others. Lesser-known victims—sometimes called "invisible victims"—often come from vulnerable and at-risk groups. American Indian women, for example, are at the highest risk of experiencing victimization and have been exposed to many different forms of trauma throughout history. These include forced relocation, boarding schools, sterilization, and even genocide.

In this chapter, Professors Kathleen Fox and Christopher Sharp, along with Kayleigh Stanek, Turquoise Devereaux, and Connor Stewart, all of Arizona State University, address the plight of invisible victims. Drawing on research about murdered and missing Indigenous women in North America, the coauthors explain how national and local policies fail to serve victims of crime and offer several recommendations—further research, additional funding, fixing jurisdictional challenges—to address the problems that face this lesser-known issue and underserved community.

Chapter 9: Firearm Violence

Firearm violence is a major public health concern in the United States. According to the Centers for Disease Control and Prevention, firearm injuries account for approximately 74% of all homicides.[25] Moreover, the majority of mass murders are committed with a firearm. Given these facts, the general public and some lawmakers are calling for strategies to reduce and prevent firearm violence.

In this chapter, Professor Jesenia Pizarro and Karissa Pelletier of Arizona State University join with Professor April Zeoli of Michigan State University and Anne Corbin to heed that call. They propose three evidence-based practices to reduce and prevent gun violence: (1) permit-to-purchase licensing laws; (2) firearm relinquishment for individuals prohibited from ownership; and (3) extreme risk protection orders. Drawing on studies that estimate the likely effects of these measures, the coauthors describe the merits of such proposals and advocate for the implementation of policies that will keep firearms from those at greatest risk of using them improperly and illegally.

Chapter 10: Rural Justice

Our national conversation about criminal justice often ignores the plight of rural communities. Federal datasets focus on the largest urban counties, and decades have passed since the National Institute for Justice last reported on rural criminal justice. Meanwhile, a shortage of lawyers practicing in communities has created an access-to-justice crisis.

In this chapter, Professor Pamela Metzger of Southern Methodist University takes up those challenges, defining rural criminal justice systems, explaining how and why they have been ignored, and exploring three approaches that would better serve their justice needs. As she explains, policy makers must fund and support research that gathers better and richer information about rural criminal justice reform, engage rural systems in criminal justice reform planning, and pursue promising, practical, and actionable strategies to recruit, train, and retain rural criminal lawyers.

Chapter 11: Interplay Between the Civil and Criminal Justice Systems

Our legal system categorizes civil and criminal issues into two distinct silos. As a result, the courts, procedural protections, the provision of legal services, and information about the legal system typically focus exclusively on one side or the other. Yet individuals' lived experiences do not fall cleanly along those same lines; people often experience multiple problems at once or have an interaction with one type of legal problem that implicates or gives rise to another.

The rigid line between civil and criminal legal issues prevents us from addressing all facets of an individual's situation in a single court system. Instead, we require that people have multiple interactions with civil and criminal court systems, which can drain both their time and their resources. It becomes harder for them to address or protect against civil consequences arising from a criminal charge or conviction. By failing to inform people engaged with one sphere of the system about legal problems in the other sphere, we lose critical opportunities for intervention and education—particularly among populations in need of assistance.

In this chapter, Professor Lauren Sudeall of Georgia State University urges legal service providers to minimize the separate treatment of civil and criminal issues and to collaborate to the greatest extent possible.

Although certain doctrinal distinctions may be beyond reach, policy makers can engage in more practical applications of this idea, including rethinking how to structure the resolution of legal issues within the court system, provide legal services, and disseminate legal education to individuals and communities.

Chapter 12: The Continuing Scourge of Erroneous Convictions

In 1989, Gary Dotson became the first man exonerated by post-conviction DNA testing. More than three decades later, more than 366 people have been exonerated by DNA testing, and hundreds more have been exonerated through other evidence of innocence. Today, DNA testing is commonly conducted before trial, problems like eyewitness error and false confessions are well known, and about half the states have taken affirmative steps to prevent these problems. Some prosecutors have even acknowledged the likely existence of wrongful convictions by establishing conviction integrity units to review past cases.

Despite those gains, we have failed to address one of the deepest systemic problems that DNA exonerations have flagged: the inability of the post-trial system to quickly and effectively rectify wrongful convictions. Our system has always assumed that the question of guilt or innocence was decided correctly at trial and that post-trial systems correct error. It also assumes that appellate judges are capable of spotting cases in which innocent people have been convicted.

In this chapter, Executive Director Shawn Armbrust of the Mid-Atlantic Innocence Project shows those assumptions are wrong. Drawing on case studies, Armbrust argues that postconviction procedural barriers keep innocent people in prison, as appellate judges continue to assume the infallibility of evidence we know can be flawed. We have yet to fix these issues, she says, and in some areas have made them worse. Armbrust explains the difficulties of correcting errors and offers a series of recommendations to right the process of exoneration.

Chapter 13: Learning from Sentinel Events

What should the justice system do when an error occurs? Pointing fingers and suing for damages may provide psychic or personal relief, but unfortunately those actions may not prevent the problem from occurring again. Instead, interest has gained momentum in a practice developed by the aviation and medical communities, which organize nonblaming, all-stakeholders, forward-looking reviews of error. Known as "sentinel event reviews," these analyses focus on avoiding repetition of system failures rather than punishing individuals. A new set of initiatives is moving forward, harnessing the frontline actors' intuitive sense that wrongful convictions, mistaken releases, "near misses," and a range of "high frequency, low impact" events are "organizational accidents" that are best approached through the lens of forward-looking accountability.

In explaining sentinel events review, this chapter turns to the initial advocates at the US Department of Justice: James Doyle and Maureen McGough. The coauthors describe what sentinel review entails, explain the problems it seeks to address, explore the burgeoning research on such review, and offer a series of recommendations for implementing sentinel review across the criminal justice system. Even as the remainder of this book offers recommendations to prevent errors, it is a maxim of human nature that mistakes will still occur. Sentinel events review seeks to learn from error and helps to transform the criminal justice system into an evolving process of continual reform.

A Note on Modern Criminal Justice Policy

The informed reader will know that evidence-based justice policy is a relatively recent phenomenon, tracing its roots to the late 1980s or early 1990s[26] but really taking hold in the first decade of the twenty-first century. To appreciate why a book like this is now possible, it is important to understand the trajectory of criminal justice policy-making during that period.

Congress, beginning in the early 1980s and lasting for three decades, "consistently made federal criminal justice policy more punitive."[27] Responding to a rise in drug crime, and convinced that "we can lock up our problems and punish our way out of social challenges,"[28] Congress in 1984 passed the Sentencing Reform Act, which, among other things, abolished federal parole. Two years later, it passed mandatory minimum sentences for drug crimes, and by the mid-1990s legislators had adopted the infamous 1994 Crime Bill, which created new crimes and increased

mandatory minimum penalties. Later congresses curtailed federal habeas corpus remedies for prisoners and limited judges' discretion to
impose reduced sentences.[29] As a result, federal sentencing became the
harshest among the industrialized nations. With states following suit,
the United States reached the highest per capita incarceration rate of
any country in the world, dwarfing even such totalitarian states as Turkmenistan and gang-ridden nations like El Salvador.[30]

Reform has not been immediate; neither did evidence-based practices arise initially to blunt or dilute the punitiveness of the American
criminal justice system. Rather, EBPs were proposed to evaluate the effectiveness of justice programs and policies. Seeking to answer "what
works," criminal justice researchers took to evaluating correctional
interventions and drug programming to assess the efficacy of existing
policy.

The move was part "modernist project . . . seeking to change and
improve the world"[31] and part follow-on to the creation of a national
data-gathering operation. The latter enterprise had begun as early as
1968, when Congress created the National Institute of Law Enforcement
and Criminal Justice, but it was not until 1979 and the establishment
of the National Institute of Justice (NIJ) that Congress truly invested
funds to "support[] a comprehensive agenda in criminal justice research,
[including] large-scale data gathering and analyses, experimental programs, evaluations, and dissemination efforts required to develop and
maintain a systematic research effort in criminal justice."[32]

With more data available, and policy makers and practitioners eager
to deploy their resources most effectively, criminologists turned to a series of meta-analyses, seeking to study correctional effectiveness and,
later, crime prevention. Perhaps the most famous initiative was a 1997
report funded by NIJ that examined "what works, what doesn't, [and]
what's promising" in preventing crime.[33] Commissioned by the US Attorney General in response to Congress's call to evaluate federal grants
for crime prevention, the report brought together some of the nation's
finest criminologists and established a new "tradition dedicated to the
advancement of EBP in criminological and criminal justice circles."[34]

Since then, "the movement toward the use of evidence-based practices has [swept] the criminal justice community."[35] Moving beyond
descriptive studies, criminal justice researchers have partnered with

practitioners to evaluate "state sentencing and corrections policy and practice,"[36] bail procedures, prosecutor charging, and drug treatment, among several other topics. The effects on policy have been profound. As President Barack Obama explained in a law review article near the end of his presidency: "Throughout my time in office, using an array of tools and avenues, I have pushed for reforms that make the criminal justice system smarter, fairer, and more effective at keeping our communities safe."[37] Among these measures were "bipartisan sentencing reform legislation reducing the crack-to-powder-cocaine disparity" and "important changes to federal charging policies and practices, the administration of federal prisons, and federal policies relating to reentry."[38]

At the state level, EBP has brought changes as well. Partially in response to research questioning the effectiveness of draconian penal policy, "more than half the states have adopted significant drug law reforms in recent years."[39] New York State reduced its harsh drug penalties, Michigan abolished automatic life sentences without parole for serious drug sales, and Texas expanded diversion programs for drug possessors.[40] Several states also have adopted "parole reforms that enable eligible inmates to earn 'good time' credits in order to accelerate their release dates and/or reduce the number of technical violators who are returned to prison."[41]

Perhaps most surprising, Congress in 2018 passed and President Donald Trump signed a bipartisan federal prison and sentencing reform bill. This legislation, the First Step Act, reduces sentences for certain drug offenses and expands a "safety valve provision [that] allows federal judges to sentence below the statutory mandatory minimum punishment for certain eligible offenders."[42] In addition, the act "includes a number of provisions aimed at reforming" the Federal Bureau of Prisons and its approach to correctional programming and drug treatment.[43] All of this can be tied back to early evaluation studies and the rise of EBP in criminal justice.

Why Employ EBP?

At the heart of evidence-based reform is the recognition that criminal justice decision-making is improved when it is grounded in "well-designed and implemented research," which can "better explore the impact of policies, programs, and daily practices."[44] Rather than relying on anecdotal reports or habitual attachments to "the ways things have always been," empirical research offers "valuable information for making more objective decisions" that help improve the effectiveness, efficiency, and fairness of criminal justice processes. "Benefits from these strategies include reduced victimization, better lives [for the public and offenders alike,] and cost savings from more efficient programs. Conversely, non-evidence-based interventions are at a higher risk of failing to produce desired outcomes or even worsening problems."[45] In fact, "the concepts and conclusions of some research studies have . . . been so thoroughly assimilated in policy and practice"—including lessons on rehabilitation, criminal investigation, pretrial release, policing staffing, and domestic abuse—that some of the officials charged with implementing these policies have "forgotten where they originated."[46]

This is not to say that EBP has been easy to implement in criminal justice. Unlike in medicine, which has been keen to adopt evidence-based practice, in the justice sector the link between scientific evidence and decision-making is not always direct. In medicine, "whether an intervention works depends on if it is empirically shown to eliminate or reduce illness or injury. Thus, it is widely accepted in the medical community that scientific standards are the primary, if not only, bases for interventions."[47] By contrast, in criminal justice, "scientific standards are considered relevant but not [always] dominant."[48] Justice leaders also must contend with legal precedent, not to mention "political or ideological appeal[s]" from elected officials or the public at large. Debates about criminal justice are played out in a broader arena that is influenced by "emotions, symbols, faith, belief, and religion." As such, successful reform does not turn simply on empirical research but "must [also] take into account changes in public 'mood' or emotions over time and be sensitive to different political and social cultures."[49]

Knowing which empirical method to employ can be challenging. Within the sociolegal research community, EBP is premised on "scientific methods." According to the US Office of Justice Programs, scientific evidence is expected to be objective, observable by others, based in fact, free of bias, replicable, and generalizable to individuals or groups outside those involved in the original study.[50] The accepted "gold standard" in empirical research is the randomized controlled trial (RCT), in which a group of research subjects is randomly assigned to receive a particular intervention or treatment while a control group is left unaffected. However, RCTs are difficult to implement in the justice setting, meaning that some questions must be examined through different empirical approaches. In court, for example, it would be unacceptable to assign one group of defendants a defense lawyer while another group was unrepresented so that researchers could assess the value of indigent defense. At other times it is difficult to convince a decision maker, like a judge selecting candidates for drug court, "to suspend their usual placement criteria in favor of random assignment to a particular program or intervention."[51]

For that matter, there can be disagreement about what counts as "evidence" in EBP. Certainly, quantitative statistics, like the number of crimes committed, sentence lengths, and recidivism rates, are recognizable to most as "data," but qualitative data can be useful too. Measures such as motorists' reactions to police stops, which form the basis of procedural justice, speak to the legitimacy of the justice system. Even case studies can offer lessons, such as when officials conduct a post hoc analysis of errors in the justice process. All of these forms of evidence appear in this book, and in our view all are valid bases for considering system reform. The key in EBP—and an issue for readers to consider as they weigh the evidence presented and assess the recommendations in the following chapters—is whether the information was collected transparently and fairly by those eager to learn from the evidence rather than pushing an ideological agenda.

Even when high-quality evidence can be amassed, there is the question of how much is enough to justify a change to justice practices. "Unfortunately, there is no single satisfactory answer." A more reasonable approach focuses "less on single evaluations and more on examining the magnitude and consistency of the evidence produced by multiple studies of specific programs and initiatives."[52] Even this may not be enough to convince some skeptics. Lawyers are known to reject "empirical information [as] irrelevant to the normative goals of criminal law and procedure," and judges, in particular, are often poorly "equipped to deal with complicated social scientific data."[53]

However, the response should not be to throw up one's hands and rely on instinct, individual perception, or assumptions, all of which have been shown to be susceptible to implicit biases.[54] Legal actors and policy makers need to draw on experts to assist in assessing and explaining empirical evidence. Indeed, "the use of empirical studies makes criminal justice decisions more transparent and allows us to hold decision makers accountable for their actions."[55]

That, ultimately, is the message of this book: *EBP makes criminal justice more transparent and allows society to hold decision makers more accountable.* Criminal justice is a profession,[56] a designation that carries with it higher responsibilities. Professionals should not make decisions about people's liberty, the community's safety, or the use of tax dollars by relying on anecdotal understandings or outdated assumptions. Evidence-based practice offers a better path to accomplish what is undoubtedly a shared goal: the prevention of harm. It provides a broader and deeper depiction of criminal justice processes in addition to a timely and accurate accounting of what is happening and what works. It also shines a light on the system's frailties and shortcomings—both the failure to achieve expected goals and the unfortunate (and hopefully unintended) consequences that create inequities. If we expect the public to accept and support the criminal justice system as the best way to prevent and address harm, if we seek to foster "higher levels of legitimacy [in that system and] greater compliance with the law,"[57] then we must be prepared to apply the latest and most reliable lens to the criminal justice system and pursue reform as the evidence leads us.

NOTES

1 National Basketball Association, "Milwaukee Bucks Players' Statement."
2 National Basketball Players Association, "Joint NBA and NBPA Statement."
3 Politico, "Biden vs. Trump."
4 Ibid.
5 Jones, "Failure of the 'Get Tough' Crime Policy."
6 Goodman, Page, and Phelps, *Breaking the Pendulum.*
7 National Institute of Justice, "Crime Solutions."
8 California Courts, "Evidence Based Practice."
9 Community Resources for Justice, "Implementing Evidence-Based Policy and Practice in Community Corrections."
10 Eck et al., *Mapping Crime: Understanding Hot Spots.*
11 Foundations Recovery Network, "Alternatives to Prison."
12 Judicial Conference, *2017 Report of the Ad Hoc Committee.*
13 Dolovich and Natapoff, eds., *New Criminal Justice Thinking.*

14 Brennan Center, *Ending Mass Incarceration*.
15 Ray, "What Does Defund the Police Mean and Does It Have Merit?"
16 Legaspi, "Attorney General Jeff Sessions Wants to Revive D.A.R.E. Program."
17 Ibid.
18 In the summer of 2020, at the very height of Black Lives Matters, a clear majority of "Black Americans [said] they wanted the police presence [in their neighborhoods] to remain the same." Gallup, "Black Americans Want Police to Retain Local Presence."
19 Forman, *Locking Up Our Own*.
20 Anonymous reviewer of this book.
21 Reiman and Leighton, *The Rich Get Richer*.
22 Among other forces, one may credit the creation of the Racial Democracy Crime and Justice Network and Latina/o/x Criminology among researchers, as well as the rise of donors such as the Open Society Foundations and Arnold Ventures that are willing to support critical research.
23 US Bureau of Justice Statistics, *Prisoners in 2017*.
24 Pew Research Center, "5 Facts about Crime in the U.S."
25 FBI, "2018 Crime in the United States."
26 The early progressive era of the 1920s sought to apply research in reforming many aspects of American life, including the criminal justice system. But the close partnership between researchers and practitioners, and their reliance on *empirical* evidence to determine "what works," is a more modern phenomenon.
27 Hopwood, "The Effort to Reform the Federal Criminal Justice System," 791.
28 Daniels, "What Prosecutors and Incarcerated People Can Learn from Each Other."
29 Hopwood, "The Effort to Reform the Federal Criminal Justice System."
30 In June 2021, the US rate was 639 prisoners per 100,000 inhabitants. El Salvador, which was in second place, had a rate of 562, and Turkmenistan, which was third, reported 552 prisoners per 100,000 inhabitants. Statista, "Countries with the most prisoners per 100,000 inhabitants."
31 Freiberg and Carson, "The Limits to Evidence-Based Policy," 154.
32 Petersilia, *The Influence of Criminal Justice Research*.
33 Sherman et al., "Preventing Crime."
34 Freiberg and Carson, 154.
35 Orchowsky, "An Introduction to Evidence-Based Practices," 2.
36 Ibid.
37 Obama, "The President's Role in Advancing Criminal Justice Reform," 813.
38 Ibid.
39 Greene and Mauer, *Downscaling Prisons*.
40 Subramanian and Moreno, *Drug War Détente*.
41 Beckett, Reosti, and Knaphus, "The End of an Era?," 240.
42 Hopwood, 795.
43 Ibid.

44 Johnson et al., 2018, 2.

45 Ibid.

46 Petersilia, *The Influence of Criminal Justice Research*, vi.

47 Johnson et al., "Use of Research Evidence by Criminal Justice Professionals," 3. That is the model *within* the medical community. As the push to inoculate Americans against the coronavirus has shown, the public may be a harder sell. The latter is also true in criminal justice policy-making.

48 Ibid.

49 Freiberg and Carson, 152.

50 Orchowsky, "An Introduction to Evidence-Based Practices," 6.

51 Ibid., 7.

52 Ibid., 9.

53 Meares, "Three Objections to the Use of Empiricism," 853.

54 Kang et al., "Implicit Bias in the Courtroom."

55 Ibid.

56 Miller and Brawell, "Teaching Criminal Justice Research."

57 Meares, "Three Objections to the Use of Empiricism."

1

Body-Worn Cameras as a Mechanism for Enhancing Police Accountability and Legitimacy

MICHAEL D. WHITE AND AILI MALM

Police in the United States are under significant scrutiny for their use of force, especially in cases involving unarmed African American men.[1] In 2014–2015, the deaths of Michael Brown, Eric Garner, Freddie Gray, and Walter Scott, among others, led to public outrage, riots in some cities, and widespread calls for police reform. More recently, the deaths of George Floyd, Breonna Taylor, and Rayshard Brooks have reignited national outrage over police use of force. These tragic deaths have led to global protests and legislative efforts to reform the police at the local,[2] state,[3] and federal levels.[4] There have even been calls to defund the police.[5] This unrest highlights the long-term, persistent undercurrent of racial injustice in American policing, demonstrated by a history of abuse of authority against Black and Hispanic citizens.[6] This history of racial injustice also represents a significant threat to minority citizens' perceptions of police legitimacy.[7] Tyler defined legitimacy as "a psychological property of an authority, institution, or social arrangement that leads those connected to it to believe that it is appropriate, proper, and just."[8] The value of legitimacy lies in how it shapes citizens' behavior, as people follow the law and obey the police because they believe it is the right thing to do.[9] Low reserves of legitimacy represent a direct threat to the core functioning of the police in our society because citizens' voluntary, self-regulatory behavior falters (perhaps best demonstrated by the recent protests against police following George Floyd's death).

In this chapter, we contend that body-worn cameras (BWCs) are an essential component of any reforms designed to restore police legitimacy. We organize the chapter into three sections.

First, we review the strongest evidence that BWCs have a positive impact on policing and policing legitimacy. That positive impact arises not only from police and citizen support for BWCs but also from BWCs' positive results, such as enhanced procedural justice, demonstrated reductions in the use of force and citizen complaints, and improved investigative and courtroom evidence. We believe this body of evidence supports the argument that BWCs are an evidence-based reform. According to a 2017 report by the United Kingdom College of Policing, evidence-based policing involves researchers and police creating, reviewing, and using the best available research to guide policy and practice.[10] We also contend that these positive outcomes set the stage for enhanced police legitimacy. Second, we explain the increasingly mixed body of evidence on BWCs, offering important context for understanding this research. And third, we highlight important considerations for planning and implementing successful BWC programs.

Background

In 2014, former President Barack Obama created the President's Task Force on 21st Century Policing. The Task Force held hearings to identify best practices and recommendations for enhancing police accountability and rebuilding community trust in police legitimacy.[11] The Task Force's final report, published in May 2015, highlighted police body-worn cameras as important tools for accomplishing those goals.[12]

Since 2015, thousands of law enforcement agencies in the United States (and abroad) have adopted BWCs.[13] There are several potential explanations for this widespread adoption. First, a diverse range of stakeholders, including citizens,[14] police leadership organizations,[15] and civil rights groups (including the ACLU),[16] support the use of BWCs. Indeed, several legislative police reform efforts as recently as 2022 have proposed mandatory BWC programs.[17] Second, since 2015, the US Department of Justice (DOJ) has awarded approximately $84 million in grants to more than 400 law enforcement agencies, resulting in the deployment of nearly 90,000 BWCs across the country.[18] Third, early research studies suggest that BWCs can reduce police use of force and citizen complaints[19] and enhance investigative and prosecution outcomes.[20] Several studies also report that BWCs can improve citizens' perceptions of procedural justice[21] and increase the procedural justice of officers' behavior.[22] These studies are especially noteworthy, as procedural justice is a primary mechanism for achieving police legitimacy.[23]

However, support for BWCs is not unanimous. First, recent research demonstrates that BWCs do not guarantee positive outcomes. Several studies document no impact on the use of force and citizen complaints.[24] One study even shows that BWCs are associated with increased rates of assaults on officers.[25] Second, in some jurisdictions, officers and police unions have strongly resisted BWCs.[26] Moreover, critics have raised several concerns about BWCs, most notably the potential for privacy violations (vis-à-vis officers and citizens), as well as cost and resource requirements. And third, some critics argue that as BWCs increase internal (departmental) and external (public) scrutiny of the police, officers may engage in de-policing.[27]

By 2017, national media headlines emphasized this skepticism: "The failure of police body cameras: (*Vox* in July 2017);[28] "Body cameras aren't working. So, what's next?" (*Huffington Post* in November 2017).[29] By 2020, the cynicism around BWCs had been amplified: "Police body cameras were supposed to build trust. So far, they haven't" (*Popular Science* in June 2020);[30] "There's a renewed call for police body cameras. Here's why that may not be the right solution." (CNN in June 2020);[31] "Body cameras are seen as key to police reform. But do they increase accountability?" (*PBS NewsHour* in June 2020).[32]

The persistent crisis in police legitimacy, the mixed research findings on BWCs, and the growing anti-BWC sentiment all raise a fundamental question: Should police departments start new BWC programs? We believe the answer is "yes," and we devote the remainder of this chapter to reviewing the evidence that supports this position.

Evidence Supporting the Adoption of Police Body-Worn Cameras

Advocates of police BWCs have made numerous claims about the value of cameras for police, citizens, and the criminal justice system. While the evidence for some of those claims is scant,[33] we focus on the claims for which the evidence is strong. As we discuss each claim, we explain how it supports our argument that BWCs create a pathway to enhanced police legitimacy.

Citizens Support BWCs

Many law enforcement agencies adopt BWCs because they want to create transparency, thereby improving their relationships with the communities they serve. Therefore, clear proof that citizens support BWCs is important evidence that BWCs can help restore police legitimacy. Several studies have concluded that, among the general population, there is strong support for BWCs.[34] A handful of studies have captured attitudes among civilians who have had BWC-recorded police encounters; the results are similarly positive.[35] For example, White and colleagues interviewed 279 citizens who had recent encounters with police officers in Tempe, Arizona.[36] More than 90% of those citizens agreed or strongly agreed that all Tempe officers should wear BWCs, and 80% agreed or strongly agreed that BWCs make officers behave more professionally and citizens act more respectfully. The same researchers report similarly positive results in Spokane, Washington.[37] For example, 77% of Spokane citizens said the benefits of BWCs outweigh their costs.

The evidence about how minority community members view BWCs is decidedly more complicated. Only a handful of studies have examined minority citizens' attitudes, and the vast majority of these studies have captured attitudes of Black citizens. Some research suggests that most Black citizens want police officers to wear cameras. For example, Graham and colleagues surveyed 1,000 African Americans and found widespread support for police BWCs.[38] However, other recent studies show more mixed results. Kerrison and colleagues interviewed 68 Black Baltimore residents about BWCs.

They concluded: "While support for the implementation of BWCs was mixed, even respondents who expressed support for the program were unsure of how officers might respond to the additional surveillance measures, as well as what would be done with officers who were caught on tape abusing their power or breaking the law."[39] In one of the few studies that captures both Black and Latino attitudes, Ray and colleagues reported that white citizens had less positive attitudes regarding BWCs than Black and Latino citizens: for example, 23.5% of white respondents agreed that BWCs will create transparency between police and citizens, compared to 60% of Black and 63.6% of Latino respondents.[40]

While the complex views of minority communities warrant further exploration (especially differences across Black and Latino populations), the available evidence suggests that most people—minorities citizens included—want police officers to wear cameras because they believe that BWCs will improve police behavior and citizens' behavior. In some cities, citizens' demands for BWCs—often made by advocacy groups or local government officials—have overridden police reluctance to adopt the technology.[41] On June 19, 2020, the governor of Colorado signed a bill mandating police BWCs throughout the state.[42] Arguably, BWCs have become a prerequisite for maintaining police legitimacy in the eyes of citizens.

Officers Support BWCs

Officer attitudes about BWCs also matter if they are expected to use the technology. Thirty-seven studies have explored officer perceptions of BWCs, either predeployment (N=9), postdeployment (N=11), or both (N=15).[43] The 37 studies measure officer perceptions across a wide range of topics, from general attitudes to very specific issues such as the impact of BWCs on police–community relations and the impacts on citizen behavior. Studies vary in the issues covered, however (e.g., a study may cover some issues but not others). For example, 28 studies report an overall measure of officer attitudes about BWCs, and the majority report positive perceptions (54%).[44] Moreover, 62% of studies report positive officer attitudes about the impact of BWCs on police–community relations.

While the research shows that officer attitudes vary quite a bit predeployment, studies that examine officer attitudes before *and* after deployment often report significant positive postdeployment changes.[45] In a three-agency study, Gaub and colleagues examined officers' pre- and postdeployment attitudes toward BWCs. They reported significant positive change in two of the three agencies: "Tempe and Spokane officers, overall, increasingly recognized the positive effects of BWCs, whereas Phoenix did not see this trend."[46]

Officer perception studies show that attitudes about BWCs also vary by issue.[47] For example, studies examining officer attitudes about the evidentiary value of BWCs report very positive police attitudes. Nineteen studies examine officer attitudes about BWCs and the quality of evidence, and 16 of 19 (84%) report positive police perceptions.[48] However, officers are much more negative in their views of how BWCs impact citizen behavior. Of the 24 studies examining officer attitudes about BWCs' impact on citizen cooperation and respect, only seven report positive officer perceptions. Some pre- and postdeployment studies also show this finding. In Tempe, officer agreement with the statement "citizens will become more cooperative" declined from 65.7% to 47.5% after the department deployed BWCs.[49]

Overall, officers support BWCs; any ambivalence or opposition they have often disappears once they begin wearing them. Officer acceptance of BWCs is crucial because it protects against implementation failures, most commonly illustrated by low camera activation rates. Research shows that activation rates are higher among officers who view the technology favorably.[50] High activation rates offer another opportunity to improve perceptions of police legitimacy. An officer's failure to record an incident—especially a critical incident such as an officer-involved shooting—can quickly erode community trust in the police. In contrast, providing the public with BWC footage of a critical incident can demonstrate transparency, thereby enhancing police legitimacy. Several police departments have created formal processes for releasing BWC footage of officer-involved shootings. For example, the Los Angeles Police Department (LAPD) releases critical incident video footage within 45 days of filming, intending specifically "to increase transparency with respect to the operations of the LAPD and in doing so[] foster greater public trust."[51] Officer activation of the BWC is a crucial first step in this process.

BWCs Reduce the Use of Force

As the crisis in policing centers on the use of force, BWCs have been promoted as a mechanism to curtail excessive force. In 2014–2015, police killings of Michael Brown, Freddie Gray, Walter Scott, Tamir Rice, and others led thousands of police departments across the country to adopt BWCs. In 2020, the deaths of George Floyd, Breonna Taylor, Rayshard Brooks, and others at the hands of the police reinvigorated the debate about whether BWCs reduce the use of force.[52]

What does the research tell us? Early studies linked BWCs to dramatic reductions in police use of force. The 2013 study of the police department in Rialto, California—the first randomized controlled trial of BWCs—reported that "shifts without cameras experienced twice as many incidents of force as shifts with cameras."[53] To test the durability of this effect, Sutherland and colleagues recently revisited the Rialto study and concluded that

> the impact of cameras had survived long after the experiment ended. Our interpretation is that once cameras and any associated changes in police practice are embedded as part of the operation, they simply became 'habit' for officers.[54]

Police departments in Las Vegas, Orlando, Spokane, Tampa, and Mesa, Arizona, also experienced notable declines in the use of force after they deployed BWCs.[55] Several recent studies, including one of the Washington, DC Metropolitan Police Department (DC Metro) observed no change in use of force after officers began wearing cameras.[56] Importantly, no studies have documented an increase in the use of force after BWC deployment.[57]

By the summer of 2021, 26 published studies or reports had examined the impact of BWCs on the use of force. Thirteen of those had documented notable or statistically significant declines following camera deployment.[58] Researchers have interpreted this finding in different ways. While Lum and colleagues assert that "these study findings do not reveal a definitive conclusion that BWCs can reduce officers' use of force,"[59] we are decidedly more positive about their significance. After all, nearly 60% of studies have documented postdeployment declines in the use of force. As we note elsewhere:

> There are no absolutes. What program or strategy is effective 100 percent of the time? Medications that are approved by the US Federal Drug Administration rarely cure every single human afflicted with a disease or ailment, and many medications produce a host of unintended side effects. Programming in criminal justice is no different. Programs that are considered evidence based, such as hot spots policing, are not foolproof. Why should we expect any different with police BWCs?[60]

Moreover, two recent national-level studies have shown that BWCs reduce use of force. Miller and Chillar examined national trends in BWC adoption and concluded that "the acquisition of BWCs may reduce fatalities arising from police activities, at least in the early years following their introduction."[61] Williams and colleagues conducted a cost-benefit analysis of BWCs and concluded that "our analysis suggests the ratio of benefits to society from adoption of BWC to the costs is on the order of 5 to 1."[62]

The dynamics driving this reduction in the use of force are unknown. Advocates of BWCs highlight the civilizing effect of cameras on behavior, arguing that deterrence or social awareness theory accounts for this change: when people realize that they are being observed, they change their behavior.[63] Are these changes in officers' behavior, citizens' behavior, or both? As we discuss later in this chapter, the answer remains elusive. Regardless, BWCs' potential to reduce the use of force—and to hold officers accountable for excessive use of force—is among BWCs' most significant benefits.

The high-profile tragedies of 2014, 2015, and 2020 demonstrate the vulnerability of police legitimacy to a single use-of-force incident. If BWCs deliver on their promise of reducing the use of force, they are a critical component of a larger effort to achieve and sustain police legitimacy.[64]

BWCs Reduce Complaints Against Officers

A reduction in citizen complaints is one of the most commonly cited benefits of BWCs. We have contended elsewhere that citizen complaints, regardless of how they are adjudicated, are an important indicator of officer performance.[65] Much like use-of-force events, citizen complaints are a direct threat to police legitimacy. The larger the number of complaints, the larger the threat. Moreover, the failure to properly investigate citizen complaints and hold officers accountable for their behavior also jeopardizes legitimacy. Derek Chauvin, the officer who knelt on George Floyd's neck for nearly nine minutes, had 18 prior complaints lodged against him, but only two resulted in discipline. Multiple BWCs, including Chauvin's own device, captured George Floyd's death.

In fact, the footage from Chauvin's BWC likely expedited the department's decision to fire the officers involved and the prosecutor's decision to file homicide charges. It is unclear whether BWC footage exists for Chauvin's other encounters that generated complaints.

Research strongly suggests that BWCs reduce citizen complaints. The Rialto study documented a nearly 90% reduction in citizen complaints following BWC deployment,[66] and those effects have persisted.[67] Early BWC studies in Mesa, Arizona, and Orlando also reported large reductions in complaints.[68] The meta-evaluations conducted by Flight and colleagues similarly concluded that BWCs lead to reductions in complaints against officers.[69] Lum and colleagues concur, noting that "researchers have mostly found that officers wearing BWCs receive fewer reported complaints than do those that are not wearing the cameras."[70]

Again, the research does not shed light on the causes of this reduction in complaints. Do BWCs produce better behavior among officers, thereby leading to fewer complaints? Or is improved citizen behavior the underlying cause? Certainly, some portion of the reduction in complaints is explained by changes in citizen reporting patterns—specifically a reduction in frivolous complaints. That is to say, citizens are less likely to file false or untruthful complaints if they realize that their police encounters are being recorded.[71]

While more research is necessary, these findings are powerful, strongly demonstrating that BWCs can reduce citizen complaints against police. And, as noted above, BWCs can also provide valuable evidence to investigate those complaints. Both are important pathways to police legitimacy.

BWCs Improve the Quality of Investigations for Police, Prosecutors, and Defendants

Another benefit of BWCs is their ability to improve the collection of evidence in investigations. BWCs can provide audio and video evidence that allows for more efficient and accurate resolution of citizen complaints against officers and, further downstream, criminal cases in the court system. As compared to traditional written police reports, BWCs provide a more accurate account of incidents, limited only by the cameras' video and audio ranges. While these benefits are supported anecdotally by statements from officers, prosecutors, and judges, only a handful of studies have tested these claims. Studies about reductions in investigative time are particularly scant.[72] Braga and colleagues studied this issue in the police department in Las Vegas—the only formal cost-benefit analysis of BWCs to date—evaluated the department's investment of nearly $900,000 per year, and found a cost savings of nearly $4 million per year, the vast majority of which came from a reduction in time spent investigating citizen complaints.[73] The authors also estimated that "BWCs save over $6,200 in officer time spent investigating an average complaint, as compared to complaint investigations for officers without BWCs."[74] The Toronto Police Service found that the time required to investigate complaints against officers dropped notably if BWC footage was available, implying cost savings.[75] Clearly, we need more work in this area, as one cost-benefit study is not nearly enough. But the results from the Las Vegas study are compelling. If BWCs offer multiple pathways to enhanced police legitimacy while simultaneously saving money, the implications are profound. This intriguing possibility is especially relevant in 2020 given the current debate over "defunding" the police through forced budget reductions.[76]

The research examining the impact of BWCs on prosecution and court outcomes is a bit stronger. Seven of eight studies that empirically examined the effect of BWCs on prosecution and court processing show that BWCs have positive effects. While four of the studies are from the United Kingdom and have weak research designs, even those studies show that BWCs increase crime detection, arrests, and guilty pleas.[77] Three of the four more rigorous studies also show positive effects. In one, White and colleagues examined the impact of BWCs on misdemeanor drug and alcohol cases in Tempe, Arizona, finding that, while there was no impact on case outcomes, there was a significant reduction in adjudication time.[78] The authors suggest that BWC evidence may thus cut both ways:

> BWCs give downstream criminal justice actors a visual and auditory window into what transpired during the encounter. That window likely provides much more definitive evidence than written reports and in-person (often contradictory) testimony from officers and defendants. Sometimes

this concrete evidence benefits the police and prosecution; sometimes, it helps the defendant. As a result, the BWC evidence serves to reduce time to adjudication (as all cases are handled more quickly), but its impact on the likelihood of guilty outcomes is mixed, depending on the specifics of a given case.[79]

Two studies show that camera footage is particularly beneficial in domestic violence cases.[80] Researchers in Essex, in the United Kingdom, concluded that domestic violence investigations that included BWC footage were significantly more likely to result in criminal charges.[81] When Morrow and colleagues examined domestic violence cases in Phoenix, they found that domestic violence cases with BWC footage were more likely to end in adjudications of guilt.[82] Lum and colleagues conclude that "the findings from stronger studies also reveal that BWCs have investigative benefits."[83] We concur. The handful of studies on investigative and court outcomes show the benefits of BWC evidence.

The value of BWC evidence has important implications for police legitimacy and the legitimacy of the criminal justice system. White and colleagues note: "If BWCs do indeed implicate and exonerate, then the cameras' real evidentiary value goes far beyond quicker case processing time, and the concomitant savings to prosecutors and courts. The real value of BWCs may lie in more accurate determinations of guilt or innocence."[84]

BWCs Improve Procedural Justice

BWCs also have the potential to enhance police legitimacy by increasing procedural justice. Essentially, if members of the public believe the police have treated them fairly and with respect, they are more likely to accept police authority. Researchers posit that procedural justice encompasses four distinct elements: participation (giving voice to citizens), neutrality, dignity and respect, and trustworthy motives.[85] Five studies have examined whether BWCs produce higher levels of procedural justice.

Researchers in Los Angeles used systematic social observations such as ride-alongs with police to assess procedural justice before and after the deployment of BWCs. Their study finds significantly higher levels of procedurally just policing when officers wore cameras.[86] McCluskey and colleagues concluded: "Significant increases in procedural justice during police-citizen encounters were directly attributable to the effect of BWCs on police behavior and the indirect effects on citizen disrespect and other variables."[87] Demir and colleagues examined BWCs' impact on motorists, studying their attitudes about compliance with police directives, observing traffic laws, and cooperating with police. They reported positive effects on all three outcomes. They noted:

> BWCs generate indirect impacts on specific citizen compliance mediated through improvements in procedural justice, as well as indirect impacts on general compliance and cooperation mediated through improvements in both police legitimacy and procedural justice . . . The findings indicate BWCs provide a form of officer accountability that mere training in procedural justice might be insufficient to achieve.[88]

White and colleagues conducted a study in Spokane and found significantly higher perceptions of procedural justice among citizens who knew that they had been recorded on a BWC.[89]

However, researchers in Anaheim, California,[90] and Arlington, Texas,[91] conducted research similar to the Spokane study, using telephone surveys to ask citizens who had experienced recent face-to-face encounters with police about procedural justice. They then compared the responses from citizens who had encountered officers with and without BWCs. While there were no differences in perceptions of procedural justice in either study, the Arlington researchers failed to determine whether the citizens were aware of the camera's presence. The Anaheim study results are a bit more perplexing, as the researchers accounted for citizen awareness of BWCs. The Anaheim results could be due to the study group's smaller group size (N=59 officers), or it could simply be that, at this site, BWCs did not increase procedural justice. In short, three of the five studies examining this question found a link between BWCs and enhanced procedural justice. One study demonstrated how BWCs led to improvements in procedural justice and police legitimacy, which generated greater levels of citizen compliance. The results are very promising, but five studies are not enough. Therefore, this is perhaps the area in which there is the most urgent need for additional research on BWCs.

Why the Mixed Findings?

While the research on BWCs is persuasive, the findings are by no means unanimous. Not every study documented positive changes. Several studies documented no impact on use of force, citizen complaints, or both.[92] In their evaluation of BWCs in Washington, DC, Yokum and colleagues concluded:

> We are unable to detect any statistically significant effects. As such, our *experiment suggests that we should recalibrate our expectations of BWCs*. Law enforcement agencies (particularly in contexts similar to Washington, DC) that are considering adopting BWCs should not expect dramatic reductions in use of force or complaints, or other large-scale shifts in police behavior, solely from the deployment of this technology.[93]

Ariel and colleagues reported a troubling association between BWCs and increased rates of assaults on officers.[94] Braga and colleagues concluded that the benefits of BWCs in terms of force and complaint reductions may be offset by increases in formal activity, especially in minority communities: "Alternatively, increased enforcement activity could undermine police legitimacy if citizens view heightened arrests and citations as harmful to their communities."[95]

To assess the impact of BWCs on police legitimacy, it is important to consider the significance of the studies that produce these different results. We believe the mixed evidence on the effects of BWCs can be explained, at least in part, by three factors. Two factors relate to the implementing police agency: the agency's predeployment starting point and the agency's BWC implementation methods. The third factor relates to research issues.

The State of the Agency Before BWC Deployment

The state of a police department before BWC employment is important for interpreting BWCs' impacts on that department. Had the department recently experienced a scandal or controversial event that compromised police legitimacy? Was the department under federal oversight through a consent decree? Did the department have accountability mechanisms that were sufficient to ensure professionalism among officers?

For example, consider situational differences in the pre-BWC starting point of two agencies discussed earlier in this chapter: Rialto and DC Metro. After a significant police misconduct scandal, Rialto hired Tony Farrar as a "reform chief." Among other efforts to improve the department, Farrar implemented a BWC program.[96] In contrast, DC Metro introduced BWCs after it had been under a federal consent decree for nearly a decade.

Given these variations in the context, is it a surprise that, after BWC deployment, the Rialto department experienced immediate, large declines in citizen complaints and the use of force while the DC Metro department did not? After all, Rialto was at a nadir when the BWC program started, so its reserves of police legitimacy were likely quite low. Perhaps Rialto's large reductions in the use of force and citizen complaints reflected the agency's poor state before Chief Farrar's reforms. In DC Metro, perhaps a decade of federal oversight prior to BWC deployment had already resolved organizational deficiencies and restored police legitimacy.

More broadly, it might be the case that professional organizations with restrictively high employment criteria, robust training, effective supervision, and proper accountability systems do not experience large reductions in use of force and citizen complaints after they adopt BWCs because their officers were *already* using appropriate levels of force. Perhaps such agencies already function at a high level and are already viewed as legitimate by the citizens they serve. In other words, we may need to measure a department's pre-BWC starting point to understand how much room that agency has for improvement.

Important Considerations for Planning and Implementation

The mixed research findings about BWCs may be explained by the considerable difficulties associated with planning and implementing BWC programs. BWCs affect every aspect of police operations and have significant implications for other criminal justice stakeholders. BWCs require a tremendous investment of internal resources. Additionally, many jurisdictions have adopted BWCs in contentious political environments or after controversial incidents, which likely produced pressure for rapid deployment of BWC technology. (Recall that the Ferguson

Police Department deployed BWCs less than a month after Michael Brown's death.[97])

In addition, BWCs require significant dedicated human resources. Staff must review and redact BWC footage for public records requests, provide hardware and software technical assistance to officers, audit metadata to assess if officers are activating and using the BWCs properly, and deliver other system maintenance and support. Poor BWC program implementation can cause resistance among frontline officers and unions, create problems with technology integration and data storage, and impose unintended costs (financial and otherwise).[98] In short, BWC implementation comes with both a high degree of difficulty and significant risks if implemented poorly. Most important, poor implementation can short-circuit the potential for positive outcomes, including enhanced legitimacy.

We consider officers' BWC activation rates to be an important metric for evaluating implementation success, and we view low activation compliance as a form of implementation failure. Work by McClure and colleagues reports substantial variation in officer activation rates, from under 2% to more than 65%.[99] In a study of BWCs among Phoenix police, Katz and colleagues reported officer activation compliance of approximately 30% during the entire study period, though it declined substantially over time (from 42% to 13%).[100] There are no agreed-upon benchmarks for activation compliance, and as a result departments should work internally to identify reasonable goals that suit their individual needs. In the final main section of the chapter ("Strategies for Successful Implementation of BWC Programs"), we review some resources for improved program planning and implementation.

Research-Related Issues

A handful of decisions made by researchers can also affect the likelihood of documenting positive effects. Not all research studies are created equal, and the degree of confidence placed in a study's findings should be directly proportional to the study's methodological rigor. There are three important questions to be asked about each study. First, how rigorous was the research, including the related question, where do the study methods rank on the Maryland Scale of Scientific Methods (SMS)?[101]

Second, how did the researchers measure their outcomes? Third, how long was the study period?

Even the most rigorous studies, randomized controlled trials (RCTs),[102] may have issues. BWC studies are not conducted in a perfectly controlled setting. Officers in the treatment group (officers with BWCs) and officers in the control group (officers without BWCs) may interact regularly. They may see each other in the locker room, at roll calls, and during meal breaks. Officers from both groups may respond to the same call. When these interactions occur, the officers *without* BWCs are "exposed" to the officers *with* BWCs. This exposure, called "contamination" or "treatment spillover" in research terms, violates the integrity of the RCT design.

Researchers have documented varying degrees of contamination in RCT studies of BWC implementation. For example, in the DC Metro study, this treatment spillover occurred in 70% of calls.[103] As a result, the researchers could study only the 30% of calls that were uncontaminated. In the Las Vegas study, researchers documented a contamination rate of approximately 20%.[104] In contrast, Wallace and colleagues documented a 49% contamination rate in their Spokane study.[105]

There may be other ways to construct RCTs that evaluate BWC implementation. Using the DC Metro study as a case study, Ariel and colleagues have proposed randomizing the study of BWCs by work shifts rather than by officers.[106] Some shifts would use BWCs; others would not. In this type of shift-based randomization study, officers would move back and forth between the control and treatment groups. While this arguably would create a 100% contamination rate, Ariel and colleagues point out that shift-based randomization would allow researchers to increase sample sizes and better understand methodological issues related to the choice of treatment "units."[107] We believe there is no simple answer to how to construct the best RCTs that evaluate the use of BWCs. But we must recognize that, like pre-implementation standing and implementation strategies, methodological decisions influence the potential for significant findings.

Strategies for Successful Implementation of BWC Programs

Having established BWCs' potential to increase police legitimacy, in this section we highlight critical considerations for offices that want to deploy an effective BWC program that enhances and sustains police legitimacy.

Because BWCs are very expensive, and their costs go far beyond the initial investment in cameras and associated infrastructure, their implementation warrants significant forethought. Yet it is very difficult to project the total costs of BWC acquisition, implementation, and maintenance, and many agencies have grossly underestimated the investment—financial and otherwise—required to implement and maintain a successful BWC program. Data storage costs can run into the millions of dollars. For example, the Denver Police Department reported incurring costs of more than $6 million for the purchase of 800 cameras and the associated storage of the videos they produced.[108] Braga and colleagues estimated that the Las Vegas BWC program cost $1,097 per officer per year, for a total annual cost of $891,390.[109] Fortunately, the DOJ's Training and Technical Assistance (TTA) team have created the BWC Cost and Storage Estimator, a valuable tool that assists with the estimation of BWC program costs.[110] We strongly recommend that departments considering new BWC programs consult this important resource.

Further, proper planning and implementation are critically important for an effective BWC program. DOJ is acutely aware of the challenges associated with planning, implementing, and managing a BWC program, and early on it began to provide guidance to agencies deploying that technology. The Bureau of Justice Assistance (BJA) manages DOJ's Policy and Implementation Program (PIP), which funds BWC programs. In PIP's first five years, BJA provided more than 400 law enforcement agencies with $84 million in funding, resulting in the deployment of just over 90,000 BWCs nationally.[111] BJA also funds the TTA team, which supports agencies that receive PIP funding. The TTA resources are publicly available online,[112] and the TTA team will assist any agency that asks, regardless of whether that agency receives federal funding for BWCs.

BJA also created the National Body-Worn Camera Toolkit (Toolkit).[113] Rolled out by BJA in May 2015, the Toolkit provides law enforcement agencies with a wide range of resources about BWCs, including new research, guidance on policy and training, and information about engagement with prosecutors, advocacy groups, citizens, and other interested parties. The Toolkit includes a Law Enforcement Implementation Checklist (Checklist).[114] The Checklist serves as a best-practices guide for successful planning and implementation of a BWC program.[115] The Checklist offers six core implementation principles:

Learn the fundamentals and develop a plan.
Form a working group.
Develop policy.
Define the technology solution (specify hardware and software needs).
Communicate with and educate stakeholders.
Execute phased rollout and implementation.

Adherence to the Checklist should optimize the likelihood of successful BWC implementation. Successful implementation will, in turn, increase the potential for positive program outcomes, including enhanced police legitimacy.[116]

Finally, we urge BWC adopters to pay particular attention to one particular implementation issue: BWC activation compliance. Failure to activate BWCs, regardless of the reason, can be problematic for a police department. Low activation compliance can undermine all of the benefits generated by BWCs. Though there are no industrywide standards for activation compliance, police leaders should identify compliance rate goals at the individual, unit, and department levels (e.g., 75%) and then initiate targeted responses at low activators to achieve those goals. Additionally, recent studies have linked high levels of activation compliance to important outcomes such as reductions in the use of force and citizen complaints, which represent some of the primary pathways by which BWCs improve police legitimacy.[117] Clearly, there is no added evidentiary value if there is no video. Can we expect citizen and officer behavior to improve if the camera is not activated? Failure to activate in a critical incident can lead to public outrage and deplete reserves of police legitimacy.

For all these reasons, it is vitally important for police departments to monitor BWC activation compliance routinely. The easiest path to institutionalizing activation compliance is to build it into BWC policy as a mandatory auditing function of first-line supervisors, and many departments have done just that. White and colleagues examined the BWC policies of more than 200 agencies that have received federal funding for BWCs.[118] They note that the vast majority of federally funded agencies require supervisors to conduct periodic or random reviews of their subordinates' BWC footage to assess policy compliance (and, in many cases, also general performance).

We do acknowledge a tension between the need to monitor activation compliance on a routine basis and the resources required for such a monitoring program—especially the burden on first-line supervisors. Notably, many of BWC vendors have developed automated activation features to take the human element out of the equation (e.g., if the officer pulls the gun or Taser from the holster, the BWC is automatically activated).[119] The automated activation feature is intriguing and should be explored by agencies as a means to improve their BWC program.

Final Thoughts and Considerations

We believe we have made a strong case based on the evidence available that police departments should adopt BWC programs. The evidence suggests that BWCs generate numerous benefits, from enhanced procedural justice and increased citizen support of the police to reductions in citizen complaints. Each represents a potential pathway to enhanced police legitimacy. However, BWCs are tools—not solutions—and our expectations about their impact must be realistic. There is a long history of police use of excessive force against minority citizens, and BWCs cannot resolve the decades of mistrust and anger resulting from that history. That being said, we do believe that BWCs can and should be part of a larger portfolio of police reform efforts.

NOTES

1 Portions of this chapter are drawn from Michael D. White and Aili Malm, *Cops, Cameras, and Crisis.*

2 Hamedy and Gauk-Roger, "Los Angeles City Council Moves Forward."

3 Kelly, "Colorado Governor Signs Bill Mandating Police Body Cameras and Banning Chokeholds."

4 Cochrane and Broadwater, "Here Are the Differences Between the Senate and House Bills."

5 Ferguson, "'Defund the Police.'"

6 White and Fradella, *Stop and Frisk.*

7 Headley and Blount-Hill, "Race and Police Misconduct Cases."

8 Tyler, *Why People Obey the Law,* 375.

9 Tyler, "Psychological Perspectives."

10 U.K. College of Policing, *What Is Evidence-Based Policing?*

11 President's Task Force on 21st Century Policing, *Final Report.*
12 Ibid., 32.
13 Hyland, *Body-Worn Cameras in Law Enforcement Agencies, 2016.*
14 Sousa, Miethe, and Sakiyama, "Inconsistencies in Public Opinion"; White, Todak, and Gaub, "Assessing Citizen Perceptions of Body-Worn Cameras."
15 International Association of Chiefs of Police, *Body-Worn Cameras Model Policy.*
16 Stanley, *Police Body-Mounted Cameras.*
17 Cochrane and Broadwater, "Here Are the Differences Between the Senate and House Bills.".
18 Bureau of Justice Assistance, "Training and Technical Assistance."
19 Ariel, Farrar, and Sutherland, "The Effect of Police Body-Worn Cameras"; Hedberg, Katz, and Choate, "Body-Worn Cameras and Citizen Interactions."
20 Morrow, Katz, and Choate, "Assessing the Impact of Police Body-Worn Cameras"; Owens, Mann, and Mckenna, *The Essex Body Worn Video Trial.*
21 Demir, Braga, and Apel, "Effects of Police Body-Worn Cameras"; White, Todak, and Gaub, "Assessing Citizen Perceptions of Body-Worn Cameras."
22 McCluskey et al., "Assessing the Effects of Body-Worn Cameras."
23 Tyler, "Psychological Perspectives"; Tyler and Fagan, "Legitimacy and Cooperation"; Tyler and Huo, *Trust in the Law.*
24 Edmonton Police Service, *Body Worn Video: Considering the Evidence*; Grossmith et al., *Police, Camera, Evidence*; Yokum, Ravishankar, and Coppock, *Evaluating the Effects of Police Body-Worn Cameras.*
25 Ariel et al., "Wearing Body Cameras Increases Assaults against Officers."
26 Levenson, and Allen, "Boston Police Union Challenges Body Camera Program."
27 Wallace et al., "Body-Worn Cameras as a Potential Source of De-Policing." De-policing involves the police reducing their proactivity or "pulling back" as a result of the increased scrutiny on their profession.
28 Lopez, "The Failure of Police Body Cameras."
29 Ikem, Nkechi, and Ogbeifun, "Body Cameras Aren't Working. So, What's Next?"
30 Verger, "Police Body Cameras Were Supposed to Build Trust. So Far, They Haven't."
31 Kaur, "There's a Renewed Call for Police Body Cameras."
32 Norwood, "Body Cameras Are Seen as Key to Police Reform."
33 White and Malm, *Cops, Cameras, and Crisis.*
34 Crow et al., "Community Perceptions of Police Body-Worn Cameras"; Sousa, Miethe, and Sakiyama, "Inconsistencies in Public Opinion of Body-Worn Cameras on Police"; Wright and Headley, "Can Technology Work for Policing? Citizen Perceptions of Police-Body Worn Cameras."
35 White, Todak, and Gaub, "Assessing Citizen Perceptions of Body-Worn Cameras."
36 White, Todak, and Gaub, "Examining Body-Worn Camera Integration and Acceptance."
37 White, Todak, and Gaub, "Assessing Citizen Perceptions of Body-Worn Cameras."

38 Graham et al., "Videos Don't Lie: African Americans' Support for Body-Worn Cameras."

39 Kerrison, Cobbina, and Bender, "Stop-gaps, Lip Service, and the Perceived Futility," 281.

40 Ray, March, and Powelson, "Can Cameras Stop the Killings?"

41 Elms, "Activists, Elected Officials Push for More Body Cameras for Police"; Wilkins, "Activists Demand All Prince George's Officers Wear Body Cams."

42 Kelly, "Colorado Governor Signs Bill Mandating Police Body Cameras and Banning Chokeholds."

43 Mesa Police Department, *On-Officer Body Camera System: Program Evaluation and Recommendations*; Pelfrey and Keener, "Police Body Worn Cameras: A Mixed Method Approach"; Young and Ready, "Diffusion of Policing Technology."

44 BWC TTA, "Directories of Outcomes."

45 White, Todak, and Gaub, "Examining Body-Worn Camera Integration and Acceptance."

46 Gaub et al., "Officer Perceptions of Body-Worn Cameras."

47 Ibid.

48 Recall there are a total of 37 published studies that examine officer perceptions of BWCs, but studies vary in the topics covered. Only 19 of the 37 asked officers about BWCs and the quality of evidence. The remaining 18 studies did not cover that issue.

49 White, Todak, and Gaub, "Examining Body-Worn Camera Integration and Acceptance."

50 Young and Ready, "A Longitudinal Analysis"; Katz et al., *Phoenix, Arizona, Smart Policing Initiative.*

51 Los Angeles Police Department, *Board of Police Commissioners Critical Incident Video Release Policy*, 1.

52 Kaur, "There's a Renewed Call for Police Body Cameras."

53 Farrar, *Self-Awareness to Being Watched.*

54 Sutherland et al., "Post-Experimental Follow-Ups," 114.

55 Braga et al., *The Benefits of Body-Worn Cameras*; Henstock and Ariel, "Testing the Effects of Police Body-Worn Cameras"; Jennings et al., "A Quasi-Experimental Evaluation"; Jennings, Fridell, and Lynch, "Cops and Cameras"; White, Gaub, and Todak, "Exploring the Potential for Body-Worn Cameras."

56 Yokum, Ravishankar, and Coppock, *Evaluating the Effects of Police Body-Worn Cameras.*

57 Ariel, "Police Body Cameras in Large Police Departments"; Ariel et al., "Report: Increases in Police Use of Force"; Braga et al., "The Effects of Body Worn Cameras"; Headley, Guerette, and Shariati, "A Field Experiment of the Impact of Body-Worn Cameras (BWCs)"; Yokum, Ravishankar, and Coppock, *Evaluating the Effects of Police Body-Worn Cameras.*

58 White, Gaub, and Padilla, *Impacts of BWCs on Use of Force.*

59 Lum et al., "Research on Body-Worn Cameras," 101.

60 White and Malm, *Cops, Cameras, and Crisis.*

61 Miller and Chillar, "Do Police Body-Worn Cameras Reduce Citizen Fatalities?" 28.

62 Williams et al., "Body-Worn Cameras in Policing: Benefits and Costs," 18.

63 Wallace et al., "Camera-Induced Passivity."

64 White and Malm, *Cops, Cameras, and Crisis.*

65 Devine et al., "Minneapolis Police Are Rarely Disciplined for Complaints, Records Show."

66 Farrar, *Self-Awareness to Being Watched*; Ariel, Farrar, and Sutherland, "Effect of Police Body-Worn Cameras."

67 Sutherland et al., "Post-Experimental Follow-Ups."

68 Mesa Police Department, *On-Officer Body Camera System: Program Evaluation and Recommendations*; Jennings et al., "A Quasi-Experimental."

69 Flight, "Black Box"; Maskaly et al., "Effects of Body-Worn Cameras."

70 Lum et al., "Research on Body-Worn Cameras," 99.

71 White and Coldren, "Body-Worn Cameras."

72 White and Malm, *Cops, Cameras, and Crisis.*

73 Braga et al., *The Benefits of Body-Worn Cameras.*

74 Braga et al., "The Effects of Body-Worn Cameras," 10.

75 Toronto Police Service, *Body-Worn Cameras.*

76 Ferguson, "'Defund the Police.'"

77 Ellis, Jenkins, and Smith, *Isle of Wight*; Goodall, *Guidance*; ODS Consulting, *Body Worn Video Projects.*

78 White et al., "Implicate or Exonerate?"

79 Ibid.

80 Miller, Toliver, and Police Executive Research Forum, *Implementing a Body-Worn Camera Program*; White, *Police Officer Body-Worn Cameras.*

81 Owens, Mann, and McKenna, *Essex Body Worn Video Trial.*

82 Morrow, Katz, and Choate, "Assessing the Impact"; Katz et al., *Evaluating the Impact.*

83 Lum et al., "Research on Body-Worn Cameras," 108.

84 White et al., "Implicate or Exonerate?" 10.

85 Tyler, "Psychological Perspectives"; Tyler and Fagan, "Legitimacy and Cooperation"; Tyler and Huo, *Trust in the Law*; Tyler, Goff, and MacCoun, "Impact of Psychological Science."

86 McCluskey et al., "Assessing the Effects of Body-Worn Cameras on Procedural Justice."

87 Ibid., 208.

88 Demir, Braga, and Apel, "Effects of Police Body-Worn Cameras," 1–2.

89 White, Todak, and Gaub, "Assessing Citizen Perceptions of Body-Worn Cameras."

90 McClure et al., *How Body Cameras Affect Community Members' Perceptions of Police.*

91 Goodison and Wilson, *Citizen Perceptions of Body-Worn Cameras.*

92 Edmonton Police Service, *Body Worn Video: Considering the Evidence*; Grossmith et al., *Police, Camera, Evidence*.
93 Yokum, Ravishankar, and Coppock, *Evaluating the Effects of Police Body-Worn Cameras* [emphasis in original].
94 Ariel et al., "Wearing Body Cameras Increases Assaults Against Officers."
95 Braga et al., "Police Activity and Police-Citizen Encounters," 538.
96 Winton, "2 Rialto Police Officers Resign."
97 Hollinshed, "Ferguson Police."
98 White, Todak, and Gaub, "Examining Body-Worn Camera Integration and Acceptance."
99 McClure et al., *How Body Cameras Affect Community Members' Perceptions of Police*.
100 Katz et al., *Evaluating the Impact*.
101 Sherman et al., "Preventing Crime." The Maryland SMS rates the rigor of studies on a scale of 1 (least rigorous) to 5 (most rigorous; randomized controlled trials). A variety of factors determine a study's rating on the Maryland SMS, most notably whether there are pre- and post-test measures of the outcome of interest and whether there is a comparison or control group.
102 Randomized controlled trials randomly allocate subjects between two or more groups, treating them differently in the study to reduce outside influences or investigative biases.
103 Yokum, Ravishankar, and Coppock, *Evaluating the Effects of Police Body-Worn Cameras*.
104 Braga et al., *Benefits of Body-Worn Cameras*.
105 Wallace et al., "Camera-Induced Passivity."
106 Ariel, Sutherland, and Sherman, "Preventing Treatment Spillover."
107 Ibid.
108 Phillips, "Eyes are Not Cameras."
109 Braga et al., *Benefits of Body-Worn Cameras*.
110 Training and Technical Assistance Team, *Cost and Storage Estimator*.
111 Gaub, Todak, and White, "One Size Doesn't Fit All."
112 BWC TTA, "Resources."
113 Bureau of Justice Assistance, "Toolkit."
114 Bureau of Justice Assistance, "Checklist."
115 See also Miller, Toliver, and Police Executive Research Forum, *Implementing a Body-Worn Camera Program*.
116 White, Todak, and Gaub, "Examining Body-Worn Camera Integration and Acceptance."
117 Ariel et al., "Report"; Hedberg, Katz, and Choate, "Body-Worn Cameras."
118 White, Flippin, and Katz, *Policy and Practice*.
119 Diaz-Zuniga, "New Bodycams Start Recording"; Anthony, "New Holster."

2

A New Charge Afoot?

Improving Prosecutors' Charging Practices

JON B. GOULD, RACHEL BOWMAN, AND
BELÉN LOWREY-KINBERG

It is widely understood that prosecutors are powerful actors in the criminal justice system.[1] Yet for years, prosecutors have operated largely outside of public view, leaving judges to serve as the public face of the criminal justice system.[2] In the 1980s, state and federal governments created sentencing guidelines intended to increase uniformity. But such measures only accelerated the shift of discretionary power from judges toward prosecutors.[3] Today, some observers contend that prosecutors are the most powerful players in the criminal justice system,[4] serving as "crucial gatekeepers between the police and the courts."[5] Importantly, it is prosecutors who decide which cases even make it to a judge.

After years of prosecutors being the black box of criminal justice, the tide is turning as researchers and policy makers alike are turning a more critical eye to prosecution. We have seen the election of a new wave of progressive prosecutors, and even veteran prosecutors are increasingly open to evidence-based practices. Together, these trends bring increased research into prosecutor decision-making, from charging decisions, to alternative dispositions, to plea bargaining (which closes most cases). It is a heady time for both prosecutors and their critics, as research is now available to help guide the practice—and reform—of prosecution.

In this chapter, we offer an overview of the emerging interest in evidence-based prosecution, especially as it pertains to prosecutors' charging practices. Drawing from our research on the topic, we identify five primary areas for reform. Prosecutors should prioritize the early screening of potential cases, relying on trained, veteran prosecutors to make these judgements. They should decide on charges faster, thereby reducing the length of pretrial detention. They should refrain from charging based on a defendant's criminal history unless the elements of the crime specifically take prior offenses into account. They ought to rotate lawyers out of major crime units to avoid desensitizing them to violence and should create trainings with law enforcement to improve collaboration in charging. Finally, district attorneys (DAs) should actively recruit attorneys with diverse educational, socioeconomic, racial, ethnic, and ideological backgrounds and encourage communication among attorneys in deciding which cases warrant particular charges.

Trends in Prosecution

The twenty-first century has seen heightened attention to criminal justice reform. As concerns have risen about police violence, racial disparities in sentencing, mass incarceration, and the cost of incarceration, activists have increasingly pushed policy makers and practitioners to become "smart on crime." Rather than focusing on past debates about being "soft" or "tough" on crime, the modern movement relies on data to advance evidence-based practices in criminal justice.[6] At the height of Barack Obama's administration, for example, federal officials initiated several measures to evaluate and reform the criminal justice system. One of these programs was Attorney General Eric Holder's Smart on Crime Initiative, which called on federal prosecutors to "ensure just punishments for low-level, nonviolent convictions."[7] Among other things, this initiative compelled federal prosecutors to avoid charges that triggered mandatory minimum sentences for nonviolent crimes. In a 2013 memorandum to United States attorneys and assistant US attorneys, Eric Holder wrote:

> It is with full consideration of these factors that we now refine our charging policy regarding mandatory minimums for certain nonviolent, low-level drug offenders. We must ensure that our most severe mandatory minimum penalties are reserved for serious, high-level, or violent drug traffickers. In some cases, mandatory minimum and recidivist enhancement statutes have resulted in unduly harsh sentences and perceived or actual disparities that do not reflect our Principles of Federal Prosecution. Long sentences for low-level, non-violent drug offenses do not promote

public safety, deterrence, and rehabilitation. Moreover, rising prison costs have resulted in reduced spending on criminal justice initiatives, including spending on law enforcement agents, prosecutors, and prevention and intervention programs. These reductions in public safety spending require us to make our public safety expenditures smarter and more productive.[8]

Although the Trump Administration reversed this policy, its central tenet lives on as an early acknowledgement that prosecutorial discretion plays a central role in expanding or curbing the country's high rates of incarceration.

Along with "smart on crime" reforms at the federal level, a growing wave of state prosecutors have retired the "tough on crime" slogan for a new message of "evidenced-based" or "data-driven" prosecution.[9] Under this approach, district attorneys are pursuing programs and policies supported by empirical evidence, thereby reducing incarceration rates and saving resources.[10] Among these measures are an end to cash bail, minimizing the prosecution of low-level nonviolent offenses, decriminalizing marijuana possession, employing pretrial diversion and drug courts, and avoiding the death penalty.[11]

For the first time, prosecutor-led reforms are the topic of competitive elections. Historically, incumbent district attorneys were not only routinely reelected; the majority also went uncontested, term after term.[12] More recently, district attorneys' races have become more competitive as criminal justice reformers are recognizing the significant role district attorneys play in achieving criminal justice reform on the local level. For one, district attorneys have significant autonomy in enacting officewide policies on charging, pretrial diversion, bail, and other issues. Since approximately 95% of criminal cases are handled at the state level,[13] filling local criminal justice positions with reform-minded officials is becoming a key strategy for many progressive reformers. In recent years, major donors like George Soros have begun to fund state-level political action committees (PACs) to back district attorney candidates running on progressive platforms.[14] Other prominent voices in the push for reform-minded prosecution include Black Lives Matter activist Shaun King and the Real Justice PAC. Amid this broad mobilization for change in prosecution, there have been record turnouts in many local district attorney races, and voters have elected a new wave of progressive prosecutors.[15]

At the forefront of this surge was Kings County (NY) District Attorney Ken Thompson, who in 2013 defeated a 23-year incumbent in Brooklyn, New York.[16] During his tenure, Thompson implemented a Conviction Review Unit to review wrongful conviction claims and vowed to stop prosecuting low-level marijuana possession. He aimed for the office to become a "model and gold standard for what a progressive prosecutorial agency could look like."[17] Indeed, other cities followed suit. Wesley Bell's 2015 win in Ferguson, Michigan, Kim Foxx's 2016 win in Chicago, Larry Krasner's 2017 win in Philadelphia, and Rachel Rollins's 2019 win in Suffolk County, Massachusetts, are part of a progressive wing of the reform movement that has taken office.[18] Importantly, this movement is not limited to a particular political party or a particular type of jurisdiction.[19] Reform-minded district attorneys have won in stereotypically "liberal" places like San Francisco and in more unlikely places like Corpus Christi, Texas.[20]

Prosecutorial "reform" is not limited to newly elected or self-described "progressive" prosecutors. With evidence-based policy finding its way to the justice sector, many long-standing prosecutors are rethinking how they pursue cases and reimagining what constitutes a just outcome. They are also hiring attorneys from more diverse backgrounds, including those who have worked in public defense or civil rights law.[21] Notwithstanding the close collaboration between police and district attorneys' offices, some prosecutors have even highlighted their independence from the police and their willingness to prosecute officers who break the law.[22]

From a researcher's perspective, the most useful transformation in prosecution has been the willingness of several district attorneys to collect and share case-processing data. For example, Cook County State's Attorney Kimberly Foxx made headlines when she publicly released six years of felony prosecution data.[23] Other district attorneys have reached out to researchers to collaborate in analyzing office operations and case processing. Through these alliances, the black box of prosecution is becoming somewhat more transparent. Prominent collaborations include the Prosecutors' Center for Excellence, which seeks to identify, evaluate and implement "best practices" for prosecutors,[24] and the Institute for Innovation in Prosecution at John Jay College in New York City, which aims to "to promote data-driven strategies, cutting-edge scholarship, and innovative thinking" in prosecution.[25] Similarly, the Fair and Just Prosecution project convenes and supports newly elected district attorneys who are committed to culture change, transparency, and accountability in prosecution,[26] and the Safety and Justice Challenge's project on Advancing Prosecutorial Effectiveness and Fairness through Data and Innovation seeks to create performance metrics that can combat racial and ethnic disparities.[27] Together, these institutes and projects are reflective of the heightened attention prosecutors have received in recent years.

Reforms from the Prosecutorial Charging Practices Project

If reform is to start anywhere, it should address the first step in prosecuting a case—the decision to charge or decline a case—and, if pursuing the matter, what charges to file. Our research has been focused on prosecutor charging, much of it in collaboration with the Deason Criminal Justice Reform Center at Southern Methodist University's Dedman School of Law. Our research expands the scope of knowledge about charging decisions in two important ways.

First, this research examines midsized jurisdictions.[28] Research on prosecutors typically comes from large urban jurisdictions, places like Cook County and New York County (Manhattan).[29] However, we chose jurisdictions that are far more representative of the well over 2,300 prosecutors' offices across the country.[30] Led by Democratic and Republican district attorneys, the offices we studied can best be described as "reform-minded" even if the DAs did not run as "progressive prosecutors." These offices shared a goal of implementing "evidence-based practices" to evaluate and improve the operations of their offices.

Second, unlike previous research that focused on plea bargaining,[31] our research focuses on charging. Certainly, the prior focus on plea bargaining is understandable, since almost all criminal cases end by agreement rather than trial.[32] However, case outcomes are highly dependent upon decisions made at earlier points in the criminal justice process.[33] Prosecutors have the power to decide whether to file or drop charges, what those specific charges will be, and whether to add enhancements like weapons charges.[34] The charges that prosecutors decide to file are critically important.

From our research, we arrived at five key areas to improve, if not reform, prosecutor charging. Collectively, they address which prosecutors should be responsible for charging, when they should do it, how long the process ought to take, which factors prosecutors should consider, and how to minimize the desensitizing effects of the job on prosecutors. We do not claim that these recommendations are exhaustive, but they are evidence-based. Indeed, if prosecutors intend to employ best practices to act fairly and justly, these measures are an important step forward in improving prosecutors' charging of criminal cases.

Reform 1: Prioritize Early Case Screening by Veteran Prosecutors

A criminal case begins when law enforcement arrests a suspect. After this point, district attorneys' offices diverge as to how, and to how quickly, they approve charges. In one jurisdiction we studied, police officers must screen cases with an "on call" prosecutor before making arrests for felonies and certain violent misdemeanors. The prosecutor reviews the facts of the case and either approves the charges, modifies the charges, or declines to charge the case entirely (in which case the defendant is released). This prescreening can be done by a rotating group of prosecutors or by a dedicated charging unit, as is the practice in Harris County, Texas (Houston).[35]

Other jurisdictions use significantly different approaches. In one office we studied, prosecutors conduct a daily "jail review" to consider the previous day's arrests. During this process, prosecutors make a probable cause determination, assessing whether the allegations support the elements of the crime(s). Although exact percentages were not available, prosecutors described accepting most of the police charges, so long as the facts satisfied the legal elements. In this jurisdiction, declining to charge a case at jail review is a time-consuming process. Prosecutors said that, as a result, if they are "on the fence" about the suitability of a case, they "let it slide" and permit the case to go forward.

In yet another jurisdiction, magistrates are responsible for charging. There, police typically go straight to the magistrate for approval of charges, without any prosecutor's review. Police turn to prosecutors for help only if they are worried that the magistrate will reject their charges.

Our research suggests that dedicated screening or charging units are the most effective model for prosecutorial charging. Dedicated units have multiple benefits. They help prosecutors to identify and decline weak cases early and ensure that the appropriate charges are selected.[36] They formally establish a "pause button" in offices, encouraging prosecutors to fully assess the circumstances surrounding a crime and to use their discretion to decide which cases to pursue. In offices without screening units, some line prosecutors complained they felt pressure from the elected district attorney to charge cases in which the underlying evidence was not strong. This was not typical for lawyers in charging units, who spoke of the discretion they had to "separate the weak from the strong cases."

Charging units also allow prosecutors to weed out poor cases early in the process, reserving their office's valuable time and resources for the most important cases. In one jurisdiction that did not employ a charging unit, prosecutors estimated that one-third of cases could be declined upfront if prearrest review was implemented by dedicated screeners. According to those prosecutors, law enforcement officers "do stupid stuff" when issuing citations or making arrests, but once the cases land on their desks—weeks after the initial interchange—it is difficult for lawyers to "stop the train." In other words, early screening can act as a safeguard for defendants. If a district attorney's office can quickly decline charges that do not warrant prosecution, prosecutors can minimize defendants' unnecessary involvement in the criminal justice system. Altogether, charging units help screen out the weakest cases, reduce caseloads and costs, and shield suspects from improper charges.

Notwithstanding these benefits, reform in case screening should be implemented carefully. Ideally, offices should create a dedicated charging unit to screen cases and approve charges rather than assigning screening duties to line prosecutors more broadly.[37] We acknowledge, however, that some smaller counties may not have the resources to assign staff to a dedicated screening unit. One solution to this problem might be for smaller counties to pool their resources to fund shared screening units.[38]

In addition, we recommend that veteran prosecutors staff the charging unit. Less experienced prosecutors may struggle in a charging unit, especially if they are not fully trained. Prosecutors described charging as a difficult process to learn and as one in which they were provided with little formal training or oversight. Many prosecutors we surveyed had to learn the process on their own—only a few received formal training when hired or assigned to charging. Moreover, less experienced prosecutors tend to charge cases more severely than their veteran colleagues, who have a better perspective on the responsibilities of the job. Thus, seasoned prosecutors who can train newer prosecutors should be assigned to a charging unit.

Additionally, there should be a uniform understanding of an office's charging standards. Even within individual offices, we found that prosecutors disagreed about whether cases should be charged on the probable cause or beyond a reasonable doubt (BARD) standards. In two jurisdictions, line prosecutors complained that they received "mixed messages" from supervisors about the appropriate standard. Those lawyers also said that, in their offices, felonies were more likely than misdemeanors to be evaluated under BARD. Clear and consistent messages from the district attorney about the appropriate standard should accompany the formation of a charging unit.

Reform 2: Accelerate the Time to Charge

The Sixth Amendment of the United States Constitution guarantees defendants the right to a speedy trial. Although the Constitution does not provide an explicit definition of "speedy," federal and state laws (e.g., 18 USC § 3161, VA Code § 19.2-243) establish clear time limits. (Within the parameters of relevant state and federal statutes, several prosecutors' offices also set their own standards for case processing speed.) Although Congress intended the Speedy Trial Act to minimize pretrial delays, a lack of enforcement and the pervasive use of continuances have allowed prosecutors and defense attorneys to circumvent speedy trial regulations.[39] In 1992, the American Bar Association (ABA) declared that 98% of criminal cases should be resolved within 180 days of filing,[40] yet states continued to fall short of this benchmark.[41] Nearly 20 years later, the ABA's 2011 Model Time Standards set what it considered more realistic standards, specifying that 75% of felony cases should be resolved within 90 days, 90% should be resolved within 180 days, and 98% should be resolved within 365 days.[42] However, early evidence suggests that states are failing to meet even these modified benchmarks.[43]

In order to guarantee a speedy trial, prosecutors should move quickly to file formal charges. The ABA's Speedy Trial Standards prescribe a timetable for this key step in the process. According to Standard 12-2.6(a),

> an indictment, information, or other formal charging instrument should be filed within [30] days after the defendant's first appearance in court after either an arrest or issuance of a citation or summons, so that defendants receive prompt notice of the charges on which they will be held to answer and have adequate opportunity to prepare for pretrial motions and for trial within the speedy trial time limit period.[44]

Our research suggests that there is significant variation in how long prosecutors take to file formal charges, a disparity that is not tied to the time required to make a charging decision. According to veteran prosecutors in the jurisdictions we studied, a charging decision can be made within 10–15 minutes, yet the time from arrest to indictment in their jurisdictions ranged between 96 and 134 days.

If prosecutors can formally charge a case in 10–15 minutes, why do they wait up to 134 days to do so? Office norms explain some of this disjunction. In addition, legal factors (such as the severity of the offense and the strength of the evidence) and defendant characteristics (such as age and gender) influence the time from arrest to formal charges. We found that prosecutors charged violent offenses more quickly than nonviolent offenses, especially drug crimes. Further, prosecutors took longer to file charges against older defendants and women, two groups of defendants who they viewed as less serious offenders and thus deserving of additional consideration in charging.

Regardless of demographics, pretrial involvement with the criminal justice system is pernicious. Even if a suspect eventually avoids criminal charges, the time spent awaiting formal charges carries a myriad of consequences. For those released, costs include fees to bail bondsmen and the indignities of pretrial supervision. For those detained, there are lost wages, the possible loss of employment, and separation from families. Victims and the public are also ill-served when cases linger.

In light of the many burdens that can result from delays in the criminal justice system, we make several recommendations to speed up the formal charging process. First, district attorneys should implement office policies that set more ambitious timelines for prosecutors to file charges. If, as line prosecutors report, the formal charging is a relatively quick and straightforward process, there is no reason to delay the decision. By accelerating the timeline to file charges, district attorneys can minimize defendants' pretrial involvement in the criminal justice system while ensuring that defendants and their attorneys "receive prompt notice of the charges on which they will be held to answer" as Standard 12-2.6(a) of the ABA's Speedy Trial Standards states. (Implementing early case screening would also reduce prosecutors' caseloads, which might allow them to meet more ambitious case processing standards.)

Given the continued failure of many prosecutors' offices to meet the timelines already set by federal, state, and professional benchmarks, nothing less than a deliberate organizational change will be needed to make progress on the timeliness of charging. As a 2010 report from the National Center for State Courts details, ambitious case processing standards also provide a framework for developing court schedules and procedures that can meet those standards.[45] District attorneys committed to evidenced-based prosecution are well-positioned to evaluate their offices' case processing times and identify what factors may be slowing them down.

We also recommend that prosecutors establish and maintain strong lines of communication with local law enforcement and forensic scientists. Prosecutors routinely depend on partner agencies to charge and try cases. But charging decisions can be delayed as prosecutors wait for medical records, forensic reports, and additional information from police. In one jurisdiction we studied, prosecutors and detectives swapped case files multiple times, thereby delaying formal charges for up to 90 days. More efficient communication, including the sharing of electronic case files, can speed up case processing by avoiding a back-and-forth about the quality and scope of the available evidence.

In addition, prosecutors often rely heavily on victim cooperation, particularly in cases that are otherwise very difficult to prove (e.g., sex offenses, child abuse, and domestic abuse).[46] Prosecutors sometimes must go to extensive lengths to get in contact with victims. A lengthy process of missed calls and meetings can delay the progress of the case. And even with prompt communication, some victims refuse to testify, forcing prosecutors to drop a case. To maximize victim cooperation, prosecutors should use victims' advocates who are demographically and culturally representative of the clients they serve, and they should involve those advocates as early in the process as possible. Early collaboration with victims' advocates can help build victims' trust in the district attorney's office and, ultimately, encourage them to cooperate with the prosecution. These efforts, in turn, can help to keep cases on track for a speedy resolution.

Reform 3: Limit the Use of Defendants' Criminal History

Under federal and state sentencing laws, a defendant's criminal history is one of two legally defined criteria that help establish the ultimate sentence.[47] Under these laws, defendants with prior convictions are subject to higher sentences. Prior convictions, however, are not typically elements of a crime, and with few exceptions they do not increase the seriousness of a crime. Stealing $100, for example, usually remains a misdemeanor regardless of whether it is the defendant's first, third, or fifth attempt. Nevertheless, in our research prosecutors consistently cited criminal history one of the top-three factors they consider when deciding charges, along with the amount of evidence and the completeness of the police investigation.

Despite their uniform reliance on criminal history, prosecutors interpreted this information differently. To some prosecutors, an extensive criminal history signaled that the criminal justice system had failed the defendant and that a different approach, such as drug courts, was needed. In our research, this perspective was especially prominent among senior prosecutors and those with prior experience as defense attorneys. However, other prosecutors interpreted multiple prior convictions as red flags that signaled a defendant "doesn't [care] about any break you're going to give him." These prosecutors were more likely to "upcharge"—that is, file more serious charges against—defendants with criminal histories than those who had none. Needless to say, when such disparate approaches occur within a single district attorney's office, it raises questions about the consistent and fair administration of justice.

Other research has also concluded that criminal history is an important element in understanding charging decisions.[48] Researchers have theorized that prosecutors view criminal history as a window into a defendant's character. In particular, the "focal concerns perspective" predicts that criminal justice actors make discretionary decisions based on three factors: (1) the defendant's blameworthiness; (2) the defendant's dangerousness; and (3) the practical costs of the outcome.[49] Prosecutors may use a defendant's prior record as a proxy for whether the defendant is a danger to the community. Thus, "defendants with long and serious criminal histories will be viewed as more culpable and blameworthy than first-time defendants."[50]

Consistent with this focal concerns perspective, the prosecutors we interviewed appeared to use criminal history as a vehicle through which they gained insight into a defendant's moral character—such as whether he was a "bad guy" or undeserving of mercy. Indeed, seeking to distinguish those who made "one-time mistake[s]" from those who exhibited a "pattern of behavior," prosecutors seemed to use defendants' past records to craft stories about their dangerousness.

Moreover, we found that the *type* of criminal history matters to prosecutors, especially when the defendant is a person of color. Whereas defendants with a felony history, regardless of race, were more likely to face felony charges, minority defendants with a *misdemeanor* history were more likely to face charges than were white defendants with a misdemeanor history. This pattern suggests that minority defendants may be experiencing an additional "penalty" for a misdemeanor history that white defendants are not—a practice that only compounds racial and ethnic disadvantages since African American and Hispanic defendants are disproportionately likely to have a prior record.[51]

Elected DAs disagree about the appropriateness of weighing criminal history in charging decisions. Among the three interviewed, one asserted that criminal history is an indispensable aspect of charging, whereas the others instructed their lawyers to ignore past crimes unless they are an element of the offense (such as possession of a firearm by a convicted felon). Even in offices where the DA deemphasizes criminal history, line prosecutors candidly reported their reliance on a defendant's prior record when deciding on charges. These variations in office policies and practices reflect not only different approaches to criminal history but also the challenges that district attorneys face in ensuring line prosecutors follow their lead.

Our research reveals several concerning trends in how prosecutors use criminal history at the charging stage. There is inconsistency both between and within offices about whether and how to consider prior convictions in charging. Further, the use of criminal history in charging only compounds the penalty that defendants face for their prior involvement in the criminal justice system.

Our research suggests several promising avenues to address these challenges. First, district attorneys should establish an office policy prohibiting prosecutors from considering criminal history when they make charging decisions. To guarantee that the policy is followed, they should also implement training and supervision. Clearly articulating and communicating this policy to supervising prosecutors and to line prosecutors is a key first step. Regular training and communication will help ensure that the policy is carried out and that criminal history is considered only when it is an element of the crime.

Second, we recommend that district attorneys implement this policy by making a defendant's criminal history unavailable to charging prosecutors unless the elements of the crime require it. This can be as simple as placing "rap sheets" in a different folder of a case file or separating the bail and charging functions within the office so that prosecutors responsible for bail maintain possession of criminal history reports. Limiting the use of criminal history to relevant functions[52] will allow charging prosecutors to assess the elements of the crime and select the appropriate charge(s) without using criminal history to make a moral determination about the defendant's character.

Finally, as we will discuss in our fifth recommendation, increasing the diversity of line prosecutors may reduce the misuse of criminal history in charging. In particular, enlisting senior prosecutors and those with experience as defense attorneys may be beneficial. More experienced prosecutors, and those with defense experience, may better appreciate where it is possible to rehabilitate—not simply punish—defendants.

Reform 4: Attend to Prosecutors' Needs

Prosecuting a case is not easy for lawyers, either professionally or personally. Foremost among these challenges, many new prosecutors are assigned to charge cases with little to no formal training or guidance.

In one jurisdiction we studied, only 5% of prosecutors reported having been trained in charging when they were hired, and 65% said that they received instruction on a piecemeal basis. Some offices did not have a formal charging policy. Where there was a formal charging policy, many lawyers were unaware of its existence.

Excessive prosecutorial caseloads are also challenging. Like defense attorneys who are inundated with cases, prosecutors described being faced with so many cases that it was difficult to keep up. Prosecutors told us that they were concerned that their high caseloads might cause them to overlook evidence, select the wrong charge, decline to prosecute a case that should have been charged, or charge an innocent defendant. Our findings support Adam Gershowitz and Laura Killinger's argument that high prosecutor caseloads hinder proper charging.[53]

The high caseloads assigned to defense attorneys—who themselves may lack the time and resources to adequately defend cases—may also hinder proper charging.[54] Prosecutors explained that they depend on defense input to consider filing reduced charges or offering an alternative disposition. As one prosecutor put it: "Some defendants have a story to tell, but I can't [reject] charges without a reason or explanation, and that requires the defense [to] bring me something." Our research suggests that if defense attorneys could devote more time to individual cases before they are formally charged, prosecutors could better consider filing reduced charges. Thus, reducing attorney caseloads—for both the defense and the prosecution—should be a priority. One viable option is the charging-unit model discussed above. Another answer is increased government funding for both sets of offices.[55]

Effective charging relies on good police work. However, some prosecutors complain that law enforcement officers misapply the law (resulting in overly punitive arrests or charges) or simply conduct poor investigations that the prosecutors do not have time to rectify, in which case they must simply dismiss the charges. Among the most commonly identified problems are arresting suspects for an act that does not constitute a crime, filing investigative reports with missing information, relying on questionable witnesses, and search and seizure violations. Prosecutors' reliance on the police makes these problems one more hurdle to overcome and gives prosecutors an added incentive to provide regular training to law enforcement agencies to address these issues.

Finally, many prosecutors told us how their work impacted them emotionally. Frequent exposure to violent crime left several desensitized to violence and lacking empathy for the defendant. "We [become] good at dehumanizing the defendant and [see only] the victim," one prosecutor told us. As a result, they have difficulty considering alternatives to incarceration, pushing instead for charges and sentences that are more punitive. On a personal level, the anxiety and irrational fears that prosecutors described are akin to the symptoms of post-traumatic stress disorder. Other have described these feelings as secondary traumatic stress, or emotional trauma caused by indirect exposure to the original strain,[56] although little published work exists on the topic as it relates to prosecutors.

The psychological effects of prosecuting, starting at charging, deserve greater attention. Prosecutors who have lost empathy or have become desensitized to violence cannot fairly charge defendants or ensure that victims receive justice. On the other end of the spectrum, the secondary trauma that prosecutors experience from their interactions with victims can lead to intense physical and emotional reactions. One possible response is to rotate prosecutors out of major crime units to decrease their constant exposure to violence. Increasing awareness of this problem, providing and destigmatizing counseling services, and giving prosecutors opportunities to discuss these problems with colleagues may also help alleviate the psychological burdens of prosecution.

Reform 5: Promote Diversity in Prosecution

We recommend that district attorneys make an active effort to hire prosecutors with diverse backgrounds. Traditionally, white men have dominated the criminal justice profession in the United States. However, as the field of law has become more diverse across race, ethnicity, and gender, criminal court actors have also become somewhat more diverse.[57] Indeed, nonwhite prosecutors represented 19–30% of the lawyers in each office we studied. Although the diversification of judges and lawyers has not eliminated problems like mass incarceration or racial disparities in sentencing outcomes, there is some evidence that diversity, especially among prosecutors, may be a step in the right direction.[58] Previous research has shown that jurisdictions employing greater percentages of African Americans in their justice systems, particularly among prosecutors, tend to have smaller racial disparities in incarceration.[59] In our work on charging, we found that prosecutors of color tended to view victim input as more important and a defendant's criminal history as less important than did their white colleagues.

However, the growing racial and ethnic diversity among prosecutors may not yet be sufficient to produce broad organizational change. In the offices we studied, prosecutors of color reported dismissing fewer cases than their white colleagues—a departure from the assumption that minority decision makers will be more lenient.[60] This does not necessarily suggest that nonwhite prosecutors are "stricter" than their white counterparts. As Rosabeth Moss Kanter's work on minority representation in organizations suggests, organizational change requires more than a few "token" minority employees; it takes a "strong minority presence."[61] In other words, it may be that these offices do not yet have enough nonwhite lawyers on staff to make prosecutors of color comfortable exercising their preferred discretion. Indeed, several prosecutors of color told us that they felt pressure not to dismiss weak cases or reduce charges when they felt that the police had made a mistake.

A similar phenomenon has been observed among judges. While many hoped that the increasing diversity among judges would eliminate pervasive problems like mass incarceration and racial discrimination in sentencing, this has not yet occurred.[62] That unrealized hope may be attributed, in part, to the strength of organizational norms. As prior work suggests, the process of judicial selection and socialization may offset attitudinal differences among judges of different races.[63] So, too, the organizational incentive for prosecutors to simply charge cases may counterbalance the inclination of individual prosecutors to view cases more skeptically.

Our recommendation extends beyond racial and ethnic diversity: we also advise recruiting lawyers with defense experience. In one of the jurisdictions we studied, prosecutors with prior defense experience praised the effect of that work, saying they are better able to understand why a defendant offends and are better-positioned to suggest resolutions that target the source. This perspective "from the other side" may help prosecutors recognize when criminality is the byproduct of other underlying issues or unmet needs and assist them in crafting more creative solutions for repeat offenders. Other researchers have also suggested that electing district attorneys with defense experience has multiple benefits, including developing a respectful work relationship with the defense bar, sharing potentially exculpatory evidence, and identifying weak aspects of a case.[64]

Additionally, our findings suggest that prosecutors' ideological beliefs influence their charging decisions. We saw this most clearly when we presented a focus group of prosecutors in one jurisdiction with a potential case of resisting arrest and asked them whether and how they would charge the matter. Self-described conservatives were more likely to side with the police officer involved and say that each distinct act of the defendant—turning away from the officer, calling him expletives, pulling a hand away—constituted a separate count of resistance. Moderate and liberal prosecutors, by contrast, tended to look at the event as a whole and would have charged a single count. Hypothetical cases involving possession of marijuana or drug paraphernalia also highlighted ideological differences. Some of the more liberal prosecutors said that, unless there was evidence of other offenses, they would refuse to charge these crimes, especially since, as one prosecutor predicted, the state "is going to decriminalize marijuana in the next two years." Other prosecutors, however—those who saw themselves as "tough on crime"—were perfectly willing to charge defendants with these crimes and routinely pursued minor drug cases. Some saw these crimes as gateways to more serious offending. Others simply felt that their job was to "enforce the law whatever it is."

Having such diverse ideological perspectives within the same office can spur important conversations about the function and aim of charging. It also calls for a more deliberate determination about appropriate charging. A large body of research suggests that diverse groups tend to perform better on complex tasks, engage in more information sharing, and generate more creative solutions than less diverse groups.[65] In light of this, increasing the diversity of line staff in district attorneys' offices should help improve the quality of their decision-making in charging and processing cases. However, that diversity needs to be incorporated into accepted charging norms. The answer does not lie in divergent practices, that is, where a subgroup of progressive prosecutors in the office charges more leniently while their more conservative colleagues charge severely. Justice for victims and defendants should not turn on the demographics or ideology of the prosecutor who handles a case. Rather, sincerely reform-minded district attorneys should garner the diverse perspectives of their line attorneys and integrate them into accepted and understood charging policies.

Diversifying line prosecutors may require district attorneys to recruit differently. This could mean recruiting from more geographically diverse law schools or, in the longer term, encouraging local students of color to attend law school to pursue a career in prosecution. Building a more diverse team of prosecutors may also require an image change for prosecution. Retiring the old messages of the "war on drugs" and "tough on crime" eras and promoting evidence-based prosecution reforms may be just the vision that is needed. By espousing a new message—one that prioritizes evidenced-based practices to prevent crime and divert, treat, and rehabilitate defendants—district attorneys may be able to appeal to a broader demographic of attorneys.

Conclusion: Enacting Reform

The burgeoning community of prosecutors interested in evidence-based practices creates a significant opportunity for researchers to better understand prosecution. Among prosecutors' many roles, their charging function has received relatively little attention even though it is a crucially important stage. Prosecutors' newfound openness to collecting and sharing data gives researchers the opportunity to examine the inner workings of prosecutors' charging decisions. From our own in-depth look under the hood of prosecutors' charging decisions, we identified five areas for reform. First, we recommend that prosecutors' offices create dedicated charging units and implement early case screening systems that can efficiently eliminate cases that do not warrant prosecution, thereby minimizing defendants' unnecessary exposure to the criminal justice system and easing prosecutors' caseloads. We also encourage district attorneys to assign veteran prosecutors to these charging units, as their experience and perspective is best suited to the job of weighing charges.

Second, we find significant delays between arrest and the filing of formal charges. These delays turn on defendant and case characteristics and should be addressed. We therefore recommend that district attorneys implement more ambitious time standards for the filing of charges and that they implement training and supervision to ensure that these timelines are met. With the creation of formal screening units, prosecutors should be able to process cases more quickly, reduce pretrial detention, and meet speedy charging standards.

Third, we find that defendants' criminal history plays heavily into many prosecutors' charging decisions. In practice, prosecutors use criminal history as a measure of a defendant's character, which then becomes a guide for the appropriate charge and desired outcome for the case. Since criminal history is rarely an element of the crime but instead an explicit sentencing criterion, we recommend that district attorneys implement an office policy that prohibits factoring a defendant's criminal history into the charging decision.

Fourth, our research shows that prosecuting crime takes a toll on those who do it. Between heavy caseloads, repeated exposure to some of the darkest acts in our society, and a lack of control over the quality of the work from law enforcement and the defense bar, greater attention should be paid to the needs of prosecutors. In addition to reducing caseloads through early case screening, we recommend that district attorneys' offices rotate their prosecutors out of major crime units to avoid desensitization to violence. They should also hold regular trainings with law enforcement to improve investigations and provide clarity about the nature of charging.

Finally, we urge district attorneys to hire prosecutors from diverse backgrounds. Even in the most racially diverse office in our study, only 30% of the line prosecutors were people of color. To help ensure that the criminal justice system is as diverse as the individuals it addresses and serves, district attorneys should actively recruit prosecutors with diverse educational, socioeconomic, racial, ethnic, ideological, and professional backgrounds.

We are cognizant that change does not always come easily, especially since organizational norms and habits in prosecutors' offices are often deeply engrained. However, we are hopeful that the new era of evidence-based prosecution can replace anecdotal rationales. Importantly, reform requires consistent messages and oversight. It is not enough for a district attorney (especially a newly elected one) to announce a new office policy. Senior staff must work in unison to create buy-in before implementing the reform. Although the recent wave of reform-minded district attorneys creates an opportunity for change, lasting reform hinges on career prosecutors. They must accept the idea that evidence should shape the policies and must take an active role in culture change. Across the nation, prosecutors are riding that wave. We are optimistic that enduring change is afoot.

NOTES

1 Davis, "Prosecutorial Discretion."
2 Miller and Wright, "The Black Box."
3 Hagan, "Extra-Legal Attributes and Criminal Sentencing"; Baumer, "Reassessing and Redirecting Research on Race and Sentencing." Sentencing guidelines significantly constrained judges' discretion while leaving prosecutors' discretionary power largely untouched. Stith and Cabranes, *Fear of Judging*; Starr and Rehavi, "Racial Disparity in Federal Criminal Sentences"; Tonry, *Sentencing Matters*; Albonetti, "Sentencing under the Federal Sentencing Guidelines"; Lacasse and Payne, "Federal Sentencing Guidelines and Mandatory Minimum Sentences"; Ulmer, *Social Worlds of Sentencing*; Oppel, "Sentencing Shift Gives New Leverage to Prosecutor." Some scholars even argue that sentencing guidelines simply shifted discretionary power from judges into the hands of prosecutors because guideline ranges and mandatory minimums gave prosecutors powerful tools to leverage plea agreements.
4 Medwed, *Prosecution Complex*.
5 Miller, "The New Reformer DAs," 4.
6 Fairfax, "From Overcriminalization to Smart on Crime."
7 United States Department of Justice Archives, "The Attorney General's Smart on Crime Initiative," 1.
8 Office of the Attorney General, "Memorandum to the United States Attorneys," 1.
9 Medina, "The Progressive Prosecutors."
10 Fairfax, "The 'Smart on Crime' Prosecutor."
11 Miller, "The New Reformer DAs"; Medina, "The Progressive Prosecutors."
12 Wright, "Beyond Prosecutor Elections."
13 LaFountain et al., *Examining the Work of State Courts*.
14 Bland, "George Soros' Quiet Overhaul of the U.S. Justice System"; "George Soros/ Political Activity."
15 American Civil Liberties Union, "Primary Voter Turnout"; Otterbein, "Voter Turnout Skyrockets in Philly's District Attorney Race."
16 Austen, "Progressive D.A. Tests the Power."
17 "In Memoriam: Kenneth P. Thompson, 1966–2016," 2.
18 Austen, "Progressive D.A. Tests the Power"; Medina, "The Progressive Prosecutors."
19 Bazelon and Krinsky, "There's a Wave of New Prosecutors."

20 Austen, "Progressive D.A. Tests the Power"; Jouvenal, "Tattooed Tilt to the Left."
21 Dehghani-Tafti, "What I Believe In"; Khurshid, "Should a Top Prosecutor Have Prior Prosecutorial Experience?"; Madej, "Who Is Larry Krasner?"
22 della Cava, "New, More Progressive Prosecutors Are Angering Police."
23 Daniels, "The Kim Foxx Effect"; Jouvenal, "Tattooed Tilt to the Left."
24 "Who We Are," www.pceinc.org.
25 Institute for Innovation in Prosecution at John Jay College, "Innovation in Criminal Justice," www.prosecution.org.
26 "Our Work and Vision," https://fairandjustprosecution.org.
27 "Advancing Prosecutorial Effectiveness and Fairness," https://caj.fiu.edu.
28 "National Survey of Prosecutors," www.bjs.gov. The Bureau of Justice Assistance classified offices as serving populations of (a) 1,000,000 or more, (b) 250.000–999,999, (c) 100,000–249,000, or (d) 99,999 or less. The jurisdictions chronicled here fall into categories (b) and (c).
29 Abrams, "Is Pleading Really a Bargain?"; Cossyleon et al., "Deferring Felony Prosecution"; Kutateladze et al., "Cumulative Disadvantage."
30 Perry and Banks, *Prosecutors in State Courts, 2007—Statistical Tables.*
31 Bushway, Redlich, and Norris, "An Explicit Test of Plea Bargaining"; Kutateladze, Andiloro, and Johnson, "How Does Defendant Race Influence Plea Bargaining?"; Yan and Bushway, "Plea Discounts or Trial Penalties?"
32 Reaves, *Felony Defendants in Large Urban Counties, 2009.*
33 Free, "Race and Presentencing Decisions in the United States"; Metcalfe and Chiricos, "Race, Plea, and Charge Reduction"; Piehl and Bushway, "Measuring and Explaining Charge Bargaining"; Shermer and Johnson, "Criminal Prosecutions"; Sutton, "Structural Bias in the Sentencing of Felony Defendants."
34 Kim, Spohn, and Hedberg, "Federal Sentencing as a Complex Collaborative Process."
35 Carmichael, Gibson, and Voloudakis, "Evaluating the Impact of Direct Electronic Filing in Criminal Cases"; Gershowitz, "Justice on the Line."
36 Gershowitz, "Justice on the Line."
37 This conclusion comes from our own research and that of Gershowitz, "Justice on the Line."
38 Gershowitz, "Justice on the Line," 34.
39 Hopwood, "The Not so Speedy Trial Act."
40 American Bar Association, *Standards Relating to Trial Courts, 1992 Edition*, Section 2.50.
41 Ostrom and Hanson, *Efficiency, Timeliness, and Quality.* They found that, of nine jurisdictions studied, none met the ABA benchmark. On average, courts only resolved 68% of cases within 180 days. Further, there was significant variability between courts, with the most expeditious court studied resolving 89% of cases within 180 days and the least expeditious court studied resolving less than 50% of cases within 180 days.
42 Van Duizend, Steelman, and Suskin, *Model Time Standards for State Trial Courts.* The Model Time Standards were a collaboration of the Conference of State Court

Administrators, the Conference of Chief Justices, the American Bar Association House of Delegates, and the National Association for Court Management.

43 Office of the Legislative Auditor General, State of Utah, *A Performance Audit of the Operating Efficiency of the Utah State Court System*; Judicial Council of California/Administrative Office of the Courts, *Statewide Caseload Trends, 2000–2001 Through 2009–2010.*

44 American Bar Association, "Criminal Justice Section Standards: Speedy Trial," Standard 12–2.6(a).

45 Steelman, "State and Local Trial Courts."

46 Meeker, O'Neil, and Hayes, "Policing and Prosecuting Sexual Assault." They find that, in sexual assault cases, victim cooperation is a stronger predictor of arrest and charging than even physical evidence.

47 The offense level of the crime is the other. US Sentencing Commission, *2018 Guidelines Manual.*

48 Frederick and Stemen, *Anatomy of Discretion: An Analysis of Prosecutorial Decision Making*; Spohn and Holleran, "Prosecuting Sexual Assault."

49 Steffensmeier, Ulmer, and Kramer, "The Interaction of Race, Gender, and Age in Criminal Sentencing."

50 Kutateladze et al., "Cumulative Disadvantage," 519.

51 The Sentencing Project, *Report of The Sentencing Project to the United Nations Special Rapporteur.*

52 A defendant's criminal history is arguably germane in the risk assessment of pretrial release. Yang, "Toward an Optimal Bail System." But unless the elements of a statute specifically reference past crimes, a defendant's criminal record is irrelevant in charging.

53 Gershowitz and Killinger, "The State Never Rests."

54 Lefstein, *Securing Reasonable Caseloads.*

55 Gershowitz and Killinger, "The State Never Rests."

56 Miles-Thrope, "Trauma for the Tough-Minded Prosecutor"; Seamone, "Sex Crimes Litigation as Hazardous Duty."

57 Ward, "Race and the Justice Workforce"; Smith, *Emancipation: The Making of the Black Lawyer, 1844–1944*; George, "Court Fixing."

58 Ward, Farrell, and Rousseau, "Does Racial Balance in Workforce Representation Yield Equal Justice?"; King, Johnson, and McGeever, "Demography of the Legal Profession and Racial Disparities in Sentencing."

59 Ward, Farrell, and Rousseau, "Does Racial Balance in Workforce Representation Yield Equal Justice?"

60 Smith, *Race Versus the Robe*; Goldman, "Should There Be Affirmative Action for the Judiciary"; Welch, Combs, and Gruhl, "Do Black Judges Make a Difference?"

61 Kanter, *Men and Women of the Corporation.*

62 Steffensmeier and Britt, "Judges' Race and Judicial Decision Making," 761. Prior to much empirical research on the topic, many assumed that black judges would sentence distinctively from white judges, in that black judges would be more sym-

pathetic to traditionally marginalized groups. Johnson, "The Multilevel Context of Criminal Sentencing"; Spohn, "The Sentencing Decisions of Black and White Judges." However, the research on the effect of judicial diversity on sentencing outcomes is quite mixed, with some scholars finding that black judges tend to be less punitive on minority defendants compared to white judges. Steffensmeier and Britt, "Judges' Race and Judicial Decision Making." Others find that black judges are actually more punitive than white judges.

63 Steffensmeier and Britt, "Judges' Race and Judicial Decision Making."
64 Levine and Wright, "Prosecutor Risk, Maturation, and Wrongful Conviction Practice."
65 Sommers, "On Racial Diversity and Group Decision Making," 598. Sommers provides a detailed discussion on the effects of group diversity.

Participatory Defense as an Abolitionist Strategy

RAJ JAYADEV AND JANET MOORE

In 2007, a few families met around a table at Silicon Valley De-Bug, a community organizing hub in San Jose, California.[1] The families came to De-Bug because their loved ones were facing the possibility of going to jail or prison. Gail's son David had been racially profiled, beaten by police, and wrongfully charged with resisting arrest. Blanca was there with her 17-year-old son, Ronny, who was developmentally delayed and required 24-hour care. Police had coerced Ronny to create a fictional account of his involvement while interrogating him for a robbery charge. Christina was there for her dad, a day laborer who was picked up on a misdemeanor charge while looking for work outside a Home Depot. He now faced possible deportation due to the criminal charge.

When these families gathered at the De-Bug table, their feelings ranged from uncertain to scared. They did not know if the defense lawyers were doing the work needed to beat the prosecution's case. They did not feel they had a trusted counselor and advocate to walk with them and fight for their loved one throughout the process. No one at the table had chosen these lawyers. Like most people who face criminal charges, David, Ronny, and Christina's dad couldn't afford to hire counsel. Their cases were assigned to government-paid attorneys. And like public defense providers across the country, the attorneys were caught up in a perpetual crisis caused by lax regulation, inadequate funding, and excessive workloads. The attorneys juggled too many cases with too few resources and struggled to fulfill their basic duties to communicate, investigate, and advocate.[2]

The costs of the public defense crisis are enormous. A good lawyer is literally the first line of defense against excessive penalties and related harms that fall disproportionately on poor people and people of color.[3] US penal systems impose distinctively harsh incarceration rates, sentences, and conditions; onerous fines, fees, and forfeitures; and civil disabilities that deny people voting rights, US residency and citizenship, jobs, housing, and education.[4] Had these families not gathered at the De-Bug table, they would have faced the intimidating, anxiety-filled, confusing prospect of navigating those risks alone. Instead, they worked together to support each other. They learned to dissect police reports, locate defense evidence, and create social biography videos to share the fuller story of who their loved ones were beyond the case file. They came to court for one another, packing court dates with community presence. They met weekly to share updates and strategize next steps. Their solidarity equipped them to demand more from the public defense lawyers and to empower the lawyers by sharing new insights and energy.

Their collective effort paid off. Prosecutors dropped charges in all three cases. But the effect was greater than the results from these individual cases: as the families worked together at the De-Bug table, the participatory defense movement was born. The movement's key innovation was to inject community organizing into public defense. Celebrated by a MacArthur "Genius" award, the movement's steady growth into a national network of participatory defense hubs (40 as of publication) provides evidence that people can work together to change case outcomes, practices, policies, and—most important—themselves.[5] These changes reflect the movement's three major goals: improving public defense in specific cases and jurisdictions; rebalancing race, class, and power disparities that benefit police, prosecutors, and prisons; and creating new organizers who advance penal abolition. This approach to justice transformation aims at ending reliance on criminal legal systems as the default response to social problems by building healthy people and communities and better ways to prevent and heal harm.[6] The success of this capacity-building approach is evident in the quasi-abolitionism of wealthy white neighborhoods, where access to quality education, health care, income, housing, and transportation accompanies low rates of contact with crime, police, prosecution, and prisons. This approach also finds support in research on social determinants of health, deterrent effects of social supports and collective efficacy, remediation of structural violence inflicted on race-class subjected communities, and the resilience of the same communities, among other factors.[7]

We begin this chapter by clarifying relationships among participatory defense, penal abolition, and evidence-based criminal justice reform. We then describe the public defense crisis that sparked participatory defense, illustrate the movement's unique contribution to justice transformation, and show how policy makers, public defenders, and community members can engage with participatory defense and advance movement goals. Throughout the chapter, researchers should also see opportunities to advance knowledge about the movement by creating co-learning partnerships with participatory defense hubs.

Participatory Defense, Penal Abolition, and Evidence-Based Justice Reform

In considering relationships among participatory defense, penal abolition, and evidence-based justice reform, three closely related points bear emphasis. First, participatory defense provides the missing "people power" required to drive sustainable improvement in broken public defense systems.[8] Where isolated resistance can make things worse for people who need public defense,[9] the movement connects and amplifies the voices of people who face criminal charges, their families, and their communities. Through those connections, people transform themselves from being (at best) recipients of professional services or (at worst) fodder for carceral machinery. They become change agents who intervene at a crucial juncture in criminal cases. They convert years of potential time served into time saved, bringing loved ones home from jail, prison, and immigration detention centers. They push new practices and policies aiming to make "criminal justice" more than an oxymoron or aspiration.

Second, participatory defense is part of a social movement family that brings people power to interventions in policing, charging, bail, sentencing, and incarceration.[10] These movements have been active for years but gained broader attention during global protests that arose after Minneapolis police killed George Floyd in May 2020. These movements do not aim to patch broken systems to keep them running. Instead, they redefine public safety, advance "nonreformist reforms" that reduce reliance on carceral systems, and work toward a future in which mutually thriving, self-governing communities—those not plagued by racism and poverty—abolish the need for such systems.[11] Movement members often acknowledge that realizing these aspirations requires struggle, in part because some people disagree that such a future is possible. However, these movements insist that the abolitionist framework generates the questions and innovations necessary for justice transformation.[12]

Third, this collective critical engagement with criminal justice offers new ways to think about evidence-based system change.[13] Critical engagement analyzes power: Who defines and punishes crime? Who evaluates the success of those endeavors? Why do they hold that power—and to what effect? Some effects are unsurprising. Power often shields the powerful from criminal liability for even the gravest of harms.[14] Yet criminal legal systems have strong inertia as the default response to harm, especially when alternatives are lacking; communities often report harm from both overpolicing and unresponsive policing.[15] That inertia persists despite the lack of conclusive evidence that incarceration reduces crime or, if it does, at what cost.[16]

Naming these problems is not rejection of research; if anything, it is the logical conclusion from a holistic account of research that illustrates the overreach and failures of the carceral state.[17] Neither is it an indictment of efforts by criminal justice officials and staff to wrestle optimal outcomes from flawed systems. Instead, it is a demand for more effective interventions that emerge from co-learning research partnerships with communities as they adapt unique local experiences, knowledge, analytical frameworks, and priorities to the struggle for justice.[18] Those adaptations are necessarily fluid, partial, and iterative. For participatory defense, the important goals are improving case outcomes, public defense systems, and related policies. It is crucial, however, to remain focused on the movement's overarching aim of creating organizers who can advance justice transformation. The movement's most important metric is the people themselves, who no longer feel isolated and powerless against criminal legal systems but instead identify and advance interventions to make those systems unnecessary. Through content analysis, exploratory qualitative and statistical analyses, and interviews, in this chapter we offer evidence that participatory defense is among the most promising interventions to date into the permanent crisis of public defense.

A "Peculiar Sacredness": The Permanent Crisis of Public Defense

David, Ronny, and Christina's dad had a right to government-paid defense counsel because, like most people who face possible incarceration, they could not afford to hire a lawyer.[19] The right to public defense arises from federal and state constitutions, statutes, administrative codes, case law, and court rules.[20] From one perspective, all of these regulatory mechanisms protect fundamental life, liberty, and property interests at risk when governments target an individual for detention, interrogation, and prosecution. Those interests led the United States Supreme Court to describe the right to counsel as having a "peculiar sacredness."[21] The same interests led the Court to extend the right to public defense from the trial phase to pretrial (custodial interrogation, initial appearances, plea bargaining), sentencing, appeal, and postconviction, with an estimated annual cost of $4.5 billion.[22]

Despite the importance of public defense, systems that provide it have been in crisis for decades. As one historian put it, "the permanent crisis permanesces."[23] The crisis denies poor people their right to counsel entirely in some instances and blocks them from high-quality representation in others.[24] In *Avery v. Alabama*, for example, the Court lauded the "peculiar sacredness" of the right to counsel, then let Alabama execute Mr. Avery even though his lawyers had spent only a few hours on his defense. Before and after *Avery*, public defense has been notorious for excessive workloads, poor performance, and the chasm between law's soaring rhetoric and shameful reality.[25] From this perspective, the peculiar sacredness of public defense is how it funnels tax dollars to one group of lawyers (defenders) to make life easier for other government-paid lawyers (prosecutors and judges) by feeding a government-funded carceral machine that chews up poor people and people of color who lack the political power to fight back. Social science research sheds light on this perspective by analyzing ways that "courtroom work groups" comprising prosecutors, defenders, and judges churn cases through the system so quickly that the process becomes part of the punishment.[26] Some defenders fight that case-processing role, others acquiesce in it, and many lament it, asking: "Why don't my clients think I'm a real lawyer?"[27]

That question persists because the public defense crisis prevents even well-intentioned lawyers from fulfilling basic duties, such as communicating with people they represent; investigating facts and researching law; filing motions to secure experts and exclude illegally obtained evidence; trying cases; and minimizing convictions and sentences. These failures cause wrongful convictions, unsupported guilty pleas, overincarceration, and unwarranted civil disabilities that hinder healthy family and community life. They feed mass incarceration, magnify power disparities that favor the state, and deepen the estrangement and disenfranchisement caused by contact with criminal legal systems.[28]

These grave problems brought families to the De-Bug table in 2007. But if the problems are so clear, why do they continue? There is widespread agreement that the major reasons are structural: federalist deference to local rule; separation of powers among the three branches of government; and the lack of a powerful political champion for high-quality public defense. In other words, judges won't issue rulings that force legislatures to pay for quality defense in cases prosecutors file against poor people who have no political action committee.[29] Two judge-made legal doctrines raise especially high barriers to reform. One requires people to prove that they were denied counsel. Courts insist that the doctrine requires more than a warm body with a law degree, but winning relief is extremely difficult.[30] The second doctrine requires proof of two things in a specific case: first, that counsel failed to meet prevailing practice standards; and second, a reasonable possibility that meeting the standards would have changed the outcome. Courts have used this doctrine to find lawyers effective while asleep, habitually drunk, and—while apparently awake and sober—failing to find and use readily available evidence of innocence.[31]

Since these doctrines are so good at blocking relief, neither has generated enforceable standards for structuring and funding public defense. Systems can be funded at the federal, state, county, or municipal levels. They can rely mainly on public defense agencies with salaried attorneys or, alternatively, on private counsel who take appointments on a case-by-case basis or are under contracts to handle a set number of cases for a specific fee.[32] Pay rates often barely cover overhead. Conflicts of interest are rampant. Louisiana's system is especially perverse, but it is far from extraordinary. Funding comes mainly from fines and fees, which are disproportionately imposed on poor people. A chief defender captured this pernicious circle with dismay: "Public defenders are paid to lose."[33]

Channeling these structural, political, doctrinal, and cultural forces, courts allow conflicts of interest and excessive workloads to continue. They do so despite long-standing demands for resource parity between defense and prosecution, despite guidelines requiring defenders to re-fuse excessive caseloads, and despite workload studies and horror sto-ries from overloaded jurisdictions.[34] Judicial orders for systemic relief are rare, jurisdiction-specific, and require years of litigation; funding settlements are vulnerable to budget-conscious legislators and gover-nors.[35] Prosecutors seldom reduce demand by dismissing cases even when courts encourage it. During Missouri's lengthy litigation, the St. Louis prosecutor insisted that creating waiting lists for public defense representation was the "least-bad alternative" to dismissals.[36] Civil rights advocates objected because waiting lists delay access to counsel for months and even years; if jailed pretrial because they cannot afford bail, people lose jobs, housing, family relationships, and evidence—and those mounting losses raise pressure to take unjustifiable plea deals.[37]

Lack of defender independence compounds these problems. Stan-dards promulgated by the American Bar Association prioritize public defense independence to ease pressure from hostile judges, prosecutors, legislators, and voters.[38] Some jurisdictions respond with commissions of diverse stakeholders who establish rules for attorney qualification, training, appointment, payment, and performance. However, judges still often decide which attorneys are appointed and how much they are paid.[39] Power over defenders' paychecks chills advocacy by encourag-ing lawyers to keep the docket moving and the appointments coming. Pressure is highest where expectations of defenders are low, competition for cases is high, reimbursement rates barely keep the lights on, and attorneys can buy favorable treatment through contributions to judi-cial campaigns. These problems even mar the federal system; despite being among the best in terms of funding, training, and oversight, local cultures undermine independence, in turn influencing appointments, compensation, performance, and results.[40]

These well-recognized system deficits create justifiable mistrust among people who need public defense, their families, and their com-munities.[41] Courts deepen mistrust by appointing defense counsel instead of granting poor people the same right to choose a qualified, available lawyer that is enjoyed by those who can afford to hire counsel.[42] The result is a "meet 'em and plead 'em" stereotype of public defense lawyers who work for the government, not the person facing charges. To be sure, many defenders work extremely hard and provide top-quality representation. Too often, however, defenders and systems are overwhelmed by crushing workloads, toxic local cultures, burnout, and high turnover.[43] Too often, the process effectively erases people who need public defense. As one man described his experience:

> Once they see what you in there for, they already know. They just come down there with a paper and it's got your name on it, all your charges, all your history on it, and he's tellin' you, "We gonna plead this." Wait a minute, dude, we ain't even talk. "And if we plead this, the judge already said that he would do this." When did that happen?! Where was I at?![44]

The public defense crisis has deep roots. It resists attempted cures. It feeds the larger criminal justice crisis manifest in the 2020 global protests over race, poverty, and the meaning of public safety. These overlapping crises highlight the importance of participatory defense and its release of previously untapped people power to drive meaningful, sustainable justice transformation.

Participatory Defense Principles, Strategies, and Achievements

Understanding participatory defense requires understanding how Silicon Valley De-Bug operates. The basic principles and practices are important because, while they are not quick or easy to implement and may be unfamiliar to some readers, they are already present and effective in communities all over the country. That fact is evident from the expansion of participatory defense from a single hub in San Jose into a national network of at least 40 mutually supportive, yet independently creative, local hubs in diverse regions across the country.[45] After explaining movement principles, this section provides an overview of movement strategies, then shows how those strategies change case outcomes, practices, policies, law, and the people themselves.

Protect Your People: Participatory Defense Principles

De-Bug calls itself an "un-organization" in which community work grows organically and instinctually through a deliberate process of inclusive "slow-building" that makes everyone an architect of the institution. This allows a stronger sense of ownership and decision-making that is consensual and horizontal, not top-down. As a result, De-Bug activities run the gamut: media hub, meditation circle, criminal justice organizing model. The activities reflect De-Bug's respect for total personhood and allow for the strengths and needs of individual communities to emerge as the focus of the group. A recent immigrant may also be an emcee; a factory worker may also be a meditation expert; a formerly incarcerated person may also be an artist. Every De-Bug enterprise— from political campaigns to entrepreneurial endeavors and participatory defense—came from an individual who offered a hope, dream, or idea. The De-Bug community followed that individual's lead.

It cannot be overemphasized that it is this focus on relationships rather than projects that sustains the work. It is not romanticism but rather hardheaded pragmatism to recognize that, before De-Bug had a budget, tax ID number, or MacArthur Award, the people had each other; and also that building this level of solidarity through inclusive, horizontal decision-making is hard, slow work. Like a martial art, it is a practice. After repeating the motions over and over each day, when the skills are needed they can be applied quickly and naturally. The values become the practice, the practice becomes instinctual, and when it matters most, instincts become actions. The process takes time, effort, patience, commitment, mutual respect, care, and trust. Those capacities are present in communities across the country, generating unique strategies for change.

Principles in Action: Participatory Defense Strategies

One of the most widely used participatory defense strategies is the social biography video. This strategy is a good example of how participatory defense is slow-built. In the movement's earliest days, families like Gail's, Blanca's, and Christina's came to the De-Bug table to strategize on how to advocate for loved ones facing charges. What they wanted above all was for the judges deciding the fate of their family members to know the accused beyond the police report. Meanwhile, during the week, youth videographers were at De-Bug honing their storytelling skills. The two groups were introduced. The result was social biography videos. These short films illuminate the lives of those facing incarceration, deportation, or even execution in ways that court documents cannot. They show how the outcome of a case would affect not only the person facing charges but also his or her family and community. Instead of freezing a person in the static moment of a charged offense, these videos show the dynamic lives of loved ones who have a past, a future, and the potential for redemption and transformation like anyone else.

Sharing that information overcomes limitations that judges face when deciding another's fate. The videos take judges and prosecutors out of the sterility of the courtroom and into the complicated realities of community life they usually have no connection to; conversely, they allow compelling community narratives to penetrate the courts. Judges and prosecutors see the parking lot where a young man was forced to sleep while he was homeless. They meet the uncle who runs an auto body shop and has a job waiting for his nephew. Such insights are most likely to emerge from intimate, caring relationships. They change case outcomes from pretrial release, through plea negotiations, to sentencing and parole. As one judge put it, the videos "humanize defendants, destroy stereotypes, and leave judges with a far better understanding of the persons standing before them."[46] Gideon Project founder and MacArthur Award winner Jon Rapping describes the videos' additional, structural-reform potential: they provide an "army of advocates with a new tool to fight back against a system that has become complacent about processing people because it sees them . . . only as the crime with which they are accused."[47]

Participatory defense continues to bring new tools to that fight, slow-building interventions that change not only case outcomes but also practices, policies, laws, and the movement members themselves. Annual case reviews document how people transform years of potential time served into time saved as they analyze and challenge police reports and court records and provide new evidence to fight the prosecution's case. Additional statistical analysis illustrates the impact of building sustained community presence in the courtroom to let judges and prosecutors know that the person facing charges is not alone. Movement members identify systemic problems and solutions, engaging in court interventions, public protests, and policy advocacy. They increase trust between defenders and the people they represent, secure new resources for defenders facing overwhelming caseloads, and challenge laws and policies that generate new cases.[48]

These core principles and strategies are an evolution in public defense. They allow people facing charges, their families, and their communities to participate in, and thereby reciprocate and strengthen, efforts of public defenders. They do so by shifting the focus from the agency of lawyers and other professionals to the agency of people and communities harmed most directly by crime and criminal legal systems. Working together collectively, people and communities push, empower, and collaborate with public defenders to optimize results in specific cases and to fight for systemic solutions to systemic problems. The work starts at the table—the participatory defense hub—where community members guide and coach each other through the stress, confusion, and frustration of confronting criminal charges. The self-transformation that emerges is among the most important types of evidence of the movement's achievements.

Coming to the Table: The Transformational Power of the Participatory Defense Hub

The best way to understand the power of participatory defense is to participate. That means applying movement principles by decentering the usual focus on lawyers to highlight the self-transformation of movement members. This shift in perspective is important because it reveals self-transformation as the necessary and previously missing condition not only for achieving sustainable improvements in public defense but also for achieving broader movement goals of shifting power and eventually abolishing criminal legal systems as the default solution to social problems.

Opportunities for self-transformation arise each week during participatory defense hub meetings, which occur in community-friendly spaces such as community centers, churches, and the work spaces of nonprofit social justice organizations. On entering a De-Bug participatory defense hub meeting, you might see 13-year-old Tony sitting shyly at the edge of a conference table next to his mother. Tony was just released after 99 days in juvenile hall. He responds respectfully to the "congratulations" and "welcome home" sentiments offered by strangers around the table. Although these supporters have never met Tony, they know him through his mother's stories and from seeing his name on the participatory defense hub whiteboard. Tony is participating in the first of several ceremonies that were created by and are distinctive to participatory defense. When a family brings a loved one to the table, his or her name is written on a whiteboard. When the family brings the loved one home by helping defense lawyers obtain dismissals, acquittals, or reduced sentences, the loved ones erase their names from the whiteboard.

The crowd of 20 people breaks into applause when Tony takes the eraser to his name. Tony's mother thanks the community who supported her and her son through the darkest 99 days of their lives. She is in tears. Tony was facing years of incarceration, but thanks to participatory defense strategies, her advocacy, and the public defender's lawyering, her son will be able to have his fourteenth birthday at home. In addition to the whiteboard ceremony, Tony's story will be lifted up in a "Time Served to Time Saved" celebration. At these events, the movement honors new benchmarks by comparing the original maximum sentencing exposure that people faced with the result after participatory defense intervention. In its first 15 years of existence, participatory defense has prevented justice system actors from inflicting time served—time in a cell, isolated from family and community—and has saved over 10,200 years for defendants, families, and communities to live, work, heal, and grow together.

If tradition holds, Tony's mother will continue attending participatory defense hub meetings. She will help other families who find themselves in the frightening, stressful, and confusing position she once occupied. She will share with them what she learned from others in the participatory defense movement. In this way, the participatory defense learning process is a cumulative intelligence—each new family, each new case, informing the body of knowledge of the hub, which then is more equipped to support the next family.

There is tremendous power in bringing a community organizing ethos to the otherwise deeply isolating experience of facing charges in a criminal or juvenile courtroom. Participatory defense hub meetings are now facilitated by people who first came for their own cases or cases involving their loved ones. In 2007, Gail and Blanca were isolated, anguished mothers who felt forced to sit idly as their sons were chewed up by the courts. Today they are vocal advocates who help other families navigate daunting, complicated court processes. They train communities across the country, speaking as both mothers and organizers who have learned the power and possibility of participatory defense. In the slow-building martial artistry of participatory defense, Gail and Blanca are black belts.

Exploratory qualitative research and content analysis of publications by and about the movement indicate that the same self-transformation is happening in hubs from Birmingham to Boston, from Phoenix to Philadelphia.[49] As new groups of low-income people and Black, brown, Indigenous, and other people of color bring loved ones home from criminal legal systems, they develop new theories and practices for new interventions to shrink those systems and their race–class disparities. This release of people power may be the most important long-term evidence of participatory defense as an abolitionist force. Through mutual support, people and communities become change agents instead of service recipients. In the face of systems designed to isolate and disempower, they develop their own horizontal collective strength and bend back the entrenched institutions that threaten their freedom and in some instances their lives.

It is important to emphasize that participatory defense hub meetings are not legal clinics. Lawyers are rarely in the room. In the few locations where a lawyer might attend a meeting, the lawyer stays in the back of the room and is expected to defer to the group's discussions so that participants can fully share the stories of their loved ones, draw on the experience of other community members, and brainstorm ways to help loved ones achieve the best possible outcome. In this way, participants build the knowledge, relationships, and power needed to push, assist, and collaborate with public defense lawyers in new and more effective ways. In many respects, that is the point of the participatory defense model. From a movement-building perspective, the case outcome is not the only goal. Instead, it is equally or even more important that the process transform each participant's sense of agency. An indicator of its success in doing so is the continued participation of community members long after the case that brought them to the hub is resolved. For this reason, the participatory defense movement shuns the word "client." That label reduces people into recipients of another's services or actions. In the participatory defense model, the key actors responsible for creating change are the people who face charges, their families, and their communities.

The success of this people-power approach is clear from the movement's growth. For many participatory defense hubs, "outreach" is organic; people hear about meetings from other families, often while visiting loved ones at the local jail. Neither did the movement initiate the founding of other hubs across the country. Instead, local organizers and defenders learned about the movement and reached out for information, training, and support. This unforced movement growth is fed by a common yearning among families for support and for help navigating criminal justice systems. Families are also eager to discover how they can improve the outcome of their loved one's case. The 40 currently active participatory defense hubs provide pay-it-forward training for families and communities in how best to partner with or push the lawyers appointed to defend their loved ones. In the span of 15 years, the movement has expanded participation in the training leadership team from three to 27 while developing a comprehensive program that supplements regular local trainings with (to date) four regional skills institutes and three national gatherings—the most recent of which drew 200 participatory defense organizers who engaged in 15 separate sessions.

In addition to this numerical growth, a natural maturation of the hubs occurs when community members, by working on improving public defense in individual cases, get a good, shared "look under the hood" at the mechanics of criminal legal systems as a whole and at how race, class, and other structural factors affect system operations. With that information, movement members can identify pivot points for flexing community power and dismantling the carceral machine. Developing and leveraging this new collective wisdom and strength is a critical part of self-transformation, power-shifting, and structural change. Those processes include building on case interventions by remaking practices, policies, and laws.

System Change: From Case Outcomes to Practices, Policies, and Laws

Participatory defense knows that there are Tonys across the country waiting to come home to communities that, if equipped with the necessary knowledge, skills, and strategies, can intervene in local courtrooms to bring them home—even in places that are notoriously "tough on crime." Applying these strategies in case after case alters local practices, raising expectations for procedures and results that deserve to be called "justice." The Birmingham, Alabama, hub used social biography videos to obtain parole for four prisoners, one of whom had spent 19 years trying and failing to win release. When Gainesville, Florida, police roughed up an anti-Trump protester and arrested him on multiple charges, hub members provided defense counsel with eyewitness statements, iPhone videos, and evidence of the man's injuries; that information contributed to the dismissal of all charges. After the movement helped a Philadelphia man shrink his sentence from potentially 12 years' imprisonment to probation, he said the support was "something I had never heard of or seen. Participatory defense can help save lives. I've heard people talk about probation reform. This is *justice* reform."[50]

That statement about justice reform also captures the relationship between case interventions and broader movement goals. Each case intervention touches a systemic problem. Some problems involve crises that exacerbate underlying system breakdowns and require immediate action. In one recent example, hubs across the country protested the impact of COVID-19 on detainees and prisoners in campaigning for mass release. The campaigns were often successful, and in Massachusetts the Supreme Judicial Court specifically cited a pro se (self-represented) amicus letter from local participatory defense hub members in its release order.[51]

Other problems are so entrenched in criminal legal systems that they require constant, relentless action. Racism is an obvious example. After Kris's lawyer failed to challenge a judge's racist assumptions that his summer job was "probably selling drugs," he filed a motion to replace the lawyer. Regardless of outcome, the motion held the lawyer, judge, and system accountable by making a public record of their conduct.[52] To protest prosecutor complicity in racialized police violence, the Knoxville, Tennessee, hub mounted a social media campaign highlighting how survivors are revictimized by charges such as resisting arrest.[53] In Boston, after a prosecutor and defenders accused each other of perpetuating white privilege, hub members used meetings and letters to call both agencies to account; among other things, they demanded that prosecutors implement new bail, charging, and sentencing policies and that defenders provide a new complaint and discipline process to address problems with unresponsive or racist defender behavior.[54]

Because De-Bug is the oldest active participatory defense hub, it has had time to develop a varied range of interventions, especially in the pretrial context. For example, when hub members learned that the law required provision of public defense counsel at misdemeanor arraignments, they used public pressure to secure new funding and fill the gap.[55] De-Bug's First 24, Court Doing, and Community Release projects also aim to keep people out of jail before trial. First 24 shares collective wisdom on steps to take right after detention or arrest when loved ones often lack access to counsel. Like all participatory defense interventions, First 24 grew from lived experience in a specific case: replacing a daughter's isolation, confusion, fear, and panic when her father disappears into the system with the power that comes with care, support, practical knowledge, and prompt, effective action. Instead of staring helplessly at a phone, people can now quickly find their loved ones, get their medication to them, share vital information to bring them home, and help them start working on their cases.[56]

Court Doing likewise responded to an agonizing pretrial situation: felony arraignments that are lightning-speed assembly lines jailing people who are presumed innocent. Court Doing emerged after months of court watch, which injects community presence into courtrooms to gather data, bear witness, and demand accountability from people and processes that otherwise operate with little oversight.[57] Court watch confirmed hub member suspicions that, in their courts, bail reforms purportedly aimed at slowing and diverting the assembly line instead continued to jail and control Black, brown, and low-income communities via racially biased risk assessments, electronic monitoring, and automatic denial of bail based solely on charge level.[58]

Court Doing's ultimate aim is a uniform policy of automatic release that gives people court dates instead of detaining them. The short-term aim is to disrupt the pretrial incarceration assembly line and create pathways to freedom. Before Court Doing, pretrial release "hearings" in felony cases were over in seconds. The public defender would call the case, glance at the charge, suggest no bail or low bail, the prosecutor would respond, and in 75% of cases the judge would send the person back to jail. The few people released often had to satisfy conditions that can be difficult in themselves (finding jobs or housing) and even harder when layered with other requirements (electronic monitoring, home detention, drug tests, and other check-ins during the workday). Failure often meant jail.[59] The arraignment courtroom was filled with family and friends of those being held. They watched their loved ones marched into court in chains, heard their names called, and saw them go back to jail. They were unsure what just happened or, if bail was set, felt that the bail bond company was the only way to bring their loved one home.

Hub members slow-built Court Doing by watching this process for months before designing an intervention. Working with the public defender office, they created a form to tap and translate care and support offered by people filling the courtroom benches into pretrial freedom for their loved ones. The form asks for information about who the loved ones really are: their roles in their families and communities; what's at stake for everyone with another day of confinement; how families and communities will help loved ones get back to court.

That care and support is changing outcomes and lives. Now, at the beginning of each arraignment session, the public defender or a hub member announces that, if people in the courtroom are there for a loved one, organizers in the back will help them understand the process and how they can help. Hub members then gather information that counters and gives context to the risk assessments that judges rely on. People offer loved ones a job, a home, or rides to court. People explain that a loved one just started college and must take his young children to day care each morning. People clarify that a prior failure to appear was not an attempt to flee but was because the family moved and missed mail or because they went to court on the wrong day. These are important realities that risk assessment algorithms and assembly-line case processing can't detect.[60]

Court Doing slows the assembly line. Now, "calling cases" means calling the names of people who stand up in the courtroom and are recognized for supporting their loved ones. Public defenders use that new information to obtain pretrial freedom. Court Doing belies a key fallacy that criminal legal systems promote: that people are alone and isolated from the support they need to succeed in meeting life's challenges (including getting to court on time). If that support is not available at arraignment, the hub offers help through Community Release. This project connects people with resources such as housing, employment, treatment programs, and text reminders of court dates. Combined with social biography videos and other participatory defense advocacy, these connections counter the rationales for jailing people before trial.

Quantitative research underscores the contribution of these programs. When De-Bug and public defenders conducted a joint evaluation of cases before and after the Court Doing and Community Release interventions, the data revealed that reliance on set bail amounts dropped by almost half.[61] The rate of no-bail release quadrupled.[62] Advocacy at bail rehearings was also effective. Judges reduced bail significantly for 19 of 25 people in a three-month sample. Twelve of the 25 moved from high bail to nonmonetary release (from a high of $500,000 and an average of over $150,000). Three of the four people who were initially held without bail were also released.[63]

Despite these accomplishments, too many releases still involve unnecessary conditions. Condition-free release is the next stage of the battle for pretrial freedom. Like every battle in the long struggle for justice, the outcome of this policy debate should ultimately be determined by the communities that are most directly affected by crime and criminal legal systems and whose members often live out multiple roles as victims, witnesses, and accused. Likewise, assessment of resulting interventions must be framed from the perspectives of the same people and communities.

In addition to changing practices, participatory defense is changing policies. Movement pressure led Santa Clara County to rethink plans for jail expansion[64] and to adopt the most robust policy in the country to protect people in jail from federal anti-immigration efforts. In the latter campaign, hub members blocked an attempt to limit protections to "nonviolent" detainees while allowing agents from US Immigration and Customs Enforcement (known as "ICE") to seize and deport people categorized as "violent." Movement members used their knowledge and experience to show coalition partners that these categories deserved no deference because people are more than a category and because community intervention in all types of cases can lead to pretrial release, reduced or dismissed charges, minimized sentences, and people returning to their families and communities—in other words, because everyone deserves the presumption of innocence and the chance to present a strong defense.[65]

Another example of movement-driven policy change involves prosecutorial discretion. From young graffiti artists working out of De-Bug, movement members learned of a new charging policy that piled felony gang enhancements on top of low-level vandalism offenses involving graffiti. In response, they gathered artists of all ages to meet with prosecutors and explain that tagging was a form of artistic expression that they engaged in regularly, often with support from public and private grants. Hub members helped the artists to understand, and to explain to prosecutors, the disproportionate harm caused by the stigma of felony enhancements, particularly for young people. Although prosecutors did not formally sunset the policy after those meetings, use of the enhancement in vandalism cases has declined.[66]

Participatory defense has also pushed for statutory changes. Several focus on maintaining family relationships. Hubs across the country are supporting campaigns to pass legislation that requires judges to consider parent–child relationships before sentencing and that ends private profiteering from phone calls between families and incarcerated loved ones.[67] In California, the movement supported passage of bills that blocked prosecutors from transferring juveniles directly to adult felony court, stopped uncounseled interrogations of youth under the age of 16, and voided prosecutor-driven plea agreements that force people to surrender their right to retroactive application of beneficial future statutes or court rulings.[68] Movement members used their intimate knowledge of the suffering caused by these practices and policies in social media campaigns and personal appeals to voters, legislators, and the governor.

A Boston hub member cites such examples as illustrating how participatory defense "builds our power to move from cases to campaigns."[69] A Birmingham member says the work has "changed my life" and that she is dedicated to sharing her new knowledge to expand the hub's impact for other Alabama families.[70] De-Bug hub member Blanca had a similar experience; she was among the first families to come to the table with her son Ronny in 2007. After Blanca worked with her new community to win dismissal of the robbery charge against Ronny, she channeled that experience to change the law and protect other teens from the trauma and injustice of coercive interrogation. During that campaign, Blanca shared the terror she felt when her son disappeared and was held incommunicado for 16 hours. She explained the pain and anger she felt watching the interrogation video, as officers falsely told her son that she would be mad at him if he didn't go along with their story and that he wouldn't be able to see her unless he did so. After watching the video of officers coaching Ronny into a false confession, the governor signed the statute into law.

Changing practices and policies has another important implication: it is a form of grassroots constitutional lawmaking. At one level, participatory defense gives new meaning to the right to counsel as people experience the right in real time in individual cases. At another level, the movement can reshape how courts interpret the right. Recall that courts define the right in terms of "reasonable" performance and possibilities for different outcomes and that "reasonable" is based on prevailing practice standards. By working with and assisting public defenders, or pushing them when they falter, participatory defense raises those standards. Strengthening norms strengthens the right.[71] Participatory defense is not alone in using norm-changing as a constitutional lever. Copwatchers are community activists who use public observation, data collection, and witnessing to redefine "reasonable" expectations under the Fourth Amendment for police stops, searches, and uses of force. Bail abolitionists push to redefine the reasonableness of jailing people who are presumed innocent. Courtwatchers push to redefine the reasonable exercise of prosecutorial discretion over charging and of judicial discretion over trial and sentencing rights. Prison abolitionists and reformers push to redefine "reasonableness" under the Eighth Amendment by working to close prisons, improve prison conditions, and eradicate mandatory minimums, solitary confinement, and the death penalty.[72]

Participatory defense is included among the norm-changing projects whose every action grows from a direct, caring, intimate connection with someone who is dealing with criminal charges. As part of this movement family, participatory defense is a powerful form of democratic self-governance that opens criminal legal systems to new scrutiny and new pressure from new publics. It is a direct, collective intervention into the generation and administration of law. It subverts the disenfranchisement and estrangement that criminal legal systems inflict on low-income communities and communities of color. It offers the people power required to transform those systems and dismantle the racism and poverty they feed upon and reproduce.

Engaging with Participatory Defense as a New Paradigm

Many public defenders understand that improving public defense is a bigger task than they can tackle on their own. To be sure, defenders connect with each other, and with the people and communities they represent, through networks of client-centered, holistic, and community-oriented public defense providers.[73] It is also true that policy makers have a clear to-do list for improving public defense: ensure the independence of the defense function; create resource parity between defense and prosecution; fund defender systems at the state instead of local level; and leverage that funding to enact and enforce best practice standards for attorney hiring, training, workloads, and performance.[74]

But even the best defender-led projects cannot replicate the unique perspectives, knowledge, and power of local, grassroots social movement organizing among people who are facing charges as well as their loved ones and their communities. They cannot replicate the way that participatory defense releases people to become change agents. It is this people power that can trigger exponentially greater transformation—a cataclysmic shake-up and eventual dismantling of carceral systems—by adding a huge number of strong new voices to the justice reform and penal abolition movements. And while enacting long-delayed public defense reforms is important, those reforms alone cannot cure the harm caused by US penal exceptionalism and reliance on criminal legal systems as a solution to social problems. Sustainable justice transformation requires a new politics. Participatory defense is among the social movements that are building that new politics. These movements are reclaiming safety, working for a future that no longer unnecessarily imprisons, estranges, and disenfranchises people but instead pursues genuine crime prevention through antiracist, antipoverty capacity-building that makes quality education, safe and stable housing, health care, and minimum basic income or jobs with a living wage available to everyone.[75]

Those are the bigger, harder goals that policy makers and criminal justice officials should pursue. The first step involves asking new questions and exploring new frameworks for analysis and action. A good opening question is: What can we do to put criminal legal systems out of business? In answering that question, it is important to recognize, respect, engage with, and support efforts to reclaim safety on community terms, including efforts pursued through community organizing. The hunger for this work is evident in the growth of participatory defense. All across the country, the infrastructure and organizing IQ necessary to practice and expand participatory defense already exists and is waiting to be tapped. To do so, again, the first step is to ask a core question: Who do people turn to, confide in, or call for solace when they learn they are facing a criminal charge? Is it their family, their temple, their neighborhood association, their union? Any community touchstone can be a participatory defense hub simply by advocating for their loved ones throughout the lifespan of the adjudication process. Those community anchors already exist and often are already leveraging collective power to challenge powerful institutions that are injuring their loved ones, congregants, neighbors, or coworkers. In marginalized communities, this is how schools get fixed, police agencies are held to account, and neighborhoods obtain investments of new resources.

Participatory defense applies that community organizing intelligence and strength to penetrate and transform local court systems. Around the country, parents are sitting in courtrooms in solidarity with their children as they face a hearing. Pastors, imams, and rabbis are writing letters to judges to reduce an impending sentence. If these actions are reimagined and reintegrated as part and parcel of a larger, named practice rather than as isolated responses, then a more profound, sustained transformation can occur in public defense, in court operations, and in the broader criminal legal systems of which those functions are a part—with that transformation fueled by the people and communities most directly affected.

A few cautions are in order. First, participatory defense succeeds because it was slow-built. Just as black belts are not earned by watching action flicks, participatory defense hubs cannot grow overnight from training videos. At the same time, participatory defense should not be frozen as a static invention or program. The movement grows and gains strength organically, from the trusting, supportive relationships and respect for local knowledge of local conditions that sustain it. For similar reasons, hubs thrive best through connection with the support and wisdom of the national network. Through that relational web, the hubs and their members share commitments to training communities on move-ment principles, goals, and strategies, to creating a national culture of critical analysis and action, and to undertaking the long, slow, hard work of movement building required to accomplish those goals.

Like all social movements, participatory defense also must be pre-pared to recognize and respond effectively to rejection, co-optation, and distraction.[76] Defense lawyers, prosecutors, and judges may resent and resist the idea that community organizing offers game-changing, benefi-cial wisdom and power. Resource-hungry public defense systems may try to shift the central tasks of high-quality representation—communication, investigation, and advocacy—onto low-income communities that need good lawyering. Resource-rich supporters may try to arm the participa-tory defense movement with funding that imposes unacceptable admin-istrative or political costs, instead of disarming the carceral machine by fighting racism, poverty, and punitive responses to social problems. With eyes on the justice transformation prize, participatory defense can over-come rejection, avoid co-optation and distraction, and continue working with the broader family of social movements to replace criminal legal systems with capacity-building and a better, safer future for everyone. That work is grounded in making a conscious, careful, patient, relentless practice out of the natural, intuitive impulse of communities to fight for the freedom of loved ones. Staying faithful to that impulse can bring the incarceration era to its rightful end.

NOTES

1 The authors thank Jon Gould and Pam Metzger for the invitation to contribute this chapter and for invaluable editorial suggestions. We are also grateful for the contributions of Marla Sandys, Associate Professor of Criminal Justice at Indiana University, and of James Lee and Erin McCabe in the University of Cincinnati Digital Scholarship program. Lauren Johnson and David Wovrosh provided excellent research assistance.

2 Constitution Project, *Justice Denied*; Mayeux, *Free Justice*, 187; Sandys and Pruss, "Correlates of Satisfaction," 431–34; Pruss, Walsh, and Sandys, "Listen."

3 Indeed, the United States is a global leader in penal severity among industrialized nations. Miller, *Myth of Mob Rule*, xi–xii, 98–160.

4 Weaver and Prowse, "Racial Authoritarianism"; Miller and Stuart, "Carceral Citizenship"; Colgan, "Fines, Fees, and Forfeitures," 22–23; Love, Roberts, and Klingele, *Collateral Consequences*.

5 MacArthur Foundation, "Raj Jayadev"; Participatory Defense Network, "Hubs."

6 M4BL, "Vision for Black Lives"; Bell, "Community"; Clair and Woog, "Courts"; Kaba, *We Do This*, 115–26; Roberts, "Abolition Constitutionalism," 43–49; Simonson, "Power Lens."

7 Herrick and Bell, "Social Determinants and Structural Violence," 6–12; South, MacDonald, and Reina, "Housing Repairs and Crime"; Petersen and Krivo, *Divergent Social Worlds*, 11; Chouhy, "Social Support and Crime," 228, 228–33; Sutton et al., *Crime Prevention*, 4–9, 23–24; Weisburd et al., "Informal Social Controls," 519–20; Cross, "Normality of Black People," 132–39.

8 Simonson, "Democratizing Criminal Justice," 1609–24; Miller, *Myth of Mob Rule*, 8–9; Beckett, "Criminal Justice Reform," 250–51, 253–54; Goodman, Page, and Phelps, *Breaking the Pendulum*, 2–16, 128–32; Gould, *Innocence Commission*, 47–49.

9 Clair, *Privilege and Punishment*, 1–9, 137–41, 155–77.

10 Simonson, "Democratizing Criminal Justice," 1609–24.

11 Clair and Woog, "Courts"; Kaba, *Do This*, 81–84; see also Russonello, "Most Americans"; Bocanegra, "Community and Decarceration," 116–17, 129–30.

12 Kaba, *Do This*, 81–84, 549–59.

13 Kaba, *Do This*, 549–59; Akbar, Ashar and Simonson, "Movement Law," 871–80; Okidigbe, "Discredited Data."

14 Darity and Mullen, *Reparations*, 16–20, 77–80, 145–52, 158–64 and app. 2; Muhammad, "Forgotten Crime"; Rex, "Prosecutions and the 2008 Financial Crisis," 106–07, 112–17; Green Library Exhibit, "Samuel DuBose."

15 Forman, *Locking Up Our Own*, 9–14; Johnson et al., "Reclaiming Safety."

16 Travis, Western, and Redburn *Growth of Incarceration*, 4–7; Galle, "Rewards," 478–85; Robinson and Darley, "Does Criminal Law Deter?"

17 Moore, "Decarceral Constitutionalism." The term "carceral state" refers to the networks of policies, personnel, and practices through which governments exercise the power to police, prosecute, and punish, of which defense representation is a key feature.

18 Johnson et al., "Reclaiming Safety."

19 Harlow, *Defense Counsel*.

20 For example, public defense in Ohio is governed by the Fifth, Sixth, and Fourteenth Amendments of the US Constitution; Article 1, section 10 of the Ohio Constitution; Title I, Chapter 120 of the Ohio Revised Codes; Chapter 120 of the Ohio Administrative Code, Rule 5(A)(2) of the Ohio Rules of Criminal Procedure; and court opinions interpreting those provisions.

21 Avery v. Alabama, 308 U.S. 444, 447 (1940).

22 Moore, Jayadev, and Sandys, "Make Them Hear You," 1294–95; Wagner and Rabuy, "Following the Money."

23 Mayeux, *Free Justice*, 187 (word choice in original).

24 Constitution Project, *Justice Denied*, 2; Gross, "Right to Counsel," 831–85; Moore, "Reviving *Escobedo*," 1034–39.

25 *Avery*, 308 U.S. at 447–53; Constitution Project, *Justice Denied*; Lefstein, "Fulfilling *Gideon*'s Promise," 39–48.

26 Gonzalez Van Cleve, *Crook County*, 6–14, 52–92; Gould and Leon, "Extralegal Factors," 652–53; Moore et al., "Attorney–Client Communication," 909–10.

27 Eldred, "Ethical Blindness," 333–94; Moore and Davies, "Knowing Defense," 362.

28 Gould, *Innocence Commission*, 65; Rapping, *Gideon's Promise*, 10–19; Bocanegra, "Community and Decarceration," 116–21; Bell, "Police Reform," 2068–72, 2083–89, 2106–09; Gonzalez Van Cleve, *Crook County*, 6–14, 52–92.

29 Dripps, "Criminal Procedure," 1079–1101; Gould, "When Courts Are Indifferent."

30 United States v. Cronic, 466 U.S. 648 (1984); Primus, "Ineffective Assistance," 1614–17.

31 Strickland v. Washington, 466 U.S. 668, 687 (1984); Moore, Jayadev, and Sandys, "Make Them Hear You," 1295.

32 Davies and Worden, "State Politics," 187–220; Strong, "Special Report," 1–28.

33 Indiana Public Defender Commission, "Overhead Costs"; Jacobs, "Paid to Lose."

34 Lefstein, "Fulfilling *Gideon's* Promise," 41–48, 56.

35 Lucas, "Overview," 94–106; DuClos, "Continued Rise in Felony Caseload"; Salter, "Waiting List"; Associated Press, "Lawsuit."

36 Salter, "Waiting List"; Associated Press, "Lawsuit."

37 Associated Press, "Lawsuit"; DuClos, "Continued Rise in Felony Caseload"; Davies, Lopes, and Clark, "Unique New York," 962–86; Gross, "Case Refusal," 253–68; Heaton, Mayson, and Stevenson, "Downstream"; Petersen, "Low-Level, but High-Speed," 1314–35.

38 Joe, "Structuring the Public Defender"; Lefstein, "Fulfilling *Gideon's* Promise," 46–47.

39 Schwall, "More Bang for Your Buck," 553–78; Sukhatme and Jenkins, "Pay to Play?"

40 Gould and Leon, "Extralegal Factors," 643–86; Sukhatme and Jenkins, "Pay to Play?"; Committee to Review the Criminal Justice Act, "Report."

41 Moore et al., "Attorney–Client Communication," 909–10.

42 Hoag, "Black on Black Representation"; Moore, "Antidemocratic Sixth Amendment," 1705–67.

43 Baćak, Lageson, and Powell, "Fighting the Good Fight," 939–61.

44 Campbell et al., "Unnoticed, Untapped," 763.

45 Selvanathan and Jetten, "Marches to Movements," 81–85.

46 Albert Cobarrubias Justice Project, Social Biography Videos.

47 MacArthur Foundation, "Jonathan Rapping."

48 Participatory Defense Network, "Time Saved" (documenting sentencing reductions); Jayadev, "Freedom and Community" (documenting reductions in pretrial detention); Jayadev, "Those Who Need It Most"; Ewing, "Assist."

49 Moore, "Decarceral Constitutionalism"; Tate and Jackson, Interview; Hanora, "Email."

50 Paceley, "Power of Participatory Defense"; Gray, "Friend in Court"; Mothers in Charge (@phillymic), July 20, 2020, https://twitter.com; Godsoe, "Participatory Defense," 721.

51 FreeThemAll, "Call to Action"; Committee for Public Counsel Services, 142 N.E.3d at 528, 531 n.8 (citing letter from "the families of certain incarcerated loved ones"); James et al., Amicus Letter.

52 Noble, "Standing Up"; Jayadev, "Tales from a Trial."

53 Community Defense, "Reggie Wilson."

54 Estes, "Too White and Privileged"; Hanora, "Email."

55 Albert Cobarrubias Justice Project, "Santa Clara."

56 First 24 Project, "Your loved one." The success of First 24 prompted similar support for people whose loved ones are injured or killed by police. The First 24: Police Violence, "Your loved one has been shot or killed by police: What do you do within the first 24 hours?"

57 Simonson, "Criminal Court Audience," 2176–90.

58 Okidigbe, "Discredited Data"; Mayson, "Bias In," 2218–300; Digard and Swavola, "Justice Denied."

59 Jayadev, "Freedom and Community."

60 Gouldin, "New Perspectives."

61 Jayadev, "Freedom and Community."

62 Ibid.

63 Ibid.

64 Reese, "Santa Clara Wobbles"; Silicon Valley De-Bug, "Stopping a Jail."

65 De-Bug San Jose, "End Ice Presence"; Ramirez, "Santa Clara County."

66 Albert Cobarrubias Justice Project, "Mercury News."

67 Tennessee Code Annotated Title 40, Chapter 35, sections 3(a) & 103(7) (2020); Commonwealth of Massachusetts, Senate Bill No. 1372, "An Act Relative to Inmate Telephone Calls." January 16, 2019. https://malegislature.gov.

68 Domingo, "Undeniable Force"; Positive Youth Justice Initiative Brief, "Community," 3–4; Tull, "Proposition 57"; Cal. Welf. & Inst. Code § 625.6(a) (2017); Albert Cobarrubias Justice Project, "My Child"; Cal. Penal Code Part 2, Title 6, Chapter 4, §1016.8 (2020).

69 Hanora, Email.

70 Tate and Jackson, Interview.

71 Moore, "Isonomy, Austerity," 173–79.

72 Simonson, "Democratizing Criminal Justice"; Kushner, "Is Prison Necessary"; Appelbaum, "American Psychiatry," 406–15.

73 Anderson, Buenaventura, and Heaton, "Holistic Defense," 819–93; National Association for Public Defense, "Statement of Purpose."

74 Primus, "Defense Counsel," 121–45.

75 Kaba, Do This, 115–26; Clair and Woog, "Courts"; Petersen and Krivo, Divergent Social Worlds, 11; Chouhy, "Social Support and Crime," 228, 232–33.

76 Godsoe, "Participatory Defense," 725–30; Pennington, "One Participatory Defense Program," 603–27; Francis, "Price of Civil Rights," 275–309.

4

Abolishing Bail

CHRISTINE S. SCOTT-HAYWARD AND HENRY F. FRADELLA

Despite some recent reforms, pretrial justice systems around the United States are broken. There are too many people locked up in our nation's jails while they await trial. Most of those people—roughly 90%—are not jailed because they are too dangerous to be released pending trial but because they cannot pay the money bail set in their case. Quite simply, for most criminal defendants, pretrial "justice" does not exist.

In this chapter, we describe the main problems with bail and pretrial detention in the United States, highlighting their impact on the entire criminal justice system. We then examine the objectives of pretrial decision-making and, in light of those goals, assess current reform efforts in some states that have undertaken notable changes in their pretrial justice processes. Ultimately, we recommend the complete abolition of money bail and the establishment of a right to unconditional release for people accused of nearly all criminal offenses. Under this approach, a narrow range of pretrial release conditions could be imposed only to ensure the accused's participation in subsequent court proceedings and to mitigate any immediate and real physical threats to the victim or the public. Pretrial service agencies, which typically gather, verify, and report the information that judicial officers need to make informed pretrial release decisions, would supervise the people subject to conditional release to ensure that they comply with release conditions and remind them of upcoming court dates. Only a small minority of defendants would be eligible for pretrial detention: those charged with serious violent crimes (such as rape or murder), those who pose a real threat of physical harm, and those who pose a demonstrated risk of absconding.

The Problems with Pretrial Justice Systems That Rely on Money Bail

Bail is a guaranteed promise by an accused to show up at court hearings.[1] In exchange for being released from custody pending the resolution of criminal charges, a defendant promises to return to court as needed. This promise is commonly guaranteed by the defendant's payment of a certain amount of money and agreement to comply with conditions set by the judge. Some individuals are released unconditionally, and without bail on their own recognizance (ROR or OR) and their promise to return. Others are denied pretrial release altogether because they pose a risk of flight, a risk of failing to appear, or pose a danger to the community.[2]

The Eighth Amendment to the United States Constitution does not establish a right to bail. Rather, it guarantees that, if bail is granted, it may not be "excessive."[3] But the Eighth Amendment's limits on judicial discretion in setting the amount of bail is virtually meaningless. Although many state constitutions create a right to bail for noncapital offenses,[4] pretrial release is often dependent on legislation setting forth the offenses for which bail might be available.[5]

On any given day prior to the COVID-19 pandemic, approximately 734,000 people were locked up in jails in the United States.[6] Astonishingly, only about one-third of these individuals are serving sentences of incarceration following criminal convictions.[7] This means that nearly two-thirds of inmates were awaiting trial or are being held pending probation or parole revocation proceedings. This latter group represented roughly 480,000 people at midyear 2019.[8] Due to COVID mitigation efforts, the number of people detained in jails decreased by 34% to 549,100 in 2020, the most recent year for which official data are available. [9] However, 380,700 of those people were not serving custodial sentences, meaning that the rate of unconvicted persons detained in jails rose during the pandemic to 69.3% of all jail inmates.[10] Typically, these individuals are not detained because a court has judged them to be a risk to public safety or decided that they are unlikely to appear in court.[11] Instead, most of them—nine out of every 10 detained defendants—are there because they cannot pay the money bail that has been set in their cases.[12]

Although recent national data are unavailable, in 2009, in the 75 largest counties in the United States, 62% of felony defendants were released
prior to case disposition.[13] Most of these defendants (77%) were released
with conditions, typically financial conditions that they post monetary
bail.[14] Yet a defendant's ability to pay is rarely considered when setting
bail amounts. Many jurisdictions even rely on bail schedules, which set
presumptive bail amounts for specific offenses and have been criticized
for failing to allow for an individualized release decision.[15]

Punishing Poverty While Ignoring Danger

Conditioning pretrial release on the payment of bail creates dispropor-
tionalities in the criminal justice system. Most significant, many poor
defendants are locked up simply because they or their families cannot
afford bail. For example, Tryone Tomlin, who was arrested and charged
with possession of drug paraphernalia in November 2014, had bail set
at $1,500.[16] Unable to pay, he spent three weeks in jail before his case
was dismissed.[17] A study in New York City found that "even when bail
is set comparatively low—at $500 or less, as it is in one-third of nonfel-
ony cases—only 15% of defendants are able to come up with the money
to avoid jail."[18] Today, "the median bail amount in this country represents eight months of income for the typical detained defendant."[19] For
this reason, it is not surprising that recent studies using zip codes as
proxies for income have shown that people from low-income neighborhoods are significantly more likely to be detained pending trial than
those from higher-income neighborhoods.[20] As we discuss below, most
of these defendants are accused of relatively minor offenses and pose
little to no risk of failing to appear or reoffending. And yet reliance on
money bail permits the release of wealthy defendants who are dangerous or who may flee, simply because those defendants can afford to
post bail.[21] Consider, for instance, real estate heir Robert Durst, who
was profiled in the HBO documentary *The Jinx*.[22] Durst was arrested
for the murder of a neighbor in 2000. After bail was set at $250,000,
he promptly paid the amount and then absconded. As Durst admitted in the documentary, his intention was always to put up the money
and then flee. Although he had been suspected of foul play in his former wife's disappearance in 1982, and he had subsequently admitted

to killing and dismembering a neighbor, Durst's wealth allowed him to post bail and disappear.[23] As we will explain in more detail, people who lack financial means—especially those who are persons of color—are not able to buy their freedom and flee in the way that Durst was able to accomplish.

Commercial Bail Profiteering

Reliance on money bail in the United States means that most defendants need to come up with sometimes significant amounts to be released. Because few defendants have immediate access to that kind of money, many turn to commercial bail bond services.[24] Typically, defendants, their families, or their friends will give the bail bond company a nonrefundable payment of 10% of the bail amount set by the court. In addition, the person who signs the bail contract—the "guarantor"—agrees that, if the defendant fails to show up in court, the guarantor will be responsible for the entire amount. Sometimes the bail agent may also require that collateral be posted. In return, the bond company posts a surety bond (underwritten by an insurance company) with the court, allowing the defendant to be released.[25]

In theory, if the accused fails to appear as promised, the bail company is responsible for paying the full amount of the bail to the court. Often the bail agent is then empowered to apprehend the defendant or to use a bounty hunter's services to do so.[26] However, in reality, few commercial bail companies pay the forfeiture fees if a defendant fails to appear. Indeed, some states report that commercial bail companies pay only 1.7% to 12% of forfeitures they owe.[27]

Commercial bail is big business—worth an estimated $2.4 billion dollars annually.[28] This may explain why the industry lobbies so heavily to secure the for-profit bail system and to quash virtually every effort to reduce the use of money bail.[29] Most recently, the American Bail Coalition, funded by a number of large insurance companies, successfully placed California's 2018 bail reform legislation on hold.[30] This is not the case everywhere, and reform in certain jurisdictions has convinced some investors to move out of the bail industry.[31]

Meanwhile, corruption has plagued the commercial bail industry since its inception[32] and continues even as the trade has professionalized.[33] A 2017 report titled *Selling Off Our Freedom*, by Color of Change (a nonprofit civil rights advocacy organization) and the American Civil Liberties Union's Campaign for Smart Justice, highlights examples of fraud, bribery, and kickbacks in California, Minnesota, and New Jersey. For example, the California Department of Insurance, which regulates California bail agents, reports that complaints—ranging from fraud and misrepresentation to theft, extortion, and kidnapping—increased fourfold between 2010 and 2015.[34] In one study of a large urban county, researchers found that bail agents preyed on "poor women of color" to generate business.[35] There is no doubt that the commercial bail industry is a substantial obstacle to change.

The Downstream Consequences of Pretrial Detention

Pretrial detention causes a wide range of negative consequences that can endure beyond the resolution of the initial case. Pretrial detention deprives individuals of their liberty and subjects them to harsh conditions of confinement before they are convicted of the crime(s) with which they are charged. Although the United States Supreme Court has determined that pretrial detention is "regulation" and not "punishment," for defendants who are in jail it is difficult to see that distinction as anything other than semantic.[36] As the Vera Institute of Justice reported in 2015, "even a brief stay in jail can be destructive to individuals, their families, and entire communities."[37] Jails are often overcrowded, with poor physical and mental health care, and they have fewer educational and vocational opportunities than prisons.[38] Further, many jails have higher death rates than the national average, and the suicide rate in jails is three times the rate in prison.[39]

The high-profile cases of Sandra Bland and Kalief Browder are illustrative. Bland, whose traffic stop captured headlines in 2015, was detained because she could not pay the $500 bail set in her case. She committed suicide in jail three days after her arrest.[40] Browder spent three years in the Rikers Island jail awaiting trial. During that time, he was repeatedly assaulted by both officers and other inmates. He spent nearly two years in solitary confinement and attempted suicide twice. Prosecutors eventually dropped the charges against him, but a year after he was released, Browder killed himself.[41]

Given the conditions experienced by pretrial detainees, it is not surprising that many plead guilty, sometimes to a crime they did not commit, simply to get out of jail.[42] Fifty years of research demonstrates that pretrial detention has negative impacts on case outcomes. Controlling for factors like offense type, charge severity, and criminal history, people who are detained are more likely to be convicted (typically as a result of guilty pleas), are more likely to be sentenced to jail or prison (rather than to probation), and are more likely to be sentenced to lengthier terms of incarceration.[43] The impact of these outcomes on mass incarceration in the United States is beyond doubt.[44]

Moreover, as the Supreme Court noted in 1975, "pretrial confinement may imperil the suspect's job, interrupt his source of income, and impair his family relationships."[45] And finally, the consequences of pretrial detention fall overwhelmingly on minorities, exacerbating existing inequalities in the criminal justice system. Although there are no national data on the racial/ethnic breakdown of pretrial detainees, people of color are overrepresented in the total jail population.[46] Not only are defendants of color less likely to afford bail than white defendants;[47] most studies find that nonwhite defendants are significantly more likely to be detained pretrial than their white counterparts and more likely to have financial bail set.[48] Research suggests that this is at least in part a result of inaccurate stereotypes exaggerating the relative dangerousness of nonwhite defendants.[49]

Pretrial Justice Reform

The modern reality of bail has been distorted from its original aims. Historically, bail was designed to ensure the defendant's appearance at subsequent court proceedings.[50] Although that is still a central reason why courts impose bail, since 1984 courts have emphasized public safety, seeking to protect the community from further offenses by the accused.[51] Indeed, the federal Bail Reform Act of 1984[52] specifies that defendants charged with certain felonies "shall" be denied pretrial release if a judicial officer is persuaded, by clear and convincing evidence, that "no condition or combination of conditions will reasonably assure the appearance of the person as required and the safety of any other person and the community."[53]

In its 1987 opinion in *United States v. Salerno*, the Supreme Court upheld the constitutionality of the Bail Reform Act.[54] As a result, federal judges to this day concern themselves not only with a criminally accused person's risk of flight but also the danger that person might pose to the community if released on bail.[55] This is also true in many state systems, even in jurisdictions that contain a right to bail for noncapital offenses.[56] The "get tough on crime" era in US criminal justice morphed bail into an unreliable prognostication of future dangerousness.[57] This, in turn, made it expedient to ignore how pretrial detention exacerbates economic and racial inequalities in the criminal justice system.

State Experiments in Reform

For decades, these problems with bail were mostly unaddressed. But that is no longer the case. Just as policing, corrections, prosecution, and defense have seen new attention and reform,[58] there is a growing understanding that a wealth-based system of pretrial justice that results in high rates of pretrial detention is wrong. Reformers have called for the elimination of cash bail,[59] and several states have experimented with new approaches.[60]

Any meaningful reform must address the problems we described earlier while also accomplishing the goals of pretrial decision-making. Specifically, reform should (1) eliminate wealth-based discrimination in release outcomes; (2) abolish the commercial bail industry; and (3) drastically reduce the number of people detained pending trial. Some states have taken steps to achieve these goals, but few have done so without creating other problems. The highest-profile reforms have taken place in New Jersey, Maryland, New York, and, most recently, Illinois.

New Jersey

In 2014, New Jersey successfully enacted large-scale bail reforms that virtually eliminated money bail and the commercial bail industry.[61] The New Jersey Criminal Justice Reform Initiative (CJR), which went into effect in January 2017, shifted the state's pretrial system from one based on money bail to one based on risk of flight and dangerousness. These reforms were supported by legislators, judges, and the governor.

To help implement those reforms, voters approved an amendment to the state constitution. Before that amendment, New Jersey had been a "right to bail" state, in which judges were unable to detain a defendant to protect public safety. The New Jersey Constitution now provides:

> Pretrial release may be denied to a person if the court finds that no amount of monetary bail, nonmonetary conditions of pretrial release, or combination of monetary bail and nonmonetary conditions would reasonably assure the person's appearance in court when required, or protect the safety of any other person or the community, or prevent the person from obstructing or attempting to obstruct the criminal justice process.[62]

To implement the reforms, New Jersey worked with Arnold Ventures to develop and validate the Arnold Foundation's Public Safety Assessment (PSA), an actuarial risk assessment tool, and a Decision Making Framework, which "produces recommendations for release conditions based on the PSA risk scores and state-specific policies and guidelines."[63] Arnold Ventures is also funding a nonpartisan research organization to conduct an "independent evaluation" of the CJR's implementation effects.

Under the new law, which relies on a presumption of release, defendants must be released on their own recognizance or on an unsecured appearance bond unless other conditions are necessary to "assure an eligible defendant's appearance in court when required, [protect] the safety of any other person or the community, [and guarantee] that the eligible defendant will not obstruct or attempt to obstruct the criminal justice process."[64] Any conditions imposed (including money bail) must be the least restrictive conditions necessary to achieve those goals. In some instances, a defendant may be detained if, after a hearing, a judge finds clear and convincing evidence that neither conditions nor money bail will ensure the defendant's appearance, protect public safety, and prevent obstruction of justice.[65]

Early indications are that the reforms have been mostly successful. A 2019 report by the New Jersey courts concluded that "CJR is working as intended."[66] In 2018, money bail was imposed in only 102 cases, and more than 90% of defendants were released pretrial.[67] Importantly, in that same year, crime rates in the state fell, particularly for violent crime; the rate of alleged new criminal activity for those released pretrial remained "virtually the same."[68] While court appearance rates dropped negligibly, overall dispositions remained relatively constant, suggesting no significant increases in absconding.[69] Most notably, jail populations decreased by nearly 45%, translating into 750,000 fewer jail beds in a year.[70] That, in turn, significantly reduced racial and ethnic disparities in pretrial detention, especially among Black women.[71] Similarly, an independent analysis of the CJR's initial outcomes concluded that CJR had not negatively impacted public safety in New Jersey. Specifically, it found a significant reduction in total arrests statewide.[72]

Maryland

In 2017, the Maryland Court of Appeals (the state's highest court) unanimously amended its court rules to "promote the release of defendants on their own recognizance, or when necessary, unsecured bond."[73] As in New Jersey, Maryland's new rules require that defendants be released on their own recognizance or an unsecured bond unless a judge finds that "no permissible non-financial condition attached to a release will reasonably ensure (A) the appearance of the defendant, and (B) the safety of each alleged victim, other persons, or the community."[74]

After the rules went into effect, the number of people released on unsecured bonds increased by 4% and the number of people released unconditionally on their own recognizance increased by 6%.[75] Overall, the use of money bail dropped by 21% and, because the judge must consider the defendant's ability to pay, the "average dollar amount of bail decreased by more than $31,000." As a result, many defendants who would otherwise have been unable to afford their bonds were released from custody.[76]

Nonetheless, Maryland's reforms fail to address many of the problems associated with the continued use of money bail. First, there are still significant racial disparities in bond amounts. Even after reform, bail amounts for Black defendants have been, on average, 22% higher than those for white defendants.[77] Additionally, Maryland judges have been ordering the detention of many more defendants. According to data from the Maryland court system, these detention orders mean that Maryland has "almost the same number of people sitting in jail" as it did before bail reform.[78] Here, too, racial disparities are prevalent: as compared to their white counterparts, Black defendants are disproportionally detained, with detention rates as much as 8.8% higher for serious crimes.[79]

New York

New York is one of the most recent states to enact bail reform. New York's law, which was enacted in 2019 and went into effect in January 2020, was predicted to reduce the state's pretrial jail population by at least 40%.[80] As Insha Rahman of the Vera Institute of Justice states, New York's bail reform statute has "historic and transformative potential to end mass incarceration at the local level."[81]

The key feature of this new law is that New York's statute—unlike New Jersey's law, which *presumes* release for many defendants—*mandates* release for an estimated 90% of all arrestees. In addition, New York does not require that judges use risk assessment tools to make their release decisions. Instead, it uses a "charge-based approach" to release decisions and release conditions. For example, people arrested for misdemeanor offenses must be released either on their own recognizance or on the least restrictive nonmonetary conditions that will reasonably ensure their appearance at future court dates. Electronic monitoring of misdemeanor defendants is prohibited except in limited and specific circumstances.[82] Moreover, the prosecuting county bears the cost of pretrial release conditions; defendants "shall not be required to pay for any part of the cost of release on nonmonetary conditions."[83]

New York did not entirely eliminate money bail. Cash bail may still be set in cases involving violent felonies and/or if a judge finds that nonmonetary conditions are insufficient to ensure that an individual will return to court. However, the decision to require bond is mitigated by the fact that a judge must consider the defendant's ability to pay when setting the bond amount.[84]

New York's law had been in effect for only a few months before COVID-19 hit, and it is difficult to assess its full impact. However, in the first few months it was in effect, jail populations dropped significantly.[85] And even before the law's implementation, judges in New York City began to release more defendants on their own recognizance and saw no reduction in appearance rates.[86] Still, the law has already been heavily criticized. Opponents of reform have highlighted the release of ignominious defendants,[87] and in April 2020 New York removed some of the law's provisions, expanding the number of offenses for which bail could be set.[88]

Illinois

In February 2021, Governor J. B. Pritzker signed into law the Pre-Trial Fairness Act, part of a larger package of criminal justice system reforms initiated by the Illinois Legislative Black Caucus.[89] Although the law does not go into effect until 2023, it is the most progressive bail reform effort to date, helped by the "grassroots mobilization of more than 100 reform organizations."[90] Not only does it completely abolish money bail, making Illinois the first state in the country to do so; it also limits the use of pretrial detention as well as onerous conditions of pretrial supervision such as electronic monitoring, instead emphasizing citation in lieu of arrest for low-level offenses and release on recognizance.[91]

The key feature of the Illinois law is the presumption of release on recognizance. Detention can be imposed only "when it is determined that the defendant poses a specific, real and present threat to a person, or has a high likelihood of willful flight."[92] These restrictions ensure that there must be real, demonstrated risk of danger or failure to appear. Moreover, conditions of release are to be set only "when it is determined that they are necessary to assure the defendant's appearance in court, assure the defendant does not commit any criminal offense, and complies with all conditions of pretrial release."[93] Notably, the statute places significant restrictions on the use of electronic monitoring as a condition of release.

The provisions of the new law are strengthened by the provision of counsel to defendants at first appearance and by placing the burden on the state to prove the necessity of detention. In addition, while the use of a validated risk assessment tool is permitted to determine conditions of release, such a tool "may not be used as the sole basis to deny pretrial release."[94] Further, if a risk assessment tool is used, the defendant is entitled to be provided with information about the tool, including the scoring system used, and is also entitled to challenge the validity of that tool.

As in New York, Illinois's legislation is already being criticized by state prosecutors and law enforcement groups.[95] However, the state's elimination of money bail along with the limitations placed on the use of pretrial detention and conditions of release have the potential to substantially reduce the number of defendants detained pretrial.

Reform Proposals

While many of these state efforts, particularly Illinois's reform legislation, are good steps forward, most focus primarily on the elimination of money bail. In our view, effective reform must be broader and should address five priorities. First, as these states have established, money bail should be abolished. Second, only a limited class of defendants—those accused of select, serious crimes of violence like rape and murder—should be subject to pretrial detention, and then only after adversarial proceedings with a panoply of due process protections. Third, pretrial risk assessment instruments should be rejected as the successor "solution" to money bail. Fourth, pretrial service agencies' monitoring of defendants should be used sparingly and should be limited to practices for which there is clear empirical evidence supporting their efficacy. Finally, unconditional release should be the de facto outcome for the vast majority of defendants. Below we discuss each of these priorities in greater detail.

Abolish Money Bail

Money bail should be eliminated entirely. Without cash bail, the commercial bail industry will disappear, along with the problems it causes. Similarly, if wealth no longer determines release outcomes, a system that jails poor people *simply* because they are poor should disappear. Further, there is little evidence that money bail achieves the goals of pretrial justice.

First, we have been unable to find *any* evidence that cash bonds, compared with other types of release conditions, keep the public safer. Second, studies about appearance rates draw mixed conclusions.[96] A 2004 study found that defendants released on a commercial bond were more likely to appear than similarly situated defendants who were released on their own recognizance.[97] Similarly, a 2017 study found that defendants in Dallas County, Texas, who were released on commercial bail bonds had lower failure-to-appear rates than those who were released on other forms of financial surety.[98] However, neither study showed that it was the financial incentive itself that led to higher appearance rates. Moreover, a recent report from the New York Criminal Justice Agency showed an *increase* in appearance rates for defendants released on their own recognizance—up from 84% to 86%—even as the number of recognizance releases increased and the number of people released on money bail declined.[99]

Even if cash bail does improve appearance rates, we think there are better ways to facilitate court appearances than to require people to pay money in exchange for their liberty, especially in light of the high costs that practice imposes on the accused and society.[100] Put another way, the benefits of release outweigh the costs of nonappearance. In fact, in a 2018 analysis, Dobbie and colleagues balanced the labor market costs of a criminal conviction against the costs of failures to appear and estimated that pretrial release provides a total net benefit per defendant of between $55,143 and $99,124.[101] Additionally, abolishing cash bail addresses the racial disparities inherent in a system that premises liberty on the ability to pay.

Limit Pretrial Detention

Most reasonable people would agree that the defendants who are presumed to be most dangerous should be detained pending trial. But that is not the major problem with the bail system, in which judges issue detention orders for only 10% of all pretrial defendants.[102] Instead, the problem is that judges set bail too high, resulting in the de facto detention of those who are eligible for release but cannot afford their bail.

In some cases, excessive bail amounts are imposed unthinkingly; often this is a problem associated with bail schedules. In other cases, judges engage in what Professor Lauryn Gouldin calls "pretextual preventive detention"—they set bail so high that it is unpayable. Particularly in jurisdictions that do not allow detention based on dangerousness, this pretextual preventative detention is a response to judicial or public perceptions of a defendant's perceived dangerousness.[103] Abolishing money bail would go a long way toward alleviating this problem. Orders of preventative detention would be limited to those defendants who pose a risk of flight, nonappearance, or dangerous reoffending while on pretrial release. But the reality is trickier for at least two reasons.

First, although the Supreme Court has cautioned that pretrial preventative detention can violate due process if it is punitive, "irrational[,] or 'excessive' in relation to its regulatory goal,"[104] these amorphous limits have proven to be illusory in practice.[105] As illustrated by Maryland's postreform increase in pretrial detention, judges too frequently determine that someone is dangerous without sufficient evidence to support that conclusion. Professor Sandra Mayson has suggested limiting pretrial detention to cases in which the "defendant presents a substantial risk of serious violent crime in the pretrial phase[] and there are no less restrictive alternatives that would render the risk less than substantial."[106] Still, the phrase "substantial risk" leaves wiggle room that is likely to allow racial disparities to continue, as they did in Maryland.[107]

In fact, research suggests that very few people pose a substantial risk to public safety while on pretrial release. In a study of the 75 largest counties in the United States, researchers found that the likelihood of a defendant being rearrested for a crime of violence while on pretrial release ranged between 1% and 3% for nearly every type of crime charged.[108] The only exceptions were cases in which the defendants were charged with murder, robbery, or rape. In those cases, the violent felony rearrest rates were 6.4%, 5.8%, and 3.2%, respectively.[109] This relatively high rearrest rate for defendants facing murder charges validates "much of what has historically existed as a presumption against the release of murder defendants."[110]

In light of these extremely low rates of violent reoffending while on pretrial release, jurisdictions in the United States should guarantee a right to pretrial release for all defendants other than those charged with murder, sexual assault, armed robbery, and robberies involving serious injury to a victim. Crimes such as purse-snatching, pickpocketing, and similar types of thefts from persons—which technically qualify as robberies in some jurisdictions—should also be subject to a presumption of release.[111]

Second, judges often make pretrial release decisions hastily and without the benefit of adversarial proceedings. We suspect it would be noncontroversial, as an abstract principle, to require due process before depriving people of their liberty without a conviction.[112] But the vast majority of pretrial detainees do not have an adversarial bail proceeding with a full panoply of due process protections. Rather, most bail orders are issued at initial appearances that might last only two or three minutes and often occur without the benefit of defense counsel.[113] While the abolition of money bail might resolve the improper use of pretextual preventative detention, it will not guarantee due process in pretrial proceedings. To address those concerns, we reiterate recommendations we have published elsewhere: experienced prosecutors should screen cases, and defense counsel should be appointed to represent defendants at their first judicial appearance.[114]

Jettison Pretrial Risk Assessment

With the notable exception of New York, the states that have recently reformed their pretrial justice systems have explicitly relied on actuarial risk assessment tools, building them into their new systems. Actuarial pretrial risk assessment instruments (APRAIs) purport to be objective tools that can accurately predict whether someone poses a particular type of risk. In the pretrial context, there are three distinctive risks: a defendant's risk of flight from the jurisdiction; a defendant's risk of otherwise failing to appear in court; and a defendant's risk of committing an offense while on pretrial release. An in-depth examination of APRAIs suggests that their methods are flawed.[115]

First, most APRAIs fail to predict distinct types of pretrial risk.[116] Some tools "only provide a general pretrial failure risk score, which is a combined outcome of missing a court appearance or being rearrested."[117] Tools that do provide separate scores for risk of failure to appear (FTA) and risk to public safety still do not adequately distinguish between different kinds of FTA risks. (As Professor Gouldin points out, there are different types of FTA, ranging from fugitives fleeing a jurisdiction to evade trial and punishment to the far more common and inadvertent instances when a defendant forgets about a hearing or is unable to get transportation to court.)[118]

In addition, when an APRAI assesses a person as a high risk for reoffending or a high public safety risk, it is not always clear what that risk assessment means. Sometimes the risk refers to the probability of arrest, even for a minor offense. At other times, as is the case with the Arnold

Foundation's PSA, the risk refers to the risk of arrest for a violent crime. However, "because pretrial violence is exceedingly rare," APRAIs cannot even identify defendants "who are more likely than not to commit a violent crime."[119] Ultimately, most defendants who are APRAI-designated as high risks to public safety are not arrested for a violent crime while on pretrial release. Indeed, if APRAIs

> were calibrated to be as accurate as possible, then they would predict that every person was unlikely to commit a violent crime while on pretrial release. Instead, risk assessments sacrifice accuracy and generate substantially more false positives (people who are flagged for violence but do not go on to commit a violent crime) than true positives (people who are flagged for violence and go on to be arrested for a violent crime).[120]

Moreover, there are significant problems with the criminal history data APRAIs use to predict future behavior.[121] Because APRAIs are developed using data and mathematical tools, many people assume that they are objective and reliable. But Professor Bernard Harcourt has persuasively argued that the inclusion of criminal history in risk assessment instruments "produces a 'ratchet effect'" that amplifies existing bias in policing and case adjudication.

Harcourt argues that, because their communities are overpoliced, minority populations are arrested at higher rates.[122] Similarly, because people of color face more serious charges, they are convicted at higher rates and face more severe sentences than white people.[123] All of this means that APRAIs oversample these populations. In Professor Mayson's words: "[B]ias in, bias out."[124]

Thus, it is not surprising that APRAIs' overestimation of risk is more pronounced for people of racial or ethnic minority backgrounds. A recent PSA validation study concluded that failure to appear scores were far more accurate predictors of pretrial outcomes for white defendants than for Black defendants. The study also found that PSA scores showed "intercept differences" by race, making the average PSA score an inaccurate assessment.[125] Perhaps even more troubling, the study, on the failure to appear scale, found extreme "slope differences" by race. In other words, identical PSA scores mean different things for white and Black defendants.[126] These types of racial disparities led the Supreme Court of

Ohio to reject a recommendation that would have allowed Ohio judges to use APRAIs when making their bail determinations.[127] In sum, it is clear that APRAIs demonstrate predictive power based on aggregate data tainted by systemic bias.

Moreover, APRAIs do not predict the future behavior of any particular defendant. While APRAIs can identify defendants who share characteristics with other "high risk" or "low risk" defendants at a better-than-chance rate, "better than by chance" is not the appropriate standard for evaluating risk assessments.[128] The proper inquiry is how risk assessment tools perform compared to the individualized determinations of risk that judges have made since time immemorial.

Very few studies have addressed this question, and the handful that have are methodologically flawed.[129] For example, a study of the federal pretrial risk assessment instrument evaluated how pretrial officers assessed "a single fictitious case" but had "no actual case outcomes with which to measure 'accuracy.'"[130] While some jurisdictions that have introduced APRAIs have reported positive outcomes, those risk assessment tools have rarely been introduced in isolation. Thus, it is impossible to tell whether it was the APRAI or some other change to the system that led to the increased release rates and other positive outcomes.

Surely, more research is needed to discern which risk assessment instruments are both valid and reliable. Similarly, we need more empirical research on whether, and to what extent, particular risk assessment algorithms can increase public safety while mitigating—rather than perpetuating—racial, ethnic, and socioeconomic disparities.[131] Algorithms honed by machine learning *may* in the future help to actualize that goal.[132] For now, however, it seems clear that current APRAIs fall short of this goal. Thus, in February 2020, the Pretrial Justice Institute (PJI), which previously championed the use of risk assessment tools, withdrew its support of APRAIs. In a public statement, the PJI stated that "pretrial risk assessment tools . . . can no longer be a part of our solution for building equitable pretrial justice systems. Regardless of their science, brand, or age, these tools are derived from data reflecting structural racism and institutional inequity that impact our court and law enforcement policies and practices. Use of that data then deepens the inequity."[133] We join the Pretrial Justice Institute in calling for the abandonment of these tools that, in their current state, perpetuate systemic inequality.

Minimize Conditions and Use Pretrial Supervision and Monitoring in Limited Circumstances

Most jurisdictions that have eliminated financial release conditions still allow other kinds of conditions to be imposed, usually upon the recommendation and supervision of a pretrial services agency.

The Pretrial Justice Institute has identified four types of nonfinancial release conditions:

- *Status quo* conditions require defendants to maintain their residence, school, or employment status.
- *Problem-oriented* conditions address problems that might affect future court appearances or lead to rearrest. For example, problem-oriented release conditions might require a defendant to enroll in counseling, vocational and educational training, social services programming, or substance use disorder treatment.
- *Contact* conditions require defendants to regularly report to the pretrial services agency (or another supervision entity) by video, telephone, or in person.
- *Restrictive* conditions limit defendants' associations, movements, or actions. These conditions might require that a defendant remain in the jurisdiction, avoid contact with the complainant, honor curfews, or comply with stay away orders from certain areas, such as those where drug sales are common.[134]

Few of these conditions are specifically designed to help defendants show up for their court appearances. And compliance with many of these requirements can be challenging, particularly for poor or unemployed people.[135] In some cases, no-contact orders may force defendants to vacate their homes to avoid family members named in those orders.[136] While some pretrial services agencies have developed job training and housing placement programs to address these concerns, other agencies are without the resources to offer such services.[137]

The imposition of "numerous restrictive conditions of release for extended periods[] may be setting people up to fail."[138] Yet we know little about the effectiveness of these burdensome conditions in reducing pretrial failures. The scant research aimed at answering this question offers mixed conclusions. A large National Institute of Justice study from the 1980s found that the use of pretrial supervision reduced local jail populations and also that defendants released with pretrial supervision had slightly better appearance rates than those who were unsupervised.[139] However, supervision did not meaningfully reduce defendants' rates of reoffending.

Moreover, it is unclear which conditions of release are associated with success or failure. Among the few conditions that have been evaluated, none have been shown to reduce pretrial failures. For example, multiple evaluation studies have been unable to conclude that pretrial drug testing effectively reduces pretrial failures, even when accompanied by a corresponding system of sanctions.[140] Similarly, multiple evaluation studies have been unable to conclude that electronic monitoring effectively reduces pretrial failures.[141] Given that popular conditions of release are not empirically supported, arrestees should be unconditionally released.

Unconditional Release Is a Better Way

Given the potential pitfalls of pretrial supervision—not the least of which is oversupervision that sets up defendants for failure—ample research supports our recommendation that most individuals should be released unconditionally pending trial. Only limited conditions should be available, and they should be imposed only to ensure defendants' participation in subsequent court proceedings or to mitigate meaningful threats of physical harm to the victim or the public. To maintain and increase their already high appearance rates, jurisdictions should implement evidence-based reforms, that is, reforms that are supported by empirical research, including court notification programs (discussed below) and other similar initiatives that address the difficulties defendants face in accessing courts.

Court Notification Programs

Court notification programs that remind defendants of upcoming proceedings are an effective way to increase appearance rates without imposing additional pretrial release conditions. A study in Jefferson

County, Colorado, found that a phone call reminding defendants about their court dates reduced the FTA rate from 21% to 12%.[142] Similarly, Multnomah County, Oregon, saw a 31% reduction in FTAs when it implemented an automated reminder system.[143] And in New York, two randomized control trials studied court reminders.

The first study examined reminder phone calls and found that, when individuals who received desk appearance tickets[144] also received reminder phone calls, they were more likely to appear in court.[145] The reminder phone calls reduced the FTA rate by 37%; whether individuals received a three-day phone call, a same-day phone call, or both was not important.[146] The second study concluded that individuals who received a summons and also received a reminder text message were more likely to appear in court.[147] The most effective strategy in this study involved two reminder text messages and reduced FTAs by 26%.[148].

Given this research, other jurisdictions are moving to adopt court notification programs. For example, after promising results were shown in Hennepin County (which includes Minneapolis), Minnesota rolled out a statewide reminder system.[149] The Arizona Supreme Court's Justice for All Task Force noted similar success.[150] The Pima County (Arizona) Consolidated Justice Courts and the Glendale and Mesa municipal courts have each implemented an Interactive Voice Response system to notify defendants of upcoming court dates, missed payments, and the issuance of warrants. Each jurisdiction has experienced a reduction in the number of people failing to appear (in one case by up to 24%).

Taking Defendants to Court and Taking Court to Defendants

Some people fail to appear for court simply because getting to court is beyond their ability. They may lack transportation or have inflexible work hours that force them to choose between keeping their jobs or appearing in court.[151] To address these problems, several jurisdictions have implemented innovations that improve access to courts. For example, some courts have expanded their hours of operation to include evening and weekend hours.[152] Others are holding proceedings in "local community centers, churches, and schools" instead of in courthouses.[153]

Many innovations depend on technology. Some courts use phone apps to connect defendants to social service agencies that can assist defendants with transportation, child care, and other needs.[154] Others allow people to resolve low-level traffic violations by emailing documentation of their registration, insurance, and driver's license.[155] Courts have also innovated by allowing pretrial court appearances via videoconference technologies, such as FaceTime or Skype, that can be used for free on mobile phones.[156]

Conclusion: We Should Go Further

It is heartening that several jurisdictions are reforming their pretrial justice systems. However, the goals of pretrial justice reform require that we do more than simply replace one flawed system with another flawed system. Eliminating money bail and the commercial bond industry is an essential first step. But additional measures that reduce the number of people detained pending trial must follow. Research suggests that jurisdictions can release more defendants unconditionally without compromising public safety or reducing their already high appearance rates, especially if they implement simple tools like court notification programs. Empirical evidence supports these reforms. Courts should follow the evidence.

NOTES

1 Neubauer and Fradella, *America's Courts and the Criminal Justice System*, 292–99.
2 Neubauer and Fradella, *America's Courts and the Criminal Justice System*, 292–94; Scott-Hayward and Fradella, *Punishing Poverty*, 32–35.
3 Duker, "The Right to Bail: A Historical Inquiry," 86.
4 Scott-Hayward and Fradella, *Punishing Poverty*, 16–17.
5 Ibid., 17–29; see also United States v. Steward, 2 U.S. (2 Dall.) 343 (1795).
6 Minton and Zeng, "Jail Inmates in 2019."
7 Ibid., 6.
8 Ibid., 5.
9 Ibid. Data found at page 11.
10 Ibid., 11.
11 In 2009, just 4% of defendants in the 75 largest counties in the United States were denied bail outright. Reaves, *Felony Defendants in Large Urban Counties, 2009*, 15; Color of Change and ACLU, "Selling Off Our Freedom," 10.
12 Reaves, *Felony Defendants in Large Urban Counties, 2009*, 15.
13 Reaves, *Felony Defendants in Large Urban Counties, 2009*, 15.
14 Ibid.

15 Scott-Hayward and Ottone, "Punishing Poverty: California's Unconstitutional Bail System," 167.

16 Pinto, "The Bail Trap."

17 Ibid.

18 Ibid.; see also Phillips, "A Decade of Bail Research in New York City," 116; Prison Policy Initiative, "Detaining the Poor."

19 Prison Policy Initiative, "Detaining the Poor."

20 Heaton, Mayson, and Stevenson, "The Downstream Consequences of Misdemeanor Pretrial Detention," 762; Stevenson, "Distortion of Justice."

21 Scott-Hayward and Fradella, *Punishing Poverty*, 4–5.

22 Jarecki, dir., *The Jinx: The Life and Deaths of Robert Durst*, aired on HBO February 8, 2015–March 15, 2015.

23 Yuko, "Robert Durst Murder Trial Begins in Los Angeles," ¶ 1, 3 (noting that Durst was never charged in his wife's disappearance and was convicted only of evidence-tampering and bail-jumping in the killing and dismemberment of his neighbor).

24 Neubauer and Fradella, *America's Courts and the Criminal Justice System*, 295; Thomas, *Bail Reform in America*, 250.

25 Neubauer and Fradella, *America's Courts and the Criminal Justice System*, 295.

26 Johnson, "The Politics of the Bail System," 179; Neubauer and Fradella, *America's Courts and the Criminal Justice System*, 295.

27 New Jersey Commission of Investigation, "Inside Out"; Utah Legislative Auditor General, *A Performance Audit of Utah's Monetary Bail System*.

28 Covert, "America Is Waking Up to the Injustice of Cash Bail."

29 Color of Change and ACLU, "Selling Off Our Freedom," 40–43.

30 Scott-Hayward and Fradella, "The Bail Industry Blocks Reform—Again."

31 Kusisto, "Criminal-Justice Changes Are Squeezing the Bail-Bond Industry."

32 Thomas, *Bail Reform in America*, 16–17.

33 Fan, "Conspiracy Theories, Criminal Investigations Plentiful."

34 Color of Change and ACLU, "Selling Off Our Freedom," 36.

35 Page, Piehowski, and Soss, "A Debt of Care," 159.

36 United States v. Salerno, 481 U.S. 739, 747–48 (1987).

37 Subramanian et al., "Incarceration's Front Door."

38 Ibid., 2.

39 Vera Institute of Justice, "The State of Jails" (citing Minton and Zeng, "Jail Inmates in 2016," 1) (documenting overcrowding); Noonan, "Mortality in Local Jails, 2000–2014—Statistical Tables" (documenting deaths in jail custody).

40 Klein, "On the Death of Sandra Bland."

41 Gonnerman, "Kalief Browder, 1993–2015."

42 Raphling, "Plead Guilty, Go Home. Plead Not Guilty, Stay in Jail"; Vaughn, "Pleading Guilty to Get Out of Jail."

43 For a detailed discussion of the impact of pretrial detention on case outcomes, see Scott-Hayward and Fradella, *Punishing Poverty*, 135–43.

44 Subramanian et al., "Incarceration's Front Door," 5 ("Given the complex role jails play in compounding the manifold negative consequences of mass incarceration in America—well acknowledged today on both sides of the aisle—local policy-makers and their constituents interested in reducing recidivism, improving public safety, and promoting stronger, healthier communities might do well to take a hard look at how the jail in their city or county is used.").

45 Gerstein v. Pugh, 420 U.S. 103, 114 (1975).

46 Minton and Zeng, "Jail Inmates in 2019," 5.

47 Prison Policy Initiative.

48 Demuth, "Racial and Ethnic Differences in Pretrial Release"; Katz and Spohn, "The Effect of Race and Gender on Bail Outcomes."

49 Schlesinger, "Racial and Ethnic Disparity in Pretrial Criminal Processing," 187–88; Arnold et al., "Racial Bias in Bail Decisions," 1929.

50 Duker, "The Right to Bail: A Historical Inquiry," 35, 69; Scott-Hayward and Fradella, *Punishing Poverty*, 11–19.

51 Causey, "Reviving the Carefully Limited Exception," 85.

52 Bail Reform Act of 1984.

53 18 U.S.C. § 3142(e).

54 Salerno, 481 U.S. at 751–52 (1987).

55 Causey, "Reviving the Carefully Limited Exception," 86.

56 Scott-Hayward and Fradella, *Punishing Poverty*, 16–29.

57 Angel et al., "Preventive Detention: An Empirical Analysis"; Goldkamp, "Questioning the Practice of Pretrial Detention"; Haapanen, *Selective Incapacitation and the Serious Offender*; Harcourt, *Against Prediction*.

58 See those chapters in this book.

59 Doyle et al., "Bail Reform: A Guide for State and Local Policymakers," 12; Pretrial Justice Institute, "Replace Money Bail."

60 To be sure, reform to pretrial justice might include multiple other measures, including increased use of citation in lieu of arrest; screening of criminal cases by experienced prosecutors; the presence of defense counsel at initial appearances; expanded use of pretrial supervision and monitoring; the availability of pretrial detention with due process; and the collection and analysis of performance measures, just to name a few. See American Bar Association, *Criminal Justice Standards on Providing Defense Services*; American Council of Chief Defenders, "Policy Statement on Fair and Effective Pretrial Justice Practices"; The Constitution Project, "Don't I Need a Lawyer? Pretrial Justice and the Right to Counsel at First Judicial Bail Hearing"; National Association of Criminal Defense Lawyers, "Resolution Concerning Pretrial Release and Limited Use of Financial Bond"; National Institute of Corrections, "Measuring What Matters: Outcome and Performance Measures for the Pretrial Services Field"; Pretrial Justice Institute, "How to Fix Pretrial Justice." We have critiqued these recommendations elsewhere in Scott-Hayward and Fradella, *Punishing Poverty*, 152–200. In this chapter, however, we focus more narrowly on specific reforms that are likely to have the most im-

mediate and meaningful impacts on eliminating a wealth-based system of bail, dramatically reducing the number of people detained pending trial, and mitigating the negative effects of pretrial detention and the unnecessary costs associated with it.

61 2014 N.J. Sess. L. Serv. ch. 31 (S.B. 946) (Aug. 11, 2014) (codified at N.J. Stat. Ann. § 2A, ch. 162 and scattered sections of § 2B).

62 N.J. Const. art I. § II.

63 Anderson et al., "Pretrial Justice Reform Study," 3–4.

64 N.J. REV. STAT. § 2A:162–15 (2018).

65 Ibid.

66 Grant, "2018 Report to the Governor and the Legislature," 13–16. We note that the state reported a slight increase in the percentage of defendants charged with a new crime while awaiting trial (from 12.7% in 2014 to 13.7% in 2017) and a slight decrease in the appearance rate (from 92.7% to 89.4%), but the report cautions that, due to measurement issues, these changes are "likely to not represent meaningful differences."

67 Ibid., 7, 32.

68 Ibid., 13.

69 Ibid., 14–15.

70 Ibid., 23.

71 Ibid., 25–28.

72 Anderson et al., "Pretrial Justice Reform Study," 14.

73 MD. R. CT. 4–216(b)(1)(A).

74 MD. R. CT. 4–216(c)(1).

75 Blumauer et al., "Advancing Bail Reform in Maryland," 14–15.

76 Ibid., 11.

77 Ibid., 19.

78 Cherem and Taylor, "Bail Reform Hasn't Led to Fewer Held in Jail"; Bui, "Reforms Intended to End Excessive Cash Bail in Md. Are Keeping More in Jail Longer."

79 Blumauer et al., "Advancing Bail Reform in Maryland," 20.

80 2019 Sess. Law News of N.Y. Ch. 59 (S. 1509-C) (Apr. 12, 2019) (codified at scattered sections of N.Y. Consolidated Laws, most notably Criminal Procedure Law §§ 500.10–530.60 (2020)).

81 Rahman, "Highlights of the 2019 Bail Reform Law," 4.

82 N.Y. CRIM. PRO. L. §§ 510.10–510.40 (2020).

83 N.Y. CRIM. PRO. L. §§ 500.10(3) (2020).

84 N.Y. CRIM. PRO. L. §§ 510.30(f) (2020).

85 Lartey, "New York Tried to Get Rid of Bail."

86 Hager, "New York City's Bail Success Story."

87 Bellware, "Class, Race and Geography Emerge as Flashpoints in New York's Bail Reform Debate."

88 Lartey, "New York Tried to Get Rid of Bail."

89 McAfee and Taylor, "Illinois Criminal Justice Reform."

90 Ali, "Did Illinois Get Bail Reform Right?"

91 2021 Ill. Legis. Serv. Pub. Act 101-0652 (H.B. 3653) (amending 725 Ill. Comp. Stat. 5/ art. 110).

92 2021 Ill. Legis. Serv. Pub. Act 101-0652 (H.B. 3653) (amending 725 Ill. Comp. Stat. 5/110-2(c)).

93 2021 Ill. Legis. Serv. Pub. Act 101-0652 (H.B. 3653) (amending 725 Ill. Comp. Stat. 5/110-2(b)).

94 2021 Ill. Legis. Serv. Pub. Act 101-0652 (H.B. 3653) (amending 725 Ill. Comp. Stat. 5/110-5(d)).

95 McAfee and Taylor "Illinois Criminal Justice Reform."

96 Liu, Nunn, and Shambaugh, "The Economics of Bail and Pretrial Detention."

97 Helland and Tabarrok, "The Fugitive," 118.

98 Clipper et al., "The Link Between Bond Forfeiture and Pretrial Release Mechanism."

99 Fox and Koppel, "Pretrial Release Without Money," 3.

100 "Deprivation of an accused person's liberty prior to trial should be an exception and limited to specific circumstances in which the state has a compelling need to confine the defendant." Van Brunt and Bowman, "Toward a Just Model of Pretrial Release," 755 (1987).

101 Dobbie et al., "The Effects of Pretrial Detention on Conviction, Future Crime, and Employment," 237; Baradaran-Baughman, "Costs of Pretrial Detention," 28–30 (estimating that fine-tuning pretrial detention decisions through careful cost-benefit analyses could save up to $78 billion annually).

102 Reaves, *Felony Defendants in Large Urban Counties, 2009*, 15.

103 Gouldin, "Disentangling Flight Risk," 862.

104 Mayson, "Dangerous Defendants," 505 (citing U.S. v. Salerno, 481 U.S. at 746–48 (1987)); see also Bell v. Wolfish, 441 U.S. 520, 535 (1979).

105 Mayson, "Dangerous Defendants," 506–07; Heaton, Mayson, and Stevenson, "The Downstream Consequences of Misdemeanor Pretrial Detention," 782–83.

106 Mayson, "Dangerous Defendants," 560–61; Lippke, "Pretrial Detention Without Punishment," 122 (arguing that there should be "substantial evidence" of the defendant's guilt on a serious charge).

107 Blumauer et al., "Advancing Bail Reform in Maryland," 19–20.

108 Baradaran and McIntyre, "Predicting Violence," 529, 561.

109 Ibid., 561.

110 Ibid., 528.

111 Guthrie, "Purse Snatching as Robbery or Theft."

112 United States v. Salerno, 481 U.S. 739 (1987), would seem to require this as well.

113 Smith and Madden, "Three-Minute Justice."

114 Scott-Hayward and Fradella, *Punishing Poverty*, 168–88.

115 For example, nearly 30 prominent researchers from MIT, Harvard, Princeton, New York University, University of California, Berkeley, Columbia, and the Algorithmic Justice League signed an open statement of concern about the

dangers of using APRAIs as part of pretrial justice reform efforts. See "Technical Flaws of Pretrial Risk Assessments"; Harcourt, "Risk as a Proxy for Race"; Gust, "Civil Rights Advocates Say Risk Assessment May 'Worsen Racial Disparities' in Bail Decisions." For an in-depth examination of the pretrial risk assessment instruments and their limits, see Scott-Hayward and Fradella, *Punishing Poverty*, 77–128.

116 Gouldin, "Disentangling Flight Risk," 842; Mayson, "Dangerous Defendants."
117 "Technical Flaws of Pretrial Risk Assessments," 1.
118 Gouldin, "Defining Flight Risk," 724–37.
119 "Technical Flaws of Pretrial Risk."
120 Ibid.
121 "Technical Flaws of Pretrial Risk Assessments," 2–3; Mayson, "Bias In, Bias Out."
122 Harcourt, "Risk as a Proxy for Race," 240.
123 Technical Flaws of Pretrial Risk Assessments," 3; Editors, Law Review, "Bail Reform and Risk Assessment"; Van Cleve and Mayes, "Criminal Justice Through 'Colorblind' Lenses."
124 Mayson, "Bias In, Bias Out," 2224, n.23 ("The computer-science idiom is 'garbage in, garbage out,' which refers to the fact that algorithmic prediction is only as good as the data on which the algorithm is trained.").
125 DeMichele et al., "The Public Safety Assessment."
126 Ibid., 50.
127 Ingles, "New Ohio Bail Reform Plan Excludes Key Recommendation"; Krouse, "Ohio Supreme Court Proposes Bail Reforms That Don't Include Risk Assessments" (explaining that "a majority of the court was swayed by assertions from the American Civil Liberties Union of Ohio that risk assessment methods are racially biased).
128 Starr, "The New Profiling."
129 Ibid., 232.
130 Ibid. (criticizing Oleson et al., "Training to See Risk.")
131 Menefee, "The Role of Bail and Pretrial Detention in the Reproduction of Racial Inequalities."
132 Kleinberg et al., "Human Decisions and Machine Predictions," 241 (analyzing more than 758,000 pretrial releasees in New York City and concluding that properly designed algorithms that utilize machine learning—a more powerful and complex tool for prediction than current risk assessment instruments—"can be a force for racial equality").
133 Pretrial Justice Institute, "Updated Position on Pretrial Risk Assessment Tools," para. 2.
134 Pretrial Justice Institute, "Using Technology to Enhance Pretrial Services," 16–17.
135 For an analogous discussion of standard conditions of probation, see Doherty, "Obey All Laws and Be Good," 349–50.
136 Mahoney et al., "Pretrial Service Programs: Responsibilities and Potential," 42.
137 Ibid., 47.

138 Myers, "Eroding the Presumption of Innocence," 678.
139 Austin et al., "The Effectiveness of Supervised Pretrial Release."
140 Bechtel et al., "A Meta-Analytic Review of Pretrial Research: Risk Assessment, Bond Type, and Interventions," 461 (2017); VanNostrand, Rose, and Weibrecht, "State of the Science of Pretrial Release Recommendations and Supervision," 24; Gottfredson et al., "Evaluation of Arizona Pretrial Services Drug Testing Programs"; Visher, "Pretrial Drug Testing: Panacea or Pandora's Box?"
141 VanNostrand, Rose, and Weibrecht, "State of the Science of Pretrial Release Recommendations and Supervision," 27; Lemke, "Evaluation of the Pretrial Release Pilot Program"; Maxfield and Baumer, "Evaluation of Pretrial Home Detention with Electronic Monitoring."
142 Schnacke, Jones, and Wilderman, "Increasing Court-Appearance Rates," 89.
143 Color of Change and ACLU, "Selling Off Our Freedom," 47.
144 A "desk appearance ticket" is a form of custodial arrest used mostly in misdemeanor cases that allows the arrestee to leave the precinct and return for arraignment at a later date.
145 Ferri, "The Benefits of live Court Date Reminder Phone Calls During Pretrial Case Processing."
146 Ibid.
147 Cooke et al., "Using Behavioral Science to Improve Criminal Justice Outcomes."
148 Ibid.
149 Xiong, "In Hennepin County, Text and Email Reminders of Court Dates Reduce Number of Warrants."
150 Superior Court of Arizona, "Report and Recommendations of the Task Force on Fair Justice for All."
151 Bornstein et al., "Reducing Courts' Failure to Appear Rate," 25 (reporting that scheduling conflicts and transportation difficulties were the top reasons people failed to appear).
152 Bernal, "Taking the Court to the People," 566.
153 Ibid., 570; Turner, "Reducing Failure to Appears Through Community Outreach."
154 Tulsa, Oklahoma, Family & Children's Services, "App Launches to Reduce Failure to Appears."
155 Ibid., 569.
156 Ibid.

5

Revisiting Sentencing Reform

CASSIA SPOHN, MEGAN VERHAGEN, AND JASON WALKER

In 1971, David Rothman, one of the foremost authorities on the history and development of the US prison system, wrote: "We have been gradually emerging from institutional responses, and one can foresee the period when incarceration will be used still more rarely than it is today."[1] Two years later, the National Advisory Commission on Criminal Justice Standards and Goals, which concluded that "the prison, the reformatory, and the jail have achieved only a shocking record of failure,"[2] recommended that "no new institutions for adults should be built and existing institutions for juveniles should be closed."[3]

More than half a century after Rothman's prediction, it has not come true and the National Advisory Commission's recommendations were not followed. Their calls for reductions in the use of incarceration, which were voiced at a time when the inmate population was just over 300,000, fell on deaf ears. Rather than declining, America's imprisonment rate, which had fluctuated around a steady mean of 110 individuals per 100,000 population for most of the twentieth century, increased every year from 1975 to 2007. In fact, the state and federal prison population increased from 300,000 to 1.6 million between 1975 and 2007, a fivefold increase. Although the number of persons incarcerated declined by 6.7% from 2007 to 2017, there were still almost 1.5 million prisoners serving time in state and federal prisons in 2017.[4] Even more troubling, the rate of Black incarceration nearly tripled from 1980 to 2000. As Bobo and Johnson concluded, "at the same time that our criminal justice policies have taken on an aggressive and deeply punitive tenor, they have also fallen with special severity on minority communities, particularly on African Americans."[5]

As these figures demonstrate, the United States "has been engaged in an unprecedented imprisonment binge,"[6] with the effects felt most keenly by people of color. Most criminologists argue that these dramatic increases in the prison population were due not to increases in crime but to changes in sentencing policies and practices, including mandatory minimum sentences, three-strikes provisions, truth-in-sentencing statutes, laws allowing life sentences without the possibility of parole, and overly punitive sentencing guidelines in which the severity of the sentence is not proportionate to the seriousness of the crime.[7] Mauer, for example, stated that "the impact of these sentencing changes on prison populations has been dramatic[] and far outweighs any change in crime rates as a contributing factor."[8]

The role played by these changes in sentencing policies and practices was confirmed by a careful and methodologically rigorous analysis of growth in the prison population from 1980 to 1996,[9] which concluded that 88% of the tripling of the prison population during this time period could be explained by changes in the imposition of punishment: 51% of the increase was due to a greater likelihood of incarceration after conviction, and 37% could be attributed to longer prison sentences. By contrast, changes in the crime rate explained only 12% of the growth in incarceration. The United States Sentencing Commission reached the same conclusion regarding the increase in the federal prison population, noting that "the changes in sentencing policy occurring since the mid-1980s—both the increasing proportion of offenders receiving prison time and average length of time served—have been a dominant factor contributing to the growth in the federal prison population."[10] Similarly, a recent comprehensive analysis by the National Research Council determined that the increase in the state prison population between 1980 and 2010 was due primarily to growth in prison admission rates, especially for drug offenses, and to increases in time served, particularly for violent crimes.[11] Other work using state-level data demonstrates that growth in incarceration rates reflects an increase in the likelihood of a prison sentence given conviction, especially for offenders deemed dangerous to public safety,[12] as well as an increase over time in the length of offenders' criminal histories.[13]

These studies convincingly demonstrate that dramatic increases in state and federal prison populations since the 1970s can be attributed largely to changes in sentencing policies and practices. As a result of the sentencing reform movement in the twentieth century, the likelihood of incarceration, especially for nonviolent crimes and drug offenses, increased and prison sentences became more punitive.[14] There also is persuasive evidence that these changes *did not* produce the predicted decline in crime[15] but *did* exacerbate already alarming racial and ethnic disparities in incarceration.[16] These findings, coupled with crippling increases in correctional budgets, have led researchers, practitioners, and policy makers to conclude that it is time to pursue meaningful sentencing reform—reforms designed to ensure that punishment is proportionate to the seriousness of the crime, ameliorate disparity and discrimination in sentencing, reduce recidivism, and end mass incarceration.[17]

As the third decade of the twenty-first century unfolds, there is mounting evidence that Americans' appetite for punishment may be shrinking and that the United States must chart a different course on sentencing. At the federal level, Congress enacted three sentencing reform bills with broad bipartisan support: The Second Chance Act (2008), which authorized grants to government agencies and nonprofits to provide employment assistance, substance abuse treatment, and other services designed to reduce recidivism; the Fair Sentencing Act (2010), which reduced the 100:1 sentencing disparity for crack and powder cocaine to 18:1 and eliminated the five-year mandatory minimum sentence for possession of crack cocaine; and the First Step Act (2018), which shortened mandatory minimum sentences for nonviolent drug offenses, reduced the sentence for conviction under the federal three-strikes rule from life to 25 years, expanded the drug safety valve that allows judges to deviate from mandatory minimums when sentencing drug offenders, and made the provisions of the Fair Sentencing Act retroactive.

States are also rethinking their approach to sentencing nonviolent offenders and drug offenders; several states have passed laws designed to roll back or otherwise revise mandatory minimum sentences for these types of offenders.[18] States also have enacted legislation that downgrades felony drug offenses to misdemeanors (and some misdemeanors to infractions) and makes certain types of offenders ineligible for a prison sentence (e.g., Assembly Bill 109 in California). Although critics contend that these reform efforts are "meager" and represent little more than "nibbling at the edges" of the problem,[19] the fact that they are supported by politicians from both sides of the political spectrum and by large majorities of American citizens suggests that the time is indeed ripe for major change to sentencing policies and practices.

Our goal in this chapter is to demonstrate why it is time to revisit sentencing reform. We begin by examining the major sentencing policies and practices enacted during the past four decades: determinate sentencing and sentencing guidelines, mandatory minimum sentencing statutes, three-strikes-and-you're-out laws, truth-in-sentencing provisions, and changes to life sentences. We discuss the factors that motivated these changes and the instrumental goals they were designed to achieve. We also evaluate their impact on mass incarceration, challenge the assertion that they have produced fairer and more equitable sentencing outcomes, and discuss needed reforms.

Four Decades of Reform

Four decades of experimentation and reform transformed sentencing policies and practices in the United States. Forty years ago, indeterminate sentencing was the norm, and "the word 'sentencing' generally signified a slightly mysterious process . . . [that] involved individualized decisions that judges were uniquely qualified to make."[20] Judges had substantial though not unfettered discretion to determine the type and length of sentences, and parole boards decided how long incarcerated offenders would actually serve. Judges considered the facts and circumstances of the case and the characteristics of the offender and attempted to tailor sentences to fit individuals and their crimes. With few exceptions, judges were not required to impose specific sentences on particular types of offenders or on offenders convicted of particular types of crimes.

Concerns about disparity, disproportionality, and discrimination in sentencing—coupled with widespread disillusionment with rehabilitation and a belief that more punitive sentences were necessary to deter and incapacitate dangerous offenders—led to a series of incremental reforms that revolutionized the sentencing process. Some jurisdictions retained indeterminate sentencing; others replaced it with more tightly structured determinate sentencing or with sentencing guidelines that calculated sentences based on the seriousness of the crime and the offender's criminal history. Mandatory minimum sentencing statutes that eliminated judicial discretion and targeted violent offenders, drug of-fenders, and career criminals were enacted at both the state and federal levels, and more than half the states enacted some version of a three-strikes law. Most jurisdictions also adopted truth-in-sentencing statutes designed to ensure that offenders serve a larger portion of the sentence imposed by the judge, and many jurisdictions expanded the categories of offenders eligible for life sentences—or life without the possibility of parole—and/or altered the number of years offenders sentenced to life would have to serve before being eligible for parole. As a result of these changes, the sentencing process today is much more complex and fragmented. Sentencing policies and practices vary on a number of di-mensions, and there is no longer anything that can be described as the "American approach."

Challenging the Indeterminate Sentence

The initial focus of twentieth-century reform efforts was the indetermi-nate sentence, in which the judge imposed a minimum and a maximum sentence—in essence, a range—and the parole board determined the date of release. The parole board's determination of when the offender should be released rested on its judgment of whether the offender had been rehabilitated or had served enough time for the particular crime. Under indeterminate sentencing, sentences were tailored to the indi-vidual offender, and discretion was distributed not only to the criminal justice officials who determined the sentence but also to corrections officials and the parole board. The result of this process was "a system of sentencing in which there was little understanding or predictability as to who would be imprisoned and for how long."[21]

Both liberal and conservative reformers challenged the principles un-derlying the indeterminate sentence and called for changes designed to curb discretion, reduce disparity and discrimination, and achieve pro-portionality and parsimony in sentencing.

Liberals and civil rights activists argued that indeterminate sentenc-ing was arbitrary and capricious and therefore violated defendants' rights to equal protection and due process of law.[22] They charged that indeterminate sentences were used to incapacitate those whom correc-tional officials believed could not be rehabilitated and that offenders' uncertainty about their dates of release contributed to prison unrest. Liberal critics were also apprehensive about the potential for racial bias under indeterminate sentencing schemes. They asserted that "racial discrimination in the criminal justice system was epidemic, that judges, parole boards, and corrections officials could not be trusted, and that tight controls on officials' discretion offered the only way to limit racial disparities."[23]

Political conservatives contended that the emphasis on rehabilitation under indeterminate sentencing too often resulted in excessively lenient treatment of offenders who had committed serious crimes or had serious criminal histories.[24] They also charged that sentences not tightly coupled to crime seriousness and offender culpability were unjust.[25] These conservative critics championed sentencing reforms designed to establish and enforce more punitive sentencing standards. Their arguments were bolstered by the findings of research demonstrating that many correctional programs designed to rehabilitate offenders and reduce recidivism were ineffective for most offenders.[26]

Determinate Sentencing and Sentencing Guidelines

In 1972, Marvin Frankel, US district judge for the Southern District of New York, issued an influential call for reform of the sentencing process.[27] Judge Frankel decried the degree of discretion given to judges, which he maintained led to "lawlessness" in sentencing, and called for legislative reforms designed to curtail judicial discretion and eliminate arbitrariness and disparity in sentencing. More to the point, he pushed for the creation of a new administrative agency called a "sentencing commission" to create rules for sentencing that judges would be required to follow.

Judge Frankel's calls for reform did not go unheeded. After a few initial "missteps," in which jurisdictions attempted to *eliminate* discretion altogether through flat-time sentencing,[28] states and the federal government adopted a series of incremental structured reforms designed to *control* the discretion of sentencing judges. A number of jurisdictions experimented with voluntary or advisory sentencing guidelines based on the past sentencing practices of judges. Advocates of this reform hoped that identifying the normal penalty or going rate for certain types of offenses would reduce intrajurisdictional disparity. Other states adopted determinate sentencing policies that abolished release on parole, offered judges a limited number of sentencing options, and included enhancements for aggravating factors such as use of a weapon, presence of a prior criminal record, or infliction of serious injury. Still other jurisdictions established presumptive sentencing guidelines that incorporated crime seriousness and criminal history into a sentencing grid that judges were required to use in determining the appropriate sentence. Whereas every state and the federal system used indeterminate sentencing in 1970, by 2017 the federal government, 14 states, and the District of Columbia were operating under sentencing guidelines promulgated by sentencing commissions; four states were operating under determinate sentencing systems; and indeterminate sentencing survived in the remaining states.[29]

Supporters of sentencing guidelines claimed that guidelines would reduce disproportionate and disparate sentencing by prescribing punishments based on the facts of the case, thereby limiting the extent to which judges' biases, preferences, and philosophies of punishment would influence their decision-making.[30] Although there are a number of methodological challenges to determining whether sentencing guidelines have reduced disparity,[31] most studies of sentences imposed under state and federal guidelines conclude that guideline sentences are more consistent and more uniform.[32] There is less disparity among judges in jurisdictions with guidelines,[33] and sentences in these jurisdictions are more tightly coupled to the seriousness of the offense and the offender's criminal history.[34] These findings are not surprising; sentencing guidelines are based explicitly on crime seriousness and criminal history, and judges are required to take these two factors into account in determining the appropriate sentence. As Tonry noted in 1996, it would be "astonishing" if guidelines had not reduced disparity in sentencing.[35] Critics, however, contend that guidelines led to more punitive punishment[36] and facilitated the rise in mass incarceration that disproportionately impacted low-income and minority communities.[37] Thus, the objective of more uniformity and consistency in sentencing may have been purchased "at the price of undue severity in sentences, undue uniformity of those sentenced, and unwarranted complexity."[38]

Those who lobbied for adoption of presumptive sentencing guidelines also claimed that guidelines would structure the sentencing process, constrain judicial discretion, and thereby eliminate unwarranted disparity and discrimination. The lack of longitudinal research comparing the effects of legally irrelevant offender characteristics on sentencing before and after the implementation of guidelines makes it difficult to assess the degree to which the guidelines themselves reduced unwarranted disparity, but most research conducted in the wake of the guidelines era revealed the persistence of disparate sentencing, especially in the decision to sentence the offender to prison or not.[39] Although researchers initially found a reduction in disparities attributed to the offender's race, ethnicity, and sex in some of the first states to adopt sentencing guidelines,[40] later studies demonstrated that these legally irrelevant factors continued to play a role, challenging beliefs that guidelines would eliminate bias in the courtroom.[41]

The failure of sentencing guidelines to eliminate sentencing disparity—especially racial and ethnic disparity—led to research designed to identify policies and practices that might explain why the guidelines had not produced the intended results. Several commentators, for example, noted that sentencing guidelines severely constrain judges' discretion in deciding between prison and probation and determining the length of the sentence[42] but place only minimal restrictions on judges' decisions to reduce sentences through downward departures or on prosecutors' charging and plea bargaining decisions.[43] As Albonetti noted: "These process-related decisions offer potential avenues through which prosecutors (and judges) can circumvent guideline-defined sentence outcomes."[44] Boerner's assessment is more pointed; he argues that "what has changed is the relative power of the prosecutor."[45] As he so colorfully put it, "in jurisdictions that have adopted sentencing guidelines, three dragons of discretion have been dragged onto the plain. One (release discretion of parole boards) has been killed and one (judicial sentencing discretion) has been significantly constrained. The remaining dragon (prosecutorial discretion), however, continues to roam the plain unrestrained."[46]

The fact that disparities remain in jurisdictions with determinate sentencing and sentencing guidelines suggests that judges and prosecutors are reluctant to determine sentences based solely on crime seriousness and prior criminal record. It implies that statutorily irrelevant factors such as race, gender, age, employment status, family circumstances, and social class may be factually relevant to criminal justice officials' assessments of dangerousness, threat, and culpability. It also attests to Tonry's assertation that "there is, substantively, no way around the dilemma that sentencing is inherently discretionary and that discretion leads to disparities."[47]

Revisiting Sentence Severity and Sentencing Guidelines

It is clear that the "tough on crime" and "war on drugs" eras led to more punitive punishment overall and to increasing numbers of nonviolent offenders and drug offenders locked up and serving long sentences in our nation's prisons. To reverse these trends, we make the following recommendations:

- *Decriminalize* or legalize possession of marijuana, release offenders who are serving prison terms for marijuana possession, and expunge marijuana possession convictions from criminal records.
- *Reduce* felony drug possession offenses to misdemeanors.
- *Enact* legislation (e.g., AB 109 in California) that makes nonviolent, nonserious, and nonsex offenders ineligible for a prison sentence.
- *Expand* alternatives to incarceration—pretrial diversion, substance abuse or mental health treatment, and problem-solving courts.

We contend that these reforms will reduce mass incarceration (and the correctional budgets needed to sustain it) while protecting public safety and reducing the likelihood of recidivism. They also will allow jurisdictions to reinvest the cost savings from reducing incarceration in community-based programs and problem-solving courts that provide treatment, reduce recidivism, and protect public safety. More important, these reforms will help ameliorate the racial and ethnic disparities in punishment produced by the war on drugs.

It also is clear that determinate sentencing and sentencing guidelines, which were designed to ensure proportionality, uniformity, and fairness in punishment, have not achieved these instrumental goals. Although this is due in part to the "hydraulic displacement of discretion"[48] from judges to prosecutors, it also reflects structural features of determinate sentencing and sentencing guidelines, including punitive enhancements for aggravating circumstances, punishments pegged to the type and amount of drugs or the monetary value of property, and restrictions on judges' ability to depart downward from the guidelines when appropriate. We therefore recommend the following changes:

Reduce the punitiveness of sentences imposed under determinate sentencing and sentencing guidelines by

- ratcheting downward the sentence ranges associated with various combinations of crime seriousness and criminal history;
- reducing sentence enhancements for aggravating circumstances (e.g., possession or use of a weapon, a history of repeat offenses, lack of remorse);
- increasing sentence discounts for mitigating circumstances (e.g., the age and mental capacity of the offender, the offender's lack of criminal history); and
- raising weight and monetary thresholds for drug and property offenses, and ensuring that statutory maximums are proportionate to the seriousness of the crime.

Reduce the rigidity of determinate sentencing and sentencing guidelines by

- making more combinations of offense seriousness and criminal history eligible for probation; and
- providing judges with discretion to depart from the guidelines where appropriate.

Hold prosecutors accountable by

- requiring that they file only those charges for which there is proof beyond a reasonable doubt and a reasonable likelihood of conviction at trial; and
- requiring that plea negotiations be in writing and on the record.

Mandatory Minimum Sentencing Statutes

Mandatory minimum sentencing statutes proliferated during the tough on crime/war on drugs eras in the United States during the 1970s, 1980s, and early 1990s. Candidates from both major political parties campaigned on "tough on crime" platforms and decried overly lenient sentences imposed by "soft" judges. They championed mandatory minimum sentencing statutes that required judges to impose specified sentences on offenders convicted of certain types of crimes—such as violent offenses, firearm offenses, drug offenses, and drunk driving offenses—and on habitual or repeat offenders. State and federal legislatures responded enthusiastically to these calls for more punitive sentencing schemes. By the mid-1990s mandatory penalties had been adopted in every state, and Congress had enacted more than 60 mandatory sentencing laws covering more than 100 federal offenses.[49]

As already noted, changes in sentencing policies and practices enacted during the sentencing reform movement were intended to reduce disparities in sentencing by precluding legal actors—especially judges—from considering statutorily irrelevant factors.[50] Mandatory minimum sentencing policies, which apply to *all* offenders convicted of certain crimes or with certain types of criminal histories, were designed to achieve this goal. In imposing the sentence, the judge is to consider only the fact that the defendant has been convicted of an offense carrying a mandatory sentence. The judge is not permitted to consider the defendant's role in the offense, family situation, background characteristics, or other mitigating factors. Mandatory minimum sentencing policies also reflect the justice system's attempt to regulate criminal behavior. Rooted in deterrence and rational choice theory, mandatory minimums were a response to the nation's growing concerns over rising crime rates.[51] Public officials claimed that mandatory minimums would prevent future crime by deterring potential offenders and incapacitating those who were not deterred.[52] The problem with this argument is that there is little, if any, evidence that more punitive sentences have a deterrent effect.[53]

Although the primary objections to mandatory minimum sentencing statutes, especially those applicable to nonviolent offenses, are their excessive severity and inflexibility, opponents also charge that these statutes, like presumptive sentencing guidelines, shift discretion from the sentencing judge to the prosecutor.[54] Because sentencing for offenses carrying mandatory penalties is, by definition, nondiscretionary, and because the application of a mandatory minimum sentence depends on conviction for a charge carrying a mandatory penalty, critics charge that prosecutors, not judges, determine what the ultimate sentence will be.

The prosecutor decides whether to file a charge triggering a mandatory minimum sentence and, if so, whether to reduce the charge to one not carrying a mandatory penalty during plea negotiations. In other words, by manipulating the charges that defendants face, prosecutors can circumvent the mandatory minimum sentencing provisions.[55]

There also is evidence that mandatory minimum sentencing statutes, especially those applicable to drug offenses, disproportionately target people of color and those living in low-income communities.[56] Some scholars suggest that this is because people of color and the poor are more likely to commit crimes that trigger mandatory penalties,[57] but others contend that disparities result from the application of mandatory minimum statutes. For example, one study examined imposition of mandatory sentences in Pennsylvania, where the application of mandatory penalties is determined by the prosecutor's decision to file a charge that triggers a mandatory penalty and then to file a motion to apply the mandatory penalty.[58] An important conclusion of this study was that "prosecutors choose to apply the mandatory to eligible offenses in relatively few cases."[59] The authors also found that eligible Hispanic (but not eligible Black) offenders were substantially more likely than eligible white offenders to receive the mandatory penalty and that eligible male offenders were more likely than eligible female offenders to receive a mandatory sentence.[60] These results challenge the notion that mandatory penalties are, in fact, mandatory, as well as the assumption that they are applied without reference to legally irrelevant factors.

Revisiting Mandatory Minimum Sentencing Statutes

Mandatory minimum sentencing statutes, which arguably were designed to deter potential offenders and ensure the incapacitation of serious and dangerous offenders, came under increasing criticism as prison populations skyrocketed, correctional budgets ballooned, and racial and ethnic disparities in imprisonment worsened. (Incapacitation is the philosophy that incarcerated offenders can no longer commit crimes once imprisoned.)[61] Beginning in the late 1990s, many jurisdictions began to revise mandatory minimum sentencing statutes, either by limiting the crimes to which they applied or by reducing their punitiveness. We argue that these minimal changes are not sufficient, especially given the lack of evidence that mandatory minimums deter crime and the substantial evidence that they contributed to mass incarceration and disproportionately target people of color and those living in low-income communities. These negative effects are exacerbated by the lack of discretion accorded to judges and the unfettered discretion that prosecutors have in deciding to file a charge that triggers a mandatory minimum or to reduce the charge to one not carrying a mandatory minimum during plea negotiations. We therefore recommend the repeal of all mandatory minimum sentencing statutes. If this is not politically palatable or feasible, we recommend:

- Drastically scaling back the punishments required by mandatory minimum sentencing statutes.
- Holding prosecutors accountable by requiring that they file charges that trigger a mandatory minimum sentence only if there is proof beyond a reasonable doubt and a reasonable likelihood of conviction of that charge at trial and by requiring that plea negotiations that eliminate the mandatory minimum sentence be in writing and on the record.

Three-Strikes-and-You're-Out Laws

Three-strikes laws were developed with the goal of increasing sentences and enhancing punishment for repeat offenders by imprisoning offenders for an extended time upon conviction for a third (or, sometimes, a second) qualifying offense. They aim to reduce crime by capitalizing on incapacitation.[62] By focusing on offenders with qualifying, repeat criminal histories, three-strikes laws specifically seek to incapacitate those who pose the greatest risk for public safety.

Additionally, three-strikes laws aim to reduce crime through deterrence, with the expectation that each additional strike an offender receives will increase an offender's perceptions of the costs of crime.[63]

Currently, thirty states, the District of Columbia, and the federal system have implemented some form of a three-strikes law. However, these laws are written and applied differently depending on the jurisdiction.[64] Although many jurisdictions give offenders with their third felony conviction life sentences without the chance of parole, other jurisdictions impose more lenient sentences for a third strike. Similarly, while commonly referred to as "three-strikes" laws, jurisdictions impose the harshest sentencing penalties after offenders accumulate differing numbers of strikes, from two in South Carolina to four in Maryland. And lastly, different jurisdictions allow for different crimes to count toward an offender's strikes. Although all jurisdictions with three-strikes laws include violent felonies as strikes, some jurisdictions also count nonviolent felonies, drug crimes, street crimes, and even criminal attempts as strikes.[65] Given these differences, it is difficult to compare the effects of three-strikes laws across jurisdictions in the United States.

Although the intention of three-strikes laws is to incapacitate violent offenders and serve as a deterrent for crime generally, early research found that instrumental crimes were generally unaffected by the implementation of these laws and that violent crime may have increased rather than decreased.[66] Some studies concluded that jurisdictions with three-strikes laws experienced slight decreases in robberies, burglaries, larcenies, and motor vehicle thefts,[67] while others found that homicides increased[68] or declined at slower rates[69] in jurisdictions with three-strikes laws compared to those without these laws. (However, researchers were reluctant to attribute these declines to the laws themselves given the potential influence of other changes in sentencing policies and practices and a general decline in national crime rates). Because California enacted one of the first—and one of the harshest—three-strikes laws, researchers have focused their attention on the law's impact in California, where about 7,000 individuals, or approximately 5.4% of California's prison population, were incarcerated as a result of a third-strike conviction in 2018.[70] The results of this research are mixed, with studies suggesting that the implementation of the three-strikes law in California resulted either in a significant deterrent effect on crime,[71] minimal to no deterrent effect on crime,[72] or a criminalizing effect in which the three-strikes law was associated with increases in crime.[73] The mixed findings from California and other jurisdictions suggest that three-strikes laws have not achieved their intended instrumental effects on crime and criminal behavior.

Critics of three-strikes laws also contend that these laws have increased racial disparities in prison populations. Research has shown that three-strikes laws are applied more often to Black defendants than to white defendants, resulting in Black defendants receiving longer prison terms even after controlling for other legally relevant variables.[74] This racial disparity is most prominent in "wobbler" cases, or those where prosecutors have discretion to file the case as either a felony or a misdemeanor. In these instances, Black defendants are more likely than similarly situated white defendants to be charged with felonies and thus to have the conviction count as a second or third strike.[75]

Revisiting Three-Strikes Laws

Although touted as a major innovation, in reality three-strikes laws are simply more punitive—in some cases, much more punitive—versions of habitual offender statutes that date back to the late eighteenth century. These laws, like their predecessors, are designed to prevent crime by deterring and incapacitating dangerous criminal offenders. The results of evaluation research are somewhat mixed; most studies reveal that three-strikes laws did not reduce or deter crime but did increase unwarranted disparity in sentencing and contribute to the disproportionate number of Black men affected by mass incarceration in the United States. To mitigate these negative effects, we recommend that jurisdictions should eliminate all two-strikes and three-strikes laws. If this is not possible, we recommend revising three-strikes laws so that:

- Only serious felonies count as strikes;
- only a third or subsequent strike triggers a sentence enhancement; and
- only three strikes for violent felonies lead to a life without the possibility of parole sentence.

Truth-in-Sentencing Laws

Widespread concerns about offenders who were paroled from prison after serving only a small proportion of their sentences led to a number of interrelated reforms. Many states abolished early release from prison at the discretion of the parole board, either for all offenders or for certain categories of offenders. States also tightened policies regarding good-time reductions for satisfactory behavior in prison and earned-time reductions for participation in prison-based educational and vocational programs. At the same time, many states enacted truth-in-sentencing laws that require offenders to serve a substantial portion of the prison sentence imposed before being eligible for release. Enactment of these laws was encouraged by passage of the Sentencing Reform Act of 1984, which required convicted federal offenders to serve 85% of the sentence imposed, and the Violent Crime Control and Law Enforcement Act of 1994, which authorized grants to states that required people convicted of violent crimes to serve at least 85% of the sentence imposed by the judge.[76]

Truth-in-sentencing laws are designed to ensure that offenders, particularly violent offenders, serve a substantial portion of their sentences. Assuming that the judge does not discount the sentence he or she imposes, anticipating that the offender will serve a larger percentage of the sentence, the laws should result in longer prison terms. Data from states that enacted an 85% rule showed that the average time served by violent offenders did, in fact, increase. It went from 32 months to 82 months in Vermont, from 28 months to 50 months in Florida, and from 31 months to 47 months in North Dakota.[77]

Like three-strikes laws and mandatory minimum sentencing statutes, truth-in-sentencing laws are premised on assertions that offenders who commit violent crimes or repeat their crimes are responsible for a disproportionate amount of crime and that locking them up for long periods of time will therefore reduce the crime rate. However, critics charge that truth-in-sentencing statutes—and especially those that require offenders to serve 75% or 85% of the sentence before being released— serve as a disincentive for inmates to participate in educational, drug treatment, or other types of programming, which negatively affects the reentry process and enhances the likelihood of recidivism.

Research addressing the effects of truth-in-sentencing laws on sentencing outcomes and crime rates is fairly minimal and the results are inconsistent. Turner and colleagues' research suggested that truth-in-sentencing laws increased prison populations and correctional spending without decreasing violent crime rates,[78] but Long's research found that truth-in-sentencing laws lead to a reduction in violent crime.[79] A case study in Mississippi found that although judges changed their sentencing behavior due to truth-in-sentencing laws, sentence lengths for violent offenses decreased while sentence lengths for nonviolent and drug offenses increased.[80] There is also some preliminary work suggesting that truth-in-sentencing laws increased disparities in sentence lengths between Black and Hispanic offenders compared to white offenders.[81]

Revisiting Truth-in-Sentencing

It is clear that much more research is needed before definitive conclusions regarding the effects of truth-in-sentencing laws can be reached. Nevertheless, the lack of evidence that longer terms of imprisonment have a deterrent effect, coupled with concerns about the impact of truth-in-sentencing provisions on offenders' morale and willingness to participate in correctional programming, suggests that truth-in-sentencing laws have been counterproductive. We also believe that there is little to be gained by requiring all offenders to serve the same percentage of the sentence before being eligible for release. We therefore recommend that jurisdictions should:

- Reduce the percentage of time offenders must serve before being eligible for release to no more than 50–60% of the sentence imposed.
- Allow offenders convicted of drug offenses and property offenses to be released after serving a smaller percentage of the sentence imposed.

Life and Life Without the Possibility of Parole Sentences

The proliferation of three-strike laws, mandatory minimums, and the elimination of parole boards or discretionary parole as part of truth-in-sentencing reforms,[82] coupled with reductions in the number of individuals sentenced to death,[83] led to dramatic increases in the number of offenders incarcerated for life or for life without the possibility of parole (LWOP). The number of offenders serving life sentences increased by roughly 500% (from 34,000 to 160,000) from 1984 to 2016, significantly outpacing "even the sharp expansion of the overall prison population during this period."[84] This is especially true for LWOP sentences, which increased from 12,453 in 1992 to 53,290 in 2016.[85] Moreover, thousands more offenders are serving "virtual" life terms, or sentences that are so long they exceed a person's natural life expectancy.

In addition to the increasing prevalence of life sentences, the growing population of "lifers" in prison also reflects the fact that the meaning of "life"[86] has changed. For most of the twentieth century, a life sentence meant that the offender would serve 10 or 15 years in prison. As Gottschalk noted: "Until the early 1970s, even in a hardline state such as Louisiana . . . a 'life' sentence typically meant 10 years and 6 months."[87] The situation is very different today. Several jurisdictions, including Florida, Illinois, Iowa, Louisiana, Maine, Pennsylvania, South Dakota, and the federal system, have abolished parole, which means that any sentence to life is "the functional equivalent of LWOP."[88] Even in jurisdictions that retain discretionary parole release, offenders are often required to serve a greater amount of time before being eligible for release, and parole boards have increasingly denied offender release petitions.[89] The Sentencing Project estimates that the typical offender sentenced to life in prison with the possibility of parole will be imprisoned three decades before being released.[90] Many life sentences, in other words, "provide the offender with the theoretical possibility of release[] but in practice often result in the offender's death in prison."[91]

The stark growth in life imprisonment notwithstanding, contemporary sentencing researchers "have largely ignored the issue of long termers and lifers."[92] However, an important reality of life sentences is that they are served disproportionately by people of color. At both the state and federal levels, two-thirds of those serving life sentences are Black or Hispanic.[93] According to Nellis, racial disproportionality is even more pronounced among offenders serving LWOP sentences.[94] On the surface, these figures certainly *suggest* that life and LWOP sentences are "riddled with racial disparity,"[95] but the degree to which race affects judicial decisions to sentence offenders to life is largely unknown. This is because there is very little research that attempts to determine whether race and ethnicity impact the imposition of life sentences after accounting for other relevant case characteristics. There are no studies examining the imposition of life sentences in state courts and only two studies of life sentencing in the federal courts,[96] one of which found that Blacks and Hispanics were more likely to be eligible for life sentences under the federal sentencing guidelines.[97] Prior work suggests that racial disparities in federal sentencing tend to be most pronounced among those with the longest sentences, but as Mauer and Nellis observe, "there is much less direct evidence available" on "the impact of race on sentences of life imprisonment" relative to the death penalty or other sentencing outcomes.[98]

Although criminologists have yet to subject life sentences to the same type of scrutiny directed at the decision to sentence an offender to prison or to impose the death penalty, social scientists and legal scholars continue to debate philosophical justifications for life imprisonment. Advocates of life sentences contend that they are defensible under both retributive and utilitarian philosophies of punishment.[99] Supporters suggest that life sentences—and especially LWOP sentences—are justified because the crimes of some individuals are so heinous that they deserve to be incarcerated for life (i.e., a retributive justification) or because they deter offenders who would otherwise commit serious crimes and guarantee that dangerous individuals will be permanently incapacitated (i.e., utilitarian justifications). Critics challenge these contentions. Robinson's detailed and comprehensive analysis of life without parole, for example, leads him to conclude that these sentences do not achieve *any* of the distributive goals of punishment: general deterrence, incapacitation, or deserved punishment.[100] Hamilton's assessment is no more sanguine; as she notes, "experts strenuously contend that America's overreliance on life incarceration, considering the vast majority of offenders naturally desist, is gratuitous, unjust, and an avoidable waste of resources."[101]

Critics of life sentences describe them variously as "death-in-prison sentences,"[102] "America's new death penalty,"[103] a "living death sentence,"[104] a "different death penalty,"[105] and "death sentences by any other name."[106] These critics argue that most life sentences, and all LWOP sentences, are no less final than a death sentence and, like death sentences, violate certain basic human rights because they deny the humanity of the offender and signal "finality in spite of the possibility of change."[107] They also contend that life sentences are meted out in racially biased ways.[108] According to Capers, a "collateral effect of the turn to life without parole and de facto life as an alternative to death is that it renders race less visible, less pressing," and "less noticeable."[109] At the same time, the use of life sentences is much more common and widespread than the death penalty, so it is unclear whether the same types of inequality observed in death penalty cases apply equally to the use of life without parole.

Revisiting Life and Life Without Parole Sentences

Our primary recommendation with respect to life and LWOP sentences is that their imposition must be subject to rigorous empirical research. Little is known about the factors that judges take into account in deciding whether to impose a life sentence, the relative weights they attach to these factors, how different procedural and legal mechanisms impact life sentences, and whether and how some offenders who are eligible for life sentences escape them. We also know virtually nothing about the effects of life sentences on public safety, inmate morale, and offender recidivism. We therefore call on researchers to address these critically important issues.

We also argue that the dramatic growth in life sentences—and especially LWOP sentences—has played a major role in mass incarceration. This, coupled with lack of evidence regarding the efficacy of life or LWOP sentences and legitimate concerns about the philosophical justifications for these sentences and their deleterious effects on those serving them, leads us to recommend the following:

- Life without the possibility of parole sentences should be eliminated.
- The amount of time that offenders sentenced to life must serve before parole eligibility should be reduced and should be commensurate to the seriousness of the crime and the severity of the offender's criminal history.

Conclusion: Revisiting Sentencing Reform

The leaders of the twentieth-century sentencing reform movement believed that the enactment of sentencing guidelines, mandatory minimum sentences, three-strikes laws, truth-in-sentencing statutes, and LWOP provisions would result in more punitive, more effective, and fairer sentencing outcomes. Although the evidence is somewhat mixed, it does appear that sentences are more punitive today than they were in the past. The movement away from indeterminate sentencing and the rehabilitative ideal to determinate sentencing and an emphasis on just desserts—coupled with laws mandating life sentences or long prison terms—have resulted in harsher sentences. There also is evidence that sentences today—and particularly those imposed under

state and federal sentencing guidelines—are more uniform, less disparate, and more tightly linked to the seriousness of the offense and the
offender's criminal history. These results, however, have come at a price.
Research reveals that the changes in sentencing policies and practices
enacted since the early 1980s have resulted in dramatic increases in the
US prison population and that the uneven application of these policies
and practices has contributed to worsening racial and ethnic disparities
in punishment.

Critics of the draconian sentencing policies and practices that have
been pursued are increasingly calling on state and federal governments
to chart a different course in sentencing policy. Scholars and practitioners concerned about skyrocketing imprisonment rates, the collateral
consequences of incarceration for offenders, their families, and their
communities, and the implications of mass incarceration for communities of color are championing sentencing reforms designed to slow the
flow of people into state and federal prisons, reduce both the number of
persons now incarcerated and the lengths of sentences they are serving,
and ameliorate unwarranted racial and ethnic disparities in imprisonment.[110] Our recommendations are designed to do just that. We believe
that the time to act is now. Like Tonry, we believe that now is the time
"for remaking American sentencing into something that is fairer, more
effective, and more just; that reinforces basic social norms; and that deserves respect."[111]

NOTES

1 Rothman, *The Discovery of the Asylum*, 295.
2 National Advisory Commission, *Task Force Report on Correction*, 597.
3 Ibid., 358.
4 US Bureau of Justice Statistics, *Prisoners in 2017*.
5 Bobo and Johnson, "A Taste for Punishment," 1.
6 Austin and Irwin, *It's About Time*, 1.
7 Garland, "Introduction: The Meaning of Mass Imprisonment"; Gottschalk,
   Caught; Mauer, "The Causes and Consequences of Prison Growth in the USA";
   National Research Council, *The Growth of Incarceration in the United States*;
   USSC, *Fifteen Years of Guideline Sentencing*; Zimring, "Imprisonment Rates and
   the New Politics of Criminal Punishment."
8 Mauer, "The Causes and Consequences of Prison Growth in the USA," 11; see also
   Alexander, *The New Jim Crow*.
9 Blumstein and Beck, "Population Growth in U.S. Prison."

10 USSC, *Fifteen Years of Guideline Sentencing*, 76.

11 National Research Council, *The Growth of Incarceration in the United States*; for a similar argument, see Alexander, *The New Jim Crow*.

12 Pfaff, *Locked In*; Raphael and Stoll, *Why Are So Many Americans in Prison?*

13 King, "Cumulative Impact."

14 Tonry, *Sentencing Matters*, 54; USSC, *Fifteen Years of Guideline Sentencing*, 44.

15 Austin and Irwin, *It's About Time*, 227; Tonry, *Sentencing Matters*, 47.

16 Spohn, "Thirty Years of Sentencing Reform"; Tonry, *Malign Neglect*.

17 For example, in a speech to the American Bar Association in August 2013, United States Attorney General Eric Holder unveiled the Department of Justice's "Smart on Crime Initiative," which called for major changes to federal sentencing practices. Noting that the United States "cannot prosecute our way to becoming a safer nation," Holder stated that federal crime control efforts must also emphasize prevention and reentry and that "it is time to rethink the nation's system of mass imprisonment." However, the former Attorney General Jeff Sessions rescinded the Smart on Crime Initiative in May 2017. He ordered that federal prosecutors and law enforcement officials should ignore the direction from Holder and the Obama administration and should pursue charges that typically result in mandatory minimum sentences.

18 Subramanian and Delaney, "Playbook for Change?".

19 Tonry, "Remodeling American Sentencing."

20 Tonry, *Sentencing Matters*, 3.

21 US Department of Justice, Bureau of Justice Assistance, *National Assessment of Structured Sentencing*, 6.

22 American Friends Service Committee, *Struggle for Justice*; Davis, *Discretionary Justice*; Frankel, *Criminal Sentences*.

23 Tonry, *Malign Neglect*, 164.

24 van den Haag, *Punishing Criminals*; Wilson, *Thinking About Crime*.

25 von Hirsch, *Doing Justice*.

26 Martinson, "What Works?"

27 Frankel, *Criminal Sentences*, 1–2.

28 Walker, *Taming Discretion*.

29 For a discussion of variations among jurisdictions with sentencing guidelines, see Kelly Mitchell, "State Sentencing Guidelines."

30 Breyer, "The Federal Sentencing Guidelines and the Key Compromises Upon Which They Rest"; Kautt and Spohn, "Crack-ing Down on Black Offenders?"

31 Spohn, *How Do Judges Decide?*

32 Knapp, "What Sentencing Reform in Minnesota Has and Has Not Accomplished"; Miether and Moore, *Sentencing Guidelines*; Stolzenberg and D'Allessio, "Sentencing and Unwarranted Disparity"; USSC, *The Federal Sentencing Guidelines*.

33 Anderson, Kling, and Stith, "Measuring Interjudge Sentencing Disparity"; Hofer, Blackwell, and Ruback, "The Effect of the Federal Sentencing Guidelines on Inter-Judge Sentencing Disparity."

34 Kramer, Lubitz, and Kempinen, "Sentencing Guidelines."

35 Tonry, *Sentencing Matters*, 42.

36 Spohn, *How Do Judges Decide?*; Tonry, *Sentencing Matters*.

37 Leitman, "A Proposed Standard of Equal Protection Review."

38 Anderson, Kling, and Stith, "Measuring Interjudge Sentencing Disparity," 303.

39 For reviews of this research, see Ojmarrh Mitchell, "A Meta-Analysis of Race and Sentencing Research"; Spohn, "Thirty Years of Sentencing Research."

40 Frase, "Implementing Commission-Based Sentencing Guidelines"; Knapp, "What Sentencing Reform in Minnesota Has and Has Not Accomplished"; Kramer, Lubitz and Kempinen, "Sentencing Guidelines"; Moore and Miethe, "Regulated and Unregulated Sentencing Decisions."

41 Everett and Wojitkiewicz, "Difference, Disparity and Race/Ethnic Bias in Federal Sentencing"; Mustard, "Racial, Ethnic, and Gender Disparities in Sentencing"; Steffensmeier and Demuth, "Ethnicity and Sentencing Outcomes in U.S. Federal Courts"; Steffensmeier, Ulmer, and Kramer, "The Interaction of Race, Gender, and Age in Criminal Sentencing."

42 Restrictions on judicial sentencing discretion were loosened by a series of Supreme Court decisions that enhanced the role of both the prosecutor and the jury in sentencing. These decisions include Apprendi v. New Jersey (530 U.S. 466, 2000), Blakely v. Washington (542 U.S 296, 2004), and United States v. Booker (543 U.S. 220, 2005). The most consequential of these was the *Booker* case, which ruled that the federal guidelines were advisory rather than mandatory; although judges must still compute and take into account the recommended guideline range for each offender, they are not bound to impose a sentence within that range. The advisory nature of the guidelines has led some scholars to suggest that judges can now provide a check on prosecutorial powers that expanded during the twentieth century. Starr and Rehavi, "Racial Disparity in Federal Criminal Sentences."

43 Albonetti, "Sentencing Under the Federal Sentencing Guidelines"; Boerner, "Sentencing Guidelines and Prosecutorial Discretion"; Nagel and Schulhofer, "A Tale of Three Cities"; Stith and Cabranes, *Fear of Judging*.

44 Albonetti, "Sentencing Under the Federal Sentencing Guidelines," 790.

45 Boerner, "Sentencing Guidelines and Prosecutorial Discretion," 197.

46 Ibid., 197–98.

47 Tonry, *Sentencing Matters*, 180.

48 Miethe, "Charging and Plea Bargaining Practices Under Determinate Sentencing: An Investigation of the Hydraulic Displacement of Discretion."

49 Tonry, *Sentencing Matters*, Chapter 5.

50 See Clair and Winter, "How Judges Think About Racial Disparities," for an interesting qualitative examination of this issue.

51 Parent et al., *Mandatory Sentencing*.

52 Mascharka, "Mandatory Minimum Sentences."

53 Farrell, "Mandatory Minimum Firearm Penalties"; Schulhofer, "Rethinking Mandatory Minimums."

54 Ulmer, Kurlychek, and Kramer, "Prosecutorial Discretion and the Imposition of Mandatory Minimum Sentences."

55 For examples of this, see Loftin and McDowall, "The Deterrent Effect pf the Florida Felony Firearm Law"; Merritt, Fain, and Turner, "Oregon's Get Tough Sentencing Reform"; USSC, *The Federal Sentencing Guidelines*; USSC, *Report to the Congress: Mandatory Minimum Penalties*.

56 Beckett and Sasson, *The Politics of Injustice*; Ulmer, Kurlychek, and Kramer "Prosecutorial Discretion and the Imposition of Mandatory Minimum Sentences."

57 Parent et al., *Mandatory Sentencing*; Sklansky, "Cocaine, Race, and Equal Protection."

58 Ulmer, Kurlychek, and Kramer, "Prosecutorial Discretion and the Imposition of Mandatory Minimum Sentences."

59 Ibid., 440.

60 For similar findings, see USSC, *The Federal Sentencing Guidelines*.

61 Simon, "Criminology and the Recidivist."

62 Ibid.

63 Marvell and Moody, "The Lethal Effects of Three-Strikes Laws."

64 Austin et al., *Three Strikes and You're Out*; Turner et al., "The Impact of Truth-in-Sentencing and Three Strikes Legislation."

65 Austin et al., *Three Strikes and You're Out*.

66 Chen, "Impacts of 'Three Strikes and You're Out' on Crime Trends"; Kovandzic, Sloan III, and Vieraitis, "Unintended Consequences of Politically Popular Sentencing Policy"; Marvell and Moody, "The Lethal Effects of Three-Strikes Law."

67 Chen, "Impacts of 'Three Strikes and You're Out' on Crime Trends"; Kovandzic, Sloan III, and Vieraitis, "Unintended Consequences of Politically Popular Sentencing Policy"; Kovandzic, Sloan III, and Vieraitis. "'Striking Out' as Crime Reduction Policy."

68 Kovandzic, Sloan III, and Vieraitis, "Unintended Consequences of Politically Popular Sentencing Policy"; Kovandzic, Sloan III, and Vieraitis. "'Striking Out' as Crime Reduction Policy"; Marvell and Moody, "The Lethal Effects of Three-Strikes Laws."

69 Chen, "Impacts of 'Three Strikes and You're Out' on Crime Trends."

70 California Department of Corrections and Rehabilitation, *Offender Data Points*.

71 Iyengar, *I'd Rather Be Hanged for a Sheep Than a Lamb*; Ramirez and Crano, "Deterrence and Incapacitation"; Shepard, "Fear of the First Strike."

72 Chen, "Impacts of 'Three Strikes and You're Out' on Crime Trends"; Worrall, "The Effects of Three-Strikes Legislation on Serious Crime in California."

73 Kovandzic, Sloan III, and Vieraitis, "Unintended Consequences of Politically Popular Sentencing Policy"; Kovandzic, Sloan III, and Vieraitis. "'Striking Out' as Crime Reduction Policy"; Sutton, "Symbol and Substance."

74 Chen, "The Liberation Hypothesis and Racial and Ethnic Disparities in the Application of California's Three Strikes Law"; Sutton, "Symbol and Substance."

75 Chen, "The Liberation Hypothesis and Racial and Ethnic Disparities in the Application of California's Three Strikes Law."

76 Berry, "Life-with-Hope Sentencing"; Hoffman, *History of the Federal Parole System*.
77 US Department of Justice, Bureau of Justice Statistics, *Prisoners in 1997*.
78 Turner et al., "The Impact of Truth-in-Sentencing and Three Strikes Legislation."
79 Long, "Does Longer Incarceration Deter or Incapacitate Crime?"
80 Wood and Dunaway, "Consequences of Truth-in-Sentencing."
81 Harmon, "The Imprisonment Race"; Adelman, "The Adverse Impact of Truth in Sentencing."
82 Berry, "Life-with-Hope Sentencing."
83 Nellis, "Tinkering with Life"; Ogletree and Sarat, *Life Without Parole*.
84 Mauer and Nellis, *The Meaning of Life*, 9.
85 Nellis, *Still Life*.
86 Mauer and Nellis, *The Meaning of Life*.
87 Gottschalk, *Caught*. 354.
88 Henry, "Death-in-Prison Sentences," 68.
89 Nellis and King, *No Exit*.
90 Ibid.
91 Henry, "Death-in-Prison Sentences," 68.
92 Kazemain and Travis, "Imperative for Inclusion of Long Termers and Lifers in Research and Policy," 357.
93 Nellis, *Still Life*; USS, *Life Sentences in the Federal Criminal Justice System*.
94 Nellis, *Still Life*.
95 Ogletree and Sarat, *Life Without Parole*, 7.
96 Hamilton, "Some Facts About Life"; Johnson, Spohn and Kimchi, "Life Lessons."
97 Johnson, Spohn, and Kimchi, "Life Lessons."
98 Mauer and Nellis, *The Meaning of Life*, 103.
99 Blair, "A Matter of Life and Death"; Cheatwood, "The Life-Without-Parole Sanction."
100 Robinson, "Life Without Parole Under Modern Theories of Punishment."
101 Hamilton, "Some Facts About Life," 820–21.
102 Henry, "Death-in-Prison Sentences."
103 Ogletree and Sarat, *Life Without Parole*.
104 Cockburn, "Worse Than Death."
105 Dow, "Life Without Parole."
106 Villaume, "Life Without Parole and Virtual Life Sentence."
107 Dolovich, "Creating the Permanent Prisoner," 122.
108 Nellis and King, *No Exit*; Ogletree and Sarat, *Life Without Parole*.
109 Capers, "Defending Life," 179.
110 Tonry, "Remodeling American Sentencing"; Tonry and Melewski, "The Malign Effects of Drug and Crime Policies on Black Americans"; Alexander, *The New Jim Crow*.
111 Tonry, "Remodeling American Sentencing," 507.

6

The Limits of Recidivism Reduction

Advancing a More Comprehensive Understanding of Correctional Success

KEVIN A. WRIGHT, STEPHANIE J. MORSE, AND
MADISON M. SUTTON

Emilio was the toddler who made other parents jealous. He was playful, engaging, and helped his mother every chance he got. Then, a family member sexually assaulted him. This trauma went untreated. Emilio became shy, quiet, and isolated himself from others, vowing to never again let anyone hurt him. Emilio also struggled academically, having trouble reading, writing, and remembering things—problems that would persist into his adulthood.

Emilio was bullied and became angry. He could not understand why people made fun of him.

To cope, Emilio turned to drugs and alcohol and began to hang out with a new crowd—guys who were failures at school but successes on the streets. Soon, Emilio also became a success on the streets—and one of the most feared people in the neighborhood. By his own admission, Emilio had become an animal, asserting himself through violence and preying on the fear of others.

Then, Emilio's little brother Juan was killed. To Emilio, Juan had been perfect, and with his brother's death, Emilio truly felt that he did not understand this world. Shortly after, Emilio was arrested for possession of a dangerous narcotic. He was convicted and sentenced to serve two years in the state prison. He was 21 years old.

Emilio arrived at an overcrowded and understaffed state prison that was built two centuries earlier. The prison staff were perpetually tired, stressed, and frustrated. Many of them had taken a job at the prison because they could not find better work. Others were actively looking for new jobs that would be more rewarding and more sustainable.

Meanwhile, a crushing monotony oppressed the people who were living in the prison. Trying to convert their successes on the street into successes in prison, they lived by a code that discourages collaboration. Most were doing whatever they could to make the time pass quickly until they could return to the streets.

When Emilio arrived at this state prison, he had endured 15 years of frustration, anger, addiction, violence, and victimization. So how could a two-year prison sentence change his path? In an underresourced prison—similarly steeped in frustration, anger, addiction, violence, and victimization—what person or program could meaningfully reach Emilio? And who would be surprised if, after two years, Emilio left this prison and committed a new crime?

Historically, the primary, if not sole, measure of Emilio's success under correctional supervision would have been whether he was re-arrested, if he "recidivated." "Recidivism" is defined as officially detected, repeated, unlawful behavior after justice system involvement.[1] Most people would agree that halting undesirable behavior is one goal of punishment, so it intuitively makes sense to focus on reduced recidivism as the indicator of success for our nation's correctional facilities.[2]

We believe that recidivism matters, but we also believe that it has been approached incorrectly, for two reasons. First, it is treated as the be-all-end-all indicator of correctional success, to the exclusion of additional complementary indicators of how well our system is performing. Second, departments of correction and criminal justice agencies assume sole responsibility for recidivism reduction, to the exclusion of other social institutions that can help address challenges toward achieving a lifestyle that is free of criminal justice system involvement.

In this chapter, we propose a more comprehensive understanding of correctional success. We conceive of correctional supervision as an opportunity to enhance the lives of people who live and work in correctional facilities, through both reconceptualized recidivism reduction efforts *and* efforts to promote meaningful and sustainable crime-free alternatives. The nation's current obsession with reducing recidivism has impaired our ability to offer meaningful alternatives.

We begin by critiquing the status quo of recidivism reduction as an exclusive indicator of correctional success. Next, we reimagine a strategy for correctional success in which multiple entities share responsibility for recidivism reduction and the achievement of complementary indicators of success. We conclude with a call for academics, policy makers, and practitioners to take actionable steps to achieve correctional success.

Throughout the chapter, we challenge the meaning of "evidence-based" reform in corrections, first asking "Evidence for what?" and then suggesting that the prevailing notion of "evidence for recidivism reduction" is an important but incomplete framework for achieving correctional success. We rely on empirical evidence to document challenges associated with achieving meaningful reductions in recidivism and to highlight the many barriers to a crime-free life that are outside of criminal justice control. Based on this evidence, we suggest a new approach to achieving correctional success, one that values the lived experience and the potential of people like Emilio in conjunction with large-scale studies of what works.

The Limitations of Recidivism Reduction as a Measure of Correctional Success

Since the late 1970s, the evidence-based corrections movement has focused only on evidence for one outcome: recidivism. When Robert Martinson famously asked "What works?" in his hugely influential 1974 article for *Public Interest* on prison reform, he was asking "What works *to reduce recidivism*?" Although his larger report addressed other correctional outcomes, including vocational success and educational achievement, Martinson's article focused solely on "the effects of rehabilitative treatment on recidivism, the phenomenon which reflects most directly how well our present treatment programs are performing the task of rehabilitation."[3]

The scientific response to Martinson was swift, and then cumulative, with the data showing that something *did* work.[4] Now, decades after Martinson's article was published, there is a remarkable consensus that *what works to reduce recidivism* is correctional programming that considers the individual psychology of criminal behavior and addresses the learned antisocial attitudes and behaviors conducive to criminal behavior.[5]

But showing that *something worked* to reduce recidivism produced two unintended consequences. First, departments of corrections and their employees (and to a lesser extent treatment and service providers) became responsible for accomplishing that *something*, since changing individual attitudes and behaviors seemed to fall squarely within their control. Second, reduced recidivism became the sole indicator of whether the correctional system was working. These consequences have limited the potential success of the US correctional system.

Recidivism Reduction Is More Than a Department of Corrections Problem

Many structural components contribute to criminal behavior, and many are well beyond the control of the criminal justice system—let alone the correctional system. Intergenerational poverty, racial and ethnic discrimination, lack of access to quality education, unemployment, and housing instability all influence engagement in criminal behavior.[6] As explored in chapter 9 (on firearm violences), people recidivate when they cannot find and maintain gainful employment, when they cannot keep a safe and secure roof over their head, when their unaddressed mental and physical health problems are exacerbated by returning to society, and when drugs and alcohol relieve the stress caused by everything else previously mentioned.[7] Time spent in prison can make all of these challenges worse—that is, the person who is released may have fewer legitimate employment prospects, enjoy less access to quality housing, and face significant mental and physical health challenges.[8] So while changing individual attitudes and behaviors conducive to criminal behavior is critical to recidivism reduction, it is not enough. Recidivism is not just a criminal justice problem; it is an employment problem, a housing problem, and a physical and mental health problem.

Employment

One of the most well-known barriers to successful reentry is securing and maintaining gainful employment.[9] But correctional administrators have little power or control to help formerly incarcerated people locate work. People who are incarcerated face bleak employment prospects and outcomes upon reentry for a variety of reasons.

First, there is a selection effect whereby incarcerated people are more likely to have struggled with employment before incarceration due to the same risk factors that could have ultimately contributed to them engaging in crime.[10] Second, incarceration effectively removes people from the job market for an extended period of time, making it harder to reenter upon release.[11] Third, the stigma of incarceration creates direct barriers to employment. Officially, the mark of a felony can restrict access to certain jobs through the inability to achieve the necessary occupational licenses. Unofficially, potential employers perceive those who have been incarcerated as being different from other applicants.

Research shows that these barriers become even more challenging when accounting for differential hiring practices based on the race and gender of applicants.[12] People leaving the correctional system are shut out of the labor market because of factors that arise or occur before, during, and after their system involvement. Corrections administrators have few options to change this paradigm.

Housing

Finding housing represents a significant challenge to successful reentry, but after people are released from custody, correctional administrators have little control over their circumstances. The inability to find housing upon release is closely related to recidivism, and those who are incarcerated have several barriers related to housing when released.[13] First, people who were previously incarcerated often face financial difficulties in affording housing.[14] Additionally, due to their felony status, many previously incarcerated men and women are excluded from various public and private housing options.[15] As a result, they may be forced to live with family members and may even experience a period of homelessness.

Second, the housing that previously incarcerated people are most likely to gain access to is often less safe, less secure, and characterized by unhealthy conditions, such as increased exposure to drugs and victimization.[16] Formerly incarcerated people also end up in housing located in communities characterized by disorder and disadvantage.[17] Between having limited housing opportunities to begin with, and then having access only to housing that is of reduced quality, people released from prison often encounter instability in their living situations.[18] People leaving the correctional system are shut out of the housing market because of factors that arise or occur before, during, and after their system involvement. Again, corrections administrators have few options to change this paradigm.

Physical and Mental Health

Reentry outcomes are significantly impacted by physical and mental illness, which can complicate a person's ability to successfully navigate social and economic relationships and institutions. For a variety of reasons, people who have been incarcerated have disproportionately poorer physical and mental health compared to those who have not been incarcerated.[19] First, incarceration is a significant life event associated with acute stress that is harmful to physical and mental health.[20] Second, incarceration is a source of chronic stress in which incarcerated individuals experience exposure to harsh living conditions, violence, loss of social support, and tenuous existences alongside correctional staff over a prolonged period.[21] Third, prisons contain elevated rates of infectious diseases such as HIV/AIDS, hepatitis, tuberculosis, and COVID-19.[22]

In addition, the barriers to successful reentry discussed previously in this section also coincide to negatively impact health. Unemployment, residential instability, poverty, and diminished social support are all associated with poor health outcomes.[23] While previously incarcerated men and women are less likely to obtain a job, the jobs they obtain are also not likely to supply comprehensive health care benefits.[24] Poor physical and mental health complicates reentry, and people returning from prison are less likely to have the means to properly treat their health conditions.

Corrections administrators have an important role to play in improving health conditions and treatment during periods of confinement. But the staggering size of correctional populations in the United States means that it is hard to individualize treatment approaches for every person in the system. And addressing individual needs through cognitive behavioral therapy, for example, does little to change the landscape of the environments to which they will return.

People leaving the correctional system also struggle with physical and mental illness because of factors that arise or occur before, during, and after their system involvement. Again, corrections administrators have few options to change this broader paradigm.

The Pursuit of Recidivism Reduction Restricts the Development and Achievement of Other Indicators of Correctional Success

There is a straightforward appeal to using recidivism reduction as the sole indicator of correctional success: one number identifies the degree to which the system is working, and "working" is defined as a person not returning to that system. But existing program and policy evaluation research shows that achieving reductions in recidivism in practice is a daunting task.

Crimesolutions.gov, a clearinghouse of the National Institute of Justice, catalogs the findings of evaluation research on recidivism programs and recidivism practices, among other research on criminal justice issues. As of July 2021, of the 146 corrections and reentry programs listed, only eight were rated as effective (5%), 93 were rated as promising (64%), and 45 were rated as showing no effects (31%). Of the 52 broader corrections and reentry practices, only four were rated as effective (8%), 30 were rated as promising (58%), and 18 (35%) were rated as showing no effects.[25]

Meanwhile, high recidivism rates give the impression that whatever is being done in the name of corrections is not working. The US Bureau of Justice Statistics documented 401,288 formerly incarcerated individuals from 30 states for a period of nine years (2005–2014). Within that period, 83% of the released individuals had been rearrested, and 55% had a parole or probation violation or committed a new offense within the first five years of release, that resulted in reimprisonment.[26]

Of course, something does work to reduce recidivism, and we know a great deal about what works best for whom and under what conditions.[27] But recidivism reduction is difficult to achieve due to the over-reliance on corrections systems and the challenges in documentation. Correctional facilities are not laboratories, and it is difficult to state with certainty that a recidivism reduction was caused by a particular program or policy rather than by any number of factors that occur outside treatment. The relentless pursuit of recidivism as the sole indicator of whether correctional systems *work* has led to a narrow vision of what correctional success could be. In the process, academics, policy makers, and practitioners have been forced to limit themselves to the pursuit of a single elusive goal.

In academia, recidivism reduction permeates the approach of correctional scholars who work within the academy's traditional incentive structure. Anecdotally, we believe that higher-ranking scholarly journals reject manuscripts that cannot demonstrate how a particular initiative reduced recidivism, regardless of whether that initiative produced other important benefits. For example, a study of a program that reduces the antisocial attitudes that can be correlated with criminal behavior may never be published if the authors cannot show how that program impacted people's behaviors. Since successful publication is often a prerequisite to academic success, academic researchers understandably gravitate toward studies that measure recidivism and avoid studies that explore other indicators of correctional success.

Additionally, recidivism research often includes financial incentives that are not available for other types of corrections research. For example, most solicitations for grants investigating corrections identify recidivism as the primary (if not sole) outcome of interest. Other financial motivators arise from proprietary risk-assessment tools, which can generate hundreds of thousands of dollars. When that kind of money is at stake, it may create a vested interest in research that demonstrates that a particular tool is essential to recidivism reduction.

Finally, the exclusive focus on recidivism can produce artificial divisions and silos within academia. Some people focus their attention on yes/no, all-or-nothing recidivism measures. Others study desistance and conceive of rehabilitation as a process of stops and starts. Both approaches are needed, yet scholars often speak past one another rather than working collaboratively to produce solutions to the challenges faced by people entering and leaving prison.[28] In short, the emphasis on recidivism reduction restricts what academics study, and with whom they study, thereby inhibiting the production of new knowledge.

For policy makers, the reduction of recidivism has become synonymous with public safety. While there is bipartisan support for recidivism reduction at the federal level, there seems to be less bipartisan agreement about how to achieve that reduction.[29] Unfortunately, politics may drive policy. There is a public perception that if policy makers are reducing recidivism then they are increasing public safety. If they are not reducing recidivism, by contrast, then they are putting their constituents at risk. So electability and reelectability (when crime is at the forefront of political discourse) may depend on at least appearing to support efforts that reduce recidivism. Tough-on-crime policies thereby become tough-on-recidivism policies.

Of course, election cycles may not line up with the realities of recidivism reduction. Programs that work to reduce recidivism may not bear fruit for years. But, at least for politicians, undertaking a quick fix to prove they are "doing something" may be more appealing than a long-term investment in future outcomes, no matter how much evidence supports that investment. In short, tunnel vision about the importance of recidivism reduction may mean that politicians ignore the importance of programs that create prosocial outcomes that may take the place of criminal behavior.

For practitioners, resource-tight correctional environments make it imperative that any program or policy be evidence-based—meaning that the program or policy can be shown to reduce recidivism. Without evidence that supports recidivism reduction, there may be few correctional innovations: some programs never launch while others are discontinued. The limited opportunities for rehabilitative programming within correctional facilities are reserved for people deemed to be at high risk of recidivism. Mandatory correctional programming rules mean that these people can be placed in programs against their will. Meanwhile, incarcerated people who truly want that programming may be ineligible because their lower level of risk makes them a lower priority for treatment and services.[30] Correctional classrooms are filled with many people who do not want to be there. That, in turn, leads many staff and prison volunteers to quickly become frustrated and jaded.

In addition, the focus on recidivism means that correctional administrators are less able to focus on strategies to improve the prison environment for people who work there as well as those who live there. For example, people who are serving long sentences or who are serving life sentences are not a priority at all. Since they will never have an opportunity to "not recidivate," corrections facilities do not provide them treatment. This is a lost opportunity for correctional improvement, as those treatment programs might help these people become a stabilizing presence within the facility.[31] But correctional administrators are tasked instead with focusing on recidivism reduction—a future outcome that is largely out of their control.

Where to Go from Here

We have focused on two problems associated with using recidivism reduction as the exclusive indicator of correctional success. We argue that recidivism reduction is more than a department of corrections problem and that the never-ending attempt to reduce recidivism restricts the development and pursuit of complementary correctional successes. There are many more reasons to be concerned about an exclusive focus on recidivism reduction. Scholars have pointed out several: Recidivism is a binary outcome that answers *if* something works rather than *how well* it works; recidivism measures encourage inappropriate comparisons of dissimilar populations; and there is a pervasive assumption that low recidivism rates are desirable, but there is little critical examination of that assumption.[32]

We believe that recidivism reduction will always be a metric of correctional success, and we acknowledge the significant advancements that have been made for correctional programming that may reduce recidivism. However, we believe that multiple entities should share the responsibility of achieving recidivism reduction and that recidivism reduction should be only one of many indicators of how well our correctional system is working.

How Shared Responsibility for Recidivism Reduction Can Improve Correctional Success

To achieve correctional success, we must make recidivism reduction more than a corrections problem. Sharing responsibility for recidivism reduction will help address challenges upstream—during correctional supervision—before people reenter the community.

Employment, housing, and physical and mental health care are some of the most prominent challenges faced by people leaving prison. Social institutions within each of these domains can and should be part of efforts to reduce recidivism.

Through collaborative efforts, social institutions could reach people while they are still incarcerated in correctional facilities. Sharing the responsibility for reducing recidivism would also create opportunities for correctional facilities, departments of housing and labor, and public health agencies to focus on the problems most in their control. This early outreach would preemptively address challenges related to recidivism and also lessen the strain that these institutions would otherwise confront when incarcerated people are eventually released. We offer several examples and possibilities from our home state of Arizona to show how existing social institutions can play a role in correctional success.

Employment

By addressing barriers to sustained and gainful employment, departments of labor and workforce development agencies, community colleges and universities, and employers themselves can all be part of correctional success. Departments of labor and workforce development can provide their usual programming; it simply needs to be targeted at people under correctional supervision. For example, the Arizona Department of Economic Security has placed its Arizona@Work programming in prisons and community corrections agencies throughout the state to assist people under correctional supervision in finding and maintaining employment. Academic institutions with business schools and career development expertise can also contribute to help people under correctional supervision write their résumés, prepare for job interviews, and develop a successful pathway out of the correctional system. The W. P. Carey School of Business at Arizona State University (ASU) is developing a program in which students enrolled in its Masters of Business Administration program provide this type of training to incarcerated women. Employers can also contribute by providing training to people under correctional supervision that will allow them to transition into employment with the same organization upon release.

Televerde is a sales and marketing company that trains incarcerated women in Arizona and Indiana to become valued employees, both during and after their incarceration. Unemployment is a barrier that can lead to someone recidivating, and these organizations can help ensure that does not happen.

Housing

Community colleges and universities, departments of housing and urban development, and community housing groups can be part of correctional success by helping to address housing barriers. Social work schools and departments are uniquely positioned to identify and create solutions for people who are homeless. People have different housing challenges for different reasons, and clinical placements and internships, in particular for social work students, can ensure that social workers are addressing the unique circumstances of people who are system-involved. Departments of housing can provide their usual programming targeted at people under correctional supervision. The Arizona Department of Housing is partnering with nonprofit organizations to provide housing vouchers for people leaving prison so that they can focus on other barriers to successful reintegration knowing they have a roof over their head.

These nonprofit organizations, and other community housing advocates, can also help ensure that the housing provided to people under correctional supervision is a secure and healthy environment. The Arizona Recovery Housing Association, part of the National Alliance for Recovery Residences, works to ensure that sober living and halfway house programs are certified and accredited to provide quality care. An inability to find a home is a barrier that can lead to recidivism, and these organizations can help ensure that does not happen.

Physical and Mental Health

Community colleges and universities, departments of health and human services, and community health care clinics can be part of correctional success by addressing barriers to achieving and maintaining physical and mental health. Community colleges and universities, especially those connected to medical centers, have practicing academics and students who can provide direct mental and physical health services to people under correctional supervision. The Student Health Outreach for Wellness clinic in downtown Phoenix is a collaboration between ASU, the University of Arizona, and Northern Arizona University. Through that collaboration, students in nursing, social work, nutrition, medicine, and pharmacy provide client-centered health care to the homeless and underserved. Departments of health and human services can provide their usual programming to people under correctional supervision.

The Arizona Department of Health and Human Services has worked to ensure that people in prison are appropriately enrolled in the state's Medicaid program. Community health care and behavioral health clinics can provide services to people under correctional supervision who may need (but not seek out) medical attention, perhaps even through telemedicine. Ill health is a barrier that can lead to someone recidivating, and these organizations can help ensure that does not happen.

Correctional Programming

Corrections, of course, play a central role in the shared responsibility of recidivism reduction. The "what works" movement within correctional scholarship has offered important insights into evidence-based practices that are effective for reducing recidivism. At the center of these best practices is adherence to the principles of effective correctional intervention as specified by the Risk Need Responsivity model.[33] Cognitive behavioral therapies and multisystemic therapies have been identified as some of the most useful treatment modalities for recidivism reduction, as they are responsive to criminogenic risks and needs.[34] Using these individual approaches to correctional programming *contributes* to what works to reduce recidivism, and correctional agencies should be responsible for providing programs that adhere to these principles of effective intervention. However, correctional programming is only one part of what could work for "corrections success," broadly defined. When other institutions share the responsibility of recidivism reduction, correctional administrators are uniquely positioned to tackle other components of corrections success.

Correctional administrators should be responsible for the safety and security of people in correctional facilities. Enhanced safety and security in the form of decreased misconduct and violence can be achieved by understanding the rehabilitation needs of people in prison and by ensuring that people in prison perceive their treatment by staff as legitimate.[35] Correctional administrators should be responsible for the maintenance of the physical and structural conditions of correctional facilities. Decrepit conditions can make facilities unsafe and unhealthy, and a concern for the physical space within which people live and work should be prioritized when making budget proposals and decisions. Correctional administrators should be responsible for providing appropriate services to people under correctional supervision, in collaboration with the other groups identified above. Prioritizing effective rehabilitation programming, and providing the space and time for that programming to flourish, can contribute to a correctional environment that is supportive of people under supervision becoming something else, rather than simply creating a coercive environment to force people not to be criminal.[36] Shared responsibility for recidivism reduction means that departments of correction can focus on—and be held accountable for—the correctional environment, and an improved correctional environment may itself reduce recidivism.

The Importance of Complementary Indicators of Correctional Success

A sole focus on recidivism—no matter who is responsible for its reduction—limits opportunities to think of additional creative upstream interventions that could repair harm, empower people, and promote public safety before people rejoin their communities. People lead meaningful lives when they are internally motivated for self-growth and have the opportunity to get better at things that matter to them.[37] If the correctional system is redefined as *working* when it is yields productive members of society who lead meaningful lives, then the investigation of correctional success widens beyond criminological research to include human behavior research that seeks to ensure that people are successful business owners, loving parents, and supportive partners.[38]

"Correctional quackery" is a derisive term used to describe any treatment intervention that is not based on existing knowledge about why crime occurs and how people change their behavior.[39] In other words, correctional quackery encompasses programs that fail to address "what works" (when "working" is defined as recidivism reduction); from this perspective, programs that might increase self-efficacy, for example, are considered unworthy of pursuit if they do not reduce recidivism.[40] But recidivism reduction can and should coexist alongside other indicators of correctional success.

The federal Office of Disease Prevention and Health Promotion and the Substance Abuse and Mental Health Services Administration—which identify crime as a public health issue—have developed eight dimensions of health and wellness. We believe that those eight metrics offer suggestions for additional indicators of correctional success.

Financial wellness, for example, represents satisfaction with current and future financial situations. People in the correctional system leave the system in debt due to unpaid bills, fines, court costs, alimony and child support, and required restitution.[41] Correctional success means creating a blueprint for eliminating debt and establishing credit. *Intellectual wellness* represents recognizing creative abilities and finding ways to expand knowledge and skills. People in the correctional system have lower levels of education than the general public, and efforts to expand higher education in prison specifically are focused on a small percentage of candidates that are prepared for a college degree.[42] Correctional success here means creating pathways for educational and vocational training that match skills and abilities. *Social wellness* represents developing a sense of connection, belonging, and a well-developed support system. People in the correctional system often have fractured social relationships with partners, parents, children, and friends.[43] Correctional success means connecting people to others, and having them share in the well-being of others, to ensure that the path to becoming a contributing member of society is not a solitary endeavor.

Universities—and their faculty, staff, and students—could play a prominent role in a reimagined approach to correctional success in the United States. Aside from evaluation research, universities are most prominently featured in the correctional system through the delivery of secondary education to incarcerated people. The reinstatement of access to Pell Grants in prison is a welcome return for the role of the university in this regard. But people within the university could also assist incarcerated people who may be unprepared or uninterested in a college education.

At Arizona State University, a foundational principle of our university charter is to assume fundamental responsibility for the economic, social, cultural, and overall health of the communities we serve. The men and women who live and work in correctional facilities are part of that community, and academics should include their perspectives, contributions, and effects when we measure the success of our contributions. The mission of the ASU Center for Correctional Solutions is to enhance the lives of people living and working in our correctional system through research, education, and community engagement. Correctional success can be achieved when people in the university work alongside people in corrections to take responsibility for the economic, social, cultural, and overall health of the men and women under correctional supervision. But there is a problem with sharing the responsibility of correctional success: when it becomes everyone's responsibility, then it becomes no one in particular's responsibility. People at universities like ASU could choose to lead action on correctional success, because a holistic approach to enhancing the lives of people speaks to the heart of their mission.

The correctional system could be structured as a system of enabling environments that nurture and promote the personal growth of the people who live and work within it.[44] A person entering the system could be assessed across life domain indicators—not simply their risk for recidivism—and the goal of their time in the system could be to improve their position across these domains.[45] Correctional staff could become critical agents of support in identifying and achieving these outcomes, alongside people who have the knowledge and expertise in these areas. An investment of training and resources for corrections staff could contribute to the meaning of their work by making them part of the solution.[46]

This is especially important, since involvement in the correctional system is deeply racialized; indeed, many scholars and activists contend that mass incarceration has replaced slavery as an institution of social control.[47] Mass incarceration means that kids grow up without parents, partners and family members become burdened with new responsibilities, and communities are stripped of positive role models. Racial equity gaps are worsened by the removal and stigmatization of mothers and fathers, brothers and sisters, neighbors, employees, and mentors. It is therefore reasonable to call into question the legitimacy of a system that has caused disproportionate harm to people of color, their families, and their communities. We believe that fundamentally changing the conception of correctional success can transform that system to one of support that creates opportunities and closes racial gaps.

System involvement, especially through incarceration, is punishment enough for criminal behavior. Academics, policy makers, practitioners, and the general public all suffer when the reduction of criminal behavior is the sole goal of the correctional system. "Not criminal" is not enough. Our correctional system is successful when people leave it better than when they entered, ready to contribute to their communities.

A Model for Achieving Correctional Success

Using reduced recidivism as the main criterion of correctional success is misguided.[48] We urge a more comprehensive understanding of correctional success so that reduced criminal involvement is not the sole benchmark. Instead, there should be a shared responsibility for reduced recidivism and the pursuit of other indicators of correctional success. The responsibility of identifying and achieving those indicators could be shared by multiple organizations, including departments of correction. We therefore conclude this chapter with some concrete recommendations for academics, policy makers, and practitioners to rethink criteria for correctional success.

Academics and Correctional Success

Academics have expertise on a variety of subjects that could guide efforts to promote correctional success within the correctional system. We believe academics could:

- *Invest* the time to learn from correctional professionals and people who are incarcerated about the challenges of working and living in their facilities. Correctional facilities are neither laboratories nor data gold mines.
- *Build* multidisciplinary teams of scholars to collaborate with people in correctional facilities, including scholars of business, health and wellness, and STEM who might otherwise not enter prisons and jails.

- *Create* educational opportunities for people who are incarcerated in jails and prisons, including exploring how virtual education can overcome concerns of safety and security and limited resources.
- *Identify*, *research*, and *promote* other indicators of correctional success, especially among senior scholars who have more academic freedom to research nontraditional indicators of correctional success.
- *Consider* people who work in correctional facilities as worthy of the same level of scholarly attention as the people who live in correctional facilities and conduct research that does more than simply examine the stress of working in correctional facilities. Instead, scholars can develop, implement, and assess programs to improve workplace culture and physical and mental health.
- *Create*, *validate*, and *apply* assessment tools that go beyond risk-to-recidivate indicators to identify ways that people can achieve success in work, relationships, and health and wellness.
- *Develop* internships and clinical placement sites within correctional facilities.
- *Create* prison-to-school pipelines that identify pathways for people out of the correctional system and into the educational system.
- *Train* university faculty and staff to understand the educational challenges experienced by currently and formerly system-involved people.
- *Communicate* research outside of academia, especially to policy makers, practitioners, the general public, and people living in prison. University administrators could also incentivize efforts to share research outside the ivory tower.
- *Develop* incentive structures and accountability measures to ensure that these recommendations become part of the shared solution for correctional success.

Policy Makers and Correctional Success

Policy makers set expectations surrounding our correctional system and have a more public audience as compared to educational and correctional institutions. We believe policy makers could:

- *Create* collaborative teams of organizations, agencies, departments, and universities that share responsibility for the success of people living and working in the correctional system.

- *Supplement* recidivism reduction goals with other indicators of correctional success related to employment, housing, and mental and physical health. Give equal weight to the achievement of these goals.
- *Distribute* grant funding across additional indicators of correctional success. Create cosponsored funding among organizations and agencies typically outside of criminal justice funding, such as labor, health and well-being, and housing.
- *Consider* people who work in the correctional system the same as law enforcement and other first responders and ensure they are entitled to the same opportunities and benefits.
- *Expect* inevitable system setbacks and resist the urge to eliminate programs or policies that have high-visibility failures.
- *Avoid* developing legislation that makes high-profile events appear commonplace. Legislation named after victims can distort public perception to impact all system-involved people as a group.
- *Develop* legislation based on examples of formerly incarcerated men and women who are now successful. Create pathways for others to earn their redemption. Frame this legislation in the same vein of saving victims and costs as victim-centered legislation would. Lead the way with people-first language and other considerations for balanced presentation. "Second chances" implies randomness and risk, whereas "second opportunities" implies prospects for success. Terms like "inmates" and "returning citizens" create pejorative labels; "people" can be used instead.
- *Demonstrate* the value of indicators of success, including prevention, that require a longer period of assessment, especially among senior policy makers and politicians who are not seeking reelection.
- *Consider* taxpayer costs associated with the correctional system as investments. Frame policies and programs in terms of return on investment for taxpayers. Evaluate the opportunity costs of prison to determine whether those dollars could be better invested in other options.
- *Develop* incentive structures and accountability measures to ensure the above recommendations become part of the shared solution for correctional success.

Practitioners and Correctional Success

Practitioners are on the ground level and can most directly impact the lives of people living and working within the correctional system. We believe practitioners could:

- *Acknowledge* the unreasonable expectation that the sole responsibility of incarceration is recidivism reduction and resist the urge to cut off prisons from society when that outcome is unachieved. Prisons and jails that are closed to outsiders invite scrutiny and an assumption of something to hide.
- *Embrace* innovation in programming and policy with a focus for how both can impact correctional facilities and the success of people living and working within them now.
- *Reward* positive behavior such as clean drug tests, as opposed to punishing negative behavior such as dirty drug tests. Reward non–justice involved behavior, such as program completion, job obtainment, and progress toward goals.
- *Prepare* people to successfully leave the correctional system beginning on the day they enter the system. Reframe time spent in correctional facilities as an opportunity to improve skills and abilities to ensure success outside the correctional system.
- *Identify* ways to connect people who are incarcerated in jails and prisons with the larger community to which they will one day return, such as through enhanced visitation opportunities, reach-in employment opportunities and classes, and parenting programs.
- *Invest* the time to learn from scholars about the challenges of doing rigorous research. Effective researcher–practitioner partnerships are built on communication and shared understandings.
- *Prioritize* the well-being and morale of staff as employees. Provide training and advancement opportunities. Identify ways to incorporate the perspectives of employees in the decision-making process.
- *Hire*, *train*, and *retain* employees with backgrounds outside criminal justice, such as social work, counseling psychology, and health and human services. Create pathways for staff that do not require them to serve in security roles should they not want to do so.
- *Promote* successful cases of people who have left behind their criminal past so that both staff and people who are currently in the system see examples of success rather than examples of failure.

- *Collaborate* with law enforcement agencies and social service institutions to better prepare people who are on supervision for success.
- *Capitalize* on mentoring opportunities from currently and formerly system-involved people who best know how to navigate the challenges of the correctional system. Lifers and people who have served long sentences are especially good candidates to be a positive influence on others.
- *Develop* incentive structures and accountability measures to ensure the above recommendations become part of the shared solution for correctional success.

Conclusion

The endless pursuit of recidivism reduction permeates the entire correctional system. It suffocates innovations that could help to produce contributing members of society both during and after their correctional supervision. The evidence-based corrections movement to reduce recidivism provides a critical foundation that should continue to be a prominent component of corrections. But the exclusive focus on a single indicator—an indicator with a complex composition that is different for every individual—has created tunnel vision and represents a fool's errand for the people who could best reimagine correctional success.

Medical professionals recognize this opportunity to save later social and financial costs by investing in the success of system-involved people who are part of underserved communities.[49] It is time that academics, policy makers, and practitioners do the same. We share the responsibility of correctional success, and our prescriptions above make clear that academics must work alongside policy makers and practitioners to address the challenge together. These prescriptions will also empower the wider community. Indeed, people who are not scholars, policy makers, or practitioners can still contribute to corrections success. They can use people-first language, critically evaluate information presented to them by the media, and acknowledge the challenges faced by people who work in our correctional system. We believe relaxing the pressure of recidivism reduction can make things easier for men and women who are hoping to change their own lives and for the men and women who are hoping to help them change.

Correctional supervision is an opportunity to help create a sustainable and meaningful life for incarcerated people so that they may later *give* rather than just *take* from society.[50] Embracing this opportunity means focusing on other areas of life as important independent of whether they are related to recidivism reduction.

NOTES

1 Wright and Khade, "Offender Recidivism."
2 We refer throughout to recidivism from correctional "facilities" and from correctional "supervision" interchangeably, with a primary focus for recidivism after incarceration. Although it is important to distinguish between recidivism from jail or prison versus recidivism from probation or parole in the community, our points about correctional success apply to recidivism from both settings.
3 Martinson, "What Works?"
4 For an excellent review of the people and critical works within this accumulation of the evidence-base on what works to reduce recidivism, see Cullen, "The Twelve People Who Saved Rehabilitation."
5 Cullen et al., "What Correctional Treatment Can Tell Us." See especially Latessa, Johnson, and Koetzle, *What Works (and Doesn't) in Reducing Recidivism.*
6 Pratt and Cullen, "Assessing Macro-Level Predictors"; Sampson, *Great American City*; Wilson, *The Truly Disadvantaged.*
7 Wright and Cesar, "Toward a More Complete Model."
8 Harding, Morenoff, and Wyse, *On the Outside.*
9 Travis, *But They All Come Back.*
10 Uggen, Wakefield, and Western, *Work and Family Perspectives on Reentry.*
11 Ibid.
12 Pager, *Marked.*
13 Makarios, Steiner, and Lawrence, "Examining the predictors"; Steiner, Makarios, and Lawrence, "Examining the Effects"; LeBel, "Housing as the Tip of the Iceberg"; Western, *Homeward.*
14 Roman and Travis, "Where Will I Sleep Tomorrow?"; Visher et al., "Baltimore Prisoners' Experiences."
15 Greenberg and Rosenheck, "Homelessness in the State and Federal Prison Population."
16 Harding, Morenoff, and Wyse, *On the Outside*; Western, *Homeward.*
17 Clear, *Imprisoning Communities*; Harding, Morenoff, and Herbert, "Home Is Hard to Find"; Sampson and Loeffler, "Punishment's Place."
18 Harding, Morenoff, and Wyse, *On the Outside*; Makarios, Steiner, and Lawrence, "Examining the Predictors."
19 Massoglia and Remster, "Linkages Between Incarceration and Health"; Kirk and Wakefield, "Collateral Consequences of Punishment."
20 Massoglia, "Incarceration as Exposure"; Pearlin, "The Sociological Study of Stress."

21 Massoglia, "Incarceration, Health, and Racial Disparities"; Sakiberm et al., "COVID-19 Cases and Deaths."

22 Maruschak, "Medical Problems of Prisoners"; Maruschak and Bronson, "HIV in Prison."

23 Massoglia and Remster, "Linkages Between Incarceration and Health."

24 Western, *Punishment and Inequality*.

25 Corrections & Reentry: Recidivism. Another example of the difficulty in achieving recidivism reduction comes in the form of disappointing results from Second Chance Act programs. Signed into law on April 9, 2008, the Second Chance Act legislation authorizes federal grants from the US Department of Justice's Office of Justice Programs to reduce recidivism and improve outcomes for people returning from state and federal correctional facilities. An overview of seven of these programs evaluated with randomized experiments showed no difference in recidivism reduction for participants as compared to people not enrolled in those programs over an 18-month follow-up period. D'Amico and Kim, *Evaluation of Seven Second Chance Act Demonstration Programs*. Finally, incarceration itself, which could be considered the broadest form of correctional intervention, has been shown to not reduce (and to possibly increase) criminal behavior. Cullen, Jonson, and Nagin, "Prisons Do Not Reduce Recidivism."

26 Alper, Durose, and Markman, *2018 Update on Prisoner Recidivism*; Durose, Cooper, and Snyder, *Recidivism of Prisoners Released in 30 States*. For comparison, see Rhodes et al., "Following Incarceration."

27 Smith, Gendreau, and Swartz, "Validating the Principles," 148–69.

28 Andrews, Bonta, and Wormith, "The Risk-Need-Responsivity (RNR) Model"; Ward, Yates, and Willis, "The Good Lives Model."

29 Chettiar and Raghavan, *Ending Mass Incarceration*.

30 Olver, Stockdale, and Wormith, "A Meta-analysis of Predictors."

31 Kreager et al., "Where 'Old Heads' Prevail."

32 Butts and Schiraldi, *Recidivism Reconsidered*; Gehring, "Recidivism as a Measure of Correctional Education"; Leverentz, Chen, and Christian, *Beyond Recidivism*. On this last point, if a state chooses to incarcerate people who are a low-risk to recidivate and would be more appropriately diverted from prison, and the overall recidivism rate drops as a result when they inevitably do not return to prison, the state may claim credit for a decision that was unnecessary. We are grateful to Michael Dolny for this point.

33 Smith, Gendreau, and Swartz, "Validating the Principles," 148–69.

34 Landenberger and Lipsey, "The Positive Effects of Cognitive-Behavioral Programs."

35 Steiner and Meade, "The Safe Prison."

36 Smith and Schweitzer, "The Therapeutic Prison."

37 Ryan and Deci, "Self-Determination Theory."

38 Ward and Stewart, "Criminogenic Needs and Human Needs."

39 Latessa, Cullen, and Gendreau, "Beyond Correctional Quackery."

40 Lee and Stohr, "A Critique and Qualified Defense of 'Correctional Quackery.'"
41 Link and Roman, "Longitudinal association."
42 Pompoco et al., "Reducing Inmate Misconduct."
43 Hutton and Moran, eds., *The Palgrave Handbook*.
44 Liebling et al., "Are Hope and Possibility."
45 Wright, "Time Well Spent," 2020.
46 Lovins et al., "Probation Officer as a Coach."
47 Alexander, *The New Jim Crow*; Goodwin, "The Thirteenth Amendment."
48 Heidemann, Cederbaum, and Martinez, "Beyond Recidivism"; McNeill et al., "Reexamining Evidence-Based Practice in Community Corrections"; Visher and Travis, "Transitions from Prison to Community"; Ward and Maruna, *Rehabilitation: Beyond the Risk Paradigm*; Gottschalk, *Caught*.
49 Dumont et al., "Public Health and the Epidemic of Incarceration."
50 Wright, "Time Well Spent."

7

Community-Based Reentry

Breaking the Cycle of Reincarceration

KELLY ORIANS AND TROY RHODES

In 1988, Troy Rhodes was released from prison for the first time. He had served three years at the Louisiana State Penitentiary at Angola. He vividly recalls the first thing his parole officer told him during his intake: "You won't make it."

It was a cruel thing to say, and it was an unfair thing to say, but she was right.

There were 318,889 people released from prison in the United States in 1988.[1] Approximately a third were reincarcerated.[2] Mr. Rhodes was one of them. By the time Mr. Rhodes was again released in 2018, the recidivism rate was even worse,[3] and the size of the prison population had more than doubled.[4]

The first time Mr. Rhodes returned home, his parents were his support system (in addition to his parole officer, although she had already made clear that she had made up her mind about him). He was lucky to get a job and have a stable place to live, but it did not prevent him from abusing drugs, and, ultimately, it did not prevent an arrest that would send him to prison with a 99-year sentence.

In 2018, he was released from prison for the second time, and this time, in addition to his wife, he was greeted by a group of supporters whom, three decades earlier, it was illegal for him to associate with: six men with felony convictions, including some former bunkmates from prison. A few years earlier, this group came together to act on a plan they had begun to formulate while incarcerated: repurpose an old bail bonds office into a transitional house providing supportive wraparound services for people leaving prison. They decided to call themselves "The First 72+." One of the cofounders, Ben Smith, who served as the co-executive director of the organization up until his death in November 2020, explained it this way: "We're talking about guys that been locked up 15, 20, 25, 40 years some of them. The purpose of this place is to give them a place to get started. That's why the name of this place is The First 72+, because those first 72 hours are so crucial. After that, we plan for the long term—getting out, and staying out."

Although certainly effective (not only for Troy but also for his family, who would have otherwise been his only support network), the reentry services The First 72+ offered Troy were not particularly innovative or uncommon in the national landscape: The organization gave him a free place to stay; its members helped him get state identification and enroll in public benefits; they provided him rides; they taught him how to use a cell phone and a computer; and they helped him schedule appointments with doctors, register to vote, and get a job. What was unique though, was *who* was supporting him, as well as what was expected of *him* in return. Mr. Rhodes was expected to, as one of the cofounders, Norris Henderson, puts it, "pay it forward, to the next man up."

The purpose of this chapter is to explore the issue of reentry from incarceration through the lens of research and evidence-based best practices and to offer two proposals for reform. We rely on the definition of "reentry" as the process of reintegration into communities, families, the housing market, the job market, the health care system, the public benefits system, and the financial sector, after someone is released from incarceration in a state or federal prison.[5] Beginning with a brief historical overview of the rise of the reentry movement in the United States, we look at the relationship between reincarceration and the scourge of mass incarceration. We then identify the persistent barriers to successful reentry and interrogate how the attendant consequences of criminal convictions and incarceration all but guarantee unemployment/underemployment, housing instability/homelessness, persistent poverty, and, ultimately, reincarceration. We then explore the ways in which these barriers are evidence of systemic racism, making a case for why reentry works, and why our evidence-based proposals are also necessary to address racial injustice and achieve racial equity. This chapter is grounded in research and uses the personal and professional experiences of the authors to better illustrate the experience of reentry and the impact of our recommendations.[6]

The Problem

In this section we provide a brief historical overview of the rise of the reentry movement in the United States, including the relationship between reincarceration and the scourge of mass incarceration.

Reentry and Mass Incarceration: The History

According to census data collected on the prison population in 1890, reentry from incarceration has been a problem for more than a century.[7] In a special report published by the US Census Bureau in 1923, "Prisoners Antecedents," it was reported that approximately 60% of incarcerated people had been previously incarcerated (or otherwise institutionalized).[8] In 1939, in an address to the National Parole Conference in the White House, President Franklin Delano Roosevelt emphasized the struggle that people coming home from prison have when trying to find employment and concluded that the circumstances surrounding reentry tend to "push a man back to a life of crime unless we make it our business to help him overcome them."[9] He declared reentry to be a national problem, a problem not only for the government but also for every "average citizen in every community in the whole of the United States."[10]

Despite such strong rhetoric from the commander in chief, the first report published on the issue of reentry by the Department of Justice did not debut until 1984.[11] In it, the director of the Bureau of Justice Statistics at the time, Steven R. Schlesinger, echoed the concern of President Roosevelt, writing: "The rate at which prisoners return to confinement is a major consideration in the use of limited prison space and an indication of the efficacy of imprisonment as a strategy for crime control."[12] Still, this report spurred only limited attention to the topic of reentry.[13] Director Schlesinger served through the duration of President Ronald Reagan's two terms in office, during which time the federal government failed to invest significantly in reentry, and President Reagan's "tough on crime" policies and the "war on drugs" contributed to a doubling of the prison population.[14]

It took 16 more years and the addition of a million people to the national prison population for a United States Attorney General to direct attention to reentry.[15] Addressing research that individuals exiting prisons had higher needs than in the past but were simultaneously facing dwindling access to housing, employment, education, and mental and physical health care,[16] Attorney General Janet Reno proclaimed in 2000 that reentry from incarceration was "one of the most present problems we face as a nation."[17]

Under the administration of President Bill Clinton, the Departments of Justice, Labor, Education, Health and Human Services, and Housing and Urban Development inaugurated the Serious and Violent Offender Reentry Initiative (SVORI), which provided more than $110 million in grants to state and local governments and was evaluated by the National Institute of Justice.[18] With support from SVORI, 89 adult and juvenile reentry programs were created, at least one in nearly every state in the country.[19] The federally funded evaluation of SVORI is still considered to be the most major reentry study ever conducted. However, it failed to produce clear evidence for what is effective in reentry, and it failed to establish a clear definition of "reentry success."[20] The SVORI program was dissolved in 2007, but funding of reentry programs has continued in every successive presidential administration.[21]

Reentry, and specifically access to employment and shelter after incarceration, have since become a major concern for the private sector as well. "Fair Chance Hiring" and "Second Chance Hiring" policies (hiring people with criminal records) are gaining broader traction; in 2019, for example, the Society for Human Resource Management, with 800,000 human resources professionals in its membership, launched a campaign to promote the recruitment and hiring of those with criminal records.[22] As that trade group explained, "business leaders . . . cannot afford to overlook [the] 1 in 3 adults in the United States that currently has a criminal background." Core Civic (formerly the Corrections Corporation of America), the largest owner of private prisons, jails, and detention centers, in 2015 made a $13.5 million investment in "residential reentry properties" (where people nearing release from incarceration serve the remainder of their sentences, known colloquially as "halfway houses").[23] In a press release announcing the acquisitions, the company noted that the purchase of these properties "aligned with needs we're hearing from governments around the country[] and provides an attractive real estate investment."[24] It seems that reentry offers lucrative business deals, just like mass incarceration.[25]

Yet despite considerably greater attention to the perils of the reentry process, and greater public and private investment in supporting people during reentry, the unemployment rate among formerly incarcerated people is greater than 27%, compared to a national rate of 5.2%—even though they are more active job seekers than their peers who have not been incarcerated.[26] Of those who are able to find employment, over 90% are earning wages that keep them at or below the poverty line.[27] Formerly incarcerated people are dramatically more likely to be homeless immediately following release and housing-insecure in the years following.[28] The most common cause of death after release from incarceration is drug overdose—occurring at a rate 12.7 times higher than the general population.[29] At least 20% of people leaving prison report being food-insecure—twice the rate of the general population.[30] And 83% people released from state and federal prisons are reincarcerated within a few years.[31]

Barriers to Successful Reentry Immediately Following Release and in the Long Term

From the perspective of someone facing prosecution and incarceration, the criminal justice system is extremely unpredictable. Court dates are constantly (and sometimes inexplicably) reset; most of the decisions are made following conversations at the bench (or in chambers), conversations that the defendant is not personally a part of;[32] trial dates and plea agreements come and go; the mood of a judge and prosecutor (and therefore one's fate) can change by the day (sometimes minute); and, once incarcerated, an inmate can be moved to different dorms or even entirely different prisons with little or no notice to him or his family.[33] It doesn't get any more predictable on the way out. In Louisiana, as in many other states, people often cannot even be certain of the day they will actually leave, sometimes being overdetained by several weeks, months, or even years.[34] Made worse, no matter how long someone has spent in prison, the burden is on them to find a ride home—or they will be given a bus ticket.

The next and most serious obstacle the recently released face is establishing their legal identity. When someone does not have valid identification, and they do not know when they are going to get it, they also do not know when they are going to be able to get a job, get food stamps, get a cell phone, or see a doctor.[35] Without an ID they can't even rent a hotel room, even if they can come up with the money to rent one.[36] Thankfully, the importance of access to state identification for people leaving prison has gained increased attention and action.[37]

Accurately timing release, finding a ride home, getting something to eat, finding a place to sleep that night, and securing government identification are the obstacles confronted immediately following release.[38] After that, one must begin to build a life in the face of nearly 45,000 legal collateral consequences of a criminal conviction regulating where people with criminal convictions can live, where they can work, how they can engage in the financial sector, how they can associate with their friends and family, and what resources they can access.[39]

In trying to secure longer-term housing, private landlords are largely free to refuse to rent to someone with a prior conviction, and public housing authorities have also been largely free to prohibit people recently released from prison from leasing a unit or joining a family member's lease.[40] A 2004 empirical study demonstrated that people recently released from prison experience homelessness at a far greater rate than the general public.[41]

Fortunately, more regulations have been adopted that limit housing discrimination against the formerly incarcerated.[42] However, a 2014 survey of the previously incarcerated across 14 states revealed that 79% of respondents reported being either categorically ineligible for rental housing or denied rental housing on the basis of their felony conviction,[43] and according to a 2018 study, formerly incarcerated people are still 10 times more likely to be homeless than the general public.[44] The prevalence of homelessness and housing instability experienced by formerly incarcerated people is certainly fed by the prevalence of joblessness. Research indicates that, five years after release, nearly 67% of formerly incarcerated people are still unemployed or underemployed.[45] Fortunately, these startling statistics have not gone completely unaddressed by the federal government.[46]

Although access to employment and housing are fraught with barriers, some formerly incarcerated people are ultimately able to secure low-wage jobs and rental housing.[47] However, once there, they are often stuck. Consideration of conviction history in lending decisions for mortgages and business loans is widely prevalent and unregulated.[48] Such discrimination functionally excludes formerly incarcerated people, as well as their families, from accessing two of the most fundamental tools to develop wealth and thereby escape substandard housing and employment.[49]

Disparate Impact

The Sisyphean burdens of reentry are not borne equally across race and income. Despite making up 13% of the US population,[50] African Americans constitute 38% of the incarcerated population.[51] Hispanics represent 18% of the general population[52] but 30% of prisoners.[53] Incarcerated individuals were significantly more likely than others to have lived in poverty just before their incarceration.[54] Incarceration, reincarceration, and the collateral consequences of criminal convictions have a disparate impact on people of color and people living on low incomes.[55] Audit studies reveal that Black rental applicants with felony convictions are treated worse than white applicants with otherwise identical applications and felony convictions.[56] Similarly, in the job market, an audit study conducted by Dr. Devah Pager revealed that Black applicants with felony convictions receive fewer callbacks than white applicants with felony convictions.[57] Worse still, because incarceration is often multi-generational,[58] the collateral consequences impact not only the person carrying the criminal record or "doing the time" but also entire families. As a result, incarceration functions as a permanent stratifying social institution, excluding millions of families of color and families living on low incomes from participating meaningfully in our communities.[59]

Navigating this stratification and exclusion is a struggle known particularly well by women, especially women of color.[60] In fact, 44% of Black women have family in prison (compared to 12% of white women).[61] The team at The First 72+ often talks about how "before there was a First 72+" there were moms, wives, sisters, grandmothers, girlfriends, former girlfriends, and daughters who were bearing this burden—the financial, emotional, and social burden of supporting someone when they are incarcerated[62] and of helping them build a life upon release.[63]

What Can We Do About It? Two Evidenced-Based Reforms to Improve Reentry

First, we need to clarify that, although the reentry process is often discussed as though the community of people leaving prisons and reentering communities is monolithic, it is not. Accordingly, reentry support needs to be tailored to reflect the diversity in individuals' experiences, needs, and backgrounds.[64] Traditionally, "risk and needs assessment tools" have been used to assist correctional staff and staff of reentry programs in identifying assets and vulnerabilities of people nearing release from incarceration.[65] Unfortunately, these tools have proven to be unreliable[66] and racially biased.[67] Although the instruments may be capable of improvement, in our experience they need to be based on the judgment and knowledge and experience of returnees' peers and their community, whose input is essential to predict risk. Additionally, as has already been discussed, across the literature on reentry, there is very little agreement about the definition of "reentry success" and, conversely, "reentry failure." At a most basic level, the criminal justice system measures reentry success relative to whether or not clients "recidivate," which is defined as any future contact with the criminal justice system (i.e., arrests, pretrial detention, new convictions, and time served in jail or prison). But merely avoiding contact with the criminal justice system is not synonymous with "success" (and is also not entirely in the control of the individual but is instead largely determined by policing practices); true success after incarceration has to be self-defined. Formerly incarcerated people must be empowered to define their own goals relative to housing, employment, family reunification, physical and mental health, use of public benefits, and financial security.

Recommendation One: Repeal "Offender No-Association Policies" and Invest in Community-Based Reentry Services Led by Formerly Incarcerated People

Even as more research is needed on reentry,[68] the clear consensus is that formerly incarcerated people benefit from connecting with, staying connected to, and supporting other people who have been involved in the criminal justice system.[69] These benefits include greater self-esteem and satisfaction with their life and lower risk of rearrest.[70] In social science research, this concept is often referred to as a "therapeutic community,"[71] "wounded healers,"[72] "helper therapy,"[73] or "mutual help groups."[74] At The First 72+, they call it "us helping us." Mr. Rhodes describes his first night home at The First 72+ as feeling like he was arriving "at an embassy," a place that could "keep [him] safe in this new 'free' world, but kept [him] connected to [his] old world in a very important way." Mr. Rhodes credits the "us helping us" model of The First 72+ for not only giving him a place to stay and support with finding gainful employment but also keeping him from going back to prison by empowering (and obligating) *him* to help the "next man up."

In 1965, Professor Donald R. Cressey referred to the transformational impact that helping someone else can have on the person providing the help as "retroflexive reformation."[75] In 2004, Professor Cressey's theory was tested with a group of 228 formerly incarcerated people in New York, finding that the "helper principle should be recognized for its potential in facilitating recovery and reintegration of formerly incarcerated persons."[76] As Cressey has contended, and as studies have confirmed, and as Mr. Rhodes experienced personally, peer support during the reentry process has a positive impact not only for the person in the early stages of transition but also for people who are continuing their transition home.[77] Indeed, as additional research indicates, "one of the characteristics that appears to best distinguish between successfully and unsuccessfully reformed ex-prisoners is the individuals' engagement in mentoring, parenting, and other 'generative' activities designed to 'give something back.'"[78] From our experience at The First 72+, we know this is true because, for people further along in their transition, providing this support gives them a sense of purpose and accountability, as well as a new identity, while reinforcing their commitment to stay focused and out of prison.[79]

Although thriving in Louisiana,[80] The First 72+'s creation of therapeutic communities would be discouraged and unlawful in many jurisdictions. More than half the states in the country have centuries-old laws and administrative policies that prohibit formerly incarcerated people and people with felony convictions from associating upon release.[81] In spite of research indicating that formerly incarcerated people significantly benefit from connecting with—and staying connected to—

other people who have been involved in the criminal justice system,[82] appellate courts across the country have consistently sided with the supervising authorities who argue that "offender non-association policies" prevent collusion and criminal activity and upheld these policies as a permissible denial of someone's First Amendment rights.[83]

These courts have been shortsighted; encouraging the involvement of formerly incarcerated people in reentry programming also encourages the development of organizations and programs that are mindful of the systemic and structural racism in the reentry process.[84] Reentry efforts led by formerly incarcerated people are more likely to appreciate these systemic barriers while also ensuring that people are appropriately held accountable for the choices that *are* in their control.[85]

For decades prior to the recent interest in criminal justice reform,[86] currently and formerly incarcerated people and their families have been organizing their communities and speaking up about how incarceration has not only failed to keep our communities safe but also actually made our communities less safe.[87] The contemporary criminal justice reform movement did not manifest from the leadership of elected or appointed officials, and so, to ensure that this era of reform is effective and does not result in attendant obstacles and barriers that further entrench the cycle of incarceration, we must look beyond the traditional definition of what it means to be an "expert." Experience can also lend itself to expertise. And when coupled with technical skills training and professional development, skilled practitioners who are also credible messengers can be developed.[88] Therefore, it is imperative that formerly incarcerated people be allowed to work together and be empowered to lead our communities away from the failed policies and procedures that created, and have maintained, mass incarceration.

Recommendation Two: Formerly Incarcerated People Should Have Tax Funded Temporary Guaranteed Income Immediately Upon Release, Administered by and in Partnership with Community-Led Nonprofits and Local Government

Both times Mr. Rhodes was released from prison, he was sent home with "gate money."[89] In 1988, it was a $10 check; in 2018, it was a debit card with the remaining balance from the nominal "incentive wages" that he had earned from the various jobs he worked in prison.[90] In each case, the money was not enough to meet even the most basic needs that someone recently released from prison has during his first few days home, such as food, transit fare, a cell phone, a place to stay, state identification, clothing, medication, and hygiene products. So, like so many people released from prison, even those who are even lucky enough to have family and friends to support them, he depended on his wife and already overburdened nonprofit organizations.[91]

Access to stable income is imperative for people coming home from prison. Without it, the newly released can, and do, go back to prison.[92] When the first SVORI evaluation was completed in 2004, one of the consistent themes identified across 89 adult reentry programs was that people leaving prison "need financial assistance."[93] And yet until just recently, the idea of providing temporary guaranteed income (TGI) to people leaving prison has been largely untested and disregarded as a reentry service.[94]

WHAT IS TEMPORARY GUARANTEED INCOME?

Temporary guaranteed income (TGI) is often associated with universal basic income (UBI), where governments provide an equal amount of cash to everyone on a regular basis with no strings attached.[95] The idea has been around since the 1600s and was even entertained (with conditions) by President Richard Nixon's administration with the proposed Family Assistance Plan in 1969 (which would go on to fail on the floor of the United States Senate).[96] It has recently regained popularity in the United States, particularly when presidential candidate Andrew Yang made UBI a cornerstone of his 2020 campaign,[97] and in June 2020, when Michael D. Tubbs, then-mayor of Stockton, California, founded Mayors for Guaranteed Income (MGI).[98] Since MGI was founded, mayors from 59 cities have signed on, and 10 cities have launched pilots.[99] In July 2021, California lawmakers approved the country's first state-funded guaranteed income program, focused specifically on people who are pregnant and on youth aging out of the foster care system.[100] In the context of reentry, TGI would provide a source of income that is often unavailable to formerly incarcerated people immediately following release and during the first year home.

HOW CAN TEMPORARY GUARANTEED INCOME IMPROVE REENTRY?

In our experience, people leaving prison need at least $350 to get through the first 24 hours home. These funds are necessary to pay for food, a place to stay (or to contribute to household bills), a cell phone, clothes and shoes, a state identification card, and hygiene products. After that, individuals need a job to cover the ongoing expenses of housing and utilities, food, transportation, community supervision fees, cell phone bills, and medication.

However, those returning from prison have difficulty finding work, let alone earning enough to cover the most minimal of expenses. Working 40 hours per week on the federal minimum wage of $7.25 per hour yields an annual income of $15,080 before taxes. However, approximately one-third of formerly incarcerated people earn less than $15,000 during their first-year home.[101] Worse, the wait to secure even a menial position is often upward of a year.[102]

It is well known and widely accepted that one of the biggest (possibly *the* biggest) contributors to the likelihood that someone will go back to prison is difficulty finding employment.[103] However, the barriers to gainful and safe employment go beyond the legal (and largely unregulated) discrimination that is permitted (and does occur) against people with felony convictions when employers will not consider their applications or offer them an interview and an opportunity to put their history in context.[104] Even if employers are not discriminating, prison rarely provides sufficient training or education for individuals to develop a marketable skill.[105] Thus, returnees require assistance to develop a moneymaking skill set, one that will make it possible to secure *gainful* and *safe* employment in the formal economy. As Robynn Cox's research indicates, "criminal behavior is very responsive to earnings, and to a lesser extent employment. . . . If we can work toward ensuring that marginalized groups in general, and those with a criminal record in particular, are able to access good, dignified employment, we can reduce crime and the rates of recidivism."[106] Without gainful employment, formerly incarcerated people will be unable to achieve financial security and risk returning to prison.[107]

Providing guaranteed income for at least 12 months following prison would better enable returnees to afford a place to live, be able to pay bills (and help keep the peace in their homes by contributing to household bills), eat, buy medication, and get around as they make the transition. It would also empower them to build for the future by providing the space to address their physical[108] and emotional health,[109] resolve outstanding legal issues, reconcile with family, go to school, develop new marketable skills, and pursue gainful and safe employment. TGI has been shown to work for people coming home from prison. Not only do recipients use the money to meet necessities and achieve stability;[110] they also are more successful in securing full-time gainful employment, pursuing and completing educational opportunities, and ultimately achieving and maintaining financial security.[111] Additionally, they have improved mental and physical health and are better able to manage and productively utilize their time.[112]

Thus, it is no wonder that TGI programs have been launched (or are preparing to launch) in at least 33 cities for individuals released from prison.[113] Among these, in 2020, the Center for Employment Opportunities created the Returning Citizen Stimulus, providing $24.4 million to 10,488 people recently released from prison and jail, across 28 cities, in the form of recurring payments over a three-month period.[114] The evaluation of this program, released in September 2021, is the first study of a TGI program designed specifically to support formerly incarcerated people.[115] The evaluation found that the majority of recipients spent their funds on essential needs like "rent, groceries, clothing, and personal care to prepare themselves for employment."[116] Recipients also reported that the income helped them feel "some level of financial stability in the period following incarceration."[117] The evaluation concluded that temporary guaranteed income "may be a promising model for smoothing reentry from incarceration."[118]

WHY SHOULD WE GIVE MONEY TO "CRIMINALS"?
As Montrell Carmouche, director of the New Orleans Safety and Freedom Fund, puts it: "We are not criminals; we are people."[119] When considering whether or not people recently released from prison should receive TGI, it is important to weigh the costs and benefits of intervention. First, there is the cost of incarceration (and reincarceration). Researchers estimate that society loses nearly $1 trillion annually (6% of gross domestic product) to incarceration.[120] A study by the Illinois

Sentencing Policy Advisory Council found that the average cost associated with a single instance of returning to prison is $151,662.[121] Based on current recidivism trends, over five years, taxpayers in Illinois alone should expect to spend over $13 billion on reincarcerating people. So, in determining how a reentry service like TGI could possibly be funded, it is important to consider the cost of *not* providing the support, the costs we will pay anyway, and the further strain we will place on already over-burdened social services agencies.[122]

However, the cost of incarceration is not simply paid by taxpayers and social services agencies; as we mentioned earlier, it is paid by the families to whom formerly incarcerated people return. Thus, objecting to TGI for people who have committed crimes *because limited economic resources should be allocated to law abiding citizens* fails to recognize that the criminal justice system (and all of its collateral consequences and costs) does not merely impact the person who has been prosecuted.

More important than the costs of incarceration and recidivism, TGI is—to use a term coined by Nwamaka Agbo—a form of "restorative economics,"[123] which refers to investments and strategies that heal and restore historically oppressed and exploited communities and create shared prosperity and self-determination.[124] Rahkii Holman, program manager for Community Works's Restorative Reentry Pilot Program (a TGI program for people returning home from prison to the Bay Area) emphasizes that the American justice system discriminates against people of color by racially disparate arrests, prosecutions, convictions, and sentencing. As a result, he explains, TGI serves as "restorative economics in practice . . . how we signify that we care about people who have been caught up in the system."[125] Indeed, as cannabis is now becoming legalized, the resulting tax revenue presents a unique opportunity to fund TGI and "repair a semblance of the harm done by the war on drugs."[126]

IMPORTANT THINGS TO CONSIDER IN IMPLEMENTING A POLICY AROUND TGI

In 2020, the authors helped launch a TGI program in New Orleans. Over a period of 11 months, we assisted nearly 300 formerly incarcerated people with accessing and maintaining a temporary guaranteed income. From this experience, we identified two additional elements that must be considered and addressed in the development of a reentry

TGI program: community involvement and the role of conditions and benchmarks in providing TGI funds.

First, programs that provide guaranteed income to the community must be designed and led *by the community*. As we discussed above, in order to truly move past the "failed experiment of mass incarceration,"[127] policy makers and practitioners should involve people who have been directly impacted by the criminal justice system. This is particularly important when allocating financial resources, where reentry services providers must be sensitive to the structural barriers that stand in the way of clients' success—including those on a macro level as well as idiosyncratic issues at a local level. With this foundation, a community-based organization led by formerly incarcerated people can properly determine the best method to transfer money in addition to any conditions and expectations that should be tied to the payments.

Like Mr. Rhodes, many people coming home from prison do not have valid government identification, do not know how to use debit cards, are completely unfamiliar with computers and smartphones, and have limited or no experience properly filing taxes. Because accessing state identification is a complicated and lengthy process, TGI programs should rely on community-based organizations (especially ones operated by formerly incarcerated and system-involved people who are from the same neighborhoods), which are uniquely capable of verifying the identity of their clients without the need for state-issued identification. Those organizations need to be properly resourced to provide one-on-one technical training and assistance for recipients. Additionally, recipients should not be required to remit income taxes from their TGI.[128] Because more than half of formerly incarcerated people are unemployed during their first year home,[129] the entirety of their TGI will be needed to meet basic needs. If taxes are assessed, they are likely to go unpaid, and the recipient's financial security will be further destabilized by the accumulation of tax debt.[130]

An essential debate among TGI programs is what conditions, if any, to place on future payments. Professor Lucius Couloute contends that TGI payments should be entirely unconditional, citing research that putting stipulations on TGI hampers participants, who are already overburdened and underresourced, while creating unnecessary administrative costs.[131] Although reentry services, parole officers, and court-monitored supervision programs vary in their use of rules, restrictions, and requirements, one all-too-common theme is that these demands are not individualized, can sometimes be arbitrary, and often take up a lot of time with little beneficial outcome.[132]

We agree that reentry policies should not burden the formerly incarcerated. However, in our experience, when an individualized approach is taken, and when the people with the power to set stipulations come from the community (who have a shared experience and capacity for empathy), TGI presents an excellent opportunity to help strengthen individual responsibility and accountability without being paternalistic.[133] The evaluation of the TGI program in which we participated found that over 80% of recipients met the required milestones, receiving all of the available payments.[134] Nearly two-thirds met milestones related to securing employment, and one-third reached milestones related to achieving financial security.[135]

Finally, while we encourage TGI to be easily available to all people leaving incarceration, we would encourage programs to be sensitive and attentive to the ways that access to money can be a temptation for people with a prior history of substance abuse. Drug use should *not* prohibit someone from receiving TGI. However, a safety plan should be put in place to ensure that no harm results from their participation in the program.[136]

Conclusion

Reentry is not a new problem, but it requires a new approach. Although data on reentry and recidivism were limited and inconsistent from 1890–2005,[137] existing information indicates that the reentry experience over the past 130-plus years has largely not improved, that the cycle of incarceration has not been stopped (or even significantly slowed), and that our prison system still consists largely of people who have been there before.[138]

Whether or not prisons are an effective tool to make our communities healthy and safe is not a new question either.[139] However, in this moment, where society is engaged in a more earnest conversation about reimagining public safety in our communities, decarcerating our communities, and ending our dependence on incarceration, it is even more important to consider what happens when people attempt to reintegrate into their communities, the ways in which they are persistently marginalized, and the stress and struggle experienced not only by the person navigating the process but also by their families.

Reentry is often discussed as a business of "second chances." But having a *chance* implies that one has a *choice* to do the right thing or the wrong thing. Without the ability to be a part of a community, to support one's self and family, and to heal, people are not getting a second chance because they are not getting an actual "chance" at all.

The proposals offered in this chapter are not panaceas. Because the formerly incarcerated community is so diverse, what counts as an important innovation for some may not have the same net benefit for others. However, these two proposals could radically shift our current approach to supporting formerly incarcerated people and families, resulting in improved outcomes for participants and the communities to which they return, as well as greater efficiency and effectiveness for the agencies and organizations that support them. These proposals introduce organizational principles and practices that, up to this point, are too rarely seen in the reentry space: community self-control and community investment. The needs of formerly incarcerated people and their families can vary wildly based on several static and changing factors; however, the one consistent need is that people require stable access to income. In order to properly and ethically broker reentry resources, especially money, reentry services must be grounded in genuine empathy. When stable income is coupled with support from peers who can hold people accountable for the things they can control—to remain cognizant of the structural barriers that stand in the way and be expected to provide the same support once they have progressed a little further—the reentry experience can be transformed from simply an individual exercise in staying out of prison into an opportunity to build sustainable, resilient, and free communities.[140]

NOTES

1 Carson and Golinelli, "Prisoners in 2012."
2 Beck, "Recidivism of Prisoners Released in 1983."
3 Alper, Durose, and Markman, "2018 Update on Prisoner Recidivism." Thank you to Professor Carrie Pettus-Davis for directing the authors to this source.
4 Carson, "Prisoners in 2018."

5 Although our recommendations would be germane to the process of reentry from incarceration in jails, we do not focus specifically on that reentry experience. For more on the study of reentry from jail, please see Griffin and Woodward, *Routledge Handbook of Corrections in the United States.*

6 One of the authors of this piece, Troy Rhodes, served nearly 20 years in prison, over two different periods. During the second time, he helped launch a reentry program based within the prison. Upon release, he first joined The First 72+ as a resident. Today, he serves as the Housing Services Program Coordinator for the organization. The other author, Kelly Orians, served as the co-executive director until the summer of 2021 and currently directs the Decarceration and Community Reentry Clinic at the University of Virginia School of Law.

7 Cahalan and Parsons, "Historical Corrections Statistics in the United States."

8 Ibid., 62.

9 Roosevelt, "Address of the President."

10 Ibid.

11 Wallerstedt, "Returning to Prison."

12 Ibid., 1.

13 The only media coverage of the BJS report appears to be an article in the *Washington Post*: Sawyer, "Study of State Prisons Finds Recidivism Rates High in 1979."

14 Renshaw, "Prisoners in 1980"; Bessette, "Prisoners in 1988."

15 Reno, "Remarks." Attorney General Reno cited research indicating that nationwide two-thirds of people released from prison were rearrested within three years of release—approximately 330,000 people every three years.

16 Petersilia, *When Prisoners Come Home.*

17 Reno, "Remarks." Thank you to Prof. Carrie Petus Davis for directing the authors to this source.

18 Lattimore et al., "National Portrait of SVORI."

19 Latessa, Listwan, and Koetzle, *What Works (and Doesn't) in Reducing Recidivism,* 205.

20 Jonson and Cullen, *Prisoner Reentry Programs.*

21 "Fact Sheet: President Bush Signs H.R. 1593, the Second Chance Act of 2007," Washington, DC, April 9, 2008. The Second Chance Act (SCA) was first passed by President George W. Bush in 2008. The SCA created $25 million in grants to fund reentry service. "FACT SHEET: President Obama Announces New Actions to Reduce Recidivism and Promote Reintegration of Formerly Incarcerated Individuals," Washington, DC, June 24, 2016. Under President Barrack Obama $100 million in funding was allocated to education, workforce development, and reentry services. His administration also launched a fair chance hiring program, released guidance on how to apply the Fair Housing Act when creating policies around arrest and criminal conviction checks during the application process, and "banned the box" in federal hiring by prohibiting agencies from inquiring about criminal convictions and credit history until after a conditional offer of employment. "The First Step Act of 2018: An Overview," Congressional Research Service,

March 4, 2019. During his term as president, Donald Trump signed a reauthorization of the SCA, known as the First Step Act (FSA). In addition to authorizing $100 million in federal grants, the FSA reformed federal sentencing guidelines resulting in shorter sentences and early releases, as well as mandating the creation of a risk needs assessment to be used by the Federal Bureau of Prisons. Interchange between authors and Professor Carrie Pettus-Davis.

22 Society for Human Resource Management, "Top Organizations Join SHRM Initiative." Thank you to Professor Carrie Pettus-Davis for directing the authors to this source.

23 Core Civic, "CCA Announces Acquisition of Four Residential Re-Entry Facilities."

24 Ibid.

25 For more on the profitability of the prison industrial complex, see Ben and Jerry's, "How Private Companies Are Profiting from Mass Incarceration."

26 Couloute and Kopf, *Out of Prison & Out of Work*. This figure is based on a data analysis conducted by the Prison Policy Institute in 2018, so it does not consider the impact of COVID-19 on unemployment. In a 2022 report authored by Wang and Bertram titled *New Data on Formerly Incarcerated People's Employment Reveal Labor Market Injustices*, the authors confirmed that the data collected for the 2018 report has not been updated but concluded that, based on data released by the Bureau of Justice Statistics in 2021, on employment of people released from federal prisons, the employment rate of formerly incarcerated people has not improved. See www.prisonpolicy.org/blog/2022/02/08/employment.

27 Morenoff and Harding, *Final Technical Report*.

28 Couloute, *Nowhere to Go*.

29 Waddell et al., "Reducing Overdose After Release from Incarceration."

30 Landon and Jones, "Food Insecurity is Rising."

31 Alper, Durose, and Markman, "2018 Update on Prisoner Recidivism."

32 Natapoff, "Speechless."

33 Kaufman, "The Prisoner Trade."

34 Skene and DeRoberts, "State Corrections Overdetention Woes." The complaint referenced in the above article can be accessed at https://static1.squarespace.com.

35 Orians and Frampton, "In Defense of Reentry."

36 McCoy, "What Identification Do I Need for a Motel Room?"

37 According to Juleyka Lantigua-Williams, reporting for *The Atlantic*, in 2016, "Attorney General Loretta Lynch asked all state governors to provide state-issued IDs for newly released federal inmates." Additionally, The FIRST STEP Act of 2018 contains a provision intended to help ease access to ID [amends 18 U.S.C. § 4042(a)(6)]. And in 2019, Congressman Mark Takano introduced "The Restoring Access Through Identification Act," which would require the Bureau of Prisons to cover all expenses associated with obtaining an official state-issued ID after leaving prison. However, this legislation failed to receive a vote during the 2019 legislative session. According to a survey of state laws conducted by the Georgia

Justice Project in 2017, and a 2020 report prepared by Politico, only half the states currently require people to be released from prison with valid state identification. Politico, "5 New Policy Ideas."

38 For more on the first 72 hours after release, see Ball, Weisberg, and Dansky, *The First 72 Hours of Re-Entry.*

39 ABA Criminal Justice Section, *National Summit on Collateral Consequences.*

40 deVuono-powell et al., *Who Pays?*

41 Metraux and Culhane, "Homeless Shelter Use and Reincarceration Following Prison Release."

42 Orians, "'I'll Say I'm Home, I Won't Say I'm Free,'" 29. Cities have begun to address the disparate impact of the criminal justice system on communities of color by passing laws that limit the use of conviction history in hiring decisions for public sector employment and rental applications for government subsidized housing.

43 deVuono-powell et al., *Who Pays?*

44 Couloute, "Nowhere to Go."

45 Onwuachi-Willig and Ajunwa, "Combating Discrimination Against the Formerly Incarcerated in the Labor Market."

46 In 2012, the Equal Employment Opportunity Commission (EEOC) [see Enns et al.] published *Enforcement Guidance on the Consideration of Arrest and Conviction Records in Employment Decisions Under Title VII.* This guidance was inspired in part by data indicating that blanket bans on hiring people with felony convictions can have a disparate impact on people of color, in violation of Title VII of the Civil Rights Act of 1964. In place of blanket bans, the EEOC suggested that employers instead use a multifactor inquiry to determine whether or not a prohibition on hiring people with prior felony convictions was consistent with a "business necessity," where the prior criminal conviction bore a "demonstrably tight nexus to the position in question." However, on August 6, 2019, following a lawsuit from the state of Texas, the US Fifth Circuit Court of Appeals in (*Texas v. EEOC*) invalidated this guidance, finding that the EEOC was not authorized to create rules to implement Title VII. This holding now leaves protection against blanket bans in the hands of Congress and/or individual states to legislate and enforce .

47 Looney and Turner, "Work and Opportunity Before and After Incarceration."

48 Henderson, "New Frontiers in Fair Lending."

49 Ibid.

50 US Census, *Quick Facts.*

51 Federal Bureau of Prisons, *Inmate Race.*

52 US Census., *Quick Facts.*

53 Federal Bureau of Prisons, *Inmate Race.*

54 Rabuy and Kopf, *Prisons of Poverty.*

55 Craigie, Grawer,t and Kimble, *Conviction, Imprisonment, and Lost Earnings*; Mauer and Chesney-Lind, *Invisible Punishment.*

56 Greater New Orleans Fair Housing Action Center, *Locked Out.*

57 Pager, "The Mark of a Criminal Record."

58 Bowman and Mowen, "Building the Ties That Bind."

59 Wakefield and Upgen, "Incarceration and Stratification."

60 Greenwood, "The Long Recovery After a Spouse Gets Out of Prison."

61 Lee et al., "Racial Inequalities in Connectedness to Imprisoned Individuals in the United States."

62 Chan and Lin Jun, "The High Cost of Phone Calls in Prisons Generates $1.4 billion a year"; Sheppard, "A Radically Different Way to Look at Incarceration."

63 Greenwood, "The Long Recovery After a Spouse Gets out of Prison."

64 For example, reentry services vary greatly based on how long someone has spent in prison; age at time of release (and age at the time of imprisonment); access to resources and education while incarcerated; substance abuse history; mental health history/impact of incarceration on mental health; physical health; history of intellectual disabilities; and whether they have family/community support (and to what extent).

65 For more on risk and needs assessment tools, see US Department of Justice, *Public Safety Risk Assessment Clearing House*. Thank you to Professor Carrie Pettus-Davis for her research on the issue of risk needs assessments and directing the authors to this source.

66 DiBenedetto, "Reducing Recidivism or Misclassifying Offenders?" DiBenedetto contends that risk assessment tools that are conducted while a person is incarcerated perpetuate bias because they do not account for positive postrelease changes in behavior or experience. Thank you to Professor Carrie Pettus-Davis for your research on the issue of risk needs assessments and directing the authors to this source.

67 Mayson, "Bias In, Bias Out." Reporting on an investigative journalism article that received substantial attention from researchers, Mayson highlighted research evaluating nonrecidivists. In a study of thousands of nonrecidivating individuals, 44.9% of Black and African American defendants had been identified as high-risk compared to only 23.5% of their white counterparts. Conversely, among individuals who recidivated, white defendants were more likely to be deemed low-risk (47.7%) than Black and African American defendants (28%). Mayson hypothesized that criminal history, among other variables, drove these differences in risk scores. Further, she hypothesized that criminal history is biased because the Black arrest rate is two times the white arrest rate for every crime category, except for three alcohol-related crime categories. Coupled with the disparate conviction, severity in sentencing, and incarceration rates, these tools will disproportionately impact Black or African American communities. Thank you to Professor Carrie Pettus-Davis for hert research on the issue of risk needs assessments and directing the authors to this source.

68 Wright et al., "Prisoner Reentry Research From 2000 to 2010"; Jonson and Cullen, *Prisoner Reentry Programs*; Griffin and Woodward, *Routledge Handbook of Corrections in the United States.*

69 LeBel, "An Examination of the Impact of Formerly Incarcerated Persons Helping Others"; Einat, "The Wounded Healer"; Heidemann, Cederbaum, and Martinez, "We Walk Through It Together"; Cressey, "Changing Criminals"; Cressey, "Social Psychological Foundations for Using Criminals in the Rehabilitation of Criminals"; Jonson and Cullen, *Prisoner Reentry Programs*.

70 LeBel, "An Examination of the Impact of Formerly Incarcerated Persons Helping Others."

71 De Leon and Unterrainer, "The Therapeutic Community."

72 Heidemann et al., "Wounded healers."

73 Riessman, "The 'Helper' Therapy Principle."

74 De Leon and Unterrainer, "The Therapeutic Community."

75 Cressey, "Social Psychological Foundations for Using Criminals in the Rehabilitation of Criminals."

76 LeBel, "An Examination of the Impact of Formerly Incarcerated Persons Helping Others."

77 Ibid.; Maruna, *Making Good*.

78 Maruna and LeBel, "Strengths-Based Approaches to Reentry."

79 Riessman, "The 'Helper' Therapy Principle" (identifying the "helper principle" in the field of social work, which refers to the benefits the "helper" receives when engaged in in a counselor/counselee or mentor/mentee relationship); LeBel, Richie, and Maruna, "Helping Others as a Response to Reconcile a Criminal Past."

80 A standard parole condition in Louisiana is the prohibition against people on parole engaging with anyone "who is known to be involved in criminal activity." See https://doc.louisiana.gov.

81 Binnall. "Divided We Fall." Policies prohibiting people leaving prison from associating with one another date back (at least) to the English penal system of the 1850s, when people released from penal settlements would be given a "ticket to leave." Of the nine conditions on the "ticket," one prohibited the holder from associating with "notoriously bad characters."

82 LeBel, "An Examination of the Impact of Formerly Incarcerated Persons Helping Others"; Einat, "The Wounded Healer"; Heidemann, Cederbaum, and Martinez, "We Walk Through It Together"; Cressey, "Changing Criminals"; Cressey, "Social Psychological Foundations for Using Criminals in the Rehabilitation of Criminals"; Jonson and Cullen, *Prisoner Reentry Programs*.

83 Binnall. "Divided We Fall."

84 For more on the ways in which reentry service organizations' "self help" approach has disregarded structural racism, and ways that we can promote greater community and movement building within the reentry space, see Wooten, *Race, Organizations, and the Organizing Process*; Couloute, "Organizing Reentry."

85 Couloute, "Organizing Reentry."

86 Viguerie, "A Conservative Case for Prison Reform"; Chettiar and Waldman, *Solutions*.

87 For more information on the history of currently and formerly incarcerated people organizing for criminal justice reform, see Voice of the Experienced, "Our

History"; Formerly Incarcerated Convicted People and Families Movement, "Our History"; Sturm and Tae, *Leading with Conviction*.

88 For more on "credible messengers," see Credible Messenger Justice Center website; Alcorn, "Reporting for Work Where You Once Reported for Probation."

89 Rhim, "Left at the Gate," 787. "Reference to gate money can be found as far as back as 1800s England in the form of 'release gratuity.' First thought of as charity, gate money was thought to be desirable to encourage and develop, for nothing can be imagined more hopeless than the condition of a man cast out on the world with a ruined character and without friends to help him, surrounded by temptations from which he has been long removed, or open to the influence of former evil associates."

90 During the 16 years Mr. Rhodes served in prison, the highest wage he received was $0.50/ hour, working as a "social mentor" in the prison's reentry program.

91 Travis and Waul, *Prisoners Once Removed*.

92 Rabuy and Kopf, *Prisons of Poverty*.

93 Latessa, Listwan, and Koetzle, *What Works (and Doesn't) in Reducing Recidivism*, 205.

94 Baszynski, "States Should Give Temporary Guaranteed Income to People Exiting Incarceration"; Couloute. "The Case for Temporary Guaranteed Income for Formerly Incarcerated People." Prior to the publication of these pieces, the authors were able to identify only one other article making a case for TGI for returnees: Edelman, "Cash for Leaving Prison."

95 Sigal, "Everywhere Basic Income Has Been Tried, in One Map."

96 Welsh, "Welfare Reform." The guaranteed income program that was proposed as part of the Family Assistance Plan came with income conditions and work requirements (for all able-bodied men and women), with the amount provided changing relative to changes in income and employment status.

97 Yang, "The Freedom Dividend."

98 Hess, "Meet the Mayors Pushing for Guaranteed Income in 30 Cities Across the Country"; Mayors for a Guaranteed Income website.

99 Mayors for a Guaranteed Income website. None of the participating cities specifically exclude people with felony convictions or people who do not have social security numbers (Community Works Panel Discussion).

100 Beam, "California Lawmakers Approve Nation's First State-Funded Guaranteed Income Plan."

101 Couloute. "The Case for Temporary Guaranteed Income for Formerly Incarcerated People."

102 Ibid.

103 Orians, "'I'll Say I'm Home.'"

104 Pager, "The Mark of a Criminal Record."

105 George, "What Are Inmates Learning in Prison?"; Zoukis, "Nearly Half of Prisoners Lack Access to Vocational Training."

106 University of Southern California, "Ensuring Financial Stability for Ex-Convicts Reduces Rates of Recidivism."

107 Ibid., citing Professor Robynn Cox: "Research suggests that criminal behavior is very responsive to earnings, and to a lesser extent employment," she said. "If we can work toward ensuring that marginalized groups in general, and those with a criminal record in particular, are able to access good, dignified employment, we can reduce crime and the rates of recidivism."

108 Couloute, "The Case for Temporary Guaranteed Income for Formerly Incarcerated People"; Blakinger. "'I Have No Teeth.'"

109 Quandt and Jones, "Research Roundup."

110 Couloute, "The Case for Temporary Guaranteed Income for Formerly Incarcerated People"; Garcia et al., *Paving the Way Home*.

111 Couloute, "The Case for Temporary Guaranteed Income for Formerly Incarcerated People."

112 Ibid.

113 Center for Employment Opportunities, "Returning Citizens Stimulus."

114 Ibid.

115 Garcia et al., *Paving the Way Home*.

116 Ibid.

117 Ibid.

118 Ibid.

119 Private organizations and department of corrections have responded to the repeated calls by people impacted by the criminal justice system to move away from dehumanizing language and labels like "convict," "inmate," "offender," and "felon" and instead refer to people who have been arrested, or spent time in jail or prison, as "people." See, e.g., Bryant, "Words Matter: Don't Call People Felons, Convicts, or Inmates."

120 Orrell, *Rethinking Reentry*.

121 Illinois Sentencing Policy Advisory Council, *The High Cost of Recidivism*.

122 For more on how states can cover the costs for a reentry TGI program, see Couloute, "The Case for Temporary Guaranteed Income for Formerly Incarcerated People."

123 Agbo, "What Is Restorative Economics?"

124 Ibid.

125 Community Works West, "Virtual Panel."

126 Couloute, "The Case for Temporary Guaranteed Income for Formerly Incarcerated People."

127 Childress, "Why America's Mass Incarceration Experiment Failed."

128 If recipients are categorized an independent contractors and required to submit W-9s, they will be subject to self-employment tax. Internal Revenue Service, *Self-Employment Tax*.

129 Looney and Turner, *Work and Opportunity Before and After Incarceration*. According to IRS data compiled by the Brookings Institution, 52% of people leaving prison reported no income within the first year of release.

130 Although we cannot offer formal legal advice on this point, based on our experience, if the benefit is distributed through a nonprofit organization, the organiza-

tion would not be required to categorize the beneficiary as an employee or an independent contractor, so long as the payments were not made to individuals who are able to exercise "substantial influence" over the affairs of the organization, and so long as the organization keeps "adequate records and case histories to demonstrate that grants serve it charitable purposes." Internal Revenue Service, *Compliance Guide for 501(c)(3) Public Charities*, 16.

131 Couloute, "The Case for Temporary Guaranteed Income for Formerly Incarcerated People," citing Colombino, "Is Unconditional Basic Income a Viable Alternative to Other Social Welfare Measures?"

132 Examples of this from our professional experience include a failed drug test for marijuana, resulting in probation requirements to attend Alcoholics Anonymous meetings; clients being levied a $500 fine for showing up late to court; probation officers ordering people with transportation issues to show up at their office at 8 a.m. to check in; and people ordered to appear in court in the middle of the day while also expected to maintain a job.

133 Examples of effective milestones could include meeting with a behavioral health specialist; meeting with a pro bono attorney (connected to them by the host organization) to discuss legal needs that are impeding their ability to rejoin the workforce or reconcile with family; attending a technology life skills class (connected to them by the host organization); meeting with a personal banker to discuss checking/savings accounts and credit-building tools; attending a mock interview (organized for them by the host organization); attending a cooking class (connected to them by the host organization); researching education/skills based training programs and determining which might be a good fit; enrolling in and completing driving school; learning how to read the bus schedule and take the bus; preparing a résumé; completing a financial life skills class (if they have not already); and preparing a budget and financial health plan.

134 Garcia et al., *Paving the Way Home.*

135 Ibid.

136 An example of a "safety plan" for people with substance use disorder can be found at https://drugfree.org.

137 Cahalan and Parsons, "Historical Corrections Statistics in the United States," 53. As the Bureau of Justice Statistics explains, the "findings from the 2005 study cannot be directly compared to those from BJS's previous prisoner recidivism studies due to changes in the demographic characteristics and criminal histories of the U.S. prison population, an increase in the number of states in the study, and improvements made to the quality and completeness of the nation's criminal history records since the mid-1990s."

138 Alper, Durose, and Markman, "2018 Update on Prisoner Recidivism," 1.

139 Law, *Prisons Make Us Safer, and 20 Other Myths About Mass Incarceration.*

140 The authors thank Professor Carrie Pettus-Davis of Florida State University for sharing her own draft on this subject. She has been credited throughout the chapter for her important contributions.

8

Advancing Policy to Address Violence Against Underserved Victims

An Illustration of the Missing and Murder of Indigenous Women and Girls

KATHLEEN A. FOX, CHRISTOPHER SHARP, KAYLEIGH A. STANEK, TURQUOISE SKYE DEVEREAUX, AND CONNOR STEWART

Many individuals and populations are considered "underserved" in the prevention of criminal victimization. After all, victimization often leaves people with an onslaught of consequences to navigate, including personal pain or injury, psychological distress and trauma, property damage or loss, lack of productivity at work and home, financial loss, and compromised personal and professional relationships and opportunities.[1] Victimization of any kind is traumatic, but the experience is even worse when victims belong to historically oppressed groups that have generally been marginalized by the US government and the criminal justice system.

These underserved populations include people who identify as part of oppressed racial, ethnic, religious, gender, or sexual orientation groups, whereas a person's risk of victimization, consequences, and unmet needs are compounded by multigroup affiliations (e.g., American Indian LGBTQ2S).[2]

America is being wracked by law enforcement's highly publicized murder of Black people, including George Floyd and Breonna Taylor, and by white people's senseless killings of other Black people, such as Ahmaud Arbery. These racially motivated homicides have reignited widespread support for the Black Lives Matter movement and have produced nationwide community protests. For the first time in US history, three-quarters of Americans acknowledge that racism and discrimination are big problems in society.[3] Racism and discrimination remain a serious problem for people of color, some of whom feel "invisible" in all aspects of life, including policy-making, law enforcement, media attention, resource allocation, health care, and personal safety and protection.

Although we acknowledge that no underrepresented population is more deserving of redress than another, in this chapter we focus on a crisis for an underserved population that receives comparatively little media attention and may be less familiar to readers: Indigenous women and girls in the United States, particularly pertaining to their murder or disappearance. Although the media disproportionately publicizes the disappearance of white women—so much so that researchers now call this phenomenon "missing white woman syndrome"[4]—Indigenous women and girls are at far greater risk of being missing and murdered than are women from other races.

At the outset of this chapter, a brief word is needed about our use of "Indigenous," a term referring to groups that exist globally, groups that have distinct social, historical, cultural, and political rights. Two common threads across all Indigenous peoples are their (1) resolve to maintain continuity within their ancestral spaces as distinct peoples and communities with political and legal rights within those spaces and (2) collective and individual experiences with state- and church-sponsored colonization, occupation, and subjugation.[5] In the United States, Indigenous peoples are often categorized collectively as Native American, Native, Native Hawaiian, Pacific Islander, Chamorro (Guam), Taino (Puerto Rico), Alaska Native, or American Indian.[6] The US Census Bureau has an official designation of American Indian/Alaska Native, for which it collects data and the acronym "AI/AN" is often used. Some scholars point out that these broad terms portray European colonialism and do not acknowledge the diversity among various tribes.[7] Indeed, Tribal members often prefer to be identified by their specific Tribal affiliation (i.e., Apache, Cherokee, Sioux), inter-Tribal affiliation (Navajo–Hopi), and multiracial affiliation (Tohono O'odham/Chicanx). We use the term "Indigenous" to refer to enrolled citizens and descendants of AI/AN communities whose lands are ancestral to the 50 US states and who have remained there throughout time.[8] The term "Indian" has been used from a racialized lens, but herein we use this as a legal term to refer to Indigenous peoples of the United States; the term was ratified into the Constitution[9] and subsequently codified in the United States Code,[10] has been established in both federal and state case law, and is the title in an entire chapter of the Code of Federal Regulations.[11] While problematic both racially and ethnically, the term is used to recognize the unique political status of Indigenous Tribes as sovereign entities and individuals as citizens of their Tribes.

The victimization of Indigenous peoples is important to study, particularly given the historical cultural and systemic oppression this group continues to face. Indigenous peoples have endured discrimination, violence, and even genocide in the United States and abroad. The United States has oppressed Indigenous peoples in many ways, including forced relocation, removal of their children to boarding schools, adoption of Indigenous children into non-Indigenous families, loss of self-governance, introduction of patriarchy, and sterilization of Indigenous women.[12] Because these were all state-sanctioned, government-perpetrated forms of systemic violence, it is critical that the US government and its policy makers pay close attention to the victimization of Indigenous peoples—and take action now.

US systems—including the criminal justice system—were forced upon US Tribes and Indigenous peoples by colonizing settlers. The Westernized systems imposed upon Tribal Nations continue to be either unfunded or chronically underfunded. As such, this chapter is rooted in the premise that Indigenous Nations are forced to operate within the flawed US justice system, which contains oppressive policies and operations that exacerbate racial disparities. The policy recommendations presented here require some "reimagination" of the criminal justice system—but within a realistic framework under the Westernized parameters that our system operates.

The victimization of Indigenous populations is exacerbated by health crises, including the global pandemic caused by ongoing coronavirus pandemic (COVID-19). Communities of color, including Indigenous communities, are among those most impacted by the disease, particularly given that they are at increased risk for underlying health conditions but have limited health care resources.[13] Among Indigenous communities, the spread of COVID-19 has been exacerbated by the cohabitation of multiple generations, a lack of running water that prevents regular handwashing, and the prevalence of "food deserts" in tribal communities.[14]

The coronavirus pandemic, and practices aimed at reducing the risk of contracting or spreading COVID-19, may result in increased family and domestic violence among Indigenous communities. Social distancing, self-quarantining, and strict curfew and stay-at-home orders produce increased stressors, such as reduced income, potential job loss, food insecurity, prolonged periods of confinement in close quarters, and the illness and/or death of loved ones. All of these factors increase opportunities for interpersonal violence.[15]

In this chapter, we first present the prevalence of interpersonal victimization among US populations and illustrate the heightened risk of victimization among Indigenous women and girls specifically, including the murder and missing of Indigenous women and girls (MMIWG). Second, we discuss the significance of violent victimization generally and among Indigenous women and girls (including MMIWG) specifically. Third, we present the state of the research on violent victimization, again with an emphasis on MMIWG. Finally, we offer four recommendations to reduce Indigenous victimization in general and MMIWG specifically. To address the issues and the recommendations provided herein, we also provide state and federal governments a framework for meaningful consultation with Indigenous elected leaders, grassroots activists and survivors, and communities to address the systematic inequities we discuss in this chapter.

Our focus in this chapter on evidence-based criminal justice reform for Tribal Nations and Indigenous peoples is rooted in a juxtaposition between Westernized and Indigenous conceptualizations of "evidence." The cultural differences are beyond the scope of this chapter and are explained in depth elsewhere, but many acknowledge that *research itself* is a colonial mechanism among Indigenous communities given historical and contemporary experiences, the invasive and extractive nature of Western methods, lack of cultural context and understanding, unwillingness of the academy to acknowledge and uphold Indigenous epistemologies, and non-Indigenous researchers who are trained to approach knowledge from a Westernized and extractive perspective.[16] Indigenous ways of knowing are rooted in worldviews: relations with humans, animals, plants, and natural phenomenon (the seen), as well as spiritual ways, origin stories or original instructions, and ceremonial constructs (the unseen).

Therefore, doing research with Indigenous populations and determining "evidence-based" knowledge must be conducted in collaboration with Indigenous peoples to ensure that the research is culturally accurate, uses decolonizing methods, has benefits for the Tribal community, and enhances Indigenous representation and capacity-building. Given the complexities associated with non-Indigenous researchers who conduct research with Indigenous populations—as well as the few Indigenous researchers (due to the "glass ceiling" caused by colonization, racism, and oppression)—we acknowledge that some, but not all, of the evidence-based knowledge that we present in this has been produced through a Westernized approach—meaning research collected without Indigenous representation or cultural understanding.

The Problem of Violent Victimization Among Underserved Populations Such as Indigenous Women and Girls

Violent crime encompasses a wide variety of offenses (e.g., homicide, assault, rape). In this chapter we focus on gender-based violence experienced by women and girls, including intimate partner violence (IPV), stalking, and sexual assault. Notably, our discussion also centers on MMIWG. First, we briefly define some terms that encompass interpersonal victimization. *IPV* is the physical or psychological abuse of an intimate partner and can include crimes such as physical assault, emotional abuse, financial abuse, stalking, and sexual assault.[17] *Stalking* is repetitive, intrusive, unwanted, and frightening, threatening, or harassing behavior that often involves a combination of legal and illegal behaviors.[18] *Sexual assault* is forced or coerced sexual contact without the explicit consent of the victim, including rape, attempted rape, and unwanted sexual touching.[19]

Across the nation, millions of women and girls are victimized by interpersonal violence. Among women in the United States, 16% (19 million) have been stalked, 36% (44 million) have been abused by an intimate partner, and 44% (52 million) have experienced sexual violence.[20] Although less than half of all violent victimization is reported to the police,[21] in recent years the global #MeToo movement has ignited increased attention to the seriousness of sexual assault.[22]

Indigenous women and girls are violently victimized at even higher rates than women of other races and ethnicities. The statistics are chilling. Four in five Indigenous women are violently victimized in their lifetimes.[23] Community-based studies find that more than half of Indigenous women (45–59%) are subjected to sexual violence.[24] National studies also reveal incredibly high rates of interpersonal victimization of Indigenous women. The most recent National Intimate Partner and Sexual Violence Survey found that over half of Indigenous women have experienced sexual violence (55%). This rate exceeds the violent sexual victimization of white (47%), African American (38%), and Hispanic women (35%).[25] In terms of IPV, 39% of Indigenous women have been victimized, as compared to 29% of African American women, 27% of white women, 21% of Hispanic women, and 10% of Asian women.[26] Twenty-five percent of Indigenous women have been stalked, a higher percentage than white (16%), African American (14%), and Hispanic (14%) women.[27]

While much remains unknown about victim–offender relationships, the available evidence suggests that the majority of Indigenous women and girls are harmed by non-Indigenous offenders. Two-thirds of Indigenous women—including women who were physically assaulted (63%) and sexually assaulted (67%)—report that their assailant was non-Indigenous.[28] This is especially problematic because of the jurisdictional challenges that tribes face in addressing violence perpetrated in their communities by non-Indians against Indigenous women. Table 8.1 below illustrates those jurisdictional complexities, showing how they depend upon the status of the offender and victim.

TABLE 8.1. Criminal Jurisdiction in Indian Country (adapted from US Government Accountability Office 2011)

Political status of the offender	Political status of the victim	Jurisdiction
Indian	Indian	Offenses in the Major Crimes Act: federal and tribal jurisdiction. Offenses not in the Major Crimes Act: exclusively tribal jurisdiction.
Indian	Non-Indian	Offenses in the Major Crimes Act: federal and tribal jurisdiction Offenses in the General Crimes Act: federal and tribal jurisdiction
Non-Indian	Indian	Exclusively federal jurisdiction (General Crimes Act)—no tribal or state jurisdiction.
Non-Indian	Non-Indian	Exclusively states jurisdiction—no tribal or federal jurisdiction.

Note: Under Public Law 280, these jurisdictional restrictions do not apply in California, Minnesota, Nebraska, Oregon, and Wisconsin; and then Alaska upon statehood. Additionally, at the time of writing, the Supreme was considering two cases—Sharp v. Murphy and McGirt v. Oklahoma—that address federal jurisdiction in Oklahoma.

Indigenous women are also at higher risk of being murdered or going missing. While the exact scope of the problem remains unclear, in some communities Indigenous women are murdered at a rate ten times the national average.[29] The extremely high rate of MMIWG is likely an underestimate, given methodological problems such as racial misclassification by law enforcement (e.g., as white, Hispanic, or Asian); omission of Indigenous race/tribal affiliation(s) on police reports; jurisdictional differences across state, federal, and tribal lands; and barriers to accessing the data collected (if any) about MMIWG.[30] In other words, the prevalence of MMIWG is undoubtedly even higher than is currently known.

The Significance of Violent Victimization

Violence has many serious and often long-term consequences for victims, their families, and their communities. Violence experienced by Indigenous people often ripples through entire communities, sometimes for generations.[31] Survivors of violence often experience a variety of harmful physical, psychological, financial, and health outcomes.

Every year, IPV results in 2 million injuries and 1,300 deaths.[32] Among IPV incidents that result in injuries, about 500,000 also require medical attention for the victim (N=552,192).[33] The victims' resulting physical health problems may lead to reduced quality of life and increased use of health care services.[34] In addition to external physical injuries, victims can also suffer from central nervous system symptoms, which can manifest as headaches, back pain, fainting, or seizures.[35] Many victims also experience a wide array of symptoms not easily attributable to interpersonal violence, such as gastrointestinal disorders, appetite loss, viral infections, cardiac problems, sexually transmitted diseases, vaginal bleeding, pelvic pain, and urinary tract infections.[36]

Victims of interpersonal violence are also at extremely high risk for psychological and mental health consequences. Psychological symptoms can include depression, anxiety, higher levels of financial stress and unemployment, post-traumatic stress disorder (PTSD), and suicidal thoughts and attempts.[37] Victims are at a higher risk for mental health issues and substance abuse issues and also use emergency room and hospital services at higher rates.[38] PTSD means that victims may relive their trauma at any point during their lives, especially if their current lives trigger something in their memory.

Although Indigenous women and girls in the United States experience a high rate of victimization, only a handful of studies examine consequences among Indigenous victims. Those studies indicate that, for Indigenous women and girls, the impact of victimization is often compounded. For example, in a study of 30 pregnant Indigenous women, 87% had experienced physical or sexual abuse, and 30% of those who were victimized suffered from mental health problems as a result.[39] Compared to Indigenous women with no IPV history, those exposed to severe physical and sexual abuse often experience an increased risk for anxiety, PTSD, mood, and other mental health disorders.[40] Violence often leaves Indigenous survivors with needs related to their abuse-related physical injuries, including counseling for mental health concerns, medical care for health problems, and support to reconnect with their Tribal community and cultural ways of coping.[41]

History, Research, and Legislation on Violent Victimization

Contextualizing the victimization of Indigenous people necessitates a historical understanding of how criminal legal policies have been administered. Tribal sovereignty is the right of Tribes to self-govern. This right existed before European arrival and persists today. Yet Tribal sovereignty has changed over time.

Understanding Victimization Through an Indigenous Perspective of Justice: Colonialism, Civilization, and Erasure

From an Indigenous perspective, acknowledging and strengthening sovereignty is the central element in any discussion about criminal justice reform. Deloria and Lytle's 40-plus-year-old observations remain true today: "It is impossible to understand American Indians in their contemporary setting without first gaining some knowledge of their history as it has been formed and shaped by the Indian experience with Western civilization. . . . This is particularly true in the case of Indian notions of law and justice."[42] Consistent with this book's theme on *big ideas*, we highlight three big ideas that have impacted Indigenous populations in the Americas: *colonialism, civilization*, and *erasure*. Those ideas directly impact criminal justice reform and are key to contextualizing any policy recommendations designed to reduce victimization and MMIWG. Although a full analysis of these concepts is beyond the scope of this chapter, we provide a brief overview of each big idea.

COLONIALISM

Colonialism is colonizers' violent invasion of Indigenous land, people, culture, and life.[43] This practice is one of domination, involving the subjugation of one group of people over another; political and economic control over foreign territory; and transfer of settler populations from their countries of origin to the lands held by subjugated peoples.[44] The process of colonialism is colonization, which involves a process of dehumanization. In North America, colonialism was manifested by discrimination, forced relocation, forced assimilation of Indigenous peoples, and threats to their self-determination. During the early era of colonization, European colonists forced Indigenous people in the United States off their lands—often violently.[45] US colonizers subjected Indigenous peoples to enslavement, rape, and murder and justified these actions by stating that Indigenous peoples, as non-Christians, were inhuman.

The colonizers' heinous treatment of women was first described by Michele de Cuneo, recalling the rape of an Indigenous woman in 1495, during the second voyage of Columbus:[46]

> While I was in the boat I captured a very beautiful Carib woman, whom the said Lord Admiral gave to me, and with whom, having taken her into my cabin, she being naked according to their custom, I conceived desire to take pleasure. I wanted to put my desire into execution but she did not want it and treated me with her finger nails in such a manner that I wished I had never begun. But seeing that[] (to tell you the end of it all), I took a rope and thrashed her well, for which she raised such unheard-of screams that you would not have believed your ears. Finally, we came to an agreement in such manner that I can tell you she seemed to have been brought up in a school of harlots.

In the colonization process, sexual violence was one method of dehumanizing women. De Cuneo's narrative illustrates that the victimization of Indigenous women and girls is historically rooted and even considered a socially acceptable practice among some non-Indigenous groups. This has clear implications for the current MMIWG crisis.

CIVILIZATION

If there is one big idea that scholars and policy makers should understand, it is that relationships between the United States and Indigenous Tribes have long been characterized by US efforts to "civilize the Indian" or "kill the Indian, save the man" to address the "Indian Problem." The overall goal of the US government–sanctioned efforts at civilizing Indigenous peoples was to eradicate Indigenous culture among children with the intention to ultimately eradicate Tribal sovereignty. The Westernized criminal justice system was forced upon Tribal Nations in an effort to further control, subjugate, and erase Indigeneity. Essentially, these efforts have led to an institutionalized viewpoint that Indigenous peoples are victims of themselves, their own cultures and worldviews, and their traditional systems. In this way of thinking, Indigenous peoples must be civilized to have rights. So, rather than acknowledging the historical and ongoing victimization of those communities, US civilizing efforts are rationalized as beneficial for Indigenous peoples.

These "civilizing" efforts have a particular impact on Indigenous women. Unlike Western civilizations that focus on individualism and are rooted in patriarchy, many Tribes are structured as matriarchal societies. In those communities, women hold leadership roles; they are the prominent decision makers about the health and well-being of their people; and, with the power of giving life during childbirth, women are considered sacred. Colonization has imposed patriarchal gender roles in Indigenous communities. In many Indigenous communities, this has shifted the matriarchal role from that of sacred life-givers, disempowering Indigenous women within their communities and diminishing their perceived value in today's society.

ERASURE

Erasure includes the ongoing acts of ignoring Indigenous advocates, scholars, and Tribal leaders in the discourse of policy-making and reform. Through colonization and efforts to civilize the original Indigenous people of the continent, mainstream society does not hear the voices and stories of Indigenous peoples. In most state education systems, colleges, and universities—outside of specific courses or programs that are Indigenous-focused—the curricula exclude Indigenous content. This systemic exclusion has led to the erasure and marginalization of Indigenous peoples and the issues they face in the criminal justice system. Therefore, the criminal justice system is often perceived as illegitimate, corrupt, and oppressive by Indigenous peoples.[47] The invisibility of Indigenous peoples means that their victimization is largely unseen and unknown in society. Through the erasure process, even experts in criminal justice lack a basic knowledge of Tribal sovereignty; more important, they lack an understanding of how Indigenous people view and value their sovereign rights. Without a solid knowledge base of Indigenous history and sovereignty, it is impossible to conduct appropriate analyses of issues of violence perpetrated against Indigenous women.[48]

These three big ideas—*colonialism*, *civilization*, and *erasure*—are key components of the framework from which we will analyze the contemporary issue of violence against Indigenous women. (We note that, throughout American history, these three big ideas have also affected other underserved racial groups and immigrant groups.) Moreover, the act of acknowledging these big ideas undermines the ideological notion of a fair, equitable, and just nation engrained into US society. Recognizing colonialism, civilization, and erasure certainly "challenges some of the current assumptions that undergird both reformist and revolutionary approaches to the law."[49] Finally, acknowledging these three big ideas allows scholars to include the experiences and wisdom of Indigenous peoples as an evidence base for reform.

Historical Trauma and Indigenous Women's and Girls' Risk of Victimization

Historical trauma among Indigenous peoples is now a recognized consequence of colonialism, civilization, and erasure. Maria Yellow Horse Brave Heart is credited with conceptualizing the term "historical trauma," which is defined as an "unresolved grief response" that "emanates from massive cumulative trauma across generations."[50] Historical trauma perpetuates victimization in numerous ways. For example, the limited research regarding Indigenous peoples and police relations suggests that colonial police tactics and general distrust of the government often lead Indigenous communities to distrust law enforcement.[51] So, historical context (coupled with recent abuse at the hands of law enforcement) has made Indigenous women hesitant to approach formal authorities to report or seek help for their victimization.[52]

These issues surrounding law enforcement in Indian Country are primarily rooted in discrimination, oppression, and jurisdictional confusion.[53] Over- and underpolicing of Indigenous communities, by both Tribal and non-Tribal law enforcement agents, reinforce Indigenous apathy and even hostility toward the police.[54] There is a widespread belief among Indigenous women that their attackers will not be prosecuted—and this belief is not unfounded. In 2007, United States Attorneys prosecuted only 30% of the cases referred to them from Indian Country but prosecuted 56% of cases referred from non-Tribal lands.[55]

For generations, the importance of historical trauma and Indigenous victimization was not prioritized. However, in 2019, the United States enacted an unprecedented flurry of legislation devoted to addressing and reducing violence against Indigenous peoples, with a particular emphasis on MMIWG. This legislation was ignited by a long-standing US grassroots movement and Canada's National Inquiry into MMIWG, which concluded that MMIWG is a "deliberate race, identity, and gender-based genocide."[56] This MMIWG legislation informs our recommendations for reducing victimization among underserved populations such as Indigenous women and girls; we summarize its status below.

Federal and State Legislation on MMIWG

In November 2019, the US government announced two monumental MMIWG developments. First, the Department of Justice launched the National Strategy to Address Missing and Murdered Indigenous Persons.[57] This initiative aims to improve criminal investigations, expand and centralize data collection, and designate coordinators to assist with tracking and reducing MMIWG in 11 states. The states expected to have tribal coordinators include Alaska, Arizona, Michigan, Minnesota, Montana, Nevada, New Mexico, Oklahoma, Oregon, Utah, and Washington. Second, an executive order established an MMIWG federal task force to improve criminal justice databases, trauma-informed responses to survivors, and educational outreach about MMIWG for Tribes and the general public.[58]

This federal legislation was preceded by several state laws addressing MMIWG. As of early 2022, 16 states had passed legislation to reduce MMIWG, including Alaska, Arizona, California, Hawaii, Idaho, Minnesota, Montana, Nebraska, New Mexico, North Dakota, Oklahoma, Oregon, South Dakota, Utah, Washington, and Wyoming. Other states had introduced such legislation as of early 2022 (e.g., Colorado, New Jersey, and New York). While state MMIWG legislation is vitally important and long overdue, most remain unfunded mandates with unrealistic goals and few resources.[59]

Policy Recommendations For Reducing Violent Victimization

In this final section, we provide four recommendations to reduce violent victimization: increasing funding to Tribes to address violence against women; addressing jurisdictional challenges and limitations; reauthorizing the Violence Against Women Act; and implementing policies to track the scope of and to reduce MMIWG. We discuss each in turn below.

Policy Recommendation One: Increase Funding for Tribes and Other Entities Serving Tribal Communities to Address Violence Against Indigenous Women

To improve the safety of Indigenous peoples and communities, adequate funding should be allocated to Tribes and other entities serving Tribal communities. The lack of funding for community-based and culturally specific programs is perhaps the biggest disconnect between policy and practice. For example, the Indian Child Protection and Family Violence Prevention Act (Public Law 101-630) was passed in 1990 and authorized funding for child abuse and family violence prevention as well as a national resource center to address family violence and child abuse. According to the act, the programs were to emphasize unique Indian culture and community involvement in the prevention and treatment of child abuse and family violence, including construction and renovation of facilities to establish family violence shelters and establish innovative and culturally relevant programs. After 30-plus years, no funds have been appropriated for these programs except for a one-year appropriation for the resource center.[60] Adequate long-term funding for Tribes and other entities serving Tribal communities is needed to overcome the long history of chronic underfunding of Indigenous programs by the US government.

In 2003, the United States Commission on Civil Rights (the Commission) published a report affirming the nation's long history of neglect, discrimination, and persistent underfunding of Indigenous communities.[61] Consistent with the statistics provided earlier in this chapter, the Commission found that Indigenous peoples were more than twice as likely to be victims of crime. However, per capita spending on law enforcement in Indigenous communities was roughly 60% of the national average. The Commission also found that Tribal courts were insufficiently funded. The result has been understaffed police departments, overcrowded correctional facilities, unprepared court systems, and underserved victims, families, and communities.

In the decade following the Commission's report, funding increased. However, it was still insufficient to overcome the backlog of public safety needs caused by decades of neglect.[62] Fifteen years later, the Commission's follow-up report revealed that while "funding for public safety in Indian Country has increased, it does not meet the public safety needs in Indian Country."[63]

The crisis of the victimization of Indigenous women and girls is highly complex. Solving that crisis requires an accurate understanding of how decades of neglect have impaired the ability of many Tribal justice systems to ensure public safety. Because we recommend increased funding for Tribes and other entities to address violence against Indigenous women and girls, including MMIWG, we must respond to those critics who argue against "throwing more money at the problem" of Indigenous victimization.

Initiatives that require increased funding have shown demonstrable success in reducing the victimization of Indigenous peoples.[64] For example, the Tiwahe Initiative[65] is an interagency collaboration that funds a comprehensive wraparound program designed to reduce Indigenous victimization, unemployment, substance use, and overincarceration and to support women's and children's shelters.[66] The Tiwahe Initiative was implemented with tremendous success in four Tribal communities. Two years after the Tiwahe Initiative's implementation, violent crime in the four communities dropped 35%.[67] Three years after implementation, violent crime was down 56%.[68] Despite this success, the 2018 budget submitted by Donald Trump's administration to Congress would have eliminated funding for this initiative. However, Congress continues to fund it. Based on the program's success, we recommend allocating continued and additional funding to scale up the Tiwahe Initiative (among other programs) to serve more Tribal Nations.

Funding should be sufficient for Tribes to operate police departments, correctional facilities, courts, shelters, diversion programs, and prevention programs that address family violence. Rather than expecting Tribes to use their limited existing funds for new initiatives, new funding should be provided as such initiatives develop. We recommend dedicated funding for training and technical assistance, creating and maintaining service provider networks, improving data collection, and conducting and disseminating research. In March 2020, in the 116th Congress, the Senate passed two bills: Savannah's Act (S.227) and the Not Invisible Act (S.982). Both offer promising steps toward solutions that will reduce MMIWG and violence against Indigenous women and girls.[69]

Policy Recommendation Two: Continue to Address Jurisdictional Challenges and Limitations

Tribal nations should have jurisdiction to appropriately address violence against Indigenous women and girls (including MMIWG) that occurs on Tribal lands. The federal government recognizes Tribal sovereignty through treaties, statutes, and executive actions that regulate internal and social relations. Where once this power was absolute for Tribal Nations, early treaties sometimes addressed their jurisdiction over crimes. Three federal laws are central to the federal exercise of criminal jurisdiction: the 1817 General Crimes Act, the 1885 Major Crimes Act, and the 1953 Public Law 280. United States Supreme Court decisions have established the states' lack of jurisdiction over Tribal lands. However, they have also limited Tribes' ability to prosecute non-Indians for crimes committed in Indian Country. This jurisdictional limitation has created challenges for Tribes, limiting their ability to address violence perpetrated by non-Indigenous offenders against Indigenous women and girls.

Recall that non-Indigenous offenders are quite common, representing two-thirds of the known perpetrators targeting Indigenous women.[70] In 2013, reauthorization of the Violence Against Women Act (VAWA) allowed tribes to acquire Special Domestic Violence Criminal Jurisdiction (SDVCJ) to prosecute non-Indian offenders who commit acts of domestic violence and dating violence and who violate protection orders on tribal lands. But the Tribes that established SDVCJ faced difficulties prosecuting non-IPV sexual assaults and the violation of protective orders.[71] Additionally, SDVCJ does not extend to the crimes of stalking, child victimization, and human trafficking. To address these loopholes, we recommend that tribal prosecutorial authority be extended to the crimes listed above.

Policy Recommendation Three: Reauthorize VAWA to Provide Technical Assistance to Tribal Nations but Limit the Imposition of the American System

Congress should reauthorize VAWA and, while funding all victims, should specifically fund Tribal grant programs to protect Indigenous peoples and their communities. As described above, the 2013 Violence Against Women Reauthorization Act attempted to address jurisdictional limitations by giving Tribes the authority to investigate, prosecute, convict, and sentence Indigenous as well as non-Indigenous offenders in Indian Country who assault Indigenous intimate partners or violate protection orders. But VAWA's 2013 restoration of Tribal jurisdiction did not apply to Alaska Native Villages. Moreover, VAWA expired in December 2018, and—as of April 2022—its reauthorization was at the beginning of the legislative process. Although VAWA has strong support from President Joseph Biden, there is some uncertainty that VAWA will pass in the Senate given the current gridlock between Democrats and Republicans. Importantly, the 2021 version of the act provides increased provisions and safeguards for homeless women, transgender women, and Indigenous women. Specifically, for Indigenous women, this version of the bill provides increased accountability and reaffirms Tribal Nations' sovereignty and authority to prosecute non-Indigenous offenders who commit crimes on tribal lands.[72]

It is also important that VAWA be culturally competent and recognize the unique ways in which Tribal Nations operate. Specifically, Tribal legal systems must meet legal standards to have jurisdiction based on the way the VAWA bill stood as of August 2021, the aforementioned Special Domestic Violence Criminal Jurisdiction.[73] As of this writing, only 18 of the 574 federally recognized Tribes are known to be exercising this special jurisdiction and are meeting the specific requirements under federal law that would allow them to access VAWA funds to assist Indigenous victims in their communities who experience violence. This gap must be addressed, as should the expense that Tribes face under VAWA that frustrate their prosecution of crimes against children, alcohol and drug crimes, and crimes that occur within the criminal justice system.[74] Additionally, Congress should consider ways that expand VAWA's reach to better support Indigenous communities while also limiting the imposition of American system.

We underscore the recommendations of the National Congress of American Indians[75] that Congress should: (1) reauthorize VAWA's tribal grant programs to ensure funding for Tribal nations who are exercising jurisdiction under VAWA; and (2) address the unique barriers to safety for Alaska Native women by providing all Indigenous communities with access to all VAWA programs.[76] Additionally, these recommendations should recognize the unique Tribal sovereignty of all Tribal Nations within the United States and maintain their systems of justice while minimizing the imposition of the American system and colonization.

Funding should be provided for community-based services that offer resources to Tribal communities and other entities serving Indigenous peoples. Due to limited funding, Tribal communities sometimes lack the infrastructure to provide safe, confidential housing and services, leading to homelessness and increased MMIWG. Indeed, there is a profound link between homelessness (sometimes a result of IPV) and sex trafficking among Indigenous women.[77] Few Tribes have their own victim services agencies or domestic violence shelters. For example, among Arizona's 22 federally recognized Tribes, there are only 10 Tribe-operated victim service agencies.[78] And among the 574 federally recognized US

Tribes, fewer than 60 (10%) have their own domestic violence shelters.[79] Investing resources into coalitions that serve Indigenous communities is vital for improving community education and safety.

For example, the Southwest Indigenous Women's Coalition (SWIWC) assists Tribal communities in Arizona to build capacity for domestic violence and sexual assault services. SWIWC maintains and publicizes a list of community victim-services on and off Tribal land. It also engages in community outreach and training. Investing in coalitions serving Indigenous communities, like SWIWC, will help enable Tribal communities to address and prevent victimization and MMIWG.

Policy Recommendation Four: Implement Policies to Track the Scope of and Reduce MMIWG

Due to methodological limitations, the available data on MMIWB is undoubtedly an underrepresentation of the problem. To minimize the gaps in data and better understand the prevalence of victimization generally and MMIWG specifically, we offer the following policy recommendations.

Law enforcement agencies, on and off Tribal land, should be provided with funds for training to enhance cultural competency and teach best practices for tracking Indigenous victims. Current practices by law enforcement agencies contribute to the problems associated with tracking missing and murdered Indigenous people (MMIP). While racial misclassification is a pervasive problem nationwide, its occurrence can be reduced by training officers on culturally appropriate ways of asking about tribal affiliation. Some law enforcement agencies do not even feature an Indigenous racial category on police reports (e.g., the official census designation of American Indian/Alaska Native). Further, many law enforcement agencies are not required to complete an incident report for missing adults. This hampers any effort to compare the rates at which Indigenous peoples go missing compared to those from other races/ethnicities. Only a handful of states require law enforcement to register missing persons with the NamUs national database.[80] Requiring law enforcement agencies to document incident reports for missing persons and record missing persons with NamUs would help more accurately track this data.

State legislation should promote awareness of, and develop policies to prevent, MMIP generally and MMIWG particularly. While about one-quarter (N=14) of US states have legislation directed at MMIWG/MMIP, most of the legislation includes unfunded mandates.[81] Limited or no funding means that inadequate time and resources are devoted to MMIWG/MMIP. From our partnership with Arizona's legislatively mandated Study Committee on MMIWG (HB2570), we can attest that this rewarding work is painstaking, labor-intensive, and filled with challenging roadblocks. When there is no funding, or limited funding, tied to MMIWG legislation, the state sends a clear message about the relative importance it places on reducing MMIWG. While the unfunded mandate to investigate MMIWG is preferable to no mandate at all, all states must enact *funded* MMIWG/MMIP legislation so that adequate time and resources may be allocated to this work. After all, MMIWG legislation is a critical step toward saving lives and improving community safety.

Research on MMIWG/MMIP should be funded, conducted, and disseminated. Comparatively little empirical research has investigated the victimization of Indigenous people, including MMIWG. Research from the academic community is desperately needed to answer the many unresolved questions surrounding the disappearance and murder of Indigenous persons. Research must not only establish the scope of the problem; it should also provide the circumstantial attributes and theoretical underpinnings of MMIWG so that culturally appropriate policies can be effectively tailored to reduce MMIWG. Research on Indigenous people's victimization should be done in close consultation with Indigenous collaborators and partners (academic and nonacademic alike) to ensure cultural accuracy and appropriateness.

Conclusion

In closing, it is possible to reduce the victimization of Indigenous women and girls, including MMIWG, and criminal justice reform is necessary to that process. Indigenous communities must be included in all aspects of criminal justice reform, particularly those addressing victimization and MMIWG. The voices of the people who will be impacted by reforms must be heard, and their perspectives must be acknowledged.

The demonstrated importance of engagement by Black families, communities, and leaders in addressing police brutality directed against them holds true for criminal justice reforms that will impact Indigenous peoples. Policy reformers must include grassroots social justice advocates, survivors, and elected policy makers and community leaders. MMIWG policy and legislation started at the grassroots level. Engaging Indigenous communities is the only way that criminal justice policy reforms will effectively reduce victimization and MMIWG and improve the safety of Indigenous women, girls, and communities.

NOTES

1 Langton, "Socio-Emotional Impact of Violent Crime."
2 Whereas "LGBTQ" stands for people who identify as lesbian, gay, bisexual, transgender, and questioning/queer, the added "2S" represents "Two Spirited," or Indigenous peoples who identify as LGBTQ.
3 Russonello, "Why Most Americans Support the Protests."
4 Stillman, "The Missing White Girl Syndrome," 491; Slakoff, "Media Messages Surrounding Missing Women and Girls," 80; Wanzo, "The Era of Lost (White) Girls," 99.
5 United Nations (n.d.), *Who Are Indigenous Peoples?*.
6 Yellow Bird, "What We Want to Be Called," 1; Sanders, "Indigenous Peoples," 4; Weaver, "Indigenous Identity," 240.
7 Yellow Bird, "What We Want to Be Called," 1; Sanders, "Indigenous Peoples," 4.
8 Yellow Bird, "What We Want to Be Called," 1; Sanders, "Indigenous Peoples," 4; Weaver, "Indigenous Identity," 240.
9 See Article 1, Section 8, Clause 3 of the US Constitution, authorizing Congress the power "to regulate commerce with foreign nations, and among the several states, and with the Indian tribes," and Article 1, Section 2, Clause 3, excluding "Indians not taxed" from taxation by the states.
10 See Title 25 of the United States Code (Indians).
11 See Title 25 of the Code of Federal Regulations (Indians).
12 Fox, "The Murder and Missing of Indigenous Women and Girls."
13 Dyer, "Covid-19: Black People and Other Minorities are Hardest Hit in US"; van Dorn, Cooney, and Sabin, "COVID-19 Exacerbating Inequalities in the US," 1243.
14 Silverman, "Navajo Nation Surpasses New York State for the Highest Covid-19 Infection Rate in the U.S."; Hoover, "Native Food Systems Impacted by COVID."
15 Hilleary, "COVID Spread May Put Native Americans at Increased Risk of Violence."
16 Smith, "The National Intimate Partner and Sexual Violence Survey."
17 Breiding, "National Intimate Partner and Sexual Survey."
18 Fox, "Method to the Madness," 74.
19 Bureau of Justice Statistics, "National Crime Victimization Survey."

20 Smith, "The National Intimate Partner and Sexual Violence Survey."

21 Morgan, "Criminal Victimization."

22 Tippett, "The Legal Implications of the Metoo Movement," 229.

23 Rosay, "Violence Against American Indian and Alaska Native Women and Men," 2016.

24 Malcoe, "Intimate Partner Violence and Injury in the Lives of Low-Income Native American Women"; Yuan, "Risk Factors for Physical Assault and Rape among Six Native American Tribes," 1566.

25 Breiding, "National Intimate Partner and Sexual Survey."

26 Ibid.

27 Ibid.

28 Bachman, "Violence Against American Indian and Alaska Native Women and the Criminal Justice Response."

29 Ibid.

30 Fox, "The Murder and Missing of Indigenous Women and Girls."

31 Ibid.

32 Breiding, "Prevalence and Risk Factors of Intimate Partner Violence in Eighteen U.S. States/Territories," 112.

33 Tjaden, "Extent, Nature, and Consequences of Intimate Partner Violence."

34 Breiding, "Prevalence and Risk Factors of Intimate Partner Violence in Eighteen U.S. States/Territories," 112; Britt, "Health Consequences of Criminal Victimization," 63; Campbell, "Health Consequences of Intimate Partner Violence," 1331; Kramer, "Prevalence of Intimate Partner Violence," 19; Macmillan, "Violence and the Life Course," 1; Thompson, "Intimate Partner Violence," 447.

35 Campbell, "Health Consequences of Intimate Partner Violence," 359.

36 Ibid.

37 Britt, "Health Consequences of Criminal Victimization," 63; Campbell, "Health Consequences of Intimate Partner Violence," 1331; Capaldi, "A Systematic Review of Risk Factors for Intimate Partner Violence," 231; Koss, "Relation of Criminal Victimization to Health Perceptions Among Women Medical Patents," 147; Macmillan, "Violence and the Life Course," 1; Slep et al., "Identifying Unique and Shared Risk Factors for Physical Intimate Partner Violence," 227.

38 Breiding, "Prevalence and Risk Factors of Intimate Partner Violence in Eighteen U.S. States/Territories," 112; Britt, "Health Consequences of Criminal Victimization," 63; Campbell, "Health Consequences of Intimate Partner Violence," 1331; Koss, "Relation of Criminal Victimization to Health Perceptions Among Women and Medical Patients," 147; Kramer, "Prevalence of Intimate Partner Violence," 19; Macmillan, "Violence and the Life Course," 1; Thompson, "Intimate Partner Violence," 447.

39 Bohn, "Lifetime Physical and Sexual Abuse," 333; Wahab, "Intimate Partner Violence and Sexual Assault," 353.

40 Burnette and Cannon, "It Will Always Continue Unless We Can Change Something," 1; Duran, "Intimate Partner Violence and Alcohol, Drug, and Mental Disorders," 11.

41 Fox, "Identifying the Needs of American Indian Women Who Sought Shelter," 251.
42 Deloria, *American Indians, American Justice*, 1.
43 Wolfe, "Settler Colonialism and the Elimination of the Native," 387.
44 Kohn, "Colonialism."
45 Helgesen, "Allotment of Justice," 441.
46 Stannard, "American Holocaust," 84.
47 Smith, "The Moral Limits of the Law."
48 Deloria, *American Indians, American Justice*.
49 Smith, "The Moral Limits of the Law," 71.
50 Yellow Horse Brave Heart, "The Return to the Sacred Path," 287.
51 Perry, "Impacts of Disparate Policing in Indian Country," 263.
52 Perry, "From Ethnocide to Ethnoviolence," 231; Perry, "Nobody Trusts Them!" 411; Perry, "Impacts of Disparate Policing in Indian Country," 263.
53 Ibid.
54 Ibid.
55 Helgesen, "Allotment of Justice," 441.
56 National Inquiry Into Missing and Murdered Indigenous Women and Girls, "Reclaiming Power and Place," 5.
57 Office of Public Affairs, "Attorney General William P. Barr Launches National Strategy."
58 Office of Press Secretary, "Executive Order on Establishing a Task Force."
59 Fox, "The Murder and Missing of Indigenous Women and Girls."
60 National Indian Child Welfare Association, *Child and Family Policy Update*.
61 US Commission on Civil Rights, "A Quiet Crisis."
62 Ibid.
63 US Commission on Civil Rights, "Broken Promises," 7.
64 Ibid.
65 *Tiwahe* means "family" in the Lakota language (Ortiz, *Tiwahe Initiative*).
66 Ortiz, *Tiwahe Initiative*.
67 US Commission on Civil Rights, "Broken Promises."
68 Ibid.
69 For a legislative overview, see Fox, "The Murder and Missing of Indigenous Women and Girls."
70 Bachman, "Violence Against American Indian and Alaska Native Women and the Criminal Justice Response."
71 US Commission on Civil Rights, "Broken Promises."
72 Barajas, "Here's the Latest on the Violence Against Women Act."
73 NCAI, *VAWA 2013's Special Domestic Violence Criminal Jurisdiction (SDVCJ) Five-Year Report*.
74 Ibid.
75 The National Congress of American Indians (NCAI) a nonprofit organization, advocates for a bright future for generations to come by taking the lead to gain

consensus on a constructive and promising vision for Indian Country. Founded in 1944, the NCAI is the oldest, largest, and most representative American Indian and Alaska Native organization serving the broad interests of tribal governments and communities.

76 National Congress of American Indians, *Policy Update*.
77 Stark and Hudon, "Colonization, Homelessness, and the Prostitution and Sex Trafficking of Native Women."
78 Southwest Indigenous Women's Coalition, "Resources."
79 LaPorte, "National Workgroup on Safe Housing for American Indian and Alaska Native Survivors."
80 Spamer, "Solving the Missing Indigenous Person Data Crisis."
81 Fox, "The Murder and Missing of Indigenous Women and Girls."

9

Using Evidence-Based Practices to Prevent Firearm Violence

JESENIA M. PIZARRO, KARISSA R. PELLETIER, APRIL M. ZEOLI, AND ANNE M. CORBIN

Firearms are a significant contributor to injury and death in the United States. According to the Centers for Disease Control and Prevention, approximately 100,000 individuals are injured with a firearm every year, and an additional 36,000 are fatally wounded.[1] Firearm injuries and death not only affect those who are injured. Research also has demonstrated that victims' families and friends are secondary victims, as they experience psychological distress and strain due to the injury or death of loved ones.[2] In addition to the human toll, firearm violence and injuries also have economic effects on society. A recent analysis suggests that gun violence costs an average of $229 billion per year due to medical and criminal justice expenses, loss of income, and pain and suffering of victims.[3] Moreover, crimes involving firearms may increase levels of fear among citizens[4] and decrease their trust of the police and other criminal justice agencies when offenders are not apprehended.[5] As a result, responding to firearm violence with effective prevention strategies and tactics is essential.

A promising approach is legislation to restrict firearms from individuals considered to be at high risk of using those weapons for illegal activities or self-injury. However, given the rights granted to American citizens under the United States Constitution, legislators and policy makers must be cautious not to overstep in limiting access to weaponry. In this chapter, we present a set of recommendations that can save American lives without infringing on the constitutional rights of law-abiding citizens who do not pose a risk to themselves or others. We start the chapter with a discussion of firearm legislation in the United States. We proceed to describe firearm violence in the country, as well as research of its nature and prevention, before concluding with a set of recommendations that have shown promise at decreasing firearm violence and injury and can pass constitutional muster.

The three strategies we discuss in this chapter are: permit-to-purchase licensing laws; firearm relinquishment for individuals prohibited from possession; and extreme risk protection orders. Permit-to-purchase licensing laws generally require individuals to apply for a firearm purchase permit in person at a local law enforcement agency, regardless of whether they want to purchase from a licensed dealer, an unlicensed dealer, or a private seller. To prevent unauthorized individuals from purchasing a firearm, this practice involves a criminal background check and may involve other measures such as fingerprinting. Firearm relinquishment laws require individuals who are forbidden to possess firearms—typically due to criminal convictions or domestic violence (DV) restraining orders—to relinquish any firearms they already possess.

Finally, extreme risk protection orders allow civil courts to temporarily suspend firearm rights for individuals who are legally able to own firearms yet are at high risk for committing violence against themselves or others, and to confiscate any firearms they possess, until the order is lifted.

Firearm Legislation in the United States

The United States is set apart from other industrialized countries by the protections it grants its citizens to own and use a firearm. The Second Amendment to the Constitution grants Americans the right "to keep and bear arms." However, there are limits to this right. The National Firearms Act of 1934 was the first federal regulation of the manufacture and transfer of firearms and imposed criminal and tax requirements on the purchase of machine guns, silencers, and sawed-off shotguns.[6] In 1938, the Federal Firearms Act was expanded to regulate the interstate exchange of firearms and ammunitions by requiring a federal firearm license and prohibiting the transfer of firearms to felons.[7]

Three decades later, the Federal Gun Control Act (GCA) of 1968[8] defined criteria that disqualify an individual from lawful firearm possession. Specifically, the GCA bars individuals from purchasing and possessing a firearm if they have been convicted of a crime punishable by one year or more of imprisonment; have been convicted of a misdemeanor DV offense; are currently the subject of a DV restraining order; have been adjudicated as mentally deficient or involuntarily committed to a mental institution; are fugitives from justice; are addicted to or use controlled substances; have been dishonorably discharged from the military; are illegal immigrants; and/or have renounced their US citizenship. Additionally, anyone under 21 years of age is prohibited from purchasing a firearm from a federally licensed distributor; however, individuals who are 18 years and older are allowed to possess a handgun, and those between age 18 and 20 can purchase firearms from unlicensed private distributors and private sellers according to federal law. Moreover, under federal law there is no established minimum age for the possession of long guns (i.e., shotguns, rifles, and carbines) or long-gun ammunition; individuals 18 years of age and older can purchase a long gun from a federally licensed dealer; and unlicensed dealers and private sellers can sell a long gun to anyone regardless of age.[9] In 1993, the Brady Handgun Violence Prevention Act (Brady Act) was appended to the GCA.[10] The Brady Act requires federally licensed dealers to complete a background check on purchasers. Individuals who meet the GCA's disqualifying criteria cannot legally purchase a firearm from a federally licensed dealer but may be able to do so from an unlicensed dealer.

States have also enacted firearm restrictions, with some adopting legislation that is stricter than federal law. For example, some states prohibit individuals with multiple convictions for alcohol-related offenses from possessing guns for periods of 1 to 5 years (e.g., Alaska, California, Maryland, Massachusetts, and the District of Columbia),[11] and the majority of states now have time-limited firearm prohibitions for individuals who were convicted of serious crimes as juveniles.[12] In Arizona, for example, juveniles convicted of an offense that would have been considered an adult felony cannot own a firearm for 10 years after their adjudication date or release from detention.[13] In California, these individuals are barred until their thirtieth birthday,[14] and in Connecticut such individuals are barred for life.[15] Several states (e.g., California, Connecticut, Massachusetts, and New York) and the District of Columbia have also increased the minimum legal age to purchase a firearm from a nonlicensed dealer to 21 instead of the federally allowed age of 18 to mirror the GCA's provisions governing licensed dealers.[16]

Firearms Regulation and the Supreme Court

Overriding federal and state efforts to regulate firearms is the Second Amendment to the Constitution and the United States Supreme Court's interpretation of its contents. In 2021, the Court prepared to hear arguments on a Second Amendment case for the first time in over a decade.[17] A brief history sets the context for what Supreme Court jurisprudence means for state regulation of firearms.

For the first 200 years following the adoption of the Second Amendment, the Supreme Court seemed reluctant to concretely define the scope of state power over the right to bear arms. In the 1960s, when the Court held that the Fourteenth Amendment's Due Process Clause incorporates much of the Bill of Rights, it never discussed the Second Amendment.[18] The Court's cautious treatment of Second Amendment questions ended in 2008 with the landmark *Heller* ruling.[19] In *Heller*, justices limited the power of the District of Columbia to regulate firearms within its borders by holding that law-abiding individuals have the right to keep firearms in their homes for self-defense purposes.[20] In 2010, the Court extended these protections to citizens of the 50 states,[21] and in 2016 the Court expanded the scope of its Second Amendment rulings to include any weapon that could be considered a "bearable" arm, even if that weapon had not existed when the Second Amendment was drafted.[22]

In 2019, the Court considered a challenge by the New York State Rifle & Pistol Association (NYSRPA) to a New York City rule that prohibited the transport of private firearms outside city limits, regardless of the purpose.[23] The Court granted certiorari to consider whether the ban violated the Second Amendment, the right to travel, or the Commerce Clause.[24] While the case was pending, New York City changed its rule to allow for such transport, rendering the case moot. However, rather than dismissing the challenge as resolved, the Court remanded the case back to the state Court of Appeals (New York's highest court) to consider whether the NYSRPA suffered damages.

Since the New York case, an additional conservative justice has been confirmed to the Court, giving conservatives a six-member majority. This shift in the Court's makeup has prompted speculation that the justices are poised to expand the rights of gun owners. Lending dimension to this speculation is the fact that the Court on April 26, 2021,[25] agreed to hear arguments on another NYSRPA case[26] focusing on an individual's application to carry a firearm outside the home for the purpose of self-defense.

If the Court agrees to further restrict firearm regulation, it will have to grapple with the fact that, since *Heller* (2008), federal courts have steadily supported states' rights to establish the parameters of the self-defense right, which encompasses the bulk of the Second Amendment's rationale, according to *Heller*.[27] Although this may countenance maintaining the status quo, the Court's increasingly conservative members may view the New York case as a tempting opportunity to establish new precedent. However, regardless of its result, the case reminds us that all legislation and rulemaking on firearm violence is open to potential reconsideration by the courts.

The Problem of Firearm Violence in the United States

Just as the United States is exceptional in its protection of gun rights, it is also notorious for its high rates of firearm injury and victimization. From 1999 to 2017, approximately 600,000 Americans lost their lives as a result of a firearms.[28] The bulk of these deaths were suicides (59%), followed by homicides (39%) and deaths that were unintentional or whose causes were undetermined (2%).[29] More recent statistics from the CDC indicate that, in 2018, approximately 40,000 people suffered a fatal injury from a firearm in the United States.[30] Of these, approximately 61% were suicides, 35% were homicides, and 2% were unintentional deaths.[31] National crime data reported in the Uniform Crime Reporting System present a grim relationship between firearms and crime. In 2018, 74% of homicides, 39% of robberies, and 26% of aggravated assaults were committed with a firearm.[32] Moreover, the vast majority of suicides and mass murders are committed with a firearm.[33] Research has also found a relationship between firearms and accidental injuries.[34] Indeed, thousands of people are unintentionally injured with a firearm every year in the United States.[35]

Firearm suicides, victimization, and offending are not equally distributed across the population. Some individuals are more at risk than others to offend or be victimized, and these patterns shift depending on the type of firearm use or outcome. Research suggests that past violent and criminal behavior is predictive of future firearm crime and victimization. For example, one study found that legal firearm purchasers with a criminal history of misdemeanor offenses were five times more likely to engage in a violent crime with a firearm than those without such a history.[36] Individuals who are involved in criminal networks, such as gangs, and have criminal associates also have increased odds of using a firearm in a violent crime or to be victimized by one,[37] and access to a firearm increases the risk of intimate partner homicide by men who are already known to be violent.[38] Alcohol and drug use/dependency are also risk factors for victimization and firearm crimes.[39]

The risk factors for harm to self, including suicidality, are different from risk of harm to others. Research has found that approximately 90% of individuals who commit suicide suffer from depression or other mental disorders.[40] Prior suicidal behavior and ideation and substance use are also risk factors for suicide.[41]

Access to Firearms in the United States

Prior studies have linked firearm-arm related crime and unintentional firearm injuries to the ready availability of firearms.[42] Current estimates suggest that there are approximately 393 million firearms in circulation in the United States.[43]

Firearms can be obtained from primary or secondary markets or by illegal means such as theft.[44] Primary markets involve the sale and distribution of firearms by federally licensed gun dealers. Research suggests that approximately 60% of gun sales occur in the primary market, but only approximately 14% of individuals who use a firearm during the commission of a crime obtain their weapons from this market.[45] Secondary markets involve the transfer of guns between individuals after purchase on the primary market. Secondary markets are not governed by federal law and are largely unregulated, unless they occur in a state that has enacted legislation specifically regulating them.[46] When a firearm is acquired from the secondary market in a state that does not regulate these purchases, purchasers are not required to undergo background checks, and there are usually no records maintained about the transaction. In this way, the secondary market facilitates firearm access for individuals who are prohibited from purchasing them. While approximately 20% of all gun sales occur in the secondary market,[47] approximately 80% of firearms used in crimes come from unlicensed secondary-market sellers.[48]

Offenders may also obtain a firearm is through criminal activity such as theft. Hundreds of thousands of firearms have been stolen from individuals who purchased their firearm legally through primary and secondary markets. Studies suggest that anywhere between 250,000 and 600,000 guns are stolen every year.[49]

The secondary market appears to be the preferred method for firearm acquisition among individuals who are prohibited from legally purchasing and owning a firearm, as well as those who plan to use the weapon in an illegal act.[50] Using data from a national survey of state prison inmates, Vittes and colleagues found that over 95% of offenders obtained firearms through a source that did not require a background check.[51] Specifically, studies have found that criminals rely on a diverse set of pathways for acquiring guns, which include corrupt licensed dealers, unlicensed sellers, straw purchasers, residential theft, and theft from firearm dealers, carriers, or manufacturers.[52] Studies that have focused on crimes committed with firearms have found that individuals who cannot obtain a firearm legally may obtain one through a straw purchase from an unlicensed dealer or private sellers in states that do not require background checks.[53] Social networks also appear to be a source of firearms used in the commission of crimes.[54] A qualitative study of active offenders in four Los Angeles jails found that most obtained firearms through their social network, purchased them illegally, or received them as a gift.[55] Research that has examined firearm acquisition by juvenile offenders also suggests that youths most often obtain their firearms from friends.[56] Juveniles also acquire firearms via pathways such as straw purchases, corrupt licensed dealers, unregulated dealers, gun shows, and theft.[57]

Preventing Firearm Violence

In light of the research evidence that elucidates who is at the highest risk for victimization, offending, and self-harm, and how these individuals get access to firearms, it is possible to design specific strategies that limit the access of these individuals to firearms, in turn saving lives. This section outlines three legislative strategies that can reduce the accessibility of firearms to risky individuals: permit-to-purchase licensing laws, firearm relinquishment laws, and extreme risk protection orders.

As mentioned earlier, the Federal Gun Control Act (GCA) of 1968[58] defines criteria that disqualify an individual from lawful firearm possession These include a felony or DV conviction, addiction to controlled substances, and adjudicated mental deficiency, among others.[59] Although one panel of a federal appellate court has recently invalidated the GCA's age requirements for handgun sales,[60] the GCA largely still stands as enacted more than 50 years ago. In 1993, the GCA was strengthened with the addition of the Brady Handgun Violence Prevention Act (Brady Act), which requires federally-licensed dealers to complete a background check on purchasers.[61] Federally-licensed dealers cannot sell firearms to individuals who are disqualified under the GCA.

However, research suggests that these laws do not prevent access to firearms by a majority of the individuals who are most at risk of using a firearm in a violent act. This is because individuals can access and purchase firearms through unregulated secondary markets or illegal means.[62] Unfortunately, current legislation mostly regulates primary markets. As a result, it is important to explore strategies and legislation that will address secondary markets and target other ways to decrease access to firearms for individuals at risk of using weapons to harm themselves and others.

Promising Statutes

There are a number of laws at the federal, state, and local levels that can help stem firearm violence in the United States. These include permit-to-purchase licensing, firearm relinquishment, and extreme protection orders.

Permit-to-Purchase Licensing Laws

The Brady Act opens a regulatory gap between the purchase of a firearm from a federally licensed dealer—in which the buyer must pass a criminal background check—and purchases from a secondary market, in which no check is required. To close this gap, some states have enacted comprehensive background check laws (CBCs).[63] CBCs require that secondary market sellers conduct a point-of-sale background check before selling a firearm to an individual. Generally, a federally licensed firearm dealer performs these background checks on behalf of private sellers. Research examining CBCs found that private sellers' compliance with the background checks is inconsistent.[64] Specifically, when Castillo-Carniglia and colleagues examined the adoption of CBCs in Colorado, Delaware, and Washington, they found that CBCs were associated with an increase in background checks only in Delaware.[65] Moreover, research examining the relationship between CBCs and homicide and suicide rates concluded that the repeal of CBCs in Indiana and Tennessee was not associated with increases in homicide and suicide rates.[66] These findings suggest that CBCs do not have a significant effect on intentional firearm fatalities.

Some states have gone beyond CBCs, enacting permit-to-purchase laws (PTPs)[67] that apply when an individual seeks to purchase a firearm from a licensed dealer *or* a private seller.[68] The majority of state PTPs require that individuals apply for purchasing permits in person at a local law enforcement agency (e.g., a police department or sheriff's office). This in-person application is one of the key differences between CBCs and PTPs, and it may be particularly important in ensuring that prohibited individuals do not purchase firearms. Prohibited persons who might otherwise offer fake identification or attempt a straw purchase (i.e., having someone else purchase the firearm for them) with a dealer or private seller might be deterred by the prospect of committing those illegal acts in front of law enforcement.[69] Additionally, some PTPs require law enforcement to fingerprint the purchaser, which increases the chances that a prohibited purchaser would be caught when using a fake identity. PTPs may also include a waiting period between applying for and receiving a permit to purchase or license. For example, Hawaii mandates a 14-day waiting period between application and issuance of a firearm permit.[70]

Studies that have examined the effects of PTPs have generally found mixed support. Although one 13-state study found that such laws had no effect on firearm homicide rates,[71] other studies have reported that they reduce statewide homicide rates. In addition, research on urban violence has found that firearm homicides decreased after the enactment of

PTPs.[72] Similarly, two studies examining the effect of a Connecticut PTP found a 40% reduction in firearm homicides during the first 10 years following its enactment.[73] Additionally, the repeal of PTPs has been associated with an increase in firearm homicides. Following the repeal of Missouri's PTP, firearm homicide rates increased there between 17% and 27%.[74] Other researchers have found similar increases following states' repeal of PTPs.[75] Overall, this research suggests that PTPs may help reduce firearm-related homicides.

The research examining PTPs' effect on suicide rates is scant but promising. The one study that has examined this relationship found positive results. In that research, Crifasi and colleagues used a synthetic control model to study whether Missouri's repeal or Connecticut's enactment of a PTP was associated with firearm suicide rates.[76] The model estimated that Connecticut's PTP was associated with a 15.4% decrease in firearm suicide rates, while Missouri's repeal of its PTP was associated with a 16.1% increase in firearm suicide rates.[77]

Firearm Relinquishment Laws

While PTP laws attempt to prevent prohibited individuals from purchasing firearms in the secondary market, firearm relinquishment laws attempt to remove firearms from newly prohibited individuals who may already have a firearm. At present, few states have passed legislation requiring prohibited individuals to relinquish their firearms.[78] Those that have done so focus primarily on individuals with a current DV restraining order (DVRO) or, less commonly, a DV misdemeanor conviction.[79] Verifying relinquishment can be challenging. In some states, individuals who are the subject of a DVRO must relinquish all firearms for the duration of the court order.[80] Other states, such as Tennessee, require a sworn affidavit by defendants attesting to their compliance with the DVRO firearm relinquishment law.[81] Still other states, such as California and Connecticut, have legislation that falls into both of these categories.[82]

Unsurprisingly, states' relinquishment processes also vary.[83] For example, California's DVRO firearm relinquishment law requires newly prohibited persons to relinquish their firearms immediately upon a law enforcement officer's request or within 24 hours of being served with the DVRO.[84] The owner may transfer the firearms to a licensed firearm dealer, instead of relinquishing it to law enforcement, but must file a receipt of this transfer with the justice system within 48 hours of being served with the order. In contrast, Connecticut's firearm relinquishment law requires prohibited persons to turn over their firearms to a law enforcement agency, a federally licensed firearm dealer, or another person who is not prohibited.[85] If the prohibited person wants to exercise this third option, a law enforcement agency must run a background check on the new possessor of the firearms prior to the transfer. After transfer, the prohibited individual must provide the law enforcement agency with proof of relinquishment. Deadlines for firearm relinquishment also vary by state, from 24 hours to 72 hours or longer.[86]

A growing body of research is evaluating the impact of these relinquishment laws. One study considered an initiative in two California counties through which law enforcement screened DVRO respondents for firearm possession and required their relinquishment. The researchers concluded that safe recovery of firearms from DVRO respondents was effective.[87] Other studies have considered DVRO firearm relinquishment laws and intimate partner homicide (IPH). Two panel studies examining state IPH trends found that states with firearm relinquishment provisions in their DVRO firearm laws experienced an associated 10–14% decrease in IPH.[88] Although the literature examining the impact of firearm relinquishment laws is still thin, the burgeoning research suggests that this is a promising strategy to reduce intimate partner homicide. It is possible that this reduction in injury may be seen in other areas of firearm violence as well.

Extreme Risk Protection Orders

Firearm suicides, victimization, and offenses are not equally distributed across the population. Some individuals are especially at risk to harm themselves or others, depending upon the type of firearm used or their background or condition. Knowing these risk factors, it is possible to prevent such individuals from easily accessing firearms.

As we mentioned above, research suggests that past incidents of violent and criminal behaviors are predictive of future use-of-firearm crimes and victimization. For example, one study found that legal firearm purchasers with a criminal history of misdemeanor offenses were five times more likely to engage in a violent crime with a firearm than those without such a history.[89] Individuals who are involved in criminal networks, such as gangs, and have criminal associates also are more likely to use a firearm in a violent crime.[90] Access to a firearm increases the risk of IPH by violent male intimate partners,[91] and use or dependence on alcohol and drugs is also a risk factor for victimization and offending in a firearm-related crime.[92]

And also as discussed above, the risk factors for harm to self, particularly suicide, are different from risk of harm to others. Research has found that approximately 90% of individuals who commit suicide suffer from depression or another other mental illness.[93] Prior suicidal ideation or behavior and substance use are also risk factors for suicide.[94]

Some states have used behavioral risk indicators to legislate extreme risk protection orders (ERPOs).[95] ERPOs are a tool intended to reduce the risk of firearm violence for those who can otherwise legally purchase or possess firearms. Modeled on DVRO firearm restrictions (which, as discussed above, have been found to reduce IPH),[96] ERPOs are civil court orders that remove access to firearms for those who are at high risk for committing violence against themselves or others but who are otherwise legally entitled to possess firearms.[97] Law enforcement officers and, in some states, clinicians or family and household members can petition the court for an ERPO that will temporarily restrict an at-risk person's access to firearms. When the threat of violence is imminent, ERPOs may be implemented when alternative measures such as arrest and psychiatric hospitalization are inappropriate or have been proven to be ineffective.[98]

Connecticut enacted the first risk-based gun removal law in the nation in 1999,[99] and Indiana followed suit in 2004.[100] However, the majority of ERPO laws are recent enactments, most coming after January 2016.[101] Given the recency of ERPOs, there is limited research on their efficacy. However, the emerging research suggests that ERPOs may be effective at preventing firearm suicide. For example, Swanson and colleagues analyzed individual-level data on firearm removal cases in both Connecticut and Indiana to estimate whether the orders saved lives.[102] Their results suggested that, in Indiana, firearm removals saved one life for every ten removals. They also found a reduction in firearm suicides in Connecticut. Kivisto and Phalen examined Connecticut's and Indiana's risk-based firearm removal laws. They found that Indiana's law was associated with a 7.5% reduction in firearm suicides over a 10-year period. After Connecticut's ERPO was updated in 2007, that law was associated with a 13.7% decrease in suicides.[103]

Perhaps the most commonly discussed use of ERPOs is the prevention of mass shootings, and it is in the wake of mass shootings that many states have passed these laws. Wintemute and colleagues examined 159 ERPO petitions in California (known there as "gun violence restraining orders") and found that 21 petitions detailed threats of a mass shooting.[104] Those ERPOs were approved, and as of this writing none of the potential mass shootings had been carried out.

Recommendations

As evidenced from the research, existing laws can help decrease firearm victimization and self-harm, but these laws are not in place in all states. There are four primary challenges. First, while the federal government has attempted to address firearm violence with the GCA, multiple loopholes in that law allow dangerous individuals to acquire and maintain possession of firearms. The Brady Act requires a criminal background check only if purchasers buy a gun from a licensed firearm dealer, and few states have enacted laws that require background checks for secondary market purchases. This allows the sale and distribution of firearms to individuals who would be barred from purchasing a firearm in the primary market. Second, while some states have enacted PTP laws to govern the secondary markets, there is no consistency among the states regarding which persons are barred from purchasing a firearm. Individuals banned from purchasing firearms in one state can simply purchase them in another state, which creates a loophole in states with more restrictive policies.[105] Third, there is a gap in laws that require relinquishment of firearms by individuals who possess a firearm but become disqualified from possession. Finally, individuals who are legally able to purchase and possess firearms may temporarily become at high risk for firearm violence.

PTPs, firearm relinquishment laws, and ERPOs can help close these loopholes. Research has found that these laws are associated with decreases in firearm homicide and suicides. As a result, we make several recommendations.

First, *states should enact PTPs that are consistent with the GCA.* As indicated in the review above, the Brady Act's requirement that federally licensed firearm dealers conduct a prepurchase background check can be circumvented in some states when buyers purchase a gun from a private seller. Expanding permit-to-purchase licensing laws throughout the 50 states would close this loophole, preventing prohibited individuals from purchasing and possessing a firearm, which in turn could reduce firearm violence.[106]

Second, *states should require the relinquishment of firearms by those who become disqualified from ownership.* In many jurisdictions across the nation, when individuals become prohibited from firearm possession, they are allowed to maintain possession of their firearms by default; no one from the justice system is responsible for monitoring firearm relinquishment. To safeguard citizens from those the justice system has disqualified from gun possession, states need to address this relinquishment gap. Given the promising results of research examining the effect of firearm relinquishment laws on IPH,[107] these laws might have the potential to reduce other types of firearm violence.[108]

Third, *states should enact extreme risk protection order laws to prevent gun access by those who are at high risk of committing gun violence.* These civil orders temporarily restrict the firearm rights of those otherwise legally able to purchase and possess firearms when those individuals are at high risk or in crisis. While this is a relatively new legislative tool, the research thus far suggests these orders may reduce firearm suicides and have been used to prevent mass shootings.[109]

Legal Implications for Recommendations

The Supreme Court's Second Amendment jurisprudence has critical implications for our recommendations to prevent firearm violence. Since the Court has historically upheld state authority to regulate firearm possession, it stands to reason (short of banning an entire class of firearms altogether) that the Court would defer to a state's regulation requiring private purchasers to apply in person for a firearm permit through a local law enforcement agency. Such a regulatory body rests within the states' Tenth Amendment police power (i.e., the power to provide for the welfare and safety of the citizenry) and comports with the Court's precedent of allowing states to determine *how* firearms are regulated. Naturally, this could all change with the Court's decision during the 2021–22 term; however, that would require a major departure from the Court's own precedent.

One creative challenge to PTP laws could involve the Commerce Clause given that the sale of a firearm reasonably relates to commerce. However, prior efforts to tie the Commerce Clause to firearm possession have been largely unsuccessful, as evidenced by the Court's 1995 decision in *United States v. Lopez*.[110] *Lopez* provided the Court with its first Commerce Clause challenge since the New Deal and presented a discrete question on the federal Gun Free School Zones Act of 1990 (GFSZA): In creating the GFSZA, did Congress exceed its Commerce Clause authority? As enacted, the GFSZA prohibited individuals from knowingly possessing a firearm in a location they know, or should reasonably know, to be a school zone.[111] The Court ruled that the statute exceeded congressional power under the Commerce Clause because, even though Congress has the authority to regulate interstate commerce, the GFSZA was not sufficiently related to commerce to justify its constitutionality. Post-*Lopez* cases heard by lower federal courts have demonstrated mixed recognition of a tenuous relationship between firearm possession and the Commerce Clause. However, because the issue in *Lopez* involved possession (not sale) of homemade machine guns, a more narrowly tailored regulation concerning firearm sales might withstand judicial scrutiny.[112]

For the reasons described above, states are empowered with the Tenth Amendment police power to make laws for the welfare and safety of their citizens. Among these duties should be the relinquishment of weapons by those who become disqualified to own them. Not only are states best situated to carry out enforcement of this particular type of law; disqualification rests on the wrongdoer's misbehavior and not the weapon itself. As such, it would be difficult to imagine the Court accepting for review a case in which the issue focuses on a state applying its authority to reinforce its own laws.

While unlikely, based on the reasons already discussed, it is possible that the Court could be open to hearing challenges to the ERPO laws recommended in this chapter. ERPOs provide an outright—albeit temporary—ban by a state or municipality against an individual from possessing a firearm. As indicated in the *Heller* decision, the Court appears willing to intervene when states employ outright bans to regulate firearm possession. However, the prohibitions under ERPOs apply only to particular individuals threatening the welfare and safety of a state's citizenry, an area over which states have broad authority under the Tenth Amendment. In addition, the Court's 2009 decision in *United States v. Hayes*[113] recognized the constitutionality of a federal law that prohibited firearm possession by individuals convicted of domestic violence, even such misdemeanor acts as pushing or grabbing.[114] For that matter, ERPOs are temporary, thereby deflating any argument that their impact is tantamount to an outright ban on firearm possession.

Still, there are indicators that the Court, now more than ever, is open to hearing cases on the Second Amendment and may be interested in expanding related gun rights.[115] While it is unclear how many justices are eager to tackle Second Amendment cases, at least three—Justices Alito, Gorsuch, and Thomas—all wrote that they would have sided with the gun owners in the 2019 New York City case had the Court not sent it back to the state court.[116] Additionally, even though Justice Kavanagh added his voice to the majority opinion in that case, he encouraged his fellow justices to consider accepting future Second Amendment cases he believed the Court would have the opportunity to face before too long.[117] It is reasonable to imagine that Justice Barrett might follow the lead of her fellow conservative justices to solidify the required 5–4 majority. *That the Court is willing to hear cases challenging either the Second Amendment or state authority to regulate it could pose a threat to the feasibility of this chapter's recommendations.*

At the time this volume was going to press, the Supreme Court had not released its decision on the *Bruen* case, though oral arguments were presented on November 3, 2021. In addition, even though four petitions have invited the Court to consider related Second Amendment questions in the 2022 term, none of them has been granted at the time of this writing. Among the questions these cases invite the Court to consider are whether the Second Amendment applies outside the home (*Young v. Hawaii*); the scrutiny level of Second Amendment cases related to firearm possession inside the home (*P.Z. v. New Jersey*); how or whether courts should defer to federal agency interpretation of statutes when applied to criminal laws (*Aposhian v. Garland*); and the scrutiny level of state laws that impeded federal rights (*Hatch v. Minnesota*).[118]

As it gears up for a session with several new justices—all of whom lean conservative—the Court may prove itself less predictable than its history and jurisprudence indicate. Regardless, the research shows that the recommendations presented here are promising and practicable, leaving their feasibility in the hands of the nine justices.

Conclusion

Firearm-related violence and injuries are a public health concern in the United States. Thousands of lives are lost, and many more are injured every year, harming the victims' families, friends, and communities and society as a whole. It is imperative to address this problem and to implement legislation that will help decrease firearm violence. This chapter has summarized three strategies that show promise at saving lives: PTPs, firearm relinquishment laws, and ERPOs. These laws are associated with decreases in homicides and suicides and have the potential to prevent mass shootings. Moreover, based on previous court decisions, our recommendations ought to pass constitutional muster. However, in the event that the current Court diverges from its own precedents in its upcoming New York decision—for instance, by constricting states' firearm regulatory authority—lawmakers at the federal, state, and local levels will have to find creative ways to tailor their efforts accordingly if they wish to reduce firearm violence and save lives.

NOTES

1 CDC, "Fatal Injury Reports 2020"; CDC, "Nonfatal Injury Reports 2020." It is important to note that the CDC warns that its estimates of nonfatal firearm injuries may be "unstable and potentially unreliable"; however, we use them here since they are the best available statistics of firearm injuries.
2 Armour, "Journey of . . . , 2020."
3 Follman et al., "The Cost . . . , 2015."
4 Kruger et al., "Assault Injury . . . , 2007."
5 Pizarro, Terrill, and LoFaso, "The Impact . . . , 2020."
6 National Firearms Act of 1934, 48 Stat. 1236. Revised 1938, 52 Stat. 1250.
7 52 Stat. 1250.
8 18 U.S.C. § 922.
9 18 U.S.C. § 922.

10 107 Stat. 1536.

11 Alaska Stat. § 11.61.200; Cal. Welf. & Inst. Code §§ 5250,5260,5270.15; Md. Code
    Ann., Pub. Safety §§ 5–101(g) and 5–134(b); Mass. Gen. Laws ch. 140, §§ 129B;
    D.C. Code Ann. § 50–2201.05(b).

12 Alaska Stat. § 11.61.200(a)(10); Ariz. Rev. Stat. § 13–3113; Cal. Penal Code §§ 23515,
    29800–30010; Conn. Gen. Stat. §§ 53a-217; Fla. Stat. §§ 790.23; ss. Gen. Laws ch.
    140, §§ 129B; Utah Code § 76-10-503(1).

13 Ariz. Rev. Stat. § 13–3113.

14 Cal. Penal Code §§ 23515, 29800–30010.

15 Conn. Gen. Stat. §§ 53a-217.

16 Cal. Penal Code § 27505; Conn. Gen. Stat. § 29–36f(a); Mass. Gen. Laws ch.
    140, §§ 130, 131E(a); N.Y. Penal Law § 400.00(1)(a). Honorably discharged US
    military or New York National Guard personnel are excluded; D.C. Code Ann. §
    7–2502.03(a)(1).

17 Totenberg, "Supreme Court to Take Up 1st Major Gun Rights Case in More Than
    a Decade.".

18 Incorporation of the Second Amendment would occur nearly 50 years later in
    McDonald v. City of Chicago, 561 U.S. 742 (2010).

19 D.C. v. Heller, 554 U.S. 570 (2008).

20 Ibid.

21 McDonald v. Chicago, 561 U.S. 742 (2010).

22 Caetano v. Massachusetts, 136 S. Ct. 1027 (2016).

23 N.Y. Rifle & Pistol Assoc. v. City of New York, 140 S. Ct. 1525 (2020).

24 Ibid.

25 Supreme Court website.

26 N.Y. State Rifle & Pistol Ass'n, Inc. v. Beach, 19-156-cv- (2d Cir. Aug. 26, 2020).

27 Erickson, "Second Amendment Federalism."

28 Goldstick et al., "US Firearm Related Mortality, 2020."

29 Ibid., 1648.

30 CDC, "Fatal Injury Reports 2020."

31 Ibid; the remaining 2 percent were legal interventions.

32 FBI, "Crime in the United States, 2018."

33 Duwe, "A History . . . , 2014"; Anglemyer et al., "The Accessibility . . . , 2014."

34 Levin and McKnight, "Firearms and . . . , 2017."

35 CDC, "Nonfatal Injury Reports 2020."

36 Wintemute et al., "Prior Misdemeanor . . . , 1998."

37 Cook et al., "Underground Drug . . . , 2007"; Sheley & Wright, "Motivations for
    Gun . . . , 1993."

38 Campbell et al., "Risk Factors . . . , 2003."

39 Wintemute, "Alcohol Misuse . . . , 2015"; Galea et al., "Drugs and . . . , 2002."

40 Mościcki, "Epidemiology of . . . , 2001."

41 Hawton et al., "Risk Factors . . . , 2013."

42 Monuteaux et al., "Firearm Ownership . . . , 2015"; Miller et al., "Firearm Availability . . . , 2001."

43 Karp, "Estimating Global . . . , 2018."

44 Cook and Ludwig, "Guns in America . . . , 2006"; Cook et al., "Regulating Gun . . . , 1995."

45 Harlow, *Firearm Use . . . , 2002*; Koper, "Crime Gun Risk . . . , 2014"; Wintemute, "Where the . . . , 2002."

46 Cook and Ludwig, "Guns in America . . . , 2006."

47 Miller et al., "Firearm Acquisition . . . , 2017."

48 Vittes, Vernick, and Webster, "Legal Status . . . , 2013."

49 Cook et al., "Regulating Gun Markets . . . , 1995"; Hemenway, Azrael, and Miller, "Whose Guns . . . , 2017."

50 Cook et al., "Regulating Gun Markets . . . , 1995"; Koper, "Crime Gun Risk . . . , 2014," Cook et al., "Sources of Guns . . . , 2015."

51 Vittes, Vernick, and Webster, "Legal Status . . . , 2013."

52 Braga et al., "Interpreting the Empirical . . . , 2012."

53 Wintemute, "Frequency of and Responses . . . , 2013."

54 Cook et al., "Sources of Guns . . . , 2015."

55 Chestnut et al., "Not an Iron Pipeline . . . , 2017."

56 Ash et al., "Gun Acquisition and Use . . . , 1996."

57 Braga and Kennedy, "The Illicit Acquisition . . . , 2001."

58 18 U.S.C. § 922.

59 However, those between age 18 and 20 can purchase firearms from private distributors according to federal law.

60 Fritze, "Law Banning Handgun Sales to Americans Under 21 Violates Second Amendment, Court Rules."

61 107 Stat. 1536.

62 Webster and Wintemute, "Effects of Policies . . . , 2015."

63 See Giffords, "Universal Background Checks . . . , 2020," for a list of states.

64 Castillo-Carniglia et al., "Comprehensive Background . . . , 2018."

65 Ibid.

66 Kagawa et al., "Repeal of Comprehensive . . . , 2018."

67 Naturally, if the Supreme Court decides that a state's denial of an individual's application for a permit to carry a firearm outside the home for self-defense is a violation of that individual's Second Amendment rights, that outcome could heavily impede the mitigation effect (and constitutionality) of permit-to-purchase laws.

68 See Giffords, "Licensing," for a list of states.

69 Webster and Wintemute, "Effects of Policies . . . , 2015."

70 Haw. Rev. Stat. Ann. §§ 134–3(a), 134–2(e).

71 Gius, "Effects of Permit-to-Purchase . . . , 2017."

72 Crifasi et al., "Association Between Firearms . . . , 2018."

73 Hasegawa et al., "Bracketing in . . . , 2019"; Rudolph et al., "Association Between . . . , 2015."

74 Hasegawa et al., "Bracketing in . . . , 2019."

75 Webster et al., "Effects of the Repeal . . . , 2014."

76 Crifasi et al., "Effects of Changes . . . , 2015."

77 Ibid.

78 See Giffords, "Categories of Prohibited People . . . , 2020," for a list of states.

79 Ibid.

80 Wis. Stat. §§ 813.1285(3), (4).

81 Tenn. Code Ann. § 36-3-625.

82 Cal. Penal Code § 29810(a); Conn. Gen. Stat. § 29–36k(a).

83 Zeoli et al., "Removing Firearms . . . , 2019."

84 Cal. Fam. Code § 6389.

85 Conn. Gen. Stat. § 29–36k(a).

86 Zeoli et al., "Retracted: Analysis . . . , 2018."

87 Wintemute et al., "Identifying Armed . . . , 2014."

88 Zeoli et al., "Retracted: Analysis . . . , 2018"; Díez et al., "State intimate . . . , 2017."

89 Wintemute et al., "Prior Misdemeanor, 1998."

90 Cook et al., "Underground Drug . . . , 2007"; Sheley and Wright, "Motivations for Gun . . . , 1993."

91 Campbell et al., "Risk Factors . . . , 2003."

92 Wintemute, "Alcohol Misuse . . . , 2015"; Galea et al., "Drugs and . . . , 2002."

93 Mościcki, "Epidemiology of . . . , 2001."

94 Hawton et al., "Risk Factors . . . , 2013."

95 See Giffords, "Extreme Risk Protective Orders . . . , 2020," for a list of states.

96 Zeoli et al., "Retracted: Analysis . . . , 2018"; Vigdor and Mercy. "Do Laws, 2006"; Zeoli and Webster, "Effects of . . . , 2010."

97 Shen, "A Triggered . . . , 2018"; Wintenmute et al., "Extreme Risk . . . , 2019."

98 Frattaroli et al., "Gun Violence . . . , 2015" Roskam and Chaplin, "The Gun . . . , 2017"; Swanson, "Understanding the . . . , 2019."

99 Conn. Gen. Stat. § 29–38c(a).

100 Ind. Code Ann. § 35-47-14-2.

101 Frizzell and Chien, "Extreme Risk . . . , 2019."

102 Swanson et al., "Implementation and . . . , 2017"; Swanson et al., "Criminal Justice . . . , 2019."

103 Kivisto and Phalen, "Effects of . . . , 2018."

104 Wintemute et al., "Extreme Risk . . . , 2019."

105 Olson et al., "American Firearm . . . , 2019."

106 Crifasi et al., "Association Between . . . , 2018"; Hasegawa et al., "Bracketing in . . . , 2019"; Rudolph et al., "Association Between . . . , 2015"; Webster et al., "Effects of . . . , 2014."

107 Zeoli et al., "Removing Firearms . . . , 2019"; Díez et al., "State Intimate . . . , 2017."

108 Hemenway, "Reducing Firearms . . . , 2017."

109 Kivisto and Phalen, "Effects of . . . , 2018"; Wintemute et al., "Extreme Risk . . . , 2019."

110 U.S. v. Lopez, 514 U.S. 549 (1995).

111 Ibid.

112 U.S. v. Rybar, 103 F.3d 273 (3d Cir. 1996).

113 U.S. v. Hayes, 555 U.S. 415 (2009).

114 U.S. v. Castleman, 572 U.S. 157 (2014).

115 At the time of this writing, the Court is prepared to consider a Second Amendment challenge to a New York law prohibiting concealed carry permits.

116 Higgens, "Supreme Court Eyes More Gun Cases."

117 Ibid.

118 The four named cases are: *Young v. Hawaii*, 20-1639, 915 F.3d 681 (2019); *P.Z. v. New Jersey*, 21-175 [J.S.] v. [P.Z.], No. FV-03-001864-18, Superior Court of New Jersey (judgments entered May 25, 2018, June 1, 2018, and June 5, 2018); *Aposhian v. Garland*, 21-159, 958 F.3d 969 (2020); and *Hatch v. Minnesota*, 21-667, *State v. Hatch*, File No. A20-0176 (Minn. Sup. Ct. filed Aug. 4, 2021).

10

Rural Criminal Justice Reform

PAMELA R. METZGER

Rural communities across the United States confront a criminal justice crisis. Rural residents have the same rights as their metropolitan peers. But rural criminal justice systems are too geographically remote to take advantage of many criminal justice resources, have caseload volumes that are too small to independently support "best practices," and have too few experienced criminal law professionals to meet local needs.[1] The consequences of geographic isolation, small scale, and professional scarcity ripple across rural criminal justice systems and reach far beyond any courthouse door or prison wall.

Police officers, lawyers, judges, and corrections staff in these regions are stretched thin by their need to serve large geographic areas. Courts sometimes meet infrequently, forcing defendants to wait for weeks before they can see a lawyer or obtain pretrial release. Courts sometimes meet in outdated buildings with cramped courtrooms that—even before the COVID-19 pandemic—could scarcely accommodate the ordinary rigors of criminal procedure. Lawyers may be scarce and experienced criminal practitioners scarcer still. Little wonder, then, that rural incarceration rates continue to rise even as urban rates decline.

While our national conversations about criminal justice research and reform focus almost exclusively on urban legal systems, the success of criminal justice reforms in the United States turns, in part, on rural criminal justice systems. Nearly 20% of the nation's population lives in nonmetropolitan areas,[2] and those areas are increasingly important drivers of mass incarceration.[3] And as the COVID-19 pandemic illustrates, there are no clean dividing lines between rural, urban, and suburban criminal justice systems. A rural jail that serves as a prisoner transfer station can quickly become a COVID-19 "super-spreader facility," pumping the national prison pipelines full of people who contracted the novel coronavirus during their brief rural stay.[4]

In this chapter I begin with a brief summary of the rural demographic and economic trends that help shape rural criminal systems. Then, rural criminal justice systems are defined and described by their operational characteristics: geographic isolation, small scale, and professional scarcity. I offer two examples of how the challenges of rural criminal justice short-change rural residents and communities. To underscore the national importance of investing in rural justice reform, I will highlight how rural jails and prisons impact the entire nation. I conclude by offering three big ideas for advancing criminal justice reform in rural settings.

Rural Criminal Justice Systems

Where is rural America located? And what are rural criminal justice systems? There are no simple answers, but one might begin by attempting to define "rurality." Unfortunately, there is no national consensus about which statistical criteria best define that term.[5] Most definitions use statistical measures—such as population density or proximity to urban areas—but there is no unanimity about which measures matter.[6] There are more than a dozen federal agency definitions of "rural," and all of them are different.[7]

In lieu of adopting a single definition of "rurality," one might instead summarize characteristics of rural America that exist regardless of which statistical definition one employs. Most rural communities in the United States are becoming poorer, less educated, and even more sparsely populated.[8] Rural residents are less likely to have completed a four-year college degree than their urban counterparts[9] and are more likely to be poor or uninsured.[10] One in three rural counties has a poverty rate above 20%.[11] Since 1990, over 3 million people have moved away from rural areas.[12] Because younger residents led the exodus,[13] the median rural age is now 51— six years older than the median urban age of 45.[14] Contrary to stereotype, US rural communities are racially and ethnically diverse. In the Black Belt of southern Alabama and Mississippi, some rural communities are more than 70% African American.[15] Over half of American Indian and Alaska Native people live in rural and small-town areas,[16] and Hispanic people are increasingly moving to rural areas.[17]

Rural economies face "slow-to-recover labor markets, population loss accelerated by urban migration, and an aging workforce," which taken together reduce local sales, income, and property tax revenues.[18] Limited internet access slows educational and occupational opportunities (22% of rural residents lack access to broadband service).[19] Rural communities struggle to recruit and retain professionals in areas such as law, industry, and medicine.[20]

Services often associated with criminal justice reform—such as medical and psychiatric treatments and educational and occupational therapies—are scarce and prohibitively far away in rural America.[21] Sixty percent of rural residents live in "mental health professional shortage areas," where there are too few mental health care providers to satisfy the local need.[22] About half of nonurban areas have no psychologist, 65% have no psychiatrists, and 81% have no psychiatric nurse practitioners.[23] And while rural areas have been hit particularly hard by the opioid epidemic,[24] more than 50% of rural counties do not have anyone licensed to provide medication-assisted treatment for opioid addiction.[25] All these factors create a grim foundation for rural criminal justice operations and reforms.

Defining Rural Criminal Justice Systems

Until very recently, there has been a marked absence of research and scholarship focusing on rural criminal legal systems. Rural policing and rural jails have attracted some scholarly attention, but comprehensive research on rural criminal *systems*—from arrest to court process to corrections to reentry—has been almost nonexistent. However, the Deason Criminal Justice Reform Center (Deason Center) at the SMU Dedman School of Law has begun to fill that research gap.

As the nation's only university research center committed to exploring STAR (small, tribal, and rural) criminal legal systems, the Deason Center is an important resource for rural justice practitioners and scholars. Its interdisciplinary researchers investigate rural criminal process and procedure, with a particular focus on the right to counsel and early-stage criminal procedure.[26] The Deason Center convenes research roundtables and online webinars that engage rural communities and rural legal professionals from all stages of the criminal process and from all areas of the nation.

In 2018, the Deason Center convened the nation's first summit addressed solely to rural criminal justice. That summit explored the challenges and opportunities that inhere in rural criminal legal systems. A second summit, held in 2019, focused on the intersection of criminal justice, substance use disorders, and mental illness in the rural United States. At each summit, a well-respected group of rural prosecutors, criminal defense attorneys, judges, law enforcement officers, corrections professionals, and community members joined criminal justice researchers and reformers to discuss the challenges and opportunities that inhere in the nation's rural justice systems.

An important outcome of the rural summits was the recognition that rural criminal justice systems often breach, blur, or transcend the boundaries associated with statistical and geographic measures of rurality. Put another way, it is accurate to say that the borders of rural criminal justice systems are porous. A statistically rural area that shares criminal justice resources with an adjacent metropolitan community may have a legal system that resembles that of its urban neighbor. Criminal justice systems in isolated areas at the outer boundary of a statistically metropolitan county may bear scant resemblance to the system that operates in the county's city center. Meanwhile, urban and suburban justice systems "export" their incarcerated populations to rural jails and prisons, creating complex relationships across demographic lines.

Acknowledging this reality, the Deason Center developed an operational framework to characterize criminal legal systems as rural or not. That framework relies upon three operational characteristics that distinguish rural systems from their urban and suburban counterparts:

- *Long Distances*: Geographic isolation precludes ready access to criminal legal agencies and resources.
- *Small Scale*: Caseloads and budgets are too small to independently support best practices.
- *Professional Scarcity*: Too few local criminal law professionals to meet local needs.[27]

While no two systems are alike, rural justice systems experience distance, scale, and professional scarcity in similar ways.

How Distance, Scale, and Scarcity Impact Rural Criminal Justice Systems

Geographic isolation increases the operational and opportunity costs for rural justice systems and delays the provision of criminal justice services. Victims struggle to reach police and to access emergency medical care.[28] Law enforcement must ration its physical presence—patrolling one area may mean lengthy delays responding to emergency calls in another area.

Treatment and support services that might improve public safety and increase reentry success are prohibitively far away.[29] Rural criminal defendants may be incarcerated hundreds of miles from their families and defense counsel.[30] A lack of public transportation exacerbates all of these challenges. Topography, weather, and even wildlife encounters can delay rural court proceedings, such as when a court reporter, while en route to work, hits a deer and needs to have her car towed.[31] Remote court proceedings using video technology might be one solution, but in some areas extreme weather conditions and challenging terrain can make it difficult to install and maintain broadband technologies.

With their small populations—and small budgets—rural communities struggle to acquire criminal court resources that urban systems take for granted. They may operate without case management systems and other basic essentials of criminal practice such as interpreters,[32] criminal history reports,[33] and even transcripts of proceedings.[34] Rural criminal courts convene in outdated buildings with inadequate security and insufficient space for confidential and secure legal practice.[35] Victims may share waiting rooms with defendants, and jurors may meet uncomfortable proximity to the trial lawyers arguing before them.

As if all of this were not difficult enough, many rural communities are professional deserts—large areas where few (if any) professionals live or work[36] and even fewer practice criminal law.[37] Rural police agencies are leanly staffed, and there are few forensic experts such as pathologists and professional sexual assault examiners. Traumatized rural victims must travel long distances for forensic examinations, and investigating police officers lose valuable time during lengthy commutes.[38]

A severe shortage of rural lawyers means that there are shockingly few lawyers and judges with deep expertise in criminal law. (Indeed, initiatives to "green" these criminal law deserts are among this chapter's big ideas for reform.) While urban systems generally employ full-time prosecutors and public defenders, rural caseload volumes are often too low to justify staffed offices for prosecutors and public defense attorneys.[39] Instead, local governments hire private attorneys to handle these matters on a part-time basis. Some of these lawyers are selected through low-bid contracts. Others are paid by the hour, by the case, or by a flat fee for a set number of cases.[40] The compensation is often quite low, and the work may require long hours of travel. This dismal combination often discourages lawyers from agreeing to handle criminal matters,[41] particularly since contracts are ineligible for benefits.[42]

These lawyer shortages are more than mere inconveniences. In many instances, they can cause constitutional violations. From states as diverse as Wisconsin, Mississippi, Maine, and Texas there is mounting evidence that indigent defendants in rural communities are less likely than their urban counterparts to receive the appointed counsel services they are entitled to under the Sixth Amendment's right to counsel.[43]

Rural legal deserts (and the associated delays in providing people with court-appointed attorneys) may be one significant factor in the rise of rural incarceration rates.[44] If no lawyer is available to represent a defendant, there is nobody to argue for a defendant's pretrial release,[45] and even brief periods of pretrial detention hamper defense investigations and increase the likelihood of conviction, whether by guilty plea or by trial.[46]

The phenomenon of nonlawyer judges underscores the problematic consequences of legal deserts in rural areas. Rather than bringing lawyer-judges from other jurisdictions into rural legal deserts, some states allow non-lawyers to serve as judges.[47] In 22 states, these lay judges can sentence a person to jail.[48] In at least some of these states, lay judges *exclusively* wield this power in rural areas. For example, in Washington, lay judges have authority to impose jail sentences in areas with fewer than 5,000 people.[49]

Impacts on Rural Residents and Communities

The combined impacts of distance, scale, and professional scarcity amplify the challenges that confront rural criminal systems. First, popular urban reform strategies, such as bail reform and specialty courts, have not been adapted for rural areas. More alarming, while there have been some decreases in urban incarceration rates, similar decreases in rural areas have not occurred; incarceration rates are in fact rising. Each of these examples illustrates the challenges of rural criminal justice.

Fewer Alternatives to Pretrial Detention and Lack of Specialty Courts

While bail reform and specialty courts are common urban reform strategies, rural realities make those options impractical. In rural areas, simply obtaining a prompt bail hearing can be a challenge. Judges, prosecutors, and defense attorneys who practice in rural areas are stretched thin by the need to serve large areas with low caseload volumes. For example, in Montana, 10 district court judges handle a geographic area larger than New England and Maryland put together.[50] Consequently, many rural criminal courts meet with alarming infrequency.[51] Judges may reserve particular days (or weeks) for criminal proceedings.[52] A 2016 report out of North Carolina describes jurisdictions in which courts convene only quarterly or even less frequently.[53]

As a result, defendants can languish in jail for months because there is no court hearing scheduled for a judge to advise them of the charges, to appoint an attorney to represent them, and to set conditions for pretrial release. In one instance, a woman spent 96 days in jail in rural Choctaw County, Mississippi, without ever seeing a judge or an attorney because the small caseload volume of the local court meant that it was in session only four times per year.[54] That case was particularly tragic, as all parties agreed that the woman was innocent.[55]

Programs designed to offer alternatives to pretrial detention are scarce, and specialty courts, such as drug courts or veterans courts, are particularly rare.[56] Most specialty courts serve counties with a population of 100,000 or more.[57] A 2012 study found that communities with fewer than 3,800 people had no specialty courts at all.[58]

Where rural pretrial programs and specialty courts do exist, the challenges of rurality make them hard to sustain. These programs often require that participants engage in intensive treatment and services. For rural participants, this means traveling to frequent treatment sessions that may be prohibitively far from their homes, often with unreliable personal transportation and no public transportation options.[59] It is little wonder, then, that many rural residents cannot successfully succeed in these programs. When they fail, their reincarceration adds to the rural incarceration boom.

Overreliance on Incarceration, Fines, and Fees

A pervasive trend in urban criminal justice reform has been the rejection of policies that use the criminal justice system to fund local government. But many rural justice systems have attempted to meet local budgetary needs by *increasing* their reliance on funds generated by the criminal system.[60] Rural communities have built new jails so that they can "rent" jail beds at a profit. They also have an inordinate dependence on the ill-advised strategy of funding local government by imposing criminal fines and fees at levels that far exceed those of their urban and suburban peers.

While the rental of jail beds is on the rise across the country, between 1978 and 2013 the rate at which rural jails held people for other authorities increased 888%, from 20 to 196 people per 100,000."[61] In contrast, urban areas and suburban rates increased by 134% and 409%, respectively—still shockingly high rates, but dwarfed by rural increases. Income from "[p]er diem payments from federal agencies like the US marshals and Immigration and Customs Enforcement" provides a short term payoff, and the US Department of Agriculture offers financial incentives to support the construction of new jails.[62]

Many rural communities have also tried to increase local revenues by welcoming the construction of prisons in their areas.[63] The federal government has actively encouraged this strategy,[64] as have some economists who view prisons as reliable industries and predict significant local benefits.[65] While some communities may have realized benefits from building prisons,[66] many more have not.[67]

A 2003 study compared rural New York counties with one or more prisons to those without prisons. This study concluded that counties with prisons did not experience "significant employment advantages" or see changes in unemployment rates that were different from those experienced statewide."[68] In fact, during economic downturns, counties with prisons experienced a 64% increase in unemployment, whereas counties without prisons saw only a 55% increase. During improving financial periods, the decreases in unemployment were roughly comparable: the unemployment rate dropped 38% in counties without a prison compared to 41% in counties with a prison.

A half-dozen similar studies have produced similar conclusions.[69] There appears to be a consensus that "prisons do not boost the economy of the average rural community."[70] In 2017, Eason summarized and retheorized much of the existing literature on the prison boom in rural areas, concluding that, while new prisons may create "a short-term economic boon" in rural communities, "these effects are not lasting."[71]

Not content to rely on jail and prison income, rural governments are also heavily reliant on the counterproductive strategy of using criminal justice fines and fees to generate revenue. A 2019 Brennan Center report investigated fines and fees in Florida, New Mexico, and Texas and concluded that, "in all target counties across the three states, rural counties had higher collections per capita than other counties."[72] The authors hypothesized that, because "governments in rural areas are frequently poorly funded," they "may be more reliant on revenue generated from fees and fines" and may therefore "prioritize generating this fee and fine revenue."[73]

An investigation by *Governing* magazine offered a similar hypothesis.[74] That investigation uncovered "one rural town in Georgia that may even have . . . created a police department and a local court" to pay off its sewer services debt. In that case, over a four-month period, the newly formed police department issued enough speeding tickets to cover 150% of the police budget with the associated fines and fees.[75] Who bears the brunt of those fines and fees? Rural residents. Furthermore, poor rural residents may find themselves incarcerated if they cannot pay.

Rural Criminal Justice as Part of a National Criminal Justice Ecosystem

It should be beyond dispute that rural criminal justice reform matters because rural residents and communities matter. Yet there is an alarming lack of national interest—much less investment—in rural criminal justice. On principle, this national failure to invest in rural reform is wrong. From a practical standpoint, it is shortsighted. Placing rural incarceration trends in a national context proves that the success of national justice reform is linked to the success of rural justice reform.

Although rural counties report lower rates of crime compared to urban areas,[76] rural arrest rates since the early 2000s have been higher than those in urban and suburban communities.[77] There is little research exploring this phenomenon. What we do know is alarming. Between 2013 and 2020, rural counties saw a 27% growth in jail populations, while the county's biggest cities saw their jail populations decrease by 18%.[78] In the same period, rural counties experienced a 436% increase in pretrial detentions.[79]

Small and rural jails account for the nation's largest number of jail admissions and the most rapid increase in jail populations.[80] According to the Vera Institute of Justice, rural areas in all regions experienced steep growth between 1970 and 2013—even those in states with historically low use of pretrial detention. Rural pretrial rates in both the Northeast and Midwest regions grew more than fivefold, from 24 to 154 per 100,000 and from 30 to 194 per 100,000, respectively."[81] Meanwhile, the rural "South and West record[ed] the highest pretrial incarceration rates, at 335 and 226 per 100,000, respectively."[82]

Rural people of color, as elsewhere in the nation, are disproportionately involved in the criminal justice system.[83] But while urban justice systems have reduced racial disparities, rural disparities in incarceration have grown.[84] Data gathered by the Vera Institute show that, between 1990 and 2013, the rate of Black incarceration in rural jails increased markedly. "By 2013, there were nearly three times the number of [B]lack people held in rural jails on a given day than in 1990, increasing from approximately 14,000 in 1990 to about 38,000 in 2013."[85] During the same period, Black incarceration rates dropped in urban, suburban, and small metropolitan areas.[86] Meanwhile, women are among the most incarcerated people in rural communities.[87] As the Vera Institute notes, "between 2004 and 2014, the number of women in jail increased 43% in rural counties and 29% in small and medium metropolitan counties, while it declined 6% in urban counties."[88] Again, a lack of research into rural criminal justice hinders a complete understanding of these disparities in rural incarceration rates. But it is clear that national criminal justice reform cannot succeed if rural incarceration rates continue to rise. The COVID-19 pandemic illustrates another important connection between rural justice reform and national justice reform. The national criminal justice system depends upon rural communities to house incarcerated people (particularly federal prisoners) as they are transferred across the country from one jail or prison to another. Rural jails that provide temporary housing for prisoner transfers can also transfer diseases along with incarcerated individuals.[89] These rural jails—which operate in communities with limited resources and scarce access to infectious disease testing[90]—may be spreading communicable diseases across the nation.[91]

When prisoner transfers spread disease, the damage is not confined within prison walls. In addition to endangering prisoners—who are closely congregated and often lack personal protection equipment—the transfer of infected prisoners creates a prison disease pipeline. That pipeline endangers corrections staff and their families, as well as the communities in which they reside, and carries potentially deadly consequences for rural, suburban, and urban residents across the nation.

Three Big Ideas to Reform Criminal Justice in Rural Places

Three themes emerge from this assessment of rural criminal justice systems. First, we know too little about rural criminal justice systems. Second, we have failed to make rural systems full partners in national criminal justice reform efforts. Finally, we have failed to tackle even well-identified and tangible problems, such as the scarcity of rural criminal justice professionals, with practical and targeted solutions. To accomplish criminal justice reform, we must address each of these failures.

Recommendation One: Researchers Must Study Rural Criminal Justice Systems

To build safe, compassionate, and sustainable criminal justice systems, rural justice stakeholders and policy makers need quantitative and qualitative data about their local systems. To make informed allocations of public funds, state and national funders need to understand rural criminal justice systems' size and scale. Gathering better and richer information is essential for rural criminal justice reform.

There is a profound urban bias in the collection of criminal justice data.[92] For example, there are 3,142 counties in the United States, but the Bureau of Justice Statistics gathers data only from the 75 largest urban counties. National surveys of prosecutors have historically excluded many prosecutors working in the small local courts that serve rural areas.[93] Indeed, the most recent Census of State Court Prosecutors includes the nation's larger prosecutors' offices but excludes prosecutors who practice in municipal courts and in low-level courts that handle misdemeanors and the early stages of felony cases.[94] Similarly, the 2007 Census of Public Defender Offices collected data only from counties with a full-time public defender office, systematically excluding most smaller and rural jurisdictions that primarily rely on assigned or contract counsel to provide indigent legal services.[95] As a result, we know too little about rural criminal justice systems.

The vast majority of our "national" criminal justice data is really just urban criminal justice data. For example, there is an oft-cited statistic that fewer than 5% of felony criminal cases are resolved by trial.[96] Yet that statistic is based exclusively on data that the Bureau of Justice Statistics collected in urban jurisdictions. Do rural criminal justice systems hold jury trials at similar rates? Or do the challenges of isolated venues, small-scale systems, and criminal law deserts produce different results? No one yet knows.

When criminal justice datasets include rural areas, there are questions about the reliability of the rural data they collect. For example, the FBI's Uniform Crime Report (UCR) program includes annual data submitted by rural police agencies. However, a 2016 study exposed discrepancies between the number of crimes that rural residents reported to police and the number of crimes police reported to the UCR. The UCR's authors attributed those discrepancies to challenges in "recording and production of crime data by the police" in rural areas. They theorized that it is simply harder for rural systems to collect and keep accurate data.[97] Indeed, rural criminal justice systems do not collect the "big data" that increasingly propel urban criminal justice policy. This is not merely because they have low caseload volumes. Financial and technical constraints limit their data-collection capacity. Data technology and training may be too expensive, local personnel may be in short supply, and the caseloads themselves may seem too small to justify the work associated with data collection and analysis.[98]

Data deficits are barriers to research, funding, innovation, and reform[99] and make it difficult for rural communities to identify, much less implement, evidence-based reforms that fit the small scale of their criminal justice systems. Creating rural data instruments and collecting empirical data about rural criminal justice systems are necessary steps toward rural criminal justice reform.[100] Governments, nonprofits, and criminal justice advocates should develop and implement data collection instruments for rural criminal justice systems and stakeholders. These instruments might include censuses, surveys, administrative data reporting systems, and other data-collection tools. These data instruments should be standardized to facilitate the development of a national rural criminal justice dataset.

Plans for data collection should recognize and adapt to the realities of resource-strapped rural justice systems. The information gathered should include data categories that speak to the realities of rural criminal justice systems, such as the distance between criminal justice services or the availability of criminal justice–related services such as treatment for substance use disorder. In addition, prominent criminal justice typologies that reflect uniquely urban experiences may be ignoring important features of rural legal systems. For example, policing typologies that address departmental diversity by race may overlook important class factors that might be highly relevant to rural policing.

Wherever possible, researchers should adapt existing data tools to gather rural-relevant information. For example, the National Institute of Justice's CrimStat program (TimeStat)—which collects and analyzes spatial statistics for predictive policing—could be tweaked or repurposed to collect and analyze rural stakeholder travel time, illuminating how distance impacts rural criminal courts.[101] The Vera Institute's jail growth data instrument exemplifies this approach. National data about incarceration have primarily been collected and counted at the state level. Recognizing that state-level data were inadequate to a detailed understanding of local incarceration trends, Vera combined disparate sources of incarceration data to create a tool that provides incarceration rates on a local level. The result has been a rich data visualization tool that has become a primary source of our knowledge about rural incarceration trends. As a result of Vera's work, we can use county-level data to investigate the causes of rural incarceration rates.[102]

Recommendation Two: Rural Criminal Justice Systems Must Be Equal Participants in the Development of Criminal Legal Reforms

Even as they gather new information about rural criminal justice systems, policy makers and criminal justice reform advocates must engage rural systems in criminal justice reform planning. Important questions—"Will this work in rural areas?" and "What adaptations will be necessary for effective implementation in rural areas?" and "What can rural areas teach us?"—should be mandatory when considering any criminal justice plan. Unfortunately, these questions are asked all too rarely. As a result, rural criminal justice communities "fail" at reforms that were never truly possible for their justice systems[103] and urban areas miss important opportunities to learn from rural successes and failures.

A 2012 National Center for State Courts study by Cheesman and colleagues describes how an Arizona criminal justice reform floundered in rural areas.[104] In 2007, Arizona became the second state to require that first-time DUI offenders use interlock ignition devices to prevent impaired drivers from starting and operating a vehicle.[105] Offenders were responsible for installing, maintaining, and paying all costs associated with the device. (Maintenance included at least eight trips per year to the installer.) Failure to comply with interlock maintenance results in the suspension of the offender's driver's license until maintenance is completed. Offenders with suspended licenses who needed to drive to work, obtain health services, engage in caretaking, or attend court were granted limited driving privileges subject to their use of the ignition interlock devices. The hope was that interlocks would deter people from reoffending and that the exceptions would reduce arrests for driving with suspended licenses as well as failures to appear in court due to transportation challenges.

Unfortunately, the interlock reforms were mostly unsuccessful in rural Arizona. Costs for the devices were often prohibitive, ranging from $850 to $1,056 per year, a significant burden on poorer rural residents. Travel was another significant burden. Ignition lock service providers were "concentrated in urban counties" and "non-existent in some rural counties."[106] To obtain and maintain the ignition locks, rural defendants had to travel—often in unreliable cars—up to 150 miles each way to install and service the devices, losing work time and spending large sums on gas. Unsurprisingly, many rural residents either failed to install the interlock devices or were unable to obtain them.

Under the same Arizona statute, many DUI offenders were required to participate in counseling and treatment programs. Again, rural realities precluded successful implementation of this approach. Many of Arizona's rural communities lack local treatment options, making it difficult, if not impossible, for DUI offenders to participate in programming required by the terms of their probation.

Had anyone stopped to consider whether the DUI program was viable in rural areas, these challenges would have been easy to predict. But Arizona legislators either overlooked the realities of rural Arizona communities or "expected market forces to act to provide statewide access to ignition interlock services."[107] Based on the Arizona experience, Chessman and colleagues recommend that states considering future similar technological innovations include plans that will guarantee rural communities' access to those technologies.[108]

Organizations like the National Association of Counties (NACo) have taken essential steps in this direction, publishing guides that explore how rural communities can implement reforms that parallel those pioneered in urban areas. For example, one of NACo's guides advocates rural-viable adaptations of urban practices,[109] and its Stepping Up Initiative adapts the Sequential Intercept Model—an empirically proven approach to treating mental and substance use disorders—to rural justice systems.[110] Meanwhile, many government and nonprofit agencies are building rural-centric tools for combating the opioid epidemic.[111] These initiatives recognize that rural justice systems and rural offenders are often different than their urban counterparts.[112]

As they weigh rural constraints when planning justice reforms, researchers and policy makers should also look to rural areas for justice innovations. Notwithstanding the challenges associated with long distances, small scale, and professional scarcity, rural justice systems may enjoy some advantages in the pursuit of justice reform. Lacking large bureaucracies, rural systems can be flexible and creative in their responses to local criminal justice problems.[113] The personal connections between justice system actors and justice-involved individuals may lead them to prefer problem-solving over punishment. Further, familiarity between system actors may foster cooperation among individuals who might have a far more adversarial relationship in an urban setting.

Overlooked in the rush to implement urban reforms, rural areas have quietly experimented with their own innovative justice solutions to the common rural problems of long distances, small case volumes, and professional scarcity. For example, rural systems have innovated by using vans or RVs to provide mobile court services to residents in distant areas.[114] A "Justice Bus" serves people across the 2.8 million acres of the Cheyenne River Sioux Reservation in South Dakota. This mobile courthouse handles misdemeanors and truancy complaints and conducts arraignments and pretrial check-ins for low-level and victimless offenses.[115] Could this success be replicated in urban areas, with mobile courts traveling to high-density, high-poverty areas whose residents may lack the bus fare or child care necessary to get to court? Urban court systems would be well-advised to study this question.

The COVID-19 pandemic underscores the importance of studying rural adaptations. Rural criminal courts long ago developed strategies for adapting to distance constraints. COVID-19 unexpectedly "ruralized" all criminal justice systems by imposing the necessity of social distancing.[116] Many urban and suburban systems were not prepared for that abrupt change. As a result, many rural criminal courts took the lead in adapting to criminal practice during a pandemic.[117]

For example, COVID-19 required that many criminal proceedings either be postponed or be convened in churches, stadiums, theaters, gymnasiums, and other spaces that could accommodate social distancing. Rural criminal justice systems quickly accomplished this. Indeed, many were already holding court in places like fire stations, garages, and community centers as part of their ordinary way of doing business. When rural Bayfield County in Wisconsin (population 15,036) conducted the state's first socially distanced criminal jury selection in a high-school gym, the criminal court in Milwaukee County was still "considering" the use of alternative locations.

Like other rural criminal justice systems, Bayfield confronts budget shortfalls, lawyer shortages, and long delays in court proceedings. Its rapid adaptation to COVID-19 is therefore even more impressive. It also raises critical research questions. Do rural courts have social capital that facilitates prompt community support and cooperation? Do the smaller administrative structures of rural criminal courts promote a flexibility that urban courts lack? Answering these questions might help urban and suburban jurisdictions move more quickly in response to future crises.

Similarly, researchers and reformers could have learned much about video-based court proceedings by studying rural practice. For nearly two decades, rural criminal justice systems have used videoconferencing for court proceedings, client communications, witness interviews, and more. But researchers' failure to identify and study these rural adaptations meant that, during the COVID-19 pandemic, there was only one strong empirical study of criminal court video practices—and that study was conducted in an urban jurisdiction. What might we have learned from studying 20 years of video proceedings in rural courts? Alas, no one knows. Criminal practitioners, defendants, victims, and witnesses across the country may be paying the price.

Recommendation Three: Invest in Strategies to Recruit, Train, and Retain Rural Criminal Law Practitioners

Any strategy to increase the availability and quality of rural criminal lawyers must raise the overall number of rural lawyers and properly equip those lawyers to handle criminal cases. Work by Dr. Andrew Davies, research director at the Deason Center, suggests that adding even one attorney per 100 square miles is associated with a measurable increase in the appointment of counsel to represent indigent criminal defendants.[118] But how can rural criminal legal systems recruit these lawyers?

In a 2020 report *Greening the Desert*, the Deason Center catalogued six promising, practical, and actionable strategies to recruit, train, and retain rural lawyers generally and rural criminal lawyers particularly:

- *Provide financial incentives*: Offer loan repayment programs for educational debt, increase rural lawyer compensation rates, and, wherever possible, provide insurance and retirement benefits to rural attorneys who prosecute and defend criminal cases.
- *Regionalize full-time offices for prosecution and public defense*: Create re-

gional or multijurisdictional offices that employ full-time lawyers and provide them with organizational support and supervision to provide services
across a wide area.

- *Innovate rural training and mentoring opportunities*: Establish rural legal
  practice incubators that launch new lawyers into rural private practice
  and provide them with local attorney mentors, offer free continuing legal
  education courses for rural attorneys who accept indigent defense court
  appointments, and establish paid fellowship opportunities for new lawyers
  to work as rural prosecutors and defenders.

- *Develop law school practice partnerships*: Create collaborative law offices
  that pair practicing lawyers with law school clinics, offer pop-up law school
  programs that can provide limited scope representation (for example,
  expunging criminal records), and offer tuition reduction or tuition reimbursement for law graduates who commit to rural practice.

- *Leverage technology*: Where broadband internet services are available,
  make judicious use of video technology to reduce travel times and expedite
  routine court proceedings.

- *Create educational pipelines to rural law practice*: Expose students in high
  school, college, and law school to rural criminal law practice, provide rural
  internship opportunities, and offer early (and sometimes guaranteed) law
  school admission to applicants who commit to rural practice and maintain
  any required academic standards.

Most of these initiatives are fairly new, so there has been scant opportunity to evaluate their success. However, many are modeled on rural
medical recruitment initiatives for which there is a substantial body of
evaluative research. Like lawyers, doctors are also in short supply in
rural areas. Rural medical deserts have long prevented rural communities from "achieving and maintaining adequate levels of rural health
care,"[119] as financial disincentives and preference for urban living dis-
suade new doctors from choosing a rural practice.[120]

In response, the medical community has been successful in attending
to medical deserts by recruiting new doctors who grew up in rural areas,
sending residents to train in rural areas, and tying financial incentives
such as scholarship funds and loan forgiveness to rural practice. Indeed,
the National Health Service Corps (NHSC) has been especially adept at
recruiting doctors and other medical professionals to practice medicine

in rural areas. NHSC is a federal program that offers scholarship and loan repayment programs to medical professional in exchange for their commitment to spend two years providing medical services in under-served areas.[121] "Twenty percent of physicians assigned to rural areas through the program were still practicing in the county of their original assignment 8–16 years later, and an additional 20% were practicing in a separate rural location."[122] Considering this evidence, researchers con-cluded that using "financial incentives and special training programs" to recruit and support aspiring primary care practitioners who have "per-sonal characteristics associated with practicing in underserved or rural areas . . . should be a strategic investment for medical education and future research.[123]

Likewise, some states have experimented with similar programs to attract new lawyers to rural areas. South Dakota's Rural Recruitment Program (RRP) is a particularly promising initiative.[124] The RRP is a pilot program supported by the South Dakota Unified Judicial System, the State Bar of South Dakota, and the state legislature.[125] Through the RRP, South Dakota recruits attorneys to work in rural counties with populations of 10,000 or fewer residents. Participants commit to five years of rural practice and receive annual incentive payments that, over five years, are equivalent to 90% of the tuition and fees for a JD degree at the University of South Dakota Law School. Funding comes from the state budget (50%), the state bar association (15%), and the rural county in which the attorney is placed (35%). By all accounts, the pilot program, which is capped at 32 participants, has been successful, and many of the RRP recruits practice criminal law under the supervision of more expe-rienced criminal lawyers.

It is too early to know whether the South Dakota program and others like it will be effective in the long term.[126] However, just as the federal government has recruited doctors to rural areas through the National Health Service Corps, policy makers should make a similar investment in the recruitment and retention of lawyers who commit to practice in rural areas. Development and measurement of recruitment and reten-tion strategies are essential for rural criminal justice reform.

Conclusion

Like urban and suburban communities, rural communities are concerned about criminal justice reform. And like everyone else, they want safe streets, fair process, and equal justice. Yet they struggle with the constraints of geographic isolation, low caseload volumes, and professional scarcity. Absent meaningful reform, geography may indeed be destiny for people involved in rural criminal justice systems.

Rural communities have fewer options for pretrial release and diversion. Defendants may spend long periods in jail while waiting to see a judge or an attorney. Jails and prisons are used as tools to generate revenue, rather than as instruments of rehabilitation and reform. And rural incarceration is rising at rates that may undermine the significant reductions in incarceration achieved by many urban systems.

For too long, funders, researchers, and justice innovators have primarily focused on urban justice systems, ignoring the challenges of distance and scale that plague rural criminal justice systems and overlooking the benefits of flexibility and familiarity that are hallmarks of rural justice success. Only a committed and sustained investment in rural justice reform can address this justice crisis. To reform criminal justice in rural communities, we must invest in rural justice research, create stable and secure rural justice funding, and guarantee the availability of rural criminal lawyers and judges.

NOTES

1 Nugent-Borakove, Mahoney, and Witcomb, "Strengthening Rural Courts."
2 SMU Dedman School of Law, "Greening the Desert."
3 Ibid.
4 Hamilton, "A Super-Spreader Jail."
5 Fields, Holder, and Burd, "Life Off the Highway."
6 USDA, "What Is Rural?"
7 *Washington Post*, "The Federal Definition of 'Rural'"; Family Justice, "Enhancing Rural Reentry."
8 Porter, "The Hard Truths of Trying to 'Save' the Rural Economy." Wealthy vacation communities are notable exceptions. See also Weisner et al., *Criminal Justice System Utilization in Rural Areas*.
9 US Department of Commerce, Census Bureau, "New Census Data Show Differences Between Urban and Rural Populations."
10 Ibid.

11 *Harvard Journal of Law and Public Policy*. In rural communities like Telluride, Colorado, an influx of wealthy homeowners has increased county residents' *average* wealth. Overall, however, the overall percentage of rural people living in poverty is consistently high.

12 Parker et al., "What Unites and Divides Urban, Suburban and Rural Communities"; COSCA Policy and Liaison Committee, "Courts Need to Enhance Access to Justice in Rural America."

13 USDA, *Rural America at a Glance* (rural populations reached their lowest point in about 2010–2011; since then, they have increased slightly).

14 US Department of Commerce, Census Bureau, "New Census Data Show Differences Between Urban and Rural Populations." While COVID-19 may drive some city dwellers back to rural and small-town areas, it is difficult to imagine that pandemic-related moves will compensate for 30 years of population decline. See also United Nations News, "Coronavirus: Reshape the Urban World"; Bender, "Escape to the Country"; Miller, "People Are Fleeing Coronavirus Hotspots"; Kaeding, "Some People Are Considering Trading City Life for Rural Wisconsin."

15 Wimberly and Woolley, *The Black Belt Databook*; Barry-Jester and Kelso, "Patterns of Death in the South Still Show the Outlines of Slavery."

16 See Dewees and Marks, *Twice Invisible*.

17 Lichter, "Immigration and the New Racial Diversity in Rural America," 3–35.

18 Porter, "The Hard Truths of Trying to 'Save' the Rural Economy"; Moody's Investor Service, "Moody's: Rural America."

19 FCC, *2020 Broadband Deployment Report*; Moriarty, *Criminal Justice Technology in the 21st Century: Third Edition*.

20 USDA Economic Research Service, "Highest Level of Education Attainment" (data suggest that rural America had lower education attainment than urban).

21 Griller et al., "Reengineering Rural Justice"; McGrath, "Making 'What Works' Work for Rural Districts."

22 See Breslau et al., "Are Mental Disorders More Common in Urban Than Rural Areas of the United States?" 50–5.

23 Andrilla et al., "Geographic Variation in the Supply of Selected Behaviorial Health Providers"; Frakt, "A Sense of Alarm as Rural Hospitals Keep Closing."

24 Keyes et al., "Understanding the Rural–Urban Differences," 52–59.

25 Zeller and Coburn, "Health Equity Challenges in Rural America."

26 See also Davies and Clark, "Access to Counsel in Local Courts in Rural New York State," 15.

27 Metzger and Guggenmos, "COVID-19 and the Ruralization of U.S. Criminal Court Systems." See also Nugent-Borakove, Mahoney, and Whitcomb, "Strengthening Rural Courts" ("Large geographic distances, sparse populations, small staff sizes in courts and justice agencies, and limited resources (including legal, social, and health services) constitute a core set of challenges for rural courts. These are magnified by lack of specialization among justice system practitioners and service

providers, professional isolation of practitioners, and the often-close interrelation-
ships between community members and justice system personnel.")

28 King et al., "EMS Services in Rural America."
29 Griller et al., "Reengineering Rural Justice."
30 Cochran et al., "Spatial Distance, Community Disadvantage, and Racial and Eth-
    nic Variation," 220–54; Mumola, *Incarcerated Parents and their Children.*
31 McKeon and Rice, "Administering Justice in Montana's Rural Courts," 205.
32 Minnesota Judicial Branch, "Access and Service Delivery 2 Committee"; see also
    Oregon State Bar, *Task Force on Access to State Courts.*
33 See, e.g., Cheesman et al., "Ignition Interlock," noting: "Rural judges and magis-
    trates do not always have adequate information about DUI offenders' criminal
    history (including DUIs) at the time of sentencing."
34 Ducker Worldwide, "2013–2014 Court Reporting Industry Outlook Report," 11.
35 Bell, "Circuit Judges Become Scarce"; Commission on Rural Courts, "Judicial
    Council of the State of Nevada," 6–8; Special Commission on the Future of NY
    State Courts, "Justice Most Local," 14.
36 SMU Dedman School of Law, "Greening the Desert."
37 Davis, "Discretionary Justice"; Pruitt et al., "Legal Deserts."
38 Hanzlick, "The Conversion of Coroner Systems to Medical Examiners in the US,"
    279–83; Scientific Working Group of Medicolegal Death Investigation, "Increasing
    the Supply of Forensic Pathologists"; United States GAO, *Sexual Assault.*
39 Farole and Langton, *County-Based and Local Public Defender Office, 2007,* table 2,
    showing that the median population of a jurisdiction in which a public defender
    office operates is approximately 117,000.
40 Primus, "Culture as a Structural," 1769; Alabama State Bar, "Part-time Judges;
    Part-time Assistant District Attorneys"; Fairfax, "Delegation of the Criminal Pros-
    ecution Function"; Lawrence et al., "Prosecutor Priorities"; Paquette, "America's
    Rural Lawyer Shortage."
41 Smith, "Defense Attorneys Await a Pay Increase."
42 Romero, "Profit-Driven Prosecution"; Sixth Amendment Center, "The Right to
    Counsel in Indiana"; Sixth Amendment Center, "The Right to Counsel in Rural
    Nevada."
43 Davies and Clark, "*Gideon* in the Desert," 245–72; Sixth Amendment Center,
    "Maine Report"; Sixth Amendment Center, "The Right to Counsel in Texas";
    Sixth Amendment Center, "Wisconsin"; Metzger, "Rural Justice System Low
    on Pretrial Resources"; Metzger, "Why Rural Americans Struggle for Equal
    Justice."
44 Kalb, "Gideon Incarcerated"; Metzger and Hoeffel, "Criminal (Dis)Appearance,"
    392; Kang-Brown and Subramanian, "Out of Sight," 13; see, e.g., Bronner, "No
    Lawyer for Miles"; Chief Justice Cherry, "2017 State of the Judiciary Message."
45 Pishko, "The Shocking Lack of Lawyers in Rural America."
46 On court delay and its impact on attorney–client contact, see Colbert, "Prosecu-
    tion Without Representation," 333–453; Miller, "Rural Courts are Fertile Ground."

For the impact of pretrial detention on the likelihood of pleading guilty, see Dobbie, Goldin, and Yang, "The Effects of Pre-Trial Detention on Conviction, Future Crime, and Employment," 201–40.

47 Trenkner, "Constitutional Restrictions," 562.

48 Arizona (Ariz. Rev. Stat. §§ 22–301(A)(1), 22–402(B), 22–403(A)); Colorado (Colo. Rev. Stat. § 13-6-203(2) & 3(3)); Montana (Mont. Code §§ 3-10-202-204); Delaware (Del. Code tit. 10 § 1302(b); tit. 11, § 5917); Indiana (Ind. Code §§ 33-35-1-4, 33-35-2-3(2), 33-35-2-8(b)); Kansas: (Kan. Stat. § 12-4104, 4105); Louisiana (La. Rev. Stat. § 33:441. La. Const. art. 6, § 24(A)(2)) Mississippi (Miss. Const. art. 6, § 171; Miss. Code § 21-23-5 & 7); Missouri (Mo. Rev. Stat. § 479.020(1), § 479.200(1)); New Hampshire (N.H. Rev. Stat. § 599:1); Nevada (Nev. Rev. Stat. §§ 4.010(2) and (3)); New Mexico (N.M. Stat. §§ 35-2-1(D), 35-3-4(A), § 35-14-2(A), 35-14-3); New York (N.Y. Const. art. 6, § 20(c); N.Y. Crim. Proc. L. § 170.25(1)); North Dakota (N.D. Cent. Code § 40-18-01(1)); Ohio (Ohio Rev. Code § 1905.01, § 1905.03); Oregon (Or. Rev. Stat. §§ 3.050, 51.050, § 51.240(1)(e)(B) and (C), 221.339(2)); South Carolina (S.C. Code §§ 22-1-10(B) and 22-3-540); Texas (Tex. Gov't Code § 26.045(a) & (c), Tex. Const. art. 5, §. 6(a) and 15. See also Masquelette v. State, 579 S.W.2d 478, 479–80 (Tex. Ct. Crim. App. 1979)); Utah (Utah Code §§ 78A-7-106(1) and 118(1), 78A-7-201(2)); Wyoming (Wyo. Stat. § 5-9-208(c)(xviii)); Washington (Wash. Rev. Code § 3.50.020; 3.50.040); West Virginia (W. Va. Code § 50-2-3, §§ 50-1-4, 8-10-2(c)).

49 Wash. Rev. Code § 3.50.020; 3.50.040.

50 McKeon and Rice, "Administering Justice in Montana's Rural Courts," 202.

51 Curtis and Davies, *Counsel at First Appearance* (unpublished report on file with the Deason Center). Among 1,017 town and village judges surveyed in rural upstate New York, 67% presided in courts scheduled to convene at least weekly, while the remainder met less often; 4% met only monthly. An older report on lower-level courts in Indiana reported: "About 20% are in session less than two hours a week, and another 7% are virtually full time." Lamber and Luskin, "City and Town Courts," 59–83, quote from page 66.

52 Levin and Haugen, "Open Roads and Overflowing Jails," 10; Bell, "Circuit Judges Become Scarce."

53 National Center for State Courts, *Implementation of a Criminal Caseflow Management Plan*; North Carolina Judicial Branch, "North Carolina Commission on the Administration of Law and Justice."

54 Jauch v. Choctaw County, 874 F.3d 425 (2017).

55 See also, Jones, "Does Our County Really Need a Bigger Jail?"

56 See, e.g., McGrath, "Making 'What Works' Work," noting the success of evidence-based treatment programs and "availability issues" that arise in rural areas; Wodahl, "The Challenges of Prisoner Reentry," 42.

57 Strong and Kyckelhahn, *Census of Problem-Solving Courts, 2012*, table 2.

58 Ibid., 5.

59 See, e.g., Kashef, "Barrier to Rural Opiod Treatment." Rural treatment programs face other barriers. Rural residents have reported higher levels of embarrass-

ment and concerns about lack of privacy regarding mental health treatment, and in close-knit rural communities, familiarity can compromise the anonymity of program participants.; Pullen and Oser, "Barriers to Substance Abuse Treatment," 891–901.

60 Kang-Brown and Subramanian, "Out of Sight," 18.

61 Ibid., 14.

62 Heiss and Norton, "The Hidden Scandal of US Criminal Justice?"

63 Kilborn, "Rural Towns Turn to Prisons"; Kang-Brown and Subramanian, "Out of Sight," 14; Eason, "Mapping Prison Proliferation," 1015–28; Hoyman and Weinberg, "The Process of Policy Innovation," 95–112.

64 King, Mauer, and Huling, "Big Prisons, Small Towns."

65 Kilborn, "Rural Towns Turn to Prisons"; Kang-Brown and Subramanian, "Out of Sight," 14; Eason, "Mapping Prison Proliferation"; Hoyman and Weinberg, "The Process of Policy Innovation."

66 Kilborn, "Rural Towns Turn to Prisons."

67 Besser and Hanson, "The Development of Last Resort," See also Farrigan and Glasmeier, "The Economic Impacts of the Prison Development Boom," 274–99; King, Mauer, and Huling, "Big Prisons, Small Towns," 1.

68 King, Mauer, and Huling, "Big Prisons, Small Towns," 1.

69 Besser and Hanson, "The Development of Last Resort"; Meagher and Thompson, "So You Think a New Prison Will Save Your Town?"

70 Eason, "Prisons as Panacea or Pariah?" 7 (summarizing the literature). Some researchers believe that prisons "negatively impact rural communities by limiting other types of development beyond future prison facilities."

71 Ibid. (summarizing the literature).

72 Menendez et al., "The Steep Costs of Criminal Justice Fees and Fines," 9.

73 Ibid.

74 Maciag, "Addicted to Fines."

75 Ibid.

76 Kong-Brown and Subramanian, "Out of Sight," 7.

77 Rad, Yang, and Wunschel, "The Arrest-Jail Admission Gap."

78 Yoon, Schmidt, and Haskell-Hoehel, "The Party Platforms."

79 Rad, Yang, and Wunschel, "The Arrest-Jail Admission Gap."

80 Kang-Brown and Subramanian, "Out of Sight."

81 Ibid., 13.

82 Ibid.

83 Jensen, "At the Razor's Edge."

84 Keller and Pearce, "A Small Indiana County"; Levin and Haugen, "Open Roads and Overflowing Jails," 4.

85 Subramanian, Riley, and Mai, "Divided Justice," 18.

86 Ibid.

87 Neath, "Understanding Jail Growth in Rural America."

88 Kang-Brown and Subramanian, "Out of Sight," 13.

89 This phenomenon is not new: the "abrupt transfer of inmates from one location" has long been identified as a factor that "complicates the diagnosis of infection, interruption of transmission, recognition of an outbreak, performance of a contact investigation, and eradication of" any contagious disease. Bick, "Infection Control in Jails and Prisons," 1047–55.

90 Heath, "Urban-Rural Divide."

91 Hamilton and Blakinger, "'Con Air' Is Spreading COVID-19."

92 Hansen and Lory, "Rural Victimization and Policing," 1–12; Weisner et al., *Criminal Justice System Utilization in Rural Areas*; Shackford, "Is Criminal Justice Reform Leaving Small and Rural Communities Behind?"; Kang-Brown and Subramanian, "Out of Sight," 2.

93 DeFrances, *State Court Prosecutors in Small Districts, 2001.*

94 Perry and Banks, *Prosecutors in State Courts.*

95 Farole and Langton, *County-based and Local Public Defender Offices, 2007.*

96 Cohen and Kyckelhahn, *Felony Defendants in Large Urban Counties, 2006.*

97 Berg and Lauritsen, "Telling a Similar Story Twice?" 61–87.

98 Strom, "Research on the Impact of Technology," 4–6, 7–5.

99 See, e.g., US Department of Justice, *Innovations in Community-Based Crime Reduction (CBCR)* ("there is little research and evaluation of 'hot spots' policing theory in rural and tribal areas").

100 See, e.g., Saunders, Cahill, and Taylor, *Feasibility of a Survey Panel*, ix ("there are no readily available sampling frames for small, rural, and border courts and community corrections agencies").

101 Levine, "CrimeState: A Spatial Statistics Program."

102 Levin and Haugen, "Open Roads and Overflowing Jails," 4.

103 See, e.g., Kang-Brown and Subramanian, "Out of Sight," 16.

104 Cheesman et al., "Ignition Interlock."

105 Ibid.

106 Ibid., 20.

107 Ibid., 27.

108 Wodahl, "The Challenges of Prisoner Reentry," 42 (noting that policy makers need to address the necessity of improving the availability of treatment services in rural areas).

109 Vetter and Clark, "The Delivery of Pretrial Justice in Rural Areas."

110 National Association of Counties, "The Stepping Up Initiative."

111 See, e.g., USDA, *Rural Community Action Guide.*

112 See, e.g., Dickson, Wasarhaley and Webster, "A Comparison of First-Time and Repeat Rural DUI Offenders," 421–37. ("the pattern of differences between rural first-time and repeat DUI offenders may be different from the pattern found in prior urban-based studies").

113 Vetter and Clark, "The Delivery of Pretrial Justice in Rural Areas."

114 Loeffler and Wanamaner, "The Ten Guiding Principles of DWI Courts"; *Big Valley News*, "Lassen County Superior Court."

115 Woessner, "Mobile Courtroom Provides Justice."
116 Metzger and Guggenmos, "COVID-19 and the Ruralization of U.S. Criminal Court Systems."
117 Ibid.
118 Davies and Clark, "*Gideon* in the Desert," 245–72.
119 Caryl, "Malpractice and Other Legal Issues," 173.
120 Goodfellow et al., "Predictors of Primary Care Physician Practice Location," 1313–21 (Predictors, P. 1: 2248).
121 National Health Service Core, "About Us."
122 Goodfellow et al., "Predictors of Primary Care Physician Practice Location" (Predictors, P. 1: 2248).
123 Ibid.
124 South Dakota Unified Judicial System, "Rural Attorney Recruitment Program"; Pruitt et al., "Legal Deserts."
125 South Dakota Legal Self-Help, "Rural Attorney Recruitment Program"; Pruitt et al., "Legal Deserts."
126 SMU Dedman School of Law, "Greening the Desert."

11

Rethinking the Civil-Criminal Distinction

LAUREN SUDEALL

In the legal world, we operate on the premise that our civil and criminal justice systems are distinct. As a result of this siloed approach, courts, court rules, procedural protections, legal services, and legal communications typically turn or focus exclusively on one side of this divide or the other.[1] Yet individuals' lived experiences do not always fall cleanly along those lines—they may experience sanctions differently than the law has categorized them or encounter one situation that gives rise to civil and criminal legal issues. Today, civil sanctions are increasingly punitive, while fines and incarceration are no longer distinctly criminal consequences. These realities undermine historical rationales for the civil-criminal divide and make the justifications for that divide increasingly incoherent.

The civil-criminal divide presents more than a conceptual or theoretical problem. The rigid line between civil and criminal legal issues prevents us from addressing all facets of an individual's situation in a single court system. Instead, we require that people have multiple interactions with civil and criminal court systems, which can drain both their time and their resources. It becomes harder for them to address or protect against civil consequences arising from a criminal charge or conviction. By failing to inform people engaged with one sphere of the system about legal problems in the other sphere, we lose critical opportunities for intervention and education—particularly among populations in need of assistance. Because people do not silo their problems into criminal and civil categories, they face additional barriers to obtaining assistance: people go to the wrong legal systems and find courts and legal providers who may be ill-equipped to redirect them. The resulting frustration and the inability to find the help they need may give some people a cramped view of the law's potential to address their problems.

In this chapter, I explain how the civil-criminal distinction influences our understanding of the legal system and explore the problems it creates for litigants and those assisting them. In doing so, I employ a broad definition of "evidence-based" reform. In my view, evidence relevant to criminal justice reform consists not only of quantitative data, such as the likelihood of recidivism and incarceration rates, but also of qualitative and even perceptual data, which shed light on how the system works (or doesn't) and how and why quantitative data are generated. In the context of this chapter, I focus specifically on how the civil-criminal distinction fails to align with—and may even exacerbate—the lived experience of many system-impacted individuals, demonstrable primarily through qualitative data. I encourage readers to question the civil-criminal distinction and to ask: What would happen if we didn't view the two as distinct? To what degree are the differences between civil and criminal justice a function of the separation we have chosen to create rather than any inherent distinction? And is the civil-criminal divide born more from a need to organize the courts and service providers than it is to resolve problems most effectively for litigants? I conclude that a merged vision of civil and criminal justice may better align with the understanding and experiences of system-impacted individuals and may better equip the legal system to respond to their problems.

In this chapter I call on systemic actors and service providers to minimize the different treatment of civil and criminal issues and to collaborate to the greatest extent possible, wherever the civil-criminal distinction creates barriers to justice for individuals or inefficiencies for courts. Even if doctrinal divisions persist, policy makers can engage in practical applications of this idea, rethinking how to structure the resolution of legal issues, provide legal services, and disseminate legal education to individuals and communities.

An Overview of the Civil-Criminal Divide

Within the legal system, civil and criminal justice problems are typically siloed into two distinct categories. The civil realm typically involves disputes between private parties, whereas the criminal realm pits individuals against the state.[2] Criminal law is a vehicle to punish those who wrong society, impose "just deserts" on the wrongdoer, and deter others from engaging in similar misconduct.[3] In contrast, civil law is seen as compensatory, providing a remedy for "individuals or entities harmed by other individuals or entities[] in order to make them whole."[4]

This long-standing division is paramount in the legal system's organization, dictating nearly every aspect of how we interpret and process disputes. Procedural protections are distributed according to the civil-criminal distinction—even those provided for by the United States Constitution. For example, the Sixth Amendment's guarantees of an attorney and an impartial jury and the Fifth Amendment's protection against self-incrimination apply only in criminal cases.[5] A panoply of other protections turns on this divide, including speedy trial rights, certain evidentiary rules, protections against unnecessary detention, advisals of fundamental rights,[6] and restrictions on when and how often one can be liable based on the same conduct.[7] Judges' daily court dockets typically include only civil or criminal cases. Legal services are also siloed: public defense systems provide indigent defendants with criminal defense services, and legal aid providers handle poor people's civil legal issues.[8]

The Problems with a Siloed Approach: Practical, Doctrinal, and Conceptual

Because the civil-criminal distinction permeates all aspects of the legal system, as well as how people interact with that system, it causes practical, doctrinal, and conceptual problems. The civil-criminal distinction misaligns with our current realities and lived experiences. Maintaining this distinction frustrates our ability to address legal issues effectively.

Practical Problems

For litigants and actors on the ground, the siloed approach to the civil-criminal divide has immediate and significant consequences. The sharp distinction drawn between civil and criminal legal issues ignores how these two systems interact and how legal problems (and their attendant or underlying circumstances) surface in individuals' lives. Legal problems categorized as criminal may result from—or give rise to—civil legal issues. Failure to honor civil legal obligations can result in criminal consequences. Yet from a litigant's perspective, these legal issues may stem from the same circumstances and may meld together in lived experience.[9] For example, an individual who is evicted and loses her housing may face criminal sanctions for behaviors associated with homelessness, such as camping or panhandling.[10] Her homelessness, in turn, can "interfere with employment opportunities" and "may exacerbate mental-health and chemical-dependency issues," undermining the possibility of rehabilitation and increasing the odds of criminal reoffending. Conversely, an individual convicted of a criminal offense may face civil collateral consequences. She may be deported or become ineligible for naturalization. She may lose the right to vote. She may become ineligible for public benefits, including public housing or a driver's license. She may be ineligible for employment or to procure a permit necessary for doing business. The obligation to pay criminal fines and fees can impair her ability to pay rent, increasing the chances of an eviction and recidivism.[11] Criminal convictions can also affect family relations, including custody and visitation determinations.[12]

Collateral consequences—legal disabilities that stem from a criminal arrest, prosecution, or conviction but are distinct from the actual sentence imposed—highlight the practical incoherence of the civil-criminal divide. While some consider collateral consequences to be "the most significant part of the criminal justice system," they are not subject to the procedural protections typically afforded in criminal proceedings.[13] The separation in the legal system between civil and criminal means that the collateral consequences of criminal convictions are not generally considered part of the criminal process.[14] But without legal protections like the right to counsel, there is a risk that collateral consequences will be imposed erroneously or in violation of existing law.[15]

Viewing collateral consequences through the lens of those who experience them provides more reason to question the law's dogmatic categorization of them as civil matters. The defining question emerging from case law is whether the collateral consequence is punitive; that is to say, if a civil consequence is adequately punitive in either purpose or effect, it may be understood as a criminal punishment and thus subject to prohibitions on double jeopardy or ex post facto laws, in addition to the array of procedural protections reserved for criminal cases.[16] The courts' decision to define a consequence as "punitive" or not may have legal significance but may not align with individuals' personal, lived experience:

Mandatory barriers in occupational licensing can cause a person to lose their chosen field of work. Mandatory deportation tears individuals from the only family and country they know. Losing financial aid can end a person's educational experience, with profound effects on future employment and financial prospects. Individuals will often experience these consequences as punitive—often as more punitive than any sentence imposed in the criminal case—even if courts have not characterized them as such.[17]

Convictions also have informal collateral effects on housing, employment, and mental and physical health.[18] Wayne Logan has suggested that these informal collateral consequences can have equal, if not more significant, impact than formal collateral consequences. Indeed, informal collateral consequences affect not only criminally convicted individuals but also third parties, including their family members.[19] Family members of registered sex offenders, for example, are more likely to experience adverse consequences relating to their safety and their economic and emotional well-being.[20] Similar patterns occur when people face civil judgments; one loss can snowball into others.[21]

When the line between civil and criminal sanctions is blurred—as, for example, in the increasingly punitive realm of school discipline—the effect of collateral consequences is no less; school disciplinary action can cause significant financial and emotional harm to children and their families.[22] Thus, as Kathryn Sabbeth has contended, the threat of collateral consequences is no different from that posed by many civil matters, and both contexts demand a need for legal representation.[23]

Applying the civil-criminal distinction to collateral consequences also fails to address cyclical aspects of legal problems: addressing collateral consequences is often critical to successful reentry following release from incarceration.[24] But by structuring the legal system around the civil-criminal distinction, we lose the ability to address how these civil and criminal issues relate to one another as well as the underlying circumstances that give rise to these problems. Roscoe Pound observed in 1959 that when a court treats a range of family problems "as a series of single separate controversies [it] may often not do justice to the whole or to the several separate parts. The several parts are likely to be distorted in considering them apart from the whole."[25] Yet because the legal system is divided, both courts and service providers may find it difficult to address issues holistically.

The domestic violence context provides a concrete example demonstrating several aspects of the problem. Multiple civil and criminal cases may arise from the same act of violence. Yet the separation between civil and criminal courts can make it difficult for domestic violence victims to most effectively address a range of legal issues related to the violence. A victim of domestic violence may choose to prosecute her partner criminally and, at the same time, may need a civil protective order.[26] If she is married, she may also need to file for divorce. If she has children, she may need to resolve custody issues, determine child support, or possibly protect her children from abuse.[27]

For each action she files, the victim will need to visit a separate clerk's office, filing a different set of procedures in each case—likely an unfamiliar and time-intensive process.[28] In each action, she will have to deal with different actors—for example, a prosecutor in the criminal case and a civil defense attorney (or no lawyer at all) in the civil actions. Because she cannot address all of these issues in one forum, the timing of one court may impede her progress in another court. Certain civil matters may be processed quickly, whereas the criminal case may move more slowly, in part because of the procedural protections afforded to the alleged abuser.[29] If a particular court orders relief, it is unlikely to have coordinated the terms or breadth of that relief with the other courts considering her legal needs. The result may be contradictory court orders or periods in which domestic violence protection orders lapse.[30]

From the perspective of domestic violence respondents, the civil-criminal line is also troubling. While a respondent may be subject to a civil order of protection, there may be criminal consequences for violating that order.[31] But because the order is civil, respondents may have no right to criminal representation to advise them about the terms of that order or their required compliance with it.[32]

Separating domestic violence cases into civil and criminal silos can also strain judicial resources. It is inefficient for several judges to handle cases that involve the same children and the same respondents.[33] In many instances, there may be poor communication across legal forums, leaving judges ill-informed about the nature and status of proceedings pending before other judges.[34] As a result, judges may be forced to rely on litigants for information about related cases; many of those litigants are unrepresented by counsel and may have an inaccurate understanding of those other proceedings. Family court judges may be unaware of parallel criminal cases, even when the facts and circumstances of those cases could have a substantial bearing on the disposition of family court cases. Criminal judges may likewise lack access to relevant facts from family court proceedings. Judith Moran contends that the "resulting information gap leads to inconsistent decisions that can compromise child safety and family functioning."[35] Catherine Ross provides a more specific anecdote:

> Imagine a case in which the parents file for divorce in domestic relations court, and then engage in a protracted custody battle over their eight-year-old daughter. During the course of the proceedings, the mother alleges that the father has sexually abused the daughter. Her complaint is reported to state authorities, who initiate a dependency action in another court, because they believe the mother has failed to protect the daughter adequately. They also refer the case to prosecutors who initiate a criminal action against the father in yet a third court. This jurisdiction also has a domestic violence court that is looking into allegations that the father physically abused the mother. Now the family is involved in four proceedings before four different judges, with different teams of lawyers, all of whom need information from the daughter regarding what she witnessed between her parents, what, if anything, her father did to her, whether she has a preference regarding custody, and if so, what it is, and so on.[36]

Although not solely responsible, the division and subsequent hierarchy imposed upon the civil and criminal legal systems may partially explain why racial inequalities in the criminal system have historically received more scholarly attention than those in the civil system. Although many have written about the relationship between race and criminal justice,[37] race and racial inequality have been vastly understudied in the literature addressing civil access to justice.[38] Effective solutions to racial inequality in the criminal sphere may still feel distant, but we have yet to even fully describe or understand the myriad ways in which race intersects with the civil legal system.

One might contend that the "civil" and "criminal" labels, despite internal inconsistencies and pragmatic concerns, serve an important signaling function. Paul Robinson has suggested that these two labels simplify and streamline communications for ordinary people whose lives are "full of concerns and pressures having little to do with the law. If the legal system hopes to communicate with the average person, the communication must be clear and simple."[39] Thus, he contends, "creating a special criminal label and widely disseminating the notion that this label has a different, condemnatory meaning" can help convey important information about the legal system.[40]

However, recent research suggests that many people do not fully understand the difference between the civil and criminal spheres. As Sara Sternberg Greene has aptly explained, lawyers' and scholars' application of the civil-criminal division contrasts with how nonlawyers experience and navigate the legal system:

> Scholars who study the legal system typically fall into one of two broad camps: those who study the civil legal system and those who study the criminal legal system. These two groups rarely come together at academic conferences; rarely work together on research projects; and, for the most part, see themselves as studying two very distinct systems and bodies of law. While this may be true from a legal standpoint, for most poor respondents there is little difference between the two systems. Court is court. The law is the law. Lawyers are lawyers. Judges are judges.[41]

For example, when asked about seeking a lawyer for assistance with an eviction, many respondents stated that "they would have to seek help from a public defender."[42] Most respondents in Greene's study believed that they were entitled to a lawyer for any legal problem—whether civil or criminal.[43]

My research on the civil legal needs of indigent criminal defendants—conducted in partnership with Ruth Richardson—demonstrates similar confusion among criminal defendants. Our research, which was based on interviews with public defenders, social workers, and their clients, suggests that even those currently engaged with the criminal legal system may not wholly appreciate the distinction between the civil and criminal systems.[44] Some defendants we interviewed did not understand how their legal rights would differ in the civil and criminal contexts.[45] When defendants did perceive a distinction, they were more likely to view civil issues as nonlegal (rather than simply assigned to a different part of the legal system).[46] Many respondents were unaware that their civil problems could be addressed with legal assistance or that such help was even available.[47] Few had attempted to seek civil legal assistance, and no one interviewed had successfully obtained it.[48] Our research also demonstrated that differences in how the system treats civil and criminal issues may lead self-represented individuals to misunderstand civil legal matters, underestimating the importance of the proceedings and/or their own rights in the civil process.[49]

Public defender clients who understand the civil-criminal distinction may be hesitant to raise civil issues with their lawyer, viewing such issues as unrelated to their criminal case—even if the lawyer should be informed of those issues or could address them while handling the criminal case.[50] Defendants who do not understand the distinction may experience frustration that their public defender cannot address other issues they may be facing. This research suggests that one unintended effect of the civil-criminal distinction may be that individuals have an incomplete understanding of the legal system's full scale or capacity, putting them at a disadvantage in marshaling the resources needed to address their problems effectively (if at all).

In addition, research by Sendhil Mullainathan and Eldar Shafir demonstrates how the intense use of mental capacity by people living in poverty to address their immediate needs—like food, shelter, and employment—leaves little room to focus on other issues.[51] As a result, such individuals often suffer from limited bandwidth and may find it difficult to make important decisions.[52] The artificial civil-criminal divide may confuse individuals who are already experiencing high levels of stress and make it harder for them to navigate a time-consuming legal system.[53]

A final practical consequence of the civil-criminal distinction is that very little research exists at the nexus of the two. As Sara Sternberg Greene has noted, scholars typically follow the same siloed pattern as the system itself, studying either the civil or the criminal justice system in isolation.[54] Even research that touches on both still tends to adopt the premise of two separate spheres, focusing on either the civil or the criminal system while exploring how an aspect of one system impacts the other. Thus, even though anecdotal data from practitioners suggest a clear link between the two realms,[55] the existing research offers insufficient information to allow us to assess the full impact of the civil-criminal divide.

Doctrinal Problems

The civil-criminal distinction is rooted in the Constitution, which was written when civil and criminal disputes and sanctions were far more differentiated than they are now and which affords greater procedural rights in the criminal context.[56] Perhaps because of their connection to the concepts of punishment and violations committed against the state, criminal offenses have traditionally been accompanied by more severe sanctions, including the loss of personal liberty. The courts' refusal to extend "criminal" rights to the civil context is based in large part on their general assumption that the two spheres are distinct in nature and their specific assumption that deprivation of liberty is a uniquely severe form of punishment.

One example of this phenomenon is the United States Supreme Court's 1981 decision in *Lassiter v. Department of Social Services.*[57] In *Lassiter*, the Court held that the Constitution did not require the state to provide an attorney for an indigent mother who was fighting the state's (civil) effort to terminate her parental rights.[58] To justify its decision, the Court emphasized that the appointment of counsel is typically required only when a person is at risk of the deprivation of physical liberty.[59] In dissent, Justice Blackmun delved more deeply into the civil-criminal distinction, noting the Court's willingness to require certain procedural protections in civil matters that it considered to be "quasi-criminal."[60] Justice Blackmun compared *Lassiter* with the case of *Little v. Streater*, decided earlier that year, which held that an indigent putative father had the right to a state-paid paternity test in a paternity action.[61] Justice Blackmun concluded that the positions of the litigants—one attempting to disprove a parental relationship and the other attempting to preserve a parental relationship—was not significant enough to warrant such differential treatment.[62]

Regardless of Justice Blackmun's argument, the deprivation of liberty has continued to serve as a judicial touchstone justifying differential treatment of legal issues and differential allocation of procedural protections, including the appointment of state-funded counsel.[63] Yet as Kathryn Sabbeth has emphasized, the loss of liberty no longer differentiates between civil and criminal cases: "In immigrant removal, civil commitment, and civil contempt proceedings, a loss of physical liberty is also at stake. Hearings regarding revocation of parole or probation violations, too, are classified as civil, though if the individual loses, she will go to prison."[64]

Even if incarceration is in fact a more severe sanction—a premise questioned by some Justices[65]—and even if incarceration is more common in criminal cases, those facts do not necessarily support the civil-criminal divide. Paul Robinson has questioned whether the need to provide additional safeguards for more severe sanctions justifies the existence of two distinct systems:

> If differential safeguards were the reason for the distinction, why have societies not simply required more safeguards for more severe sanctions within a single system? Why waste the criminal law's special procedural safeguards on the large number of less serious criminal cases in which the sanction is no greater than would be available under civil law—a fine, a restraining order, or the like?[66]

More broadly, scholars have criticized the body of Supreme Court case law devoted to defining which proceedings are "criminal" and therefore warrant heightened protections, finding such case law "confusing and lacking in a general theoretical framework."[67] One scholar describes the Court's attempts to distinguish between civil and criminal statutes as "a jurisprudential Frankenstein's monster—a patchwork assembled from disparate parts, unwieldy and unpredictable, and suffering from a distressing but justified inquietude about its reason for existing."[68]

The Court's willingness to look beyond the civil-criminal distinction and instead consider the nature of the proceeding or sanction at issue has vacillated over time. In some cases, the Court's analysis has been driven by a determination of where a sanction falls along the civil-criminal spectrum. For example, in *Padilla v. Kentucky*,[69] the Court held that defense counsel was constitutionally ineffective for failing to inform the defendant about the deportation consequences of his criminal plea. The Court reasoned that, although removal proceedings are civil, deportation is "intimately related to the criminal process" and is therefore difficult to divorce from the conviction.[70] In contrast, in applying the Eighth Amendment's Excessive Fines Clause to civil forfeiture cases, the Court held that the determinative fact was not whether the forfeiture was considered civil or criminal but whether it was understood as punishment.[71] Just four years later, in a case deciding that the protection against double jeopardy—being tried twice for the same offense—applies only in criminal and not civil cases, the Court rejected such an approach, deeming it "unworkable."[72]

Technological developments have increased the visibility and impact of civil consequences and have changed how people experience them.[73] These changes, in addition to the integration of these consequences into plea-bargaining and sentencing, have led state and federal lower courts to redefine previously civil sanctions as criminal.[74] Although primarily in dicta (commentary) rather than holdings, the Supreme Court has increasingly recognized the same distinction. Concurring in a recent case involving a void-for-vagueness challenge to a federal immigration statute, Justice Gorsuch noted:

> [T]oday's civil laws regularly impose penalties far more severe than those found in many criminal statutes[.] Ours is a world filled with more and more civil laws bearing more and more extravagant punishments. Today's "civil" penalties include confiscatory rather than compensatory fines, forfeiture provisions that allow homes to be taken, remedies that strip persons of their professional licenses and livelihoods, and the power to commit persons against their will indefinitely. Some of these penalties are routinely imposed and are routinely graver than those associated with misdemeanor crimes—and often harsher than the punishment for felonies.[75]

Despite such acknowledgments, the Supreme Court clings to the civil-criminal distinction with few exceptions,[76] using it to limit the application of procedural protections and to restrict expansion of the doctrine.

Conceptual Problems

Setting aside the doctrinal flaws of such an approach, the conceptual line between civil and criminal—and the justification for drawing that line where it lies—is far more blurred than systemic divisions might otherwise suggest. To provide one potentially provocative example: Is shoplifting from a local merchant to feed one's family so different from failing to pay rent to a landlord after one has lost a job? I am not suggesting that we criminalize the latter activity but merely highlighting what some might see as the lack of a clear conceptual—or even moral— distinction between the two behaviors.

These lines have become particularly hard to draw when it comes to defining "punishment"—an allegedly key conceptual difference between "civil" and "criminal" actions. Although punishment and incarceration are typically associated with criminal law, they are not unique to that context. As Carol Steiker has observed, attempts to define "punishment" in a way that "make[s] our two-track [civil and criminal] procedural system work . . . ha[ve] been conceptually muddled, to say the least."[77] People can face civil commitment due to mental illness[78] or be criminally prosecuted and incarcerated for failing to honor civil obligations, including payment of child support.[79] Similarly, some criminal offenses result in penalties other than incarceration, such as fines or probation restrictions. Most defendants convicted of felonies will never serve time in prison—roughly 60% receive probation or probation with jail time.[80] And most misdemeanor convictions will never result in incarceration at all.[81] As more dramatic sanctions—such as capital or corporal punishment—are applied with decreasing frequency or have been eliminated, it has become harder to categorize any given sanction as "distinctly punitive . . . [because] confinement and monetary fines are [both] used for civil restraint and criminal punishment."[82]

As Susan Klein points out, the line between the *purposes* of civil and criminal law is increasingly blurred. It is not always clear whether a sanction imposed in the civil context is intended to compensate the harmed party or to send a message to society. Similarly, it is sometimes unclear whether a punishment imposed in the criminal context is intended to protect public safety or to make the victim whole. Klein asks: "[D]oes the state revoke a drunken driver's license to punish the driver and deter him and others from similar conduct, or to ensure highway safety, or a little bit of both?"[83] Further blurring the civil-criminal distinction, a driver's license can be suspended in many states both as a criminal punishment and as a civil sanction for nonpayment of fines and fees.[84] This begs the question of whether the license suspension serves as punishment or some other purpose.

Kenneth Mann's description of increasingly common "middle ground" or "hybrid" sanctions reflects this conceptual blurring of civil and criminal consequences.[85] Although the civil system is said to provide compensatory relief, civil monetary sanctions may sometimes be nonremedial deterrents that are intended as punishments, even though they are based in civil law and procedure.[86]

The criminal system has similarly strayed from its traditional focus on morality and blameworthiness. For example, "public welfare" offenses—often intended to "heighten the duties of those in control of particular industries, trades, properties or activities that affect public health, safety or welfare"[87]—impose strict liability for various regulatory offenses. With a strict liability offense, the law does not require that offenders have any particular mens rea (criminal intent or "guilty mind"); offenders are punished regardless of their moral blameworthiness. Similarly, two of the criminal justice system's primary purposes are rehabilitation and deterrence. But those goals are not advanced by a system that segregates civil legal issues that have a significant impact on a defendant's ability to engage or re-engage in criminal activity.[88]

In a related vein, Carol Steiker has noted the victim's rights movement's incremental success in giving victims and restitution more prominent roles in the criminal process.[89] Although victims are technically not parties in criminal cases, the victim's rights movement has increasingly shifted the understanding of criminal actions away from a public proceeding against "the People" and toward a "quasi-private dispute between the victim and defendant resembling a civil action."[90] Civil collateral consequences that arise from criminal convictions are similarly problematic for the claimed conceptual differences between criminal and civil cases.

Collateral consequences are typically not considered criminal punishment,[91] yet civil justifications for their imposition—such as deterrence and public safety—may not hold water.[92] In an interesting twist on

the civil-criminal distinction, civil consequences may merge punitiveness (seen as inherently criminal) with the private (rather than public)
nature of civil disputes.[93] For example, as Jenny Roberts has explained,
while sex offender registration schemes are often touted as nonpunitive
ways to increase public safety, empirical evidence has undermined their
public safety rationale.[94] And while they may not involve punishment by
the state, sex offender registration laws expose registrants to punishment
in the form of shaming and exclusion by private individuals.[95]

Another conceptual justification for the civil-criminal distinction
is the argument that criminal proceedings invoke the "enormity and
weight" of state power by pitting an individual against the government.[96]
Yet as Kathryn Sabbeth has contended, this alleged conceptual distinction is unpersuasive. First, the state is a party to many civil actions, including actions that the state initiates, such as termination of parental
rights, eviction from public housing, and termination of public benefits
(e.g., social security).[97] Second, while the state's power over people's lives
can make it a formidable opponent, the privatization of public services
has decreased state power and expanded private actors' control over access to utilities such as electricity, water, and the internet, as well as traditionally state-operated instruments of social control such as prisons
and police.[98]

The fluid categorization and recategorization of identical conduct—
from civil to criminal or criminal to civil—further undermines the claim
of any fundamental difference between the civil and criminal spheres.
Current examples abound—for example, traffic offenses are viewed as
civil infractions in some states and as criminal offenses in others.[99] Even
within a single state, or even a single statutory scheme, the civil-criminal
divide is increasingly unclear.

Consider, for example, Texas's 2015 change to its truancy laws. Under
the new law, truancy is no longer a criminal violation, and Texas eliminated criminal sanctions—including potential jail time—for students
who skip school.[100] Still, truant students may face fines or the revocation of their drivers' licenses. In more extreme cases, where absences are
unexcused and the schools can prove parental negligence, a criminal
complaint may be filed against the parents.

Other conduct also crosses the civil-criminal line. In 2019, Texas
largely decriminalized the failure to make payments for rent-to-own

furniture, but traces of the criminal law linger.[101] The statute still permits criminal prosecution in some cases, including those in which the person intended to steal property.[102] And as LaToya Baldwin Clark has pointed out, the criminalization of civil residency violations relating to educational residency requirements lies at the intersection of civil and criminal law and policy.[103] These overlaps and recategorizations suggest that the civil-criminal line is more superficial than inherent; they can also be extremely confusing to those navigating the system, particularly those without an attorney.

Child support laws, which Elizabeth Katz calls "criminal law in a civil guise," amply demonstrate the mutable nature of civil and criminal conduct.[104] Katz explains that, in the early twentieth century, family nonsupport was criminalized. In the 1930s, responding to costs and stigma, lawmakers rebranded these proceedings as "civil" yet retained some of their criminal characteristics, such as prosecution and state monitoring and enforcement. Katz contends that the result is a civil-criminal hybrid that relies on artificial state labels or statutory placement in civil codes to deprive obligors of criminal procedure protections.[105] To confuse matters further, noncompliance with a child support obligation may result in civil contempt or, in more extreme cases, a criminal nonsupport action taken by the state.[106] Either path may involve incarceration, yet the procedures attached to the two proceedings will differ depending upon their categorization as civil or criminal.

Ultimately, the perplexing insistence on a civil-criminal divide affects our conceptual approach to reform. Under the current system, some iterations of criminal justice reform involve reclassifying criminal issues as civil in an attempt to lessen their severity. While reclassification may mean that offenders are no longer subject to incarceration, they can still face significant consequences for violations without the procedural protections afforded by criminal law. This approach to reform merely shifts criminal system burdens to the civil system, potentially pitting these systems against each other in a battle for resources and preventing society from engaging in reform efforts based on principles rather than labels. As Robinson asks: "Would it not be more efficient to have a single system that avoids the complexity and wasteful duplication of two separate and distinct systems, a single system in which condemnation and punishment could be imposed when deserved and in which only damages could be awarded when condemnation and punishment are not deserved?"[107]

Solutions: Closing the Civil-Criminal Gap

Reforms arising from changing our current understanding of the civil-criminal divide could range from minor to seismic. Either way, reform will require a significant shift in our thinking, given the pervasive way in which we silo courts, legal services, and legal research and scholarship. Below I offer a few suggestions about how we might make reforms that reflect such a shift.

A radical proposal would be to eliminate the civil-criminal distinction. This chapter stops short of offering such a dramatic solution, acknowledging both the impracticability and infeasibility of such an approach and the distinct (if undertheorized) differences between some civil and criminal offenses. For example, most would probably agree that settling a property dispute does—and should—differ from conducting a murder trial. But with that caveat, I contend that challenging, and in some cases eliminating, the stark civil-criminal divide would benefit courts and the litigants they serve.

Rather than being driven primarily by labels, courts might organize systems based on how problems tend to arise in practice. This might mean that courts would not handle solely civil or criminal matters but instead have the jurisdictional freedom and flexibility to address issues as they arise in individuals' life circumstances. Indeed, some specialized or alternative courts already do this.[108] Still, specialization risks creating another type of fragmentation, so it is important to coordinate actions among courts. There may be concerns about having judges preside over multiple matters—in part because some litigants and some cases may benefit from an impartial decision maker without knowledge of other, unrelated issues. There may also be concerns about certain involved actors—including government attorneys—having differing interests in different institutional or court contexts.[109]

While these concerns are valid, I suggest that they are not inherent to the civil-criminal divide. Rather, the culprit is the relative importance we have placed on cases in either category and the resultant procedures and rules that have proliferated in each context. The above concerns could be addressed through a combination of ethical and professional rules and through judicial discretion, recognizing that some issues may be better resolved by another judge. Concerns about conflicting interests or differing levels of procedural protections could be solved by increasing protections across the board or by calibrating protections to the needs of a particular problem without regard to its civil or criminal label.

In terms of systemic reform, this approach would suggest that a change in labels alone—for example, making traffic offenses civil rather than criminal—would mean very little. Indeed, under the current system, shifting an offense from one category to another through decriminalization may deprive people of procedural protections. Alternatively, we might emphasize "delegalization"—removing certain offenses from civil *and* criminal legal systems and instead using the legal system as a vehicle to direct individuals to relevant social and supportive services. Reducing distinctions between civil and criminal offenses and asking instead whether *any* legal sanction is appropriate might encourage us to be more thoughtful about when and whether punishment is needed. Recent efforts to eliminate sanctions for marijuana possession and to create drug courts that focus primarily on treatment may provide good models for such a shift. At its best, this approach might encourage lawmakers and policy makers to develop more creative remedies, unrestricted by labels placed on individuals' actions or by outdated definitions of punishment.

From a doctrinal angle, the law should recognize that the stakes in civil cases can be just as high as in criminal cases and that incarceration is not always the best demarcation for identifying those cases worthy of appointed counsel.[110] Maintaining a civil-criminal distinction can prevent us from assessing the real value of legal interventions—including the assignment of counsel—that generate benefits not only in their own sphere but also in others. For example, as Kathryn Sabbeth has contended, making legal counsel available to improve access to housing and employment may "ultimately have a larger impact on criminal defendants, individually and in the aggregate—including both actual defendants and potential defendants—than counsel in criminal proceedings."[111] Rather than focusing on whether an offense is civil or criminal, we might focus on the complexity of the case, the severity of the possible penalty as interpreted more broadly (beyond incarceration), and/or the value of providing counsel in a given case. By removing labels that often serve as a shortcut, we might be forced to examine why and when certain protections—such as the right to counsel and stricter evidentiary rules—are necessary.[112]

Practical reforms might institute new ways of delivering legal services. A recent study by James Anderson, Maya Buenaventura, and Paul Heaton explored the impact of holistic defense on criminal justice outcomes.[113] The researchers defined "holistic defense" as a defense model that addresses "the enmeshed, or collateral, legal consequences of criminal justice involvement (such as loss of employment, public housing, custody of one's children, and immigration status), as well as underlying nonlegal issues that often play a role in driving clients into the criminal justice system in the first place."[114] Ultimately, the study found that defendants served by the holistic defense model were less likely to be detained pretrial, less likely to receive custodial sentences, and more likely to receive shorter sentences.[115]

As to collateral consequences, several scholars have advocated for an evolved definition of "punitiveness" based either on popular understandings of the sanction[116] or the lived experiences of those impacted by it.[117] Carol Steiker has suggested a blend of these approaches, proposing a three-part inquiry to determine whether a particular consequence should be considered punishment such that criminal procedural protections apply: (1) What does the state intend? (2) What is the effect on the individual? and (3) What would the community understand the sanction to mean?[118] In a similar vein, whether legal procedures and protections should apply to collateral consequences should turn not on their label as "civil" or "criminal" but instead on a more objective determination of their importance or effect, much as the tests suggested by those scholars propose.

Minimizing the civil-criminal distinction would also have ramifications for legal education and how we train lawyers. In our current system, we train lawyers to view everything they learn as part of the same siloed system, starting with teaching law students about two disconnected realms governed by two distinct sets of rules and procedures (i.e., separate civil procedure and criminal procedure courses). In a revised paradigm—even if we cannot control how the legal system is organized—we can teach law students to think about problems holistically rather than seeing legal problems as falling within one bucket or another.

Social science research has shown that legal problems tend to occur not in isolation but in clusters, often appearing in patterns.[119] In addition, problems that can be addressed through legal assistance are often caused by and give rise to a range of other social, health, and emotional problems.[120] Thus, if a lawyer is to truly improve her client's well-being and prevent the damage done by repeated interactions with the legal system, she cannot conduct her practice in a civil or criminal law vacuum.

No law student or lawyer can ever be an expert in all legal areas, much less myriad topics beyond the law. Still, law schools could teach students how legal problems cluster together and educate them about the collateral concerns that may warrant consultation with another type of lawyer or with a social service provider. This type of training can be continued into the professional sphere, ensuring, for example, that legal aid lawyers are aware of calendars where criminal warrants can be cleared and that public defenders are aware of the triggers for civil legal problems. This expanded view of legal training would ideally acknowledge the relationship between legal and social problems and familiarize students with how to respond to these dynamics, even if they cannot solve them on their own.

Such an approach would, naturally, change how we conceive and organize legal practice. A paradigm that minimizes the civil-criminal distinction would likely include many kinds of lawyers—and social service providers—within the same practice. As Michael Pinard has described:

> [M]any defender offices have recognized the importance of linking criminal and civil issues. Some offices have formed civil teams that handle civil issues, such as housing and public benefits, related to the underlying criminal matter. Other offices do not have civil teams but assign identified attorneys to develop expertise in certain related areas, such as immigration. These attorneys are then responsible both for training other lawyers to recognize situations where these issues are likely to exist, and for providing any related legal services. Still other offices that do not handle civil issues have established referral relationships with relevant legal services organizations that can take on these matters.[121]

This "holistic mindset" need not and should not stop with those providing legal assistance. It could extend to how courts—which are the primary interface for litigants unrepresented by counsel—provide litigants with information. Just as siloed civil-criminal systems may lead lawyers to miss opportunities to identify and address other (sometimes underlying) issues, those silos also lead courts and social service agencies to lose intervention opportunities. If they were to recognize how problems arise in individuals' lives, courts and government agencies might take advantage of existing engagements with the court system and provide those individuals with information about a range of legal problems—not merely those problems solely within the court's or agency's direct purview—and the means to address them.[122] For example, a family law center might make criminal warrant-clearing calendars available in its waiting room. Or people waiting for their criminal cases to be called might be provided with information about how to best handle civil legal problems relating to divorce, child custody, public benefits, and eviction.

Conclusion

As the chapters in this volume make clear, there is much work to be done in thinking about how we improve the system that defines and processes criminal offenses and the people it accuses of committing them. Yet a siloed approach to justice reform—whether characterized as "criminal justice reform" or "civil justice reform"—might exacerbate or be seen as a manifestation of a broader problem. By segmenting our approach to reform, we focus on the trees rather than the forest. The problems relating to access, equality, racialization, and poverty that underlie both criminal and civil legal issues are not confined to one part of the legal system, and they are not confined to the legal realm. In contemplating how to improve criminal legal systems, we should consider how to tie these reforms to improvements in other systems, both legal and nonlegal, so that we maximize the impact of these reforms and create more meaningful improvements in the lives of individuals and communities most impacted by those systems.

NOTES

1 Although today civil and criminal proceedings are subject to very different rules, before the 1940s and federal rules reform, those systems were subject to similar rules grounded in common law. See Meyn, "Constructing Separate and Unequal Courtrooms," 5.

2 See later discussion of the flawed reliance on the private-state distinction to support the civil-criminal divide.

3 Klein, "Redrawing the Criminal-Civil Boundary," 679.

4 Ibid., 679–80.

5 In other contexts, like the Fourth Amendment, protections may apply in both civil and criminal cases, but the standards or methodologies applied in implementing those protections may differ. See, e.g., Wright, Note, "The Civil and Criminal Methodologies of the Fourth Amendment," 93 (describing how courts had applied "a stricter, more rule-oriented 'probable cause' analysis in criminal cases, but . . . a more flexible and less rule-bound 'balancing' methodology in civil cases").

6 See, e.g., American Immigration Council, *Two Systems of Justice* (describing the range of protections available in the criminal context that are not available to noncitizens in the civil immigration context).

7 Blenkinsopp, "Dangerousness and the Civil-Criminal Distinction," 12.

8 See Legal Services Corporation, "Fact Sheet."

9 Research conducted outside the American legal system has surfaced similar issues, demonstrating how some legal problems—including those relating to employment, children, and relationships—are likely to trigger additional legal problems. People, "Do Some Types of Legal Problems Trigger Other Legal Problems?" 37.

10 Rankin, "Punishing Homelessness," 101–02.

11 Colgan, "Fines, Fees, and Forfeitures"

12 Chin, "Collateral Consequences," 372.

13 Ibid.

14 Pinard, "Broadening the Holistic Mindset," 1078; Murray, "Are Collateral Consequences Deserved?" 1031.

15 For a discussion of the risks and results of wrongful collateral consequences, see Horn, "Wrongful Collateral Consequences," 315.

16 Steiker, "Punishment and Procedure," 777.

17 Roberts, "*Gundy* and the Civil-Criminal Divide," 224.

18 Logan, "Informal Collateral Consequences," 1117.

19 Ibid., 1107–09.

20 Levenson and Tewksbury, "Collateral Damage," 64–65.

21 See Albiston and Sandefur, "Expanding the Empirical Study of Access to Justice," 111–12 (describing negative consequences of civil judgments, including effects on mental and physical health).

22 Mowen, "Collateral Consequences," 840–48.

23 Sabbeth, "The Prioritization of Criminal Over Civil Counsel," 914; see ibid., 932 ("The prioritization of criminal over civil counsel exaggerates the divide between the functions these lawyers serve and neglects the significance of accessing economic and political resources for both client populations. Further, it falsely

suggests that the most valuable work of a lawyer is to ward off the intrusion of regulation, rather than to support its robust and equal application.").

24 Pinard, "Reflections and Perspectives on Reentry," 1219; Levenson and Tewksbury, "Collateral Damage," 65 (distancing from loved ones to reduce the effect of collateral consequences on them results in reduced social and economic support for offenders, potentially facilitating recidivism); Pinard, "Broadening the Holistic Mindset" 1067.

25 Pound, "The Place of the Family Court in the Judicial System," 164. Examples of the "effects of the distortion caused by fragmented courts for families include such harms as: unnecessary delays in adjudication and services; delays that have the equivalent of a multiplier effect on children because of children's sense of time (one year is half of a two year old's entire life); courts with overlapping jurisdiction issuing conflicting orders; failing to identify or protect persons at risk of domestic violence; subjecting children to the risk of becoming lost in foster care drift; repeated interviews of children by different examiners; and the related problem of calling children as witnesses when it is unnecessary to do so"; Ross, "The Failure of Fragmentation," 7–8.

26 Epstein, "Effective Intervention in Domestic Violence Cases," 23.
27 Ibid.
28 Ibid., 25.
29 Ibid., 24.
30 Ibid.
31 Stoever, "Access to Safety and Justice," 351.
32 Ibid.
33 Moran, "Fragmented Courts and Child Protection Cases," 488.
34 Ibid., 492.
35 Ibid.
36 Ross, "The Failure of Fragmentation," 8.
37 See, e.g., Forman, *Locking Up Our Own*; Stevenson, *Just Mercy*; Alexander, *The New Jim Crow*; Cole, *No Equal Justice*; Kennedy, *Race, Crime, and the Law*.
38 Brito et al., "*I Do for My Kids*."
39 Robinson, "The Criminal-Civil Distinction," 208.
40 Ibid.
41 Greene, "Race, Class, and Access to Civil Justice," 1290.
42 Ibid., 1289.
43 Ibid., 1290.
44 Sudeall and Richardson, "Unfamiliar Justice," 2131.
45 Ibid.
46 Ibid.
47 Ibid.
48 Ibid., 2146.
49 Ibid., 2131–32.
50 Ibid., 2151.

51 Shafir and Mullainathan, *Scarcity*, 29, 149, 157.
52 Schilbach, Schofield, and Mullainathan, "The Psychological Lives of the Poor," 435.
53 Ibid.
54 Greene, "Race, Class, and Access to Civil Justice," 1290; see also Sudeall and Richardson, "Unfamiliar Justice," 2107.
55 See, e.g., Philip, "Where Criminal Defense Meets Civil Action."
56 Dudley, "Getting Beyond the Civil-Criminal Distinction," 1065 (noting that the Constitution "distinguishes between civil and criminal proceedings and requires greater procedural safeguards in the latter.").
57 452 U.S. 18 (1981).
58 Ibid., 33.
59 Ibid., 26–27.
60 Ibid., 58 (Blackmun, J., dissenting) (citing Little v. Streater, 452 U.S. 1, 10 (1981) ("Although the State characterizes such proceedings as 'civil,' they have 'quasi-criminal' overtones. [State law] provides that if a putative father 'is found *guilty*, the court shall order him to stand charged with the support and maintenance of such child'; and his subsequent failure to comply with the court's support order is punishable by imprisonment" (citations and parentheticals omitted)).
61 Ibid.
62 Ibid.
63 Buskey and Lucas, "Keeping *Gideon's* Promise," 2307 ("The rule set forth in *Scott*—that a criminal defendant in state court is entitled to the appointment of counsel only if his conviction results in incarceration—remains the law today.").
64 Sabbeth, "The Prioritization of Criminal Over Civil Counsel," 907.
65 See Scott v. Illinois, 440 U.S. 367, 374 (1979) (Powell, J., concurring) (explaining that "the drawing of a line based on whether there is imprisonment (even for overnight) can have the practical effect of precluding provision of counsel in other types of cases in which conviction can have more serious consequences").
66 Robinson, "The Criminal-Civil Distinction," 203–04.
67 Dudley, "Getting Beyond the Civil-Criminal Distinction," 1043 (citing Jonathan I. Charney, "The Need for Constitutional Protections for Defendants in Civil Penalty Cases," *Cornell Law Review* 59 (1974): 491–506; J. Clark, "Civil and Criminal Penalties and Forfeitures," 379; Comment, "The Concept of Punitive Legislation and the Sixth Amendment," 290; Edwards, "Forfeitures—Civil or Criminal?" 191; Note, "Civil RICO Is a Misnomer," 1288; Note, "Enforcing Criminal Laws Through Civil Proceedings," 1055).
68 Fellmeth, "Civil and Criminal Sanctions in the Constitution and Courts," 10.
69 559 U.S. 356 (2010).
70 Ibid., 365.
71 Austin v. United States, 509 U.S. 602, 607–10 (1993).
72 Hudson v. United States, 522 U.S. 93, 101–02 (1997) (abrogating its earlier holding in *United States v. Halper*, 490 U.S. 435 (1989)).

73 Roberts, "*Gundy* and the Civil-Criminal Divide," 208, 216.

74 Ibid.

75 Sessions v. Dimaya, 138 S. Ct. 1204, 1229 (2018) (Gorsuch, J., concurring).

76 See, e.g., In re Gault, 387 U.S. 1, 41 (1967) (holding that juveniles must be appointed counsel despite the civil classification of delinquency proceedings).

77 Steiker, "Punishment and Procedure," 781.

78 Robinson, "Foreword: The Criminal-Civil Distinction," 700 n.23 (listing state civil commitment statutes).

79 Lollar, "Criminalizing (Poor) Fatherhood," 125.

80 See Chin, "Collateral Consequences," 374.

81 Ibid., 374–75.

82 Steiker, "Punishment and Procedure," 780.

83 Klein, "Redrawing the Criminal-Civil Boundary," 680.

84 See Whitelemons, Thomas, and Couture, *Driving on Empty*, 5, 15.

85 Mann, "Punitive Civil Sanctions," 1799 and n.15, 1802. Relatedly, Carol Steiker has noted: "This blurring or destabilization of the criminal-civil distinction is partly due to the increase in the sheer number of 'hybrid' legal institutions and practices: '[f]rom civil penalties to punitive damages, civil forfeiture to criminal restitution, legal devices that are arguably criminal-civil hybrids seem to be more common than they were a century ago.'" Steiker, "Punishment and Procedure," 783–84, citing Gail Heriot, "An Essay on the Civil-Criminal Distinction with Special Reference to Punitive Damages, Journal of Contemporary Legal Issues 7: 44 (1996).

86 Ibid.

87 Morissette v. United States, 342 U.S. 246, 254 (1952).

88 J. Anderson, Buenaventura, and Heaton, "The Effects of Holistic Defense on Criminal Justice Outcomes," 819.

89 Steiker, "Punishment and Procedure," 793.

90 Ibid.

91 Murray, "Are Collateral Consequences Deserved?" 1031.

92 See, e.g., Chin, "Collateral Consequences," 383 ("Without understanding the legal landscape, it is much more difficult to evaluate whether collateral consequences as a whole are fair and promote public safety both by keeping convicted persons from situations where they might present special dangers, or whether they frustrate public safety by denying some of them a reasonable opportunity to lead law-abiding lives and not recidivate."); Murray, "Are Collateral Consequences Deserved?" 1034 ("Their incapacitative- and deterrence-based rationales, and concerns for welfare maximization, allow for the convenient blurring of the criminal-civil line.").

93 Roberts, "*Gundy* and the Civil-Criminal Divide," 222.

94 Ibid., 218; Roberts also points to a recent declaration by the United States Commission on Civil Rights that "[m]any collateral consequences . . . are unrelated either to the underlying crime for which a person has been convicted or to a

public safety purpose," Ibid., 220; see also Levenson and Tewksbury, "Collateral Damage," 65.

95 Roberts, "*Gundy* and the Civil-Criminal Divide," 222.

96 Sabbeth, "The Prioritization of Criminal Over Civil Counsel," 921.

97 Ibid., 923.

98 Ibid., 926.

99 Compare GA. CODE ANN. § 40-13-21 (2019) with Hawai'i State Judiciary, "Types of Traffic Offenses," (explaining the differences between civil traffic infractions and traffic crimes).

100 Langford, "New Truancy Law."

101 Najmabadi and Root, "New Texas law."

102 Ibid.

103 L. Clark, "Education as Property," 408.

104 Katz, "Criminal Law in a Civil Guise."

105 Ibid., 1245. While acknowledging that the civil-criminal line is both "artificial and malleable," Katz proceeds assuming that it is too entrenched to discard. Ibid., 1307. She suggests that recognition of modern child support enforcement as criminal will require either the attachment of criminal procedures and protections or an affirmative decision to decriminalize child support enforcement (including, for example, the elimination of incarceration as a possible sanction). Ibid.

106 Dennis, "Criminal Law as Family Law," 312; see also Katz, "Criminal Law in a Civil Guise," 1242 (noting that all states retained criminal nonsupport prosecutions, even though most child support suits are considered "civil"); National Conference of State Legislatures, "Criminal Nonsupport and Child Support."

107 Robinson, "The Criminal-Civil Distinction," 207.

108 See Collins, "The Problem of Problem-Solving Courts"; see also MacDowell, "When Courts Collide," 188 (for arguments in favor of pluralism).

109 See MacDowell, "When Courts Collide," 118.

110 Buskey and Lucas, "Keeping *Gideon's* Promise," 2305; see also earlier discussion of *Lassiter* in this chapter.

111 Sabbeth, "The Prioritization of Criminal over Civil Counsel," 933.

112 See Lucas, "Deconstructing the Right to Counsel" (proposing an organizational, value-driven framework to determine when the right to a lawyer or other nonlawyer alternatives should apply in civil cases).

113 Anderson et al., "The Effects of Holistic Defense," 819.

114 Ibid., 821.

115 Ibid. However, the model did not appear to reduce recidivism; holistic defense clients were no more or less likely to be rearrested within 10 years of their initial arraignment. The researchers concluded that this was, at least in part, because the defendants who received holistic assistance were more likely to be released and therefore—in contrast to defendants who were incarcerated—had more significant opportunities to reoffend.

116 Singleton, "What Is Punishment?," 439.

117 Schlanger, "The Constitutional Law of Incarceration, Reconfigured," 361.
118 Steiker, "Punishment and Procedure," 810–11.
119 Currie, "The Legal Problems of Everyday Life," 24–25.
120 Pleasence et al., "Mounting Problems," 67–68.
121 Pinard, "Broadening the Holistic Mindset," 1089.
122 Sudeall and Richardson, "Unfamiliar Justice," 2150.

12

Exonerating the Innocent

It Takes a Village and a New Culture

SHAWN ARMBRUST

From its earliest days, the criminal legal system in the United States has grappled with wrongful convictions. In 1819, two Vermont brothers, Jesse and Stephen Boorn, were convicted of murdering their brother-in-law based on a jailhouse informant, false confessions, and flawed forensic science.[1] Shortly before Stephen Boorn was to be executed, the brother-in-law showed up alive, and the brothers became the first documented exonerees in the country.[2]

Although Judge Learned Hand described wrongful convictions as "an unreal dream,"[3] the Boorn brothers were not alone. In 1932, Yale Law Professor Edwin Borchard documented 64 other wrongful convictions in his book *Convicting the Innocent*, in response to a Massachusetts prosecutor who said this: "Innocent men are never convicted. Don't worry about it, it never happens in the world. It's a physical impossibility."[4] The patterns Borchard found are familiar to anyone who studies wrongful convictions today.

With high crime rates and the resulting tough-on-crime rhetoric from politicians, the lessons Borchard learned were largely forgotten by the 1970s and 1980s. Judges and policy makers were more focused on quickly solving crimes and limiting what they saw as endless appeals than on preventing wrongful convictions. Although scholars like Hugo Bedau and Michael Radelet built upon Borchard's work by writing in detail about 166 wrongful convictions,[5] the reaction to their work was mixed, with questions raised about whether the individuals included in their book were truly innocent.

In 1989, however, the debate over wrongful convictions changed forever when the convicted rapist Gary Dotson became the first person exonerated by postconviction DNA testing. For the first time, innocence could be scientifically proven. Since then, 377 more people have been exonerated based on postconviction DNA testing, demonstrating that wrongful convictions are not "an unreal dream" but instead are far more commonplace than anyone ever believed.[6]

Those exonerations have exposed harsh realities about the criminal legal system. We now know that the scientific evidence used to obtain many convictions was not so scientific; that eyewitnesses who were honestly certain about the accuracy of their identifications were mistaken; that people really do confess to crimes they didn't commit; that too many cases with "overwhelming" evidence of guilt only seemed that way because of evidence that was withheld by police and prosecutors; that the racial disparities that infect so much of the criminal legal system also lead to a disproportionate number of Black men being wrongfully convicted; and that our post-trial system is not equipped to rectify the convictions of innocent people.

Advocates and policy makers have been working to address many of those issues, with some success. Half of all states, the District of Columbia, and federal law enforcement agencies (including the FBI, DEA, and ATF) require the recording of interrogations, which helps identify false confessions before trial.[7] Eyewitness identification reforms that would help prevent eyewitness error also have been adopted in half the states.[8] In 2009, the National Academy of Sciences issued a groundbreaking report on the problems in forensic science,[9] and three states between 2019 and 2021 have taken action to regulate the use of jailhouse informants.[10] These changes are based on research and data that have challenged the fundamental assumptions we long made about the reliability of certain types of evidence, and they will go a long way toward preventing wrongful convictions.

The problem of racial bias in wrongful convictions is complex, deep-rooted, and difficult to quantify. Even here, however, there are signs of progress. There is growing awareness that cross-racial identifications are more likely to be erroneous, with high courts in three states moving to require jury instructions in cross-racial identification cases.[11] We also know that wrongful convictions involving Black defendants are 22% more likely to involve police misconduct than cases involving white defendants,[12] something that the police reform movement and federal consent decrees are helping to address. And, tragically, the continued shootings of unarmed Black people by police have shed light on the assumptions police make about the criminality of Black people—assumptions that also have contributed to far too many wrongful convictions. While it will take years to address the many ways in which racial bias has caused and will continue to cause wrongful convictions, the current movement for racial justice and criminal legal reform is beginning to make real headway on these issues.

For understandable reasons, the flaws that DNA exonerations have exposed in the post-trial process have received less attention and been more difficult to fix. The post-trial system is complex, is multilayered, and varies substantially by state, making its shortcomings difficult to address with a single legislative proposal. Moreover, policy makers and judges are easily influenced by the arguments of prosecutors and attorneys general that any reforms will lead to a flood of baseless innocence claims and the release of violent criminals. This means that there is little political will to thoroughly address these problems, that the rare efforts to fix the problems are undermined by provisions that focus on procedure instead of innocence, and that judges read those provisions as restrictively as possible.

Without real systemic change, advocates (including this author) for the wrongfully convicted have focused on appeals to individual prosecutors and attorneys general for two simple reasons: courts tend to do what prosecutors want, and unopposed motions almost always are granted. This focus, as well as the proliferation of Conviction Integrity Units (CIUs) that investigate wrongful convictions within prosecutors' offices, have largely driven the rise in exonerations after 2011. Although any increase in exonerations is good news, those results too often are more about the personality on the other side than the merits of a case. And the power of prosecutors, while vast, is not absolute and can be checked by judges and, in some cases, attorneys general.

As a result, decades after these problems were first exposed, they have not been solved. On the surface, as the number of pure DNA exonerations dwindles, advocates, policy makers, and judges need to focus on these issues before the window of opportunity closes. Doing that will require legislative action at the state and federal levels, a real examination of the procedural issues that keep innocent people in prison, and a willingness to truly prioritize accuracy of the system over issues like finality.

The Post-Trial Process: Assumptions and Shortcomings

Trial by a jury is a fundamental principle of the American criminal legal system, in part based on the idea that juries are uniquely well equipped to make decisions about guilt. As a result, the post-trial system is designed to address legal errors, not cases in which new evidence proves innocence years or decades after conviction. That process varies by state but typically involves a patchwork of legal procedures: direct appeal, where defendants can challenge things that are part of the existing trial record; motions for a new trial, for bringing forward new evidence within what usually is a short time period; postconviction or state habeas corpus, for raising constitutional violations in state court; and federal habeas corpus, for raising constitutional violations by the states in federal court. Each of these procedures is governed by a complex set of rules that prisoners largely are forced to navigate on their own, since the right to counsel guaranteed by the Constitution typically ends after the first stage (the direct appeal).

All of these rules and procedures have been informed by certain assumptions about the legal system and about prisoners: that trial courts correctly answer the question of guilt or innocence, that the sheer number of remedies available to criminal defendants means the system will catch the rare mistake, and that the vast majority of criminal defendants claim innocence and file endless appeals. Because of these assumptions, courts and legislatures have prioritized the finality of convictions and have structured the system accordingly.

It is no surprise, then, that this system has long been ill-equipped to handle claims of innocence. Postconviction DNA testing, with its ability to scientifically prove innocence, cast a harsh light on the post-trial system. The first two DNA exonerees, Gary Dotson in Illinois and David Vasquez in Virginia, received gubernatorial pardons because neither state had a mechanism for correcting the convictions in court. A few years later, also in Virginia, death row prisoner Earl Washington made headlines when DNA results proving his innocence butted up against the state's notorious 21-day rule, which prevented the courts from considering new evidence of innocence more than 21 days after conviction. Washington remained in prison for seven years after receiving the favorable DNA results and finally received a full pardon in 2000.[13]

Those cases began to cast doubt on the assumptions that helped shape our post-trial system, and the evidence provided by the cases has only been strengthened by additional evidence provided by the data gathered over the past 30-plus years. The 377 DNA exonerations recorded by the Innocence Project[14] (and the 2,640 total exonerations listed in the National Registry of Exonerations)[15] make clear that wrongful convictions occur more often than most people recognized. They also make clear that the post-trial system is not well situated to correct those errors. The scholar Brandon Garrett found that, of the first 200 DNA exonerees, only 9% of them had their convictions reversed during the post-trial process.[16]

Although prosecutors, judges, and the public assume that everyone in prison claims innocence and endlessly litigates, the data suggest otherwise.[17] In the few states that have expanded post-trial remedies for the innocent, prosecutors and attorneys general often warn that there will be a flood of baseless claims that overwhelm the courts. Again, the data suggest otherwise. In Virginia, an average of 27 petitions per year were filed in the first nine years that the Writ of Actual Innocence for Non-Biological Evidence was in effect.[18] In Texas, which passed a law in 2014 allowing defendants to challenge their convictions based on changes in forensic science, only 45 such challenges had been filed by 2019. In North Carolina, which created an independent state agency to investigate innocence claims, the agency has received fewer than 200 requests per year.[19] Garrett found that, in the 133 cases in which future DNA exonerees lost direct appeals and had written opinions, fewer than half filed state postconviction petitions. Only 23% filed federal habeas petitions, a comparatively high number; in 2000, another study found that only 1–2% of state prisoners filed federal habeas petitions.[20]

Nonetheless, the assumptions that created this system persist and act as an impediment to reform. While all 50 states now allow for postconviction DNA testing, the landscape for those without new DNA evidence—the vast majority of cases now that DNA testing is routinely conducted before trial—remains treacherous. In the few states with stand-alone remedies for those with non-DNA evidence of innocence, the path to legal relief is littered with harsh deadlines, procedural barriers, and requirements that have little to do with guilt or innocence. In the federal courts, impediments to relief actually have increased as DNA exonerations became more prevalent. Thus, even those who are later exonerated must spend years litigating arcane procedural issues that have little to do with guilt or innocence.

At the Mid-Atlantic Innocence Project (MAIP), we have freed 39 innocent people, more than most other innocence organizations. Despite our success, the contested cases that we litigate and ultimately win take an average of 7.5 years. Our current caseload includes three cases with scientific proof of innocence that have been in litigation for a combined total of 16 years. It also includes three cases where there is scientific proof of innocence but no legal remedy, resulting in a combined nine-year wait for a pardon.

In our cases, only one thing can typically break that logjam to secure an exoneration without prolonged litigation over procedural issues: prosecutors who will listen to compelling claims of innocence and file a consent motion, without raising available procedural or technical arguments that they could (and typically would) make. In most cases, judges will not independently use those rules to deny relief, allowing an innocent defendant to prevail. MAIP typically prevails in less than a year in those cases—even when the proof of innocence is less ironclad than in other cases we are litigating. As a result, the factor that most accurately predicts success in our cases is not evidence but the prosecutor or attorney general on the other side.

Conviction Integrity Units and the Rise in Exonerations

National data suggest that our experience at MAIP is not surprising. Data from the National Registry of Exonerations reveal that the annual number of exonerations in the United States spiked from 82 in 2010 to 149 in 2019, an 82% increase. That increase is largely attributable to just a few of the 55 Conviction Integrity Units that examine potential wrongful convictions from within prosecutors' offices. The percentage of exonerations that involved CIUs jumped from 5% in 2010 to 37% in each of the years 2019–2021. If CIU exonerations are removed from the total, the rise in exonerations drops more than threefold.[21]

The CIU exonerations are clustered among a few offices, with 88% (346/395) since 2010 coming from just eight of the 59 CIUs: Baltimore City, Cook County, Dallas County, Harris County, King's County, New York, Philadelphia, and Wayne County. Those are large jurisdictions, to be sure, but the population they represent is just 18% of the 15,099,714 people who live in areas covered by CIUs and just 6% of the total US population.

Although working with prosecutors on exonerations is useful, relying on CIUs to right wrongs puts a Band-Aid on a much larger wound. It can work only in those cases where prosecutors or attorneys general are willing to assist, which unfortunately is still a rare occasion. Prosecutors also cannot vacate convictions on their own. A judge ultimately must sign off, and many judges remain skeptical that wrongful convictions are a real problem.

The result is that too many innocent people spend years embroiled in Kafkaesque legal proceedings that prolong litigation and threaten public safety by keeping innocent people in prison. Stories about exonerations rarely focus on these details. With limited word counts and limited capacity to delve into complex topics, news stories typically focus on the exoneree's immediate release and perhaps the underlying causes of the wrongful conviction without addressing the arcane procedural barriers that prevented exoneration.

Procedural Barriers to Exoneration—Stories from the Cases

To provide greater context and evidence of these systemic inadequacies, in this chapter I present the procedural stories of three cases, illustrating some of the most egregious, albeit common, barriers that the innocent continue to face in seeking exoneration. These cases were not chosen because they were outliers. Rather, they were chosen because they represent some of the most difficult—but common—scenarios that innocent people face when fighting for their freedom. They were chosen because of how they differ, but also because of what they have in common. They involve three different states with three different sets of procedures: federal and state courts at various levels and different types of evidence leading to conviction and proving innocence. One individual was fully exonerated; the others pleaded guilty or are still in prison. Nonetheless, they have three key similarities: (1) clear and powerful proof of innocence; (2) strong government opposition that relied on or sought to enhance procedural barriers that have little to do with guilt or innocence; and (3) a resulting struggle for exoneration or freedom that took years or decades—if it succeeded at all. Together, they represent a much larger population and provide evidence that, across the board, the traditional approach to post-trial litigation has failed the innocent and urgently needs reform.

Danial Williams

On September 26, 2016, a federal judge wrote that "no sane human being" could find the Norfolk Four (Joseph Dick, Derek Tice, Danial Williams, and Eric Wilson) guilty of the rape and murder for which they had been convicted in Norfolk, Virginia.[22] After describing the Commonwealth of Virginia's "bizarre explanation for how [the defendants] committed the alleged offenses,"[23] the judge likened it to an even more farcical scenario: "For example, in this case the Commonwealth *could* posit that astronauts landed the space shuttle in Norfolk and committed the crime in space suits, leaving no evidence behind. No one would believe that explanation, but it is scarcely less likely than the scenario offered by the Commonwealth now."[24]

This blunt assessment forced Virginia's attorney general to abandon the fight to preserve the convictions of the Norfolk Four, setting the stage for the court to vacate the two convictions before it and for the governor to pardon all four men. This ended the Norfolk Four's nearly 20-year saga but left open two glaring questions: Why did the local prosecutor and the administrations of eight separate attorneys general spend so much time fighting to obtain and preserve the convictions when the evidence pointed so clearly to innocence? And why did those efforts work for so long?

The first question likely involves issues like tunnel vision, but it is impossible to answer without engaging in the type of nonblaming reviews that this chapter later recommends in all of these cases—something that rarely, if ever, happens and has not happened here. It is easier to understand why the government's efforts were so successful, even in the face of evidence that a federal judge said was so clear. A detailed look at the case of one of the men, Danial Williams, helps explain how easily the government, whether through prosecutors or attorneys general, can use the procedural tools at its disposal to delay justice, even when the evidence of innocence is clear. Those efforts are facilitated by the adoption of a notoriously unjust federal law that severely constrains the ability of federal courts to act in habeas cases.

On July 8, 1997, Michelle Bosko's husband returned to his apartment after a week at sea on his navy ship to find his young wife raped and murdered. Williams, also a navy sailor, lived in the building with his wife and immediately became a suspect when one of Bosko's friends said Williams was interested in Bosko and made her uncomfortable. Investigators brought Williams in for questioning that day, and he insisted that he was innocent. That changed when Detective Robert Glenn Ford entered the room. Ford, who previously had been demoted for obtaining false confessions, confronted Williams and threatened him with the death penalty. Williams, who had been awake for 21 hours and interrogated for nine, believed that a confession was his only way out of the room and finally confessed to raping and murdering Bosko.

The confession didn't match up to many details, including how Bosko was murdered. But the biggest problem surfaced when DNA tests on the rape kit excluded Williams as the source of the DNA. Rather than reevaluating their focus on Williams, detectives assumed Williams had committed the crime with someone else, and they pushed him to name his accomplice. Trying to avoid the death penalty, he named Joseph Dick. Dick, too, confessed and did not match the DNA evidence. Again, police went searching for accomplices rather than questioning their theory.

Dick named Derek Tice and Eric Wilson, who also confessed to Ford and who also didn't match the DNA. In addition to that obvious problem, all four confessions were internally inconsistent, inconsistent with each other, and inconsistent with the physical and crime scene evidence.

Williams had adamantly protested his innocence to his lawyers, and it was clear by the time he pleaded that DNA evidence from the scene did not belong to him or his three codefendants. But he had been the first of the Norfolk Four to confess to the crime. The trial court ruled that his confession was voluntary, and his lawyers told him to plead guilty so he could avoid the death penalty. On January 21, 1999, he listened to their advice.

One month later, Omar Ballard confessed to the crime via a letter to a friend; on March 4, 1999, police learned that the DNA at the scene was a match to Ballard, who had committed at least three other rapes and confessed in accurate detail to police after just 20 minutes that he had killed Bosko alone. Williams immediately sought to withdraw his guilty plea, but prosecutors insisted that the Norfolk Four had committed the crime with Ballard. On April 28, 1999, the judge denied his motion to withdraw the plea and sentenced Williams to life in prison.

With a new lawyer, Williams filed a direct appeal, but it challenged only the refusal to let Williams withdraw his guilty plea. Williams lost. Without a lawyer, he did not know that he had only one year to file state and federal habeas petitions. He did not file either.

In 2004, some of the best law firms in the country were recruited to represent the Norfolk Four, who had all either pleaded guilty or been convicted at trial. Although the clients clearly were innocent, the options weren't good. In Virginia at that time, defendants had to file motions for a new trial within 21 days of conviction and state habeas petitions within a year of direct appeal.

Actual innocence was irrelevant. By 2004, Virginia had created the Writ of Actual Innocence, applicable to cases in which DNA testing proved innocence, and the Writ of Actual Innocence for Non-Biological Evidence, applicable to cases with new, non-DNA evidence of innocence.

Neither of those writs could help Williams. The laws were controversial in tough-on-crime Virginia and were designed to be as narrow as possible. Williams wasn't eligible for the first because the evidence wasn't "new": he knew that DNA tests cleared him before his plea, and he knew the evidence linked to Ballard before his sentencing. He was not eligible for the nonbiological writ because his plea kept him from even filing one, even though 6% of DNA exonerations by that time had been in guilty-plea cases.

As a result, Williams had no legal remedy and had to seek a pardon. After filing in November 2005, Williams and his codefendants finally received an answer in August 2009: a conditional pardon for Dick, Tice, and Williams that would facilitate their release but preserve their convictions. Although Governor Tim Kaine said he thought the men were likely innocent, they had not conclusively proven it, and the victim's family was opposed to a full pardon. As a result, Dick, Tice, and Williams were released from prison but not free, living as registered sex offenders and convicted murderers.

In December 2009, Williams filed a federal habeas corpus petition in the Eastern District of Virginia,[25] alleging five flaws in his case: that his trial counsel was ineffective; his guilty plea was involuntary; police and prosecutorial misconduct resulted in his wrongful prosecution and conviction; Ford intentionally and deliberately pursued Williams's prosecution in bad faith; and he was convicted of a crime he didn't commit.

Despite the compelling evidence of innocence, Williams faced an uphill battle. The United States Supreme Court has never found it unconstitutional to incarcerate—or even execute—a person for a crime he did not commit. It also is not enough simply to prove government misconduct or ineffective assistance of counsel; to win a federal habeas case, the claimant must prove that the error would have changed the outcome at trial, a standard that is quite difficult in a case with false confessions. To make things even harder, the district court could not even consider those claims until Williams had satisfied the requirements of the 1996 Anti-Terrorism and Effective Death Penalty Reform Act (AEDPA), which has several procedural hurdles that frustrate most habeas claims.

By 2009, Williams was well beyond AEDPA's one-year deadline for filing his petition, which had expired sometime in 2001. Williams also had never litigated any of these claims in state court, so he had not "exhausted" them by fully litigating them there before filing in federal court, as the AEDPA requires. Although the Supreme Court had said petitioners with compelling evidence of innocence could file "second or successive" habeas petitions (most prisoners are limited to one), it had never extended the exception to claims that were time-barred or not fully litigated in state court. This typically means lots of litigation over procedural issues and much less consideration of constitutional claims.

This was the case in Williams's petition, which continued for seven years before the court actually considered his constitutional claims. The first delay occurred when Detective Ford was indicted in federal court in June 2010 for soliciting bribes from people charged with crimes in exchange for favorable treatment and then lying to the FBI about it. Williams's lawyers realized that Ford's indictment and conduct gave them a new habeas claim, which meant the federal court had to put the habeas on hold so Williams could "exhaust" his claims by raising them in state court—even though there was virtually no chance of winning under Virginia law. As expected, he lost in state court; 19 months after filing the initial habeas petition, Williams filed an amended petition in federal court that included the now-exhausted claims related to Ford.

In May 2012, the Commonwealth moved to dismiss the petition with a simple argument: Williams had blown past AEDPA's one-year deadline, and evidence of innocence was no excuse for doing so. As absurd as this argument sounds, a technical interpretation of AEDPA supported the Commonwealth's position. But in July 2013, more than a year after the motion to dismiss had been fully briefed (but before the federal trial court had ruled), the United States Supreme Court decided in *McQuiggin v. Perkins* that failing to meet the one-year deadline could be excused if habeas petitioners could make a credible showing of actual innocence.[26]

Virginia didn't give up. Under *McQuiggin*, passing through the "innocence gateway" requires new and reliable evidence that would persuade "the district court that, in light of the new evidence, no juror, acting reasonably, would have voted to find him guilty beyond a reasonable doubt."[27] Virginia said Williams couldn't meet that standard. The relevant evidence couldn't count as "new" because Williams knew about it before he was sentenced. The Commonwealth said the remaining evidence was unreliable and just not enough to prove innocence.

In June 2014, the court denied the motion to dismiss and said Williams could have a hearing on his innocence claim in April 2015. At the end of the two-day hearing, the judge was persuaded, declaring that "I don't think that these two men are guilty of this. If a jury heard this case now, it is difficult for me to conceive how they could find someone guilty based on the evidence that has come in."

Once again, Virginia didn't give up, suggesting that the judge needed to decide "whether an objective juror, after reviewing all of the credible evidence, could find Williams guilty of the rape and murder of Michelle Bosko *today, under any theory*, without regard to that which animated the prosecution at the time of his guilty plea" (emphasis in original).[28] This suggestion, made without any legal authority, would require innocent people to disprove their guilt under any possible theory—whether or not supported by the evidence.

Finally, in September 2016, the court found that the men satisfied the actual-innocence gateway and could have their claims considered. One month later, the state attorney general finally gave up the fight, writing that because of the court's factual findings related to actual innocence, the office "was constrained to admit" that it could not prevail on Williams's police misconduct claim. With that brief (and somewhat grudging) concession, Williams won his habeas claim, and all four men were fully cleared and compensated. As of July 1, 2020, the Writ of Actual Innocence for Non-Biological Evidence now allows petitions from those who had pleaded guilty.

Although this may sound like a delayed but happy ending, the state attorney general never acknowledged that the Norfolk Four are innocent, and the longtime lead attorney on the case remains a unit leader in the criminal appeals unit. Other than allowing those who previously pleaded guilty to challenge their convictions, nothing about the post-trial process has changed as a result of this case. There has been no public accounting of why the office fought to preserve the conviction for so long; neither has there been any examination of how the system could be improved to prevent situations like this from happening in the future.

George Seward

Danial Williams struggled to prove his innocence because of his confession, guilty plea, and failure to promptly avail himself of legal remedies. By that standard, George Seward did everything "right." He protested his innocence from the beginning, went to trial, and contested his conviction at every opportunity. Nonetheless, he, too, was thwarted for nearly two decades by the aggressive, callous, and contradictory procedural arguments of prosecutors and attorneys general. The reasons for that entrenched opposition are unclear, as in the Norfolk Four case, but the ongoing saga was aided by a judiciary that defers to the government and seems unwilling to accept the reality of wrongful convictions. Together, the government and the judiciary were able to use the multiple layers of the legal process to their advantage to prevent Seward from achieving full exoneration.

In July 1984, a white woman was raped in her home by a clean-shaven Black man in Baltimore County, Maryland. Ten weeks later, a police officer saw 19-year-old George Seward and thought he resembled the composite sketch. The victim identified Seward as her attacker in a photo array and a live lineup. None of the 19 usable fingerprints at the scene matched Seward or any of the known individuals who had been in the house; no other physical evidence connected him to the crime. At trial, the state admitted that the victim's cross-racial identification was the only evidence of Seward's guilt.

Seward insisted that he was innocent. He had been working part-time for an in-home dog grooming service before his arrest. The hours weren't regular, he was paid in cash, and he came in only when called. Although it was 10 weeks later, he told police and his lawyer that he might have been at work on the day of the crime.

Seward's employer twice told his lawyer that she couldn't remember if Seward had been working that day and didn't know where her payroll records were. She said she couldn't look for them because she was so busy caring for her husband, who was in the late stages of Alzheimer's. She told police the same thing. She said the same thing at trial, and the judge ordered her to look for the records and report back if she found anything. She did not, and Seward was convicted.

By 1996, Seward's family was able to hire a postconviction lawyer. By this time, the employer's husband also had died, and she allowed the attorney to search the records. Sure enough, Seward had been working on the day of the crime. Based on the employer's records, there was no way Seward could have traveled to the victim's home and committed the crime during the middle of the workday. This was not exculpatory DNA evidence, but the proof was solid. Plus, the case already looked like so many of the DNA exonerations that had already occurred by then: a mistaken cross-racial identification in a single-perpetrator rape case. The problems of eyewitness identification were well known in Baltimore County at that point: Kirk Bloodsworth, the nation's first DNA death row exoneree, had been convicted in Baltimore County based on the testimony of five eyewitnesses and was exonerated in 1992.

At the time, there was no way to raise a claim of innocence in Maryland based on newly discovered evidence. Seward's attorney instead argued that Seward had been denied effective assistance of counsel in violation of the Sixth Amendment, suggesting that the trial counsel's investigation was inadequate and unreasonable. The postconviction petition said that, if the attorney had tried harder, he would have found the records and Seward would not have been convicted.

The state and the trial court in which the petition was filed disagreed. The court wrote: "If requests by the Court and the State could not compel [the employer] to find these records, further attempts by defense counsel to request the records would in all likelihood also fail. Short of a search warrant, there was not much else to be done."[29] The lawyer's decision to stop investigating therefore seemed reasonable under the circumstances. Seward sought permission to appeal to the Maryland Court of Special Appeals, the state's second-highest court, but those efforts also failed. His lawyer filed a federal habeas petition, but it was dismissed within eight months.

Over the intervening years, Seward sought DNA testing, but the evidence had been destroyed. He asked to run the unidentified fingerprints through a database that did not exist in 1984; that effort, too, was fruitless. But in 2009, Maryland created a remedy for those with newly discovered non-DNA evidence of innocence: the Writ of Actual Innocence. Under the new law, "newly discovered evidence" was evidence that could not have been discovered by the defendant or his lawyer in time to file a motion for a new trial. Given the ruling on Seward's postconviction petition, the work records seemed like they should qualify. Seward's family hired another new lawyer, who filed a Writ of Actual Innocence seeking a new trial.

That new trial never happened. Although Seward won at the initial hearing—the local prosecutor conceding that the new evidence was indicative of innocence—the Maryland Attorney General's Office appealed this decision. Despite its previous argument that Seward's lawyer couldn't have done anything else to obtain the work records, the state now argued that Seward and his lawyer were not diligent *enough* in seeking the records. In fact, the attorney general wrote that "Seward acted with no diligence at all."[30]

The Court of Special Appeals agreed with the state. Despite the efforts detailed by the postconviction judge, the court found that "trial counsel made no reasonable and good faith effort to procure" the payroll records. It also chastised Seward for doing "nothing to procure [the] payroll records until 1996," although the court failed to acknowledge that Seward was in prison with no lawyer and no right to a lawyer during that time.[31] The ruling meant that Seward's lawyer was *too diligent* to be considered constitutionally defective but *not diligent enough* for the evidence to count as "newly discovered." The ruling was absurd but unsurprising from this court, which has worked hard to gut the Writ of Actual Innocence since its inception by accepting the government's harshest arguments.[32]

By this point, a deputy attorney general had begun to question the office's own arguments in the case, but it did not matter. After passing through the Maryland Court of Appeals, the state's highest court, the case was sent back to the local prosecutor, who said he would retry Seward but delay that trial for as long as possible to investigate. Although Seward initially turned down a plea offer to end the litigation, he reconsidered after a friend in prison was stabbed. For Seward, it had been four years since he initially had won the Writ of Actual Innocence and with it the promise of a new trial. But with the ongoing threat of violence in prison and his desire to see his elderly parents, Seward reluctantly took the plea so he could go home. He continues to live with the stain of criminal conviction; the Maryland Attorney General's Office continues to make arguments that aim to restrict the rights of innocent people to seek relief and delay their exoneration; and the Maryland judiciary continues to accept many of them.

Lamar Johnson

Wrongfully convicted criminal defendants are hamstrung by a legal system that gives the government seemingly endless tools to oppose their relief, by vehement government opposition, and by a judiciary that is itself hamstrung and often deferential. With limited ability to change that system, one obvious solution in these cases is to seek the support of prosecutors and attorneys general. If they don't raise procedural objections, those barriers won't stand in the way. Or so innocence advocates thought.

I have long sought to work with prosecutors, preferring consensus to litigation and winning to losing. But I have seen for several years that collaboration might not be a panacea. In 2011, I represented Thomas Haynesworth in the Virginia Court of Appeals, working alongside the conservative attorney general to free him; we won in the full court only by a single vote. In 2012, I was asked to represent Johnathan Montgomery after that same attorney general blocked the enforcement of a trial court order vacating his conviction because the order was illegal under Virginia law; a year later, Montgomery was exonerated under the correct procedure with the attorney general's consent. And in 2019, I watched as a Baltimore City judge grilled the head of Baltimore's CIU about whether the evidence proving the innocence of Kenneth McPherson and Eric Simmons was properly "new" under the Maryland Writ of Actual Innocence.

In the end, all of those men were exonerated, and the struggles to get there were quickly forgotten. But in July 2019, Lamar Johnson of St. Louis was not so lucky. That month, after 25 years in prison for a murder he didn't commit, the new CIU in St. Louis said it believed in his innocence, released a 75-page report documenting its findings, and filed a motion seeking his release. Two years later, Johnson remains in a Missouri prison. The issue: a fight over whether the local prosecutor is even allowed to seek Johnson's exoneration, a fundamental disagreement about the role of prosecutors that could have implications in other states where progressive prosecutors are seeking reform.

Johnson's conviction stemmed from the 1994 murder of Marcus Boyd, who sat on the dimly lit front porch of his apartment with a friend when he was shot and killed by two masked men. Boyd's girlfriend, who was inside the apartment and could not make out any of the shooters' features, told officers at the scene that she suspected Johnson because of a drug dispute between the two men. With that, Johnson became the primary suspect.

In July 1995, Johnson was convicted of the murder based on questionable evidence. This includes (1) the testimony of Boyd's friend, Greg Elking, who said he initially could not describe the perpetrators and identified Johnson only on the fifth try, having failed to do so in a photo array and three live lineups; (2) a jailhouse informant who said he overheard Johnson talking about the crime from another cell in the jail; and (3) evidence that police had seized a mask from Johnson's car 10 weeks before the crime. Johnson, who had insisted upon his innocence and provided a consistent alibi throughout, presented testimony from one of his alibi witnesses.

Johnson's innocence claim was bolstered shortly before he was sentenced, when his alleged co-perpetrator, Phillip Campbell, began writing letters to Johnson stating that he knew Johnson was innocent. Johnson filed a motion for a new trial, but the state objected, arguing that the letters were undated and that Johnson therefore couldn't prove they were newly discovered. Campbell also was unwilling to testify. The motion was denied.

For the next few years, Johnson challenged his conviction in multiple ways. He filed a motion to set aside his judgment based on ineffective assistance of counsel. He received a hearing on his claim that trial counsel wouldn't let him testify, but that was denied. He filed a second motion for a new trial based on prosecutorial misconduct and Campbell's decision to finally name the second perpetrator, James Howard. That also was denied, and those denials were affirmed. In April 1999, his direct appeal was rejected by the Missouri Court of Appeals.

In December 1999, Johnson filed a federal habeas petition citing four claims against the trial judge and alleging ineffective assistance of trial counsel. Three years later, in January 2003, a magistrate judge recommended dismissing all of his habeas claims. The federal judge agreed and dismissed Johnson's habeas petition in March 2003. By that time, Campbell and Howard had admitted sole responsibility for the crime. Elking also began recanting his testimony in 2003, admitting to a minister that he had not really been able to see who shot Boyd. Nonetheless, Johnson had no more legal options. This remained true when Campbell and Howard again signed affidavits admitting their involvement in 2009, when two other men signed affidavits corroborating their testimony, and when Elking signed an affidavit recanting his testimony in 2010.

That changed when Johnson's lawyers from the Midwest Innocence Project began working with the new St. Louis CIU. Among other evidence, the CIU's investigation uncovered information that had been improperly withheld from the defense at trial: that the detective had pressured and threatened Elking; Elking had been paid for his testimony; the detective told Elking who he should identify as the killer; the jailhouse informant had an extensive criminal history; and the jailhouse informant had made racist remarks about Johnson.

The CIU was convinced of Johnson's innocence, but there was a problem: Missouri law provides no clear and affirmative way for prosecutors to seek the freedom of someone they believe is innocent. Nonetheless, the CIU filed a motion seeking a new trial for Johnson. The trial court could have simply granted the motion, as most do, but this judge instead appointed the Missouri Attorney General's Office to represent the state.[33]

The Missouri attorney general had opposed Johnson in every one of his filings and also opposed relief in all 20 Missouri exoneration cases in which it was a party over the previous decade. At oral argument in Joseph Amrine's case, a lawyer from the office said Amrine should be executed even if the court thought he was innocent.[34] The state's hard line opposing relief in Johnson's case therefore was no surprise. At its most basic level, the attorney general's argument is about a deadline: Missouri rules require defendants to file a motion for a new trial within 15 days of the verdict; accordingly, the attorney general claimed, the court cannot consider a motion filed after 24 years. The CIU stated the rule is silent on whether a prosecutor can file for a new trial and, in any event, allows for exceptions when a manifest injustice has occurred.

The real disagreement involves a far more fundamental issue: what responsibility prosecutors have when they believe someone has been wrongfully convicted. The St. Louis CIU said it had an obligation to rectify them. The attorney general said the prosecutor should simply turn the evidence over to the defense; to do more would undermine the adversarial system, create conflicts of interest, and potentially undermine public trust in the system.

Instead, according to the attorney general, courts should decide on innocence claims based on pleadings filed by the defendants and tested through the adversarial process. The office cited "at least six mechanisms" under federal and Missouri laws by which an innocent prisoner can obtain relief and claimed those have been "carefully crafted over decades to strike a balance among competing interests in individual justice, judicial economy, finality, and the integrity of criminal judgments."[35] In the attorney general's view, Johnson's failure to prevail under any of those remedies did not suggest that the system failed. Rather, it "indicates that he has been afforded due process by several courts . . . and that, notwithstanding the adversarial efforts of the Attorney General's Office . . . the system is working and resulting in relief—where such relief is found to be warranted by the courts."[36]

The Missouri Supreme Court agreed with the attorney general, finding unanimously that it did not even have jurisdiction to consider the appeal.[37] According to the court, it can hear appeals only from final judgments, which occur when a court "enters a judgment of guilt and sentence."[38] In Johnson's case, that occurred in 1995, and he already exercised that right. The court emphasized that its decision was not a reflection of Johnson's guilt or innocence, because the only issue in the case was whether Johnson had the right to appeal the trial court's decision.

While the decision was pending, Missouri passed a law allowing prosecutors to file a motion to vacate a conviction or set aside a judgment.[39] This should help Johnson, but the law also allows the Attorney General's Office to appear, which could involve questioning witnesses and making arguments. Given the office's past positions, it is not surprising that it has opposed his freedom. However, as this volume was being ready to go to press (early 2022), a Missouri state judge was considering motions to vacate Johnson's conviction.[40]

Johnson's ongoing saga mirrors the hurdles faced by Williams and Seward. These innocent men—representative of many more like them— spent years working to prove their innocence, only to be stymied by a legal system that contains too many procedural roadblocks, is overly deferential to the government, and requires the presentation of different types of evidence in different proceedings, all of which still fails to provide a hearing on the ultimate issue: their innocence.

Unfortunately for Johnson, he has not yet been able to overcome those barriers. The support of the CIU should have given him a shot, but unfortunately it has only illuminated the perils of relying on individuals rather than working to change the system. His case should serve as an alarm bell for innocence advocates, progressive prosecutors, and anyone who cares about justice, and it should prompt real action to finally reform the post-trial system so it is not dependent on the willingness of prosecutors and judges to prioritize justice for the wrongfully convicted over finality.

Solutions

The English legal scholar William Blackstone famously said that it is "better that ten guilty persons escape, than that one innocent suffers."[41] This phrase is often quoted or paraphrased by professors, lawyers, and judges, and it is said to be one of the fundamental principles of our legal system. As the statistics and case studies make clear, however, our post-trial system is designed to protect convictions despite innocence, not to reverse them despite guilt. There is no magic answer that will reverse this trend, but there are measures that, taken together, offer hope. A proper response will require action by the federal government and individual state governments in addition to a real examination of the individual choices that prosecutors and attorneys general make in these cases and the values that inform those choices.

Both the data and the case studies in this chapter have provided ample evidence that the post-trial system has failed the innocent and have highlighted some of the most problematic issues, both procedural and cultural, with that system. The procedural issues include harsh deadlines in state and federal courts; a fixation by legislators, government attorneys, and judges over when evidence was discovered instead of what it proves; and an overly complicated, multilayered process that prevents innocent people from presenting all of their claims in one place, allows the government to make inconsistent arguments, and also allows the government to suggest that the plethora of proceedings means the system is fair. This chapter also has raised real questions about the choices that prosecutors and attorneys general make in these cases, the institutional incentives that contribute to these choices, and the values those offices prioritize. Because so many judges are former prosecutors and defer to government attorneys, defendants compete on an unequal playing field.

On a fundamental level, there are real questions about whether a system built on these principles and with this culture can ever truly be reformed. Our adversarial system is based on the notion that, as long as proper procedural rules are followed, the results of either a trial or a plea agreement can be taken as the truth. The volume and frequency of wrongful convictions call that fundamental principle into question and, as a result, call into question the wisdom and efficacy of the system as a whole. The legal profession, and Americans in general, take it on faith that our system and its design are the best in the world, but there is a lot we can learn from systems in other countries that could be used to design a new system or incorporate into our own.

For example, Great Britain, which also has an adversarial system, does not have our byzantine post-trial process. After direct appeal is denied, those with evidence that was not previously heard in court can seek review from the Criminal Case Review Commission (CCRC), an independent body that investigates miscarriages of justice.[42] The CCRC looks at both sentencing and facial issues, referring the most compelling cases to courts.[43] While the system is not perfect, its fundamental objective is to seek out unsafe verdicts rather than to uphold convictions on procedural grounds.

There also may be compelling lessons to be learned from inquisitorial systems. We don't (and likely can't) know whether adversarial systems produce more wrongful convictions than inquisitorial systems, but there are fundamental aspects of inquisitorial systems that may well make ours more accurate. Those include the rigorous professionalism of investigations, the notion of professional fact finders rather than lay juries, and the emphasis on factual accuracy instead of procedural justice.[44]

Even without a system redesign, however, there are important steps that can be taken to vastly improve the existing system. As an initial matter, the federal and state governments should think seriously about properly funding counsel beyond direct appeal. As the case studies in this chapter illustrate, navigating the post-trial process is incredibly complicated and can frustrate even the smartest lawyers. It is unreasonable—and emblematic of how callous our criminal legal system can be—to expect that prisoners should navigate those complex requirements on their own. Postconviction representation might be expensive and politically unpopular, but it would ensure a fairer process and ultimately could ensure that legal proceedings take less time and are more cost-effective. It would also increase trust in the workings of the criminal legal system.

On the federal level, Congress should repeal the 1996 Anti-Terrorism and Effective Death Penalty Reform Act. This widely criticized law is responsible for the harsh deadlines, procedural exhaustion requirements, and extreme deference to state court decisions that prolonged or frustrated relief for the Norfolk Four, Lamar Johnson, and so many others.

Reforming state systems is more complicated because the processes and procedures are different in every state. However, each state should have a procedure in which evidence of innocence can be considered regardless of how long after trial it was discovered. In some states, that may be a motion for a new trial with no statute of limitations. In other states, that may involve freestanding laws that allow defendants to present evidence of innocence. Still other states could adopt the North Carolina model (which was heavily influenced by the CCRC), in which an independent state agency, the Actual Innocence Inquiry Commission, investigates innocence claims outside the adversarial system.

Regardless of the procedure in each state, innocence should be the touchstone. It should not matter if the defendant pleaded guilty. Likewise, if the defendant did not present the evidence to a judge or a jury, it should not matter whether the state or the court believes the evidence could or should have been discovered earlier. If evidence can prove that the wrong person is in prison, it shouldn't matter that there is, arguably, some way that a more creative lawyer or enterprising prisoner should have discovered it. Although prosecutors and attorneys general consistently argue that changes like this would result in a flood of claims, the data offered at the beginning of this chapter suggest that opening this gate would result in a trickle, not a flood.

There are at least two templates for how this could work without overburdening the system. In North Carolina, evidence is "new" if the jury didn't hear it or it wasn't available before the defendant pleaded guilty. The District of Columbia's Innocence Protection Act defines "new" evidence as evidence that "[w]as not personally known and could not, in the exercise of reasonable diligence, have been personally known to the movant at the time of the trial or plea proceeding."[45] It further suggests that evidence is new if it was known to the defendant but couldn't be produced or obtained. Any of these standards could have helped the Norfolk Four, George Seward, and Lamar Johnson if it had been applied in their cases, and none of these measures has led to a flood of litigation from incarcerated individuals.

Finally, states should create procedures in which all relevant evidence can be considered. This is a common issue in innocence cases, where different evidence has to be presented through different procedural vehicles. In Johnson's case, for example, his alternative-perpetrator evidence was presented through motions for a new trial, but the evidence that the state withheld or that should have been discovered by his lawyer was presented in postconviction or habeas proceedings. The net result was that no court has ever considered the full scope of Johnson's case, which combined new evidence with exculpatory evidence that thoroughly discredited the state's case against him.

Once again, the North Carolina's Actual Innocence Inquiry Commission and Washington, DC's Innocence Protection Act are guideposts. In

North Carolina, the commission is extrajudicial, and actual innocence is all that matters. In Washington, DC, courts can consider "any relevant evidence."[46] Both of these are fairer to defendants—who may not, in fact, have evidence of innocence that is "new"—while also allowing the consideration of evidence of guilt that may have been suppressed before trial. In doing so, they make innocence the central question and prioritize truth over procedure.

Conclusion

These changes will be difficult to achieve without a serious examination of the individual decisions that frustrate justice in innocence cases and, ultimately, the values and culture that inform those decisions. The best way to start this process is to step back from the time pressures of litigation and legislative sessions and to engage in what two fellow contributors to this volume, James Doyle and Maureen McGough (see chapter 13), recommend: "sentinel event reviews," in which all stakeholders engage in a detailed, nonblaming review of an event that resulted in an undesired outcome and the decisions along the way that contributed to the outcome.

The nonblaming approach is particularly well suited to this issue. Line prosecutors and attorneys general are public servants who are paid less than their counterparts in private practice and see themselves, often correctly, as wearing the white hat. Like most people, they bristle when advocates on the other side suggest that they have, perhaps deliberately, made choices that kept an innocent person in prison. In most cases, the procedural arguments they make are the default arguments in cases argued by the prosecutor's office, and those arguments are designed to protect interests that the office has prioritized. Thus, they often are made reflexively, without thinking through their full consequences or the values they reflect.

Innocence advocates (including this author) also see themselves as wearing the white hat. We receive hundreds of requests per year from prisoners claiming innocence and typically spend years investigating a claim before choosing to represent someone as a client. As a result, we typically do not file until we are sure the person is innocent, and we are quick to moral outrage when those efforts are opposed—especially for reasons we see as trivial. The nature of the adversarial process sometimes obscures institutional concerns that undergird the reasons for opposing our claims, and line attorneys often are unwilling or unable to explain them.

Because sentinel event reviews occur outside the context of litigation or the compressed legislative period, they involve talking about the reasons for choices and the impacts of those choices. When stakeholders understand those things, they will be better equipped to suggest workable solutions that will ensure freedom for the innocent without unwittingly creating other problems.

On a more fundamental level, sentinel event reviews also require stakeholders to think about the values and culture that inform their decisions. In Lamar Johnson's case, the state attorney general laid out four competing values he believed needed to be balanced in these cases: *individual justice, judicial economy, finality*, and *the integrity of criminal judgments*. Like so many in his position, the attorney general's arguments make clear that he chose to prioritize finality. With an honest discussion about those priorities, about why they exist, and whether they make sense given what we know about the problem of wrongful convictions, we may be able to solve a problem that continues to persist after more than three decades of DNA exonerations.

NOTES

1 Borchard, *Convicting the Innocent*, 15–22.
2 Ibid.
3 *United States v. Garsson*, 291 F.646, 649 (SDNY 1923).
4 Borchard, *Convicting the Innocent*, vii.
5 Radelet, Bedau, and Putnam, *In Spite of Innocence*.
6 The Innocence Project website.
7 Ibid.
8 Ibid.
9 Committee on Identifying the Needs of the Forensic Sciences Community, "Strengthening Forensic Science in the United States: A Path Forward."
10 The Innocence Project website.
11 *People v. Boone*, 2017 NY Slip Op 08713.
12 National Registry of Exonerations, "Race and Wrongful Convictions."
13 Freedman, "Earl Washington's Ordeal," 1089.
14 The Innocence Project website.
15 National Registry of Exonerations.
16 Garrett, "Judging Innocence," 94.
17 Loeffler, Hyatt, and Ridgeway, Measuring Self-Reported Wrongful Convictions Among Prisoners," 259.

18 Virginia State Crime Commission, "Joint Report on Writ of Actual Innocence."

19 North Carolina Actual Innocence Inquiry Commission.

20 Garrett.

21 These data are available through the National Registry of Exonerations and are also on file with the author.

22 *Williams v. Brown.*

23 Ibid., 716.

24 Ibid., 716, n.5.

25 Dick filed at the same time as Williams. Tice's conviction had been reversed on direct appeal, and he was re-convicted in 2003. He therefore could file both state and federal habeas claims within the required time limits. His second conviction was reversed by a federal judge on September 14, 2009, based on ineffective assistance of counsel. Virginia did not attempt to retry him. Wilson was only convicted of the rape and not on parole or probation, so he was not "in custody" and could not challenge his conviction in court.

26 *McQuiggin v. Perkins*, 569 U.S. 383 (2013)

27 *Williams v. Muse*, Civil Action No. 3:09CV769 (E.D. Va. Jun. 27, 2014). Gov't Brief Addressing the Impact of *McQuiggin v. Perkins.*

28 *Williams v. Muse*, Gov't Post-Hearing Brief.

29 *Maryland v. Seward*, Brief of Appellee.

30 *Maryland v. Seward*, Brief & Appendix of Respondent.

31 *Maryland v. Seward.*

32 What's more, the Judicial Conference of Maryland later proposed legislation to eliminate the Writ of Actual Innocence.

33 Messenger, "Gardner's New Conviction Integrity Unit Alleges Perjury and Misconduct in 1994 Murder Case."

34 Smith, "Missouri's Attorney General Is Fighting for the Right to Keep an Innocent Man in Prison."

35 *Missouri v. Johnson*, Respondent's Substitute Brief.

36 Ibid., 35.

37 *State v. Johnson*, 617 S.W.3d 439 (Mo. 2021).

38 Ibid., 7.

39 Rivas, "Pending Law to Correct Wrongful Convictions Could Depend on Missouri Attorney General."

40 Zokovitch, "Lamar Johnson's Decades-old Wrongful Conviction Case on Potential Path to Trial."

41 Blackstone Commentaries, 352.

42 Criminal Case Review Commission website, https://ccrc.gov.uk.

43 Ibid.

44 Brants, "Wrongful Convictions and the Inquisitorial Process."

45 D.C. Code Sec. 22-4131.

46 Ibid., Sec. 22-4135.

13

Learning from Sentinel Events

JAMES DOYLE AND MAUREEN Q. MCGOUGH

Safety-conscious industries of the modern era such as aviation, medicine, and others have the capacity to continuously learn from prior events. Criminal justice systems in the United States—complex, wedded to tradition, and slow to change—lack that capacity. In this chapter, we explore, through a different lens of safety-oriented approaches such as sentinel event reviews, ways to encourage risk mitigation, a culture of safety, and forward-looking inquiries aimed at preventing future harms in the context of the criminal justice system.

Recently, researchers have begun to test whether examining wrongful convictions, mistaken releases, officer-involved shootings, and a range of other discordant outcomes as "organizational accidents"—that is to say, system-based events, not simple personal failures—can repay the investment required to build durable platforms for collaborative learning reviews.[1] An exploration led by the National Institute of Justice (NIJ) aims to equip state and local actors to develop, sustain, and evaluate the practice of "sentinel event reviews." A "sentinel event," as the NIJ defines it, is: "[A] significant negative outcome that signals underlying weaknesses in the system or process; is likely the result of compound errors, and may provide, if properly analyzed and addressed, important keys to strengthening the system and preventing future adverse events or outcomes."[2] These reviews are not conceived of as disciplinary *performance* reviews of practitioners. They are fully contextualized *event* reviews, conducted by teams including all stakeholders at all ranks focused on preventing failures rather than on blaming and punishing individuals.[3] In this "forward-looking" version of accountability, an account is not only a debt to be paid by a culpable actor; it is also a story to be told.[4] Yes, the cop (or prosecutor or forensic technician or defender) zigged when he should have zagged. But why? What influenced the choice?

Under what conditions was it made? Why did it seem like the best (or least bad) choice? Why wasn't it intercepted? Will the same mistaken decisions make sense to the next operator who comes along?

In this chapter, we describe what sentinel event reviews entail, explain the problems they address, explore the burgeoning research on such reviews, and describe the challenges faced in mobilizing sentinel reviews across justice systems. The focus will be on how adopting sentinel event reviews as a routine practice might enhance justice system safety—on how to assess the tantalizing possibility that nonblaming, all-stakeholders, forward-looking reviews can mitigate risk, bolster legitimacy, and promote a measure of healing.

The Big Idea: Recognizing System Complexity

If sentinel event reviews can be made routine, as they are in hospital medicine, the impact on criminal justice could be both wide and deep. Sentinel event reviews are a practical expression of the recognition that criminal justice operates as a complex adaptive system. That conceptual turn is potentially transformative. The goal is not to develop a device for generating tweaks to system practices but rather to instigate, nourish, and sustain a culture change. What is being tested here is whether the practice of sentinel event reviews can be a "key driver of the development and perpetuation of the safety cultures built by the aviation and medical industries."[5] Can we make "the errors themselves the mechanism for learning and change"?[6] Can criminal justice become an environment in which all actors can know and fulfill their individual responsibility for a just collective outcome?

These questions weigh heavily in the current climate. In the wake of the police murder of George Floyd and the ensuing protests, there have been unprecedented demands for defunding the police and reimagining the provision of public safety services altogether. But without an orientation toward learning—either from the errors of the past or the inevitable errors of a reimagined system of the future—the complex, interconnected factors that drive unjust outcomes likely will not be identified, understood, or remedied in any meaningful way.

Like the space shuttle *Challenger* launch decision,[7] a "wrong patient" surgery,[8] or the Chernobyl meltdown,[9] wrongful convictions, mistaken releases, self-harm in custody, and unnecessary shootings by (or of) police are system errors.[10] Miscarriages of justice result from mistakes and decisions, no one of which is independently sufficient to cause the event; they combine with each other and with latent system weaknesses and then—but only then—inflict harm. To the traditional question "Who is responsible?" safety commentators would answer: "Everyone involved, to one degree or another, if not by acting themselves, then by failing to anticipate, intercept, or correct another's action."

"Everyone" in this context includes individuals far from the scene of the event who did the hiring and training, set the caseloads, shaped the jurisprudence, imposed the budgets, and created the environmental pressures on the actors at the sharp end. Dr. Lucien Leape, one of the pioneers in medicine's patient safety movement, summarized this perspective: "While an operator error may be the proximate 'cause' of the accident, the root causes were often present within the system for a long time. The operator has, in a real sense, been 'set up' to fail by poor design, faulty maintenance, or erroneous management decisions."[11] No system can survive without disciplining conscious rule violators, but disciplining conscious rule violators is a bad place to stop.[12]

Disciplinary processes (when they occur[13]) generate information in a story-like format, but as Susan Bandes has pointed out, their tendency is to present atomized anecdotes, blind to system implications:

> The conventional story of blame and purposeful misconduct dangerously misdescribes the way governmental misconduct works, by disaggregating it into a series of individual, anecdotal acts. Government causes harm not through the misdeeds of a single malevolent person who wants to harm a specific individual, but through the collective decision-making of numerous people many of whom are acting in good faith. Few have affirmatively to act in bad faith, because all of the incentives are skewed in favor of simply not acting at all.[14]

The phrase "criminal justice system" is everywhere, but what sort of system do we mean?

Sometimes "system" seems to refer to an enigmatic ecosystem—a pond or a swamp where local actions produce mysterious impacts on the far shore. Sometimes "system" denotes a mechanical construction of gears and switches—a linear, sequential, Newtonian arrangement of discrete causes that generate automatic effects, easily captured in a timeline, flow chart, or fishbone diagram. One domino falls; it knocks over the next.

An alternative explanatory paradigm has begun to gain traction. It understands the criminal justice system not as a chaotic wetland and not as a "complicated" machine with many parts, like a jet airliner at rest. In this conception, criminal justice, like a jet airliner *in operation*, is a complex adaptive system in which the frontline operators are engaged in "sense-making" in a dynamic environment.[15] The shifting, overlapping (and often conflicting) goals, conditions, and influences that buffet actors on the sharp end and produce mistakes are not determinative, as failed switches or frozen gears would be; their impact is probabilistic. The effects are not linear and sequential; everyone's actions are affecting everyone else's actions simultaneously. While it is true that "upstream" police are affecting the "downstream" prosecutors, the police decisions are affected by the prosecutors' requirements, and both groups are affected by what they anticipate in the courtroom. All the actors are responding to pressures from caseloads, budgets, politics, and media. A "bad apple" explanation is not sufficient. Even identifying a freestanding "rotten barrel" (e.g., a corrupt or incompetent police department or crime lab) will almost never provide either an adequate diagnosis or an effective treatment. Safety (or its opposite) cannot be found in a single component or silo any more than wetness can be found in single molecule of H_2O. There is no "eureka part" that can fully explain the problem. Complexity requires an understanding not only of components but also of their interactions.

One insight that safety specialists derive from this approach is expressed in their maxim "the absence of accidents is not proof of safety." As Charles Perrow put it, Murphy's Law is mistaken: everything that could go wrong usually *doesn't*, and then we draw the wrong conclusion.[16] In this view, the absence of a disaster proves only that the probabilities inherent in various unsafe conditions and acts have not coalesced today; it does not prove that they are not present or that they will not coalesce tomorrow.

Professor Boaz Sangero has argued there is a "Hidden Accidents" principle at work in criminal justice that makes mistakes hard to see and often impossible to prove.[17] Unless and until shocks such as the first round of the DNA exoneration cases deliver a slap to the system's face, many unsafe decisions and practices in criminal justice go unremarked.

This is unsettling, but the useful converse of the maxim is that, when some unusual event *does* make a dangerous condition evident, the narrative that the event embodies can be, as patient safety advocate Dr. Donald Berwick contended, a "treasure."[18] Careful examination of a discovered event through a safety lens will reveal not only a defective component (e.g., hair comparison or coercive interrogation) or a lone dishonest human (e.g., a prosecutor who hides Brady material) but also an extensive "influence map" of overlapping and interactive dangers and weaknesses that can be addressed and mitigated before the next practitioner confronts them.[19]

Data is indispensable, but there are limits to what one can see by studying outputs; the same output may result from a huge variety of confluent influences and conditions.[20] The safety argument for sentinel event reviews is that it is from "processes like these—detailed explications of individual cases, deeply situated in complex contexts—that insights leading to useful reductions in hazards are likely to emerge."[21]

The safety paradigm, as Richard Leo notes (writing about exoneration cases), can:

> Move us beyond individual or single-cause explanations of wrongful convictions to more systemic and etiological ones that emphasize routine mistakes, feedback loops, reciprocal impacts, interaction effects, latent conditions, and cumulative error, among other factors to more accurately understand the causes and cures of wrongful convictions.[22]

This approach can encompass the unspectacular—"cold cases" that stay cold too long, fruitless stops and frisks, distended sentences for trivial violations, and "near miss" and "good catch" events where disaster was averted at the last moment by special skill or simple good luck.

A Productive New Lens

Scholarship employing this safety-oriented etiology of error can be strikingly productive. In studies of fatal police shootings, for example, this wider lens has enabled inquiry beyond the character and performance of the cop who pulled the trigger to expose issues in crime control strategies, dispatch, training, supervision, tactics, hiring, trauma treatment, and racial biases.[23] Applied to episodes of police investigative failure, it has illuminated the influence of tunnel vision and other cognitive biases, media and prosecution pressure, training and supervision gaps, and organizational cultures.[24] In exoneration cases involving violations of *Brady v. Maryland*, examination from this perspective brings to the foreground distorted incentives, cognitive pressures, culturally embedded role expectations, and failures in inspection and supervision.[25] A searching examination that compares wrongful convictions with "near misses" has identified and catalogued an array of conditions and latent weaknesses that appear to have been influential across cases.[26]

Following a preliminary reconnaissance, the National Institute of Justice began a methodical investigation of three questions regarding the potential of local sentinel event reviews predicated on this safety-oriented conception of the justice system: (1) Could they be done? (2) Would they be effective in minimizing errors? and (3) Could they be institutionalized and sustained as in aviation and medicine?[27] Recognizing that the NIJ was in the unusual (and uncomfortable) position of building something in order to evaluate it, the NIJ carefully documented progress as its Sentinel Events Initiative unfolded, publishing readouts of stakeholder reactions as the initiative harvested them and compiling a growing bibliography of the safety-oriented research that informed the inquiry.[28]

The process began with the convening of a preliminary roundtable involving stakeholders from across a range of roles and ranks: prosecutors, researchers, forensic scientists, crime survivors, and police. The advice elicited during that effort was reflected in a publication[29] that set out the NIJ's understanding of the concept and included reaction pieces from the stakeholders who attended the conference.

As one might expect when a novel initiative is incubated in a federal agency dedicated to research, development, and evaluation, these pilot efforts spurred concurrent social science research projects designed to explore specific aspects of sentinel event review development and implementation.[30] The NIJ focused on creating an evidence-based framework to support program development, including research on interdependent investigative failures and the application of the sentinel event review model in a range of outcome contexts including self-harm in jails, wrongful convictions, and homicides and nonfatal shootings.

The NIJ funded researchers at Texas State University to explore wrongful convictions through a sentinel events lens, with a particular focus on identifying the systemic nature of causal influences that generated investigative failures. Researchers deconstructed a sample of 275 wrongful convictions and other investigative failures and identified three classifications of causes: (1) personal issues that involved poor decision-making or flawed judgment (e.g., confirmation bias); (2) organizational problems that were inherent in the policies, procedures, training, and resources of the agency or organization (e.g., poor supervision); and (3) situational factors—characteristics of the crime and environment that were out of the control of the criminal justice actors (e.g., a media frenzy). Researchers then grouped the causal factors by their proximity to the investigative failure: proximate causes were considered primary factors, while secondary, tertiary, and high-level factors contributed to the bad outcome as enabling or influencing forces. Most important, researchers then mapped how the various factors related to each other (e.g., which factors facilitate other factors) and built a concept map that graphically displayed these relationships and interactions. This critical analysis provided a structure for understanding the interdependent, systemic nature of these causes for the purpose of forward-looking risk mitigation.[31]

The NIJ also funded a Vera Institute of Justice inquiry into the feasibility of applying the sentinel event review model in the context of suicide and self-harm in jails. Vera collaborated with leadership and staff across four jail systems: Middlesex Office of Adult Corrections and Youth Services in Middlesex County, New Jersey; the Spokane County Detention Services in Spokane County, Washington; the Pinellas County Sheriff's Office in Pinellas County, Florida; and the Middlesex Sheriff's Office in Middlesex County, Massachusetts. The study included an exploration of the sites' existing responses and review mechanisms for suicide and self-harm and identified barriers against as well as facilitators for the implementation of sentinel event reviews to replace or augment existing efforts. Researchers reviewed administrative data and policies, conducted interviews with jail leadership and staff, and partnered with attorneys from the law firm Clifford Chance to analyze the legal landscape of liability, discovery, and public records requests in each jurisdiction.[32] Results indicated that current approaches to reviewing in-custody self-harm and death are often adversarial and fail to account for the perspectives of multiple stakeholders, including medical services contractors and frontline correctional staff. At the same time, the hierarchical structures of most correctional institutions militate against the development of a full factual picture of an event. Vera's researchers concluded that implementing sentinel event reviews to explore these outcomes in jails was both feasible and likely to improve on existing efforts. They identified three key areas that must be addressed to support and sustain nonblaming, forward-looking, multistakeholder reviews in this context: (1) appropriately coordinating with external vendors contracted to provide health care services and synchronizing accountability systems; (2) improving collaboration and effective communication among all levels of staff and empowering line staff to contribute to review processes (as most review processes currently exclude them); and (3) reorienting organizational culture toward safety and away from blame, overcoming resistance to change, and encouraging staff to approach bad outcomes such as suicide and self-harm as preventable events. The analyses of the legal landscapes in each jurisdiction confirmed the salience of challenges regarding confidentiality (particularly with regard to sharing individual health information) and liability, but researchers determined these to be navigable obstacles rather than absolute bars to implementation.

The NIJ funded researchers from Michigan State University, Indiana University, and the Milwaukee Homicide Review Commission to apply a sentinel event model to firearm homicides and nonfatal shootings in Detroit, and Indianapolis, and Milwaukee. This project aims to build on the proven success of homicide and shooting reviews, applying the sentinel event review model for a deeper dive into preventable firearm violence while leveraging expanded input from across stakeholder groups. This project experienced initial delays due largely to the fact that public systems and the agencies within them are not necessarily set up to support this type of forward-looking, collaborative analysis. The research team had to navigate hurdles related to information-sharing across agencies, confidentiality, and liability. Though limiting, these delays have also been instructive regarding likely impediments and promising practices for framing the review process to mitigate future concerns. This project is ongoing, and researchers are generating forthcoming guidance on building sentinel event reviews through a lens of prevention and intervention.

From Concept to Practice: Can All-Stakeholders Reviews Be Done?

The logic of the safety approach argues for doing something beyond applying a new analytic strategy from the researchers' detached and elevated vantage points.

Criminal justice in the United States is an intensely state and local endeavor, and the question remained whether nonblaming, all-stakeholders (and all-ranks) sentinel event reviews could ever be mobilized on a state and local basis. The NIJ's approach to this challenge was governed from the beginning by the unanimous agreement of the initial roundtable's array of stakeholders to a proposition advanced by Michael Jacobson, one of its members: "If you want to learn something, do something."[33] Field trials of the concept were regarded as crucial. Although the insights of researchers can generate new rules and best practices, the researchers cannot ensure that those new rules will be followed, or that they can be enforced, or that they will be promptly modified when changes in the frontline environment render them useless. The safety literature makes it clear that no fix imposed from above is permanent; all fixes are under immediate pressure.

Workarounds, triage, covert work rules, and "practical drift" inevitably take effect.[34] "Work as imagined" and "work as performed" diverge over time. Practitioners still have to cope with the unexpected. When the hope is to achieve safety gains on the same level as aviation or hospital-based medicine, event reviews cannot be one-off episodes on the order of a Warren Commission or 9/11 Commission inquiry convened to deal with a front-page tragedy. The reviews must be a regular, expected *practice*.

The ultimate goal of the event reviews is not to repair or replace broken components in a Newtonian construction—although those changes will certainly provide positive by-products—but to change the culture of the complex adaptive criminal justice system to a "culture of safety"[35] maintaining a higher degree of resilience.[36] Reaching that point depends on incorporating a "just culture" that treats its practitioners fairly, a "reporting culture" in which practitioners actively participate in alerting the system to anomalies, and a "learning culture" where all participants continuously pursue their individual responsibilities for a safe and just collective outcome.

A culture of safety does not see frontline practitioners as menaces but rather as crucial resources—as alert collaborators able to "stop the line" when they detect anomalies. It recognizes that error is part of the human condition; however, as James Reason pointed out, while you cannot change the human condition, you can change the conditions under which humans work.[37]

Those considerations formed the basis for recruiting three volunteer "beta sites" to provide, if not proof of concept, at least proof of plausibility. In Baltimore, law enforcement reviewed an episode of harmful off-duty misconduct. In Philadelphia, a multistakeholder group examined a near-miss event in the investigation of a notorious multiple homicide.[38] Milwaukee gathered a range of stakeholders to review the mistaken release of a young man who almost immediately committed murder upon reentry into society.[39] The Quattrone Center for the Fair Administration of Justice at the University of Pennsylvania Law School, which had organized the Philadelphia beta review, also worked independently with the Montgomery County Pennsylvania District Attorney in a review that was not all-stakeholders in format but did employ the safety-derived "organizational accident" etiology to a botched charging decision involving miscommunicated forensic data.[40]

The information return on these efforts was impressive. In Milwaukee, an all-stakeholder group, confronting a fatal release decision that would ordinarily be blamed on the judge or courtroom prosecutor, uncovered a deeply engrained but not fully understood environment of "structural secrecy" whereby no decision maker possessed at the time of decision all the relevant predictive material that was maintained within the system as a whole. A consensus approach was developed that accomplished sweeping changes in the information-sharing practices in Milwaukee. Baltimore's review, although largely confidential because it involved a personnel matter, also produced insights that Baltimore police used to adjust their policies and practices.[41]

The NIJ also funded the Quattrone Center to support the Philadelphia Event Review Team in 2015. This voluntary collaboration of criminal justice stakeholders included the Philadelphia District Attorney's Office, the Philadelphia Police Department, the First Judicial District Courts of Pennsylvania, and the Defender Association of Philadelphia. The Quattrone Center assembled these stakeholders to apply the sentinel event review model to the conviction and subsequent exoneration of George Cortez, who was convicted of murder and sentenced to life without parole in 2012. Cortez was exonerated in 2016 and released from prison. Tragically, he was murdered just two months later at the age of 36.[42]

The review team produced an event timeline and narrative and collaboratively identified the often interconnected contributing factors that combined to produce the wrongful conviction. The review identified a substantial number of contributing conditions and influences during the investigations, trial, and postconviction phases.

Contributing factors during the investigations phase included inaccurate eyewitness identification, flawed recordkeeping, and issues with cognitive biases in investigating alternative suspects. Contributing factors in the trial phase included an overburdened court and time management pressures that prioritized efficiency at the likely expense of just outcomes. Postconviction contributing factors largely pertained to evidence retention issues.

The Philadelphia review team generated consensus recommendations for improved policies and practices across all participating stakeholder groups to address and mitigate these factors. These recommendations— which account for the interconnectedness of the actions and inactions of each participating stakeholder group—are specifically designed to reduce opportunities for similar bad outcomes in the future. The inclusion of a broad range of relevant stakeholders, including individuals with decision-making authority in their agency or organization, was meant to increase the likelihood of recommendation implementation moving forward.[43]

The results of the research projects, when combined with the insights gleaned from the sentinel event beta sites and other early implementation efforts, constituted a compelling case that sentinel event reviews of various bad outcomes in criminal justice systems were challenging but feasible and would likely produce recommendations for policy and practice improvement that would increase safety and decrease risk of error reoccurrence. Further, these reviews were appropriately designed to account for the interconnected, systemic nature of common latent causal conditions and influences.

There was also extensive feedback harvested from the stakeholders who participated in the three beta site efforts that bore directly on the first question regarding the potential of local sentinel event reviews: Could they be done? The participants' observations confirmed that they saw the event reviews as doable. In addition, the stakeholders' insights into how the reviews should be done vindicated the safety advocates' assumption that the frontline workers could best be seen as resources rather than as wayward menaces. The beta site participants and their initial roundtable interlocutors plainly had seen themselves as collaborative learners.

Indications of this reality surfaced when stakeholder leaders who had participated in exploring the concept pushed to incorporate the idea on their home turf. For example, Milwaukee's elected district attorney and chief public defender argued for making sentinel event reviews a cornerstone of a reimagined system.[44] Several roundtable participants who also served on the President's Task Force on 21st Century Policing advocated for the idea in its deliberations, and sentinel event reviews were included among its final recommendations.[45]

The lessons the stakeholders learned (and taught) were set out in the NIJ publication titled *Paving the Way*.[46] Further questions, such as the potential role in reviews of "persons harmed"—including the surviving family members of fatal police shooting victims, exonerated defendants, and the original crime victims in cases that (one way or the other) later went wrong—were investigated through specialized focus groups.

Lessons Carried Forward: Challenges and Responses

On these bases, the NIJ then committed to investing in a national demonstration project and process evaluation to implement sentinel event reviews and identify basic minimum process elements that could and should be shared across jurisdictions.

While the Sentinel Event Initiative acknowledged that the specific environment, relationships, capacity, and priorities of each jurisdiction necessitate flexibility in the model, the NIJ built the demonstration project to identify the critical core elements that could and should be present for a successful review regardless of jurisdictional differences and nuances.[47]

The NIJ recognized that its Sentinel Event Initiative was not an exploration of completely uncharted territory. There had always been scattered efforts at learning from specific bad outcomes in criminal justice—a host of after-action and critical incident reviews in the criminal justice arena that employed at least some of the essential principles of the sentinel event review process.[48] Prior to launching the demonstration project, the NIJ was committed to integrating lessons learned from its own investments with advances and insights gained from other relevant processes in the criminal justice context such as homicide reviews, elder death reviews, and domestic violence fatality reviews, as well as with any lessons learned from analogous industry efforts to employ non-blaming, forward-looking, all-stakeholder reviews.

While evidence directly supporting the broad, systematic application of sentinel event reviews in criminal justice is nascent, the routinization of these reviews in analogous complex systems such as medicine and aviation has yielded shifts in culture toward safety, quality, and learning, as well as improved outcomes. And Harvard's evaluation of the Milwaukee Homicide Review Commission—ostensibly the closest analogue to a systemized sentinel event review process in a local criminal justice system—credited the approach with slashing homicides in targeted police districts by 52% in a two-year period.[49]

In June 2017, aiming to exploit as much of this information as possible, the NIJ hosted a cumulative all-stakeholder gathering that brought together nearly 100 stakeholders from pilot sites, academic researchers, criminal justice thought leaders, policy makers, crime survivors, and subject matter experts from analogous industries to discuss lessons learned, common challenges, promising practices, messaging considerations, and likely allies and early adopters. The meeting culminated in a consensus discussion about the critical elements of building sentinel event review structures at the jurisdictional level nationwide.

This discussion coalesced around a tentative common template for sentinel event reviews that was generally consistent with the approach sketched in the Vera Institute's early report.[50] An event would be identified, and an all-stakeholders team would be assembled. A fully contextualized description of the event, including a timeline, would be developed. The contributing conditions and influences would be identified by mobilizing techniques such as fishbone diagrams and "Five

'Why's?'" inquiries. Causal connections would be made and an action plan developed and shared. The outcome would then be evaluated.

The readout from this gathering charted a course for the launch of the demonstration projects the following year.[51]

- First and foremost, the group stressed the importance of involving local stakeholders in tailoring sentinel event reviews to the local context—that a one-size-fits-all review model would likely be neither successful nor sustainable. Participants encouraged the NIJ to use the demonstration project as an opportunity to identify the key elements of an effective, sustainable review across the variable realities and capacities of each participating jurisdiction and to create a flexible baseline template to support implementation.

- Participants explored which outcomes and cases would be most appropriate for sentinel event reviews, concluding that events should be carefully selected. Jurisdictions should prioritize cases in which all relevant participants agree that the outcome presents an opportunity to learn and liability has already been determined. Cases that are recent and/or politically charged should not be reviewed. Near misses and good catches also present a valuable opportunity to learn.

- The group felt that a national training and technical assistance (TTA) provider would play a crucial role in educating jurisdictions about the process and helping them design a process that accounted for the realities of their system, culture, and community. They also discussed the importance of the TTA provider in promoting peer-to-peer learning, ensuring and sustaining active participation from multiple stakeholders, assisting in facilitating discussions and negotiating group dynamics, and ensuring the inclusion of relevant subject matter experts as needed. Policy makers and state and municipal leadership and risk management were identified as keys to both advocating for reviews and building a legislative framework that facilitates their sustained success.

- The group discussed the critical role of facilitators for the event reviews, noting that they should be considered to be a neutral convener and not aligned (or perceived to be aligned) with any particular stakeholder group; the facilitator must be steeped in the process but agnostic to the review findings. Also important are the individuals selected to take part in the review. Participants explored multiple models and stressed the importance of broad, all-ranks participation that allowed for flexibility depending on the perspectives necessary to understand causal and contributing factors.

- Participants noted the vital importance of educating review members and continually orienting them to the sentinel event review tenets and purposes. They emphasized that the criminal justice system in particular operates through a lens of retrospective blame and that a nonblaming, forward-looking orientation would be difficult for participants to trust at the outset. They noted this would likely be particularly difficult for early-career line staff who may not typically be experienced in policy and process improvement discussions.

As expected, confidentiality and information-sharing were identified as two of the most—if not the most—chronic inhibitors of establishing and sustaining sentinel event reviews. The forum participants were virtually unanimous that the first question they predicted from any colleague they approached about launching a sentinel events practice would be about confidentiality and liability.

The sense of the forum, however, was that, just as the mission of a hospital is to promote health and healing, not to avoid lawsuits, the mission of the criminal justice system is to do justice, not to avoid paying damages for any harms it had inflicted. The consensus was that, while issues of liability (and therefore confidentiality) would present a recurrent obstacle to progress in local discussions, these issues constituted one more obstacle to be anticipated and worked around, not a "deal-breaking" disqualification.[52] The forum included presentations on multiple promising practices for mitigating these challenges, including event selection, court orders, and safe harbor legislation.[53]

Into the Field

These principles informed the architecture of the NIJ's national demonstration project, which launched in early 2018. The NIJ partnered with the Bureau of Justice Assistance (BJA), mobilizing the BJA's core mission of providing jurisdictional-level training and technical assistance to support criminal justice programs and initiatives. The BJA led the solicitation and selection process of a national training and technical assistance partner, awarding $1.6 million to the Quattrone Center, while the NIJ led the development of a process evaluation to accompany site implementation.

Minneapolis was selected as the first demonstration site, bringing together the Minnesota Department of Health, the Minneapolis Health Department, and the Minneapolis Police Department for a nearly yearlong engagement applying the sentinel event review model to six overdose fatalities in the jurisdiction. Participants coalesced around the simple but critical goal of understanding the causal and related factors contributing to opioid-involved deaths with the goal of preventing future loss of life. At the conclusion of these reviews, the team developed a series of recommendations to improve interagency coordination and advance the jurisdiction's response to the opioid epidemic with a focus on improved public health outcomes, particularly for justice-involved individuals. At the time of writing, these recommendations are not publicly available. A number of additional sites across the country were in the early stages of development and implementation when the COVID-19 pandemic struck. As with most criminal justice initiatives, the demonstration project is unable to proceed as currently designed. But this unanticipated change in circumstances may provide new opportunities to apply the model to review current attempts to use a criminal justice framework to achieve public health outcomes through such efforts as enforcement of social distancing orders. These efforts to implement sentinel event reviews at the jurisdictional level have been painfully slow at times. But the tempo is not without reason, and the pace is not a reason to question the transformative potential of these reviews in criminal justice. It is important to note that these early efforts are not only creating a novel framework but also upending what are often deeply held beliefs about individual roles and how the system should (and could) work. For example, there are few occasions in our current reality to bring litigators from opposite sides of the courtroom to the same table to pursue a shared outcome. These dynamics are further complicated by the unique nuances of each jurisdiction, coupled with a deeply entrenched history of approaching all bad outcomes through the lens of retrospective blame. In many ways, sentinel event reviews go beyond an exploration of the factors tied to specific events; their implementation requires radical shifts in criminal justice agency culture and tenets.

Forward-Looking Accountability and Legitimacy

Highly publicized criminal justice failures—wanton officer-involved shootings or wrongful convictions based on prosecutorial misconduct— bring calls for accountability in the form discipline or prosecution. The failure to impose sanctions on insider rule breakers in these notorious cases breeds public frustration and alienation and undermines the trust in the law that public order requires.[54]

Sentinel event reviews are no substitute for retrospective discipline in such situations, and it would be a disastrous mistake to confuse the disciplinary and learning review processes—that is to say, to believe that they simply can be exchanged.[55] But the sentinel event reviews and the forward-looking accountability they enable could be an important complement to traditional disciplinary, tort, and prosecutorial actions.

A disciplinary process must go "down and in" to focus on the concrete misconduct of a particular individual. A safety-oriented sentinel events inquiry also seeks that information, but it goes "up and out" too—working to identify the abiding conditions and influences that a disciplinary process will tend to mute (or deride) as "excuses."[56] These features of the system, if not uncovered and addressed, will haunt future practitioners and, through them, the public.

Pursuit of a safety model in criminal justice constitutes a wager on the frontline troops: it treats them as a resource, not as a menace. It recognizes that the local motivations for practitioners' workarounds and practical drift—influences that would be repudiated as excuses in any retrospective disciplinary process—are indispensable elements of any forward-looking inquiry aimed at preventing future harms. Safety must be coproduced by the officials and the communities working together to identify harms, or else it will not be produced at all; that coproduction requires an understanding of the perspectives of all ranks, in all stakeholder roles. Just as the patient safety version of analyzing events includes the patient's family and the operating room nurse as well as the chief of surgery, the public safety incarnation must value the community and patrol officer perspectives as well as those of the assistant commissioner and the chief judge.

As things stand, the people most impacted by the justice system are least able to influence it. The safety approach could construct a participatory platform where the value we as a society give to safe workmanship—in a version of workmanship that gives due weight to the benefits of systemization and standardization—can be expressed by taking account of its opposite as well as the right of community members to be free from unnecessary intrusions and curtailments.

In the absence of the safety-oriented *event* reviews, a disciplinary *performance* review that ends inconclusively or with no sanction imposed suggests to the public that the official stance is "We don't much care whether this happens again."

Events of recent years have made it clear that the legitimacy of the criminal justice system is not something that can be assumed and then simply preserved by its officials; it must be earned—and continuously earned—by strict adherence to fair and transparent processes.

If sentinel event reviews are shown to be workable, they can provide a vehicle by which criminal justice leadership can demonstrate to the public that, regardless of what happens (or does not happen) to the frontline operator who is the disciplinary focus, the justice system's leaders will hold *themselves* accountable for learning what went wrong, why it went wrong, and how repetition of the harm can be prevented. For example, whether or not the officer in a fatal shooting is disciplined, law enforcement leaders—by immediately making and then fulfilling a public commitment to a comprehensive and transparent examination of hiring, supervision, equipment, training, dispatch, assignment strategies, organizational culture, and racial biases (implicit and explicit)—will indicate their determination to pursue the public's safety rather than their own. The National Transportation Safety Board's postcrash studies provide an instructive example: it is hard to miss the value that both the aviation community and the general public place on the clinical inquiries the board conducts and publishes.

Disciplinary processes assessing whether individual actors are to be called to "settle an account"—in the sense of paying a debt for misconduct—demand tightly circumscribed and controlled adversarial procedures to protect the rights of the accused practitioner. A forward-looking event review, in contrast, is concerned with an "account" as a story, and there is no reason to exclude community stakeholders from direct participation. There are obvious legitimacy advantages in the transparency that community stakeholder participation provides. Besides, a process that brings the community to the table guarantees that the event review (and the modifications it generates) will take full account of the iatrogenic ("from the treatment") harms that professional stakeholders might tend to overlook. A closed, technocratic, root-cause analysis, conducted exclusively by practitioners, will always risk settling on negotiated we-can-live-with-that fixes that optimize the various institutional goals of criminal justice agencies but overlook the community's interest in the price that it will pay as a result.[57] The basic logic of the sentinel events approach clears a space for actions that the criminal justice professionals do *with*—rather than for or to—the community.

This approach can play an important role in illuminating and correcting often veiled conditions and influences arising not from explicit (or even implicit) racial and ethnic biases of individual practitioners but rather from systemic biases stemming from the operation of the system-as-system. For example, after two recent deaths in police custody, Tucson, Arizona police convened an all-stakeholders Sentinel Event Review Board[58] that included community members, all-ranks police and emergency participants, and subject matter experts from mental health and other implicated disciplines. Among the many findings generated by this group were insights into a condition present in both incidents: a chronic lack of Spanish-language capacity in the emergency services communications chains. In a discipline-oriented review, these issues—with their roots in organizational structures, funding shortages, and bureaucratic cultures—would likely have been brushed aside as excuses for frontline misjudgments or misconduct and then ignored. The sentinel event review, spurred here by community stakeholder inquiry, prompted immediate changes and allowed for a formal further review after six months of progress toward correcting that system bias.[59]

By participating in collaborative learning reviews of unexpected outcomes, criminal justice practitioners can communicate they accept the notion that they "are accountable to the community for meeting even those standards of adequate workmanship that cannot be formulated in advance, and explicitly."[60] They can enhance public trust in the law and system legitimacy by showing that they care about getting things right.

Forward-Looking Accountability and Restorative Justice

Firing or prosecuting a culpable criminal justice actor may provide some degree of satisfaction to the persons they have harmed. But that is not to say that discipline and punishment are the only, or even the most effective, ways in which to pursue healing.[61] As medicine's experience with "Disclosure and Apology" initiatives in the aftermath of medical errors indicates, the inclusion of persons harmed by the treatment in forward-looking event reviews undertaken to protect others from suffering the same injuries is highly valued by patients and their families.[62] Accumulating experience in the wrongful conviction context indicates that exonerated individuals, original crime victims, and other persons harmed feel a strong need to participate in protecting others still threatened by the system's weaknesses and provides an argument for offering a similar healing opportunity in criminal justice.[63]

The sentinel event orientation also offers new potential for addressing harms to "second victims."[64] Numerous people—the eyewitness who identified the wrong man and later learned that he has been falsely imprisoned; the public defender who failed to intercept a Brady violation and saw her client sentenced to death; the ill-trained, ill-equipped, hastily dispatched cop who shoots and kills a prematurely released mental patient—may learn that they were all in a sense set up to fail by the system. Those actors also suffered trauma that no discipline and punishment of an isolated bad apple will address.

The criminal justice system is an organization that has a lot invested in its practitioners. As Sidney Dekker contends:

> Paying off the first victim and sending off the second denies the humanity and reality of the relationship that existed between the two victims. . . . Where first victims are given the impression that their lives had been entrusted to a dispensable, disposable cog in the organizational machine, what does that say about the organization's own duty ethic in relation to its patients, passengers, clients?[65]

This "second victim" awareness is one particular example of a general principle of analysis more or less dictated by the organizational accident etiology of error: the need for the perspectives of all of those implicated in the event.

Perspectives in Tension: Numbers and Narratives

The possibility of realizing the concrete dividends of sentinel events thinking in the frontline world—enhanced risk reduction, legitimacy, and restoration—is tantalizing.

Beyond those benefits, if sentinel event reviews become a regular practice, they could trigger a benign disruption in the now prevailing relationships between the field and the research communities. Scholars and researchers who have worked for decades to bring about the necessary (and tardy) recognition of the power of "evidence-based" and "data-driven" approaches to criminal justice policy[66] may well view without enthusiasm a reorientation that seems at first glance to offer only an ever-growing pile of eccentric anecdotes. The "account-as-story" foundation of the reviews does not fit comfortably into the world of grant giving, grant seeking, peer reviewing, and grant evaluating that has belatedly come to appreciate the power of statistically generated insights.

It seems at least plausible that the sentinel event reviews in individual jurisdictions can provide not only concrete benefits on the ground but also the granular "thick description" that "big data" needs.[67] Sentinel event reviews will provide a venue where researchers can supply the frontline stakeholders with research insights, but the frontline actors will simultaneously supply researchers with salient empirical questions for investigation. If implemented as routine practice, sentinel event reviews will—over time—provide a rich source of qualitative data ripe for analysis to identify trends within a jurisdiction, within a state, or even across the country. The conversation between the researchers and the front lines might be refreshed—and *continuously* refreshed—by the sentinel event practice.

NOTES

1 J. Doyle, "A Safety Model Perspective."

2 US Department of Justice, National Institute of Justice, *NIJ's Sentinel Events Initiative*.

3 Dekker, *Safety Differently*.

4 Sharpe, *Promoting Patient Safety*.

5 Klinger, "Organizational Accidents and Deadly Officer Involved Shootings."
6 Armacost, "Police Shootings."
7 Vaughan, *The Challenger Launch Decision*.
8 Chassin Becher, "The Wrong Patient."
9 Perrow, *Normal Accidents*.
10 J. Doyle, "Learning From Error In American Criminal Justice."
11 Leape, "Error in Medicine."
12 Woods, "Conflicts Between Learning and Accountability in Patient Safety."
13 Trivedi and Gonzalez Van Cleve, "To Serve and Protect Each Other."
14 Bandes, "Patterns of Injustice."
15 Dekker, "Complexity Theory"; Pupilidy and Vessel, "The Learning Review."
16 Langwiesche, *Inside the Sky*.
17 Sangero, *Safety from False Convictions*.
18 Berwick, "Continuous Improvement as an Ideal in Health Care."
19 Pupildy and Vessel, "The Learning Review."
20 Wang, "Big Data Needs Thick Data."
21 Wears and Karsh, "Thick v. Thin."
22 Leo, "The Criminology of Wrongful Conviction."
23 Klinger, "Organizational Accidents"; Armacost, "Police Shootings"; Schwartz, "Systems Failure in Policing"; Sherman, "Reducing Fatal Police Shootings as System Crashes"; Hollway, Lee, and Smoot, "Root Cause Analysis"; Thacher, "The Learning Model."
24 Shane, *Organizational Accident Theory*; Zalman and Larson, "Elephants in the Station House"; Rossmo and Pollack, "Confirmation Bias and Other Systemic Causes"; Hollway and Grunwald, "Applying Sentinel Event Reviews to Policing."
25 J. Doyle, "Orwell's Elephant."
26 Gould at al., "Predicting Erroneous Convictions."
27 Ritter, "Testing a Concept and Beyond."
28 US Department of Justice and Hertzberg, ed., "A Compiled Bibliography."
29 US Department of Justice, *Mending Justice*.
30 US Department of Justice, NIJ, "NIJ's Sentinel Events Initiative," *Strategic Plan*.
31 Rossmo and Pollack, "Confirmation Bias and Other Systemic Causes."
32 Pope and Delaney-Brumsey, *Building a Culture of Safety*.
33 US Department of Justice, *Mending Justice*.
34 Dekker, *Drift*; Snook, *Friendly Fire*.
35 Reason, *Human Error*.
36 Woods, "Resiliency Revisited."
37 Reason, *Human Error*.
38 Hollway and Grunwald, "Applying Sentinel Event Reviews."
39 Starr, "A New Way to Reform the Justice System."
40 Raper et al. "Using Root Cause Analysis Prosecutorial Error."
41 Starr, "A New Way to Reform the Justice System."
42 Philadelphia Review Team, *Report*.

43 Ibid.
44 Reed and Chisholm, *From Funnels to Large Scale Irrigation.*
45 President's Task Force on 21st Century Policing.
46 US Department of Justice, *Paving the Way.*
47 US Department of Justice, NIJ, "NIJ's Sentinel Events Initiative," *Strategic Plan.*
48 City of Tucson Police Department, *Critical Incident Review.*
49 Azrael, Braga, and O'Brien, "Developing the Capacity to Understand and Prevent Homicide."
50 Pope and Delaney-Brumsey, *Building a Culture of Safety.*
51 NIJ All-Stakeholders, 2017. Sentinel Event All Stakeholder Forum Report is available here: www.ojp.gov/pdffiles1/nij/251172.pdf.
52 Pope, and Delaney-Brumsey, *Building a Culture of Safety.*
53 NIJ, 2017.
54 Tyler and Fagan, "Legitimacy and Cooperation."
55 Woods, "Conflicts Between Learning and Accountability in Patient Safety."
56 Dekker, "The Complexity of Failure."
57 Peerally et al., "The Problem with Root Cause Analysis."
58 Tucson Sentinel Events Review Board.
59 Tucson Sentinel Events Review Board (six months).
60 Bittner, "Legality and Workmanship."
61 Braithwaite, *Restorative Justice and Responsive Regulation.*
62 Robbennolt, "Apologies and Medical Error."
63 Bazelon, *Rectify.*
64 Dekker, *Second Victim.*
65 Ibid.
66 Bach, *Ordinary Injustice.*
67 Wears and Karsh, "Thick v. Thin."

Conclusion

A Path Forward to Evidence-Based Reform

JON B. GOULD AND PAMELA R. METZGER

This book contains actionable steps to achieve criminal legal reform. Along the way, the contributors provide a vision of how criminal legal systems can continue to improve performance and offer increased fairness, compassion, and safety to communities and individuals. While the contributors address a range of topics, there is remarkable overlap in their approaches and recommendations. There is broad consensus that successful reform depends heavily on insights gleaned from existing data and research and on continued—and increased—funding and support for new data and research. The contributors agree about the importance of evaluating and reviewing criminal legal practice policy and practice on an ongoing basis. And they emphasize the need for collaborative research and reform, both across traditional stakeholder silos and among practitioners and researchers.

Ultimately, however, lasting reform will require persistent and stubborn—even relentless—pursuit of sustainable solutions that reflect the values of fair treatment and fair process that are the hallmarks of the legal system in the United States. This conclusion, therefore, not only summarizes important themes of the book but also proposes a way forward—not only for criminal justice stakeholders but also for ordinary citizens who are interested in the cause of justice reform.

Successful Reform Requires Research and Data

The importance of research and data is a pervasive theme of this book. Each of the contributors agrees that more and better empirical evidence is necessary, both to highlight policy failures and to guide evidence-based reform. Still, there are enormous criminal justice data deficits, and those deficits feature heavily in many chapters. Some authors highlight the desperate need to gather new data and conduct additional research. Others describe their own efforts to close this research gap with pioneering new research. Ultimately, funding and further research are among the most common proposals for reform.

Using Research and Data to Explain Policy Failures and Recommend Reform Strategies

Addressing the topic of sentencing reform, Cassia Spohn, Megan Verhagen, and Jason Walker (chapter 5) marshal data to demonstrate that the United States' "dramatic increases in state and federal prison populations since the 1970s can be attributed largely to changes in sentencing policies and practices" rather than to increases in crime.[1] Spohn and her colleagues place these data in a critical historical context, chronicling how well-intentioned sentencing reforms produced unintended, and disastrous, consequences. The authors identify failed policy "reforms" of the last four-plus decades—determinate sentencing and sentencing guidelines, mandatory minimum sentencing statutes, three-strikes-and-you're-out laws, truth-in-sentencing provisions, and changes to life sentences—and describe the empirical evidence of their failure.

Chapter 9, on preventing firearm violence, similarly uses data of overwhelming harm to underscore the urgent need for reform. Coauthors Jesenia Pizarro, Karissa Pelletier, April Zeoli, and Anne Corbin document the heartbreaking toll that firearm violence takes on US society, injuring 100,000 and fatally wounding 36,000 people each year.[2] Like Cassia Spohn and her colleagues, they emphasize the financial burden of the status quo, which imposes average costs of "$229 billion per year due to medical and criminal justice expenses, loss of income, and pain and suffering of victims."[3]

In their chapter on bail reform (chapter 4), Christine Scott-Hayward and Henry Fradella use national statistics about pretrial detention to illuminate the financial and human costs of the cash bail system. They contrast that data with the compelling evidence that the cash bail system is both discriminatory and ineffective. In other words, they use research and data to show that the cash bail system punishes poverty and ignores danger. Having provided firm empirical evidence that our current policies and practices are not working, Scott-Hayworth and Fradella recommend new practices—such as court notification programs—that *do* work to improve public safety, reduce public costs, and provide equal justice.

Meanwhile, the authors of the chapters on erroneous convictions (chapter 12) and sentinel event review (chapter 13) demonstrate that valuable data need not be "big data." With evidence drawn from in-depth examinations of individual cases or small datasets about criminal justice failures, the authors of these chapters propose reforms to the systems and agencies that handle the day-to-day operations of the criminal justice system.

The Need for Additional Data and Research

Pathbreaking research often requires the identification of *new* questions and the recognition of overlooked or unseen knowledge gaps. When it comes to criminal legal systems and outcomes, we often "don't know what we don't know."[4] Therefore, we need new data and research to illuminate our empirical blind spots. In their chapters about corrections and reentry, Kevin Wright, Stephanie Morse, and Madison Sutton (chapter 6, on corrections) and Kelly Orians and Troy Rhodes (chapter 7, on reentry) push policy makers and academics to consider what other questions we should ask—and answer—about strategies that can promote correctional and reentry success.

Recidivism measures a long-term result with a binary yes/no outcome. But a long-term goal, like recidivism reduction, requires interim steps to produce the desired result of criminal desistance. For that matter, it necessitates intervention after an individual is released from incarceration to ensure that they have the necessary support and resources for the transition. As Orians and Rhodes note in their chapter, there have been several initiatives to improve reentry, but the field still lacks significant analyses of interventional programming. They offer compelling evidence, much of it qualitative, for the proposals they advance. Still, the field and its potential interventions require greater study.

In her chapter on rural criminal justice reform (chapter 10), Pamela Metzger makes a similar argument for the exploration of relatively under-examined rural criminal legal systems. Metzger compares the wealth of evidence about urban systems with the relative dearth of evidence about rural systems and insightfully highlights the unfortunate consequences. When urban reforms are imposed on rural jurisdictions, a failure to recognize and respond to the unique features of rural criminal practice may doom those reforms to failure. Meanwhile, when data collection and research practice are concentrated in urban areas, practitioners and scholars never learn about—much less study—rural innovations and practices. She contends that, by replacing our blinkered approaches to research and reform with inclusive, expansive, and imaginative inquiries about overlooked topics and communities, we can increase our success in identifying and implementing evidence-based reforms.

Not content to wait for others to conduct new research, scholars like Lauren Sudeall and Jon Gould, Rachel Bowman, and Belén Lowrey-Kinberg, among others, have launched their own studies. To investigate how ordinary people experience the bifurcation of civil and criminal justice, Sudeall interviewed public defenders, social workers, and their clients. Her findings, presented in chapter 11, firmly support her proposals for increased collaboration and communication across the otherwise siloed systems of criminal and civil justice.

Meanwhile, Gould, Bowman, and Lowrey-Kinberg (chapter 2) conducted independent research with system insiders. In collaboration with the Deason Criminal Justice Reform Center, Gould and his colleagues explored prosecutorial charging practices in three jurisdictions, with the intention of subjecting hot criminal justice reform trends—such as progressive prosecution—to the cold eye of empirical research. Their results offer unique insights into reform opportunities that can be rapidly deployed in prosecutors' offices nationwide. Importantly, the concentrated nature of their research inquiry—prosecutorial charging practices—allows the coauthors to make targeted recommendations that are well within the range of changes that any district attorney can adopt. Since prosecutors are often the gatekeepers of the criminal legal system, implementing the pathbreaking research described in chapter 2 could have a significant impact on justice reform across the nation.

Successful Reform Requires Iterative Investigations and Experiments

The iterative nature of successful reform is also a prominent and persistent theme of the book. "Iterative reform" means that, as practitioners and policy makers implement new policies, procedures, treatments, or interventions, researchers must evaluate the impact of those initiatives. Unsuccessful interventions are then modified or abandoned. Successful initiatives can be refined, reapplied, and reevaluated. This iterative process creates a data-driven feedback loop that promotes perpetual learning and improvement.

As James Doyle and Maureen McGough emphasize in chapter 13, on sentinel event review, criminal justice systems have historically failed to engage in this type of continuous learning. Doyle and McGough explain how the evolving practice of sentinel event review aims to change that. Using individual criminal justice events to expose organizational and systemic flaws, sentinel event review accomplishes three important tasks. First, it *depersonalizes* criminal justice errors and near misses, replacing a "blame and shame" model that focuses on individual error with a systemic learning model that focuses on organizational culture and practice. Second, it *reorients* discussions of criminal justice error from retrospective critiques of failure to forward-looking investments in improved policy and practice. Third, it *models* the iterative learning approach that has helped to revolutionize other high-stakes systems such as aviation and medicine.

In chapter 12, Shawn Armbrust shows how sentinel event review, coupled with legislative reform, has the potential to create targeted legal strategies to reverse wrongful convictions. Armbrust describes the growth of Conviction Integrity Units (CIUs)—divisions within a prosecutor's office that consider and evaluate claims of wrongful convictions. As a way of moving forward, Armbrust recommends that CIUs draw on lessons learned from the sentinel event model. As she explains, "the nonblaming approach is particularly well suited" to prosecutor-driven assessments of wrongful conviction.[5] When case reviews "occur outside the context of litigation or the compressed legislative period, they involve talking about the reasons for choices and the impacts of those choices."[6] This means that prosecutors can "suggest workable solutions that will ensure freedom for the innocent without unwittingly creating other problems."[7] At the same time, these reviews "require stakeholders to think about the values and culture that inform their decisions," thereby offering the opportunity for "an honest discussion" of office and agency priorities and open inquiry about whether those priorities "make sense given what we know about the problem of wrongful convictions."[8] While CIUs cannot alone create widespread reform, Armbrust contends that they can create openings for collaborative discussions about much-needed changes to the legal system by which we review allegations of wrongful convictions.

Of course, iterative learning also occurs outside of sentinel event review. The chapters on firearms (chapter 9), policing (chapter 1), and reentry (chapter 4) draw heavily on other iterative strategies for reform-oriented iterative learning, including systematic reviews and meta-analyses. In a "systematic review," researchers locate "primary studies, appraising the quality of these studies, selecting studies to be included, extracting data from the studies, and synthesizing the findings" to "critically appraise the quality of the relevant primary research" on a particular topic.[9] A "meta-analysis" is a related research technique that combines the findings from multiple studies to draw conclusions about what works across a range of different environments.[10] Taken together, these two approaches help criminal justice researchers draw broad conclusions about similar studies that were conducted in different jurisdictions with different laws and different ways of practicing criminal justice.

Chapter 1, Michael White and Aili Malm's analysis of body-worn cameras (BWCs), illustrates the value of these iterative learning research techniques. Since all policing occurs in highly specific local environments, the study of BWCs in one police department might have limited value in predicting the value of implementing the practice in another police department. Fortunately, researchers have been able to conduct systematic reviews and meta-analyses of multiple studies into BWC implementation. These reviews, in turn, have enabled White and Malm to highlight "the strongest evidence that BWCs have a positive impact on policing and policing legitimacy" and explain an "increasingly mixed body of evidence on BWCs."[11] Equipped with these data, the coauthors offer nuanced recommendations and suggestions about how and why to implement a BWC program.

Successful Reform Requires Collaboration

Another frequent point of agreement among the contributors is that the traditionally siloed approach to adversarial criminal justice has hampered the cause of reform. Prosecutors and defense attorneys may be loath to cooperate, perceiving only the risks and not the rewards of consensus-based reforms. Police may be reluctant to "take instruction" from community groups. Legislators may respond to political imperatives rather than consult with experts about evidence-based solutions. Many authors in this book, therefore, underscore the necessity of collaboration among *all* stakeholders, from practitioners and policy makers to justice-involved individuals and their communities.

In some instances, reform-oriented collaboration means that lawmakers must harmonize their legislative approaches with research results. For example, in chapter 11, Lauren Sudeall proposes that legislators and judicial rulemaking bodies learn from researchers and from justice-involved individuals about the frustrations and inefficiencies of our bifurcated civil and criminal justice systems. She urges that judges and lawyers draw on that shared research to identify possible areas of cooperation that could give ordinary people a better and more intuitive experience in the civil and criminal legal systems.

In other areas of law, collaboration means that legislators must work across state and federal lines to guarantee that their intended reforms are effective. Nowhere is this issue more salient than in the area of reducing firearm violence. Legislative strategies to reduce firearm violence require that reformers navigate the Second Amendment right to bear arms and plan reforms that will succeed across a complex maze of federal and state regulations. Coordination among state and federal lawmakers will be required to close the multiple loopholes that have been created by legislation that fails to account for the legal and illegal markets that supply firearms to people across the nation.

In their chapter on the victimization of Indigenous women and girls, Kathleen Fox, Christopher Sharp, Kayleigh Stanek, Turquoise Devereaux, and Connor Stewart make similar observations about the patchwork approaches that legislatures and law enforcement agencies have adopted in their (failed) attempts to combat violence against this vulnerable population.

Fox and her coauthors emphasize, however, that meaningful reform cannot be accomplished without collaborations that actively engage impacted communities.

The participatory defense model outlined by Raj Jayadev and Janet Moore in chapter 3 exemplifies the value of broad collaboration with *all* stakeholders, from practitioners to policy makers to justice-involved individuals and their communities. Jayadev and Moore contend that criminal law reformers, rather than relying solely on the siloed communities of criminal law practitioners and policy makers, should embrace collaboration with affected individuals. The coauthors emphasize the centrality of a strategy that is "consensual and horizontal, not top-down" and that focuses on "relationships rather than projects." They urge that participatory defense, and similar collaborative and community-based reform strategies, can make "everyone an architect" of institutional reform.[12]

Successful Reform Requires Ongoing Public Commitment to Change

As this book goes to press, extraordinary changes are afoot that show promise for continuing success in criminal legal reform. Bipartisan interest and engagement suggest the possibility of durable legislative reforms, and emerging technologies offer new ways to implement these reforms. The tragic events of 2020—the murder of George Floyd (among others) and COVID-19's devastating effects on the nation's courts and correctional facilities—have generated renewed popular interest in justice reform.

Technology and data have played a central role in this phenomenon. The viral spread of videos showing police using excessive and deadly force has exposed a vast national audience to the often brutal intersection of race, ethnicity, and policing. The online harvesting of data about how COVID-19 has impacted jail and prison populations has similarly helped to humanize the plight of people who are incarcerated during the pandemic. All of this has prompted renewed questions among the general public about criminal legal policy.

At the same time, an ever-widening spectrum of social groups, politicians, celebrities, and ordinary people have become advocates for criminal justice reform. From Kim Kardashian to Colin Kaepernick, celebrities have adopted the cause of criminal justice reform. And recent elections suggest that ordinary people may increasingly be turning to electoral politics as a way to drive justice reform.

Certainly, the 2020 election was an "extraordinary milestone of civic engagement."[13] Nearly 160 million Americans voted, and compared to prior years "turnout increased in every state and in 98% of the nation's counties."[14] The highly contested presidential election, accompanied by many high-stakes senatorial elections, appears to have driven this nearly unprecedented level of democratic engagement.

In contrast, in more typical years—and particularly in purely local elections—turnout rates have been vastly lower. National election turnout rates have ranged from 56% (1972) to 66% (2020),[15] and estimates of turnout rates for local elections range from a relatively high rate of 27%[16] to as low as 11%.[17] These dispiriting turnout rates are often accompanied by significant disparities in the wealth, race, ethnicity, and age of those who do vote.[18] Perhaps these dismal local turnout numbers have even contributed to the high rates of incumbency among local criminal justice actors. "Incumbent prosecutors win re-election in 94% of the races they enter,"[19] and "hundreds of judges draw no challengers for their seats, and many judges go their whole careers without facing political opposition."[20]

Yet today it is clear that public engagement with criminal legal reform is on the upswing. Certainly, criminal justice reform won big at the 2020 ballot box. Although there were some notable electoral defeats—chief among them the defeat of California's Proposition 25 initiative on bail reform (discussed in chapter 4), there were also major victories for reformers.[21] Voters elected progressive prosecutors and endorsed ballot initiatives that were intended to reduce incarceration rates.[22] California voters rejected a movement to increase certain misdemeanor offenses to felonies and approved a measure restoring voting rights to people on parole.[23] Voters in places as diverse as South Dakota, New Jersey, Montana, and Arizona voted to legalize marijuana, and voters in Oregon and the District of Columbia went even further, legalizing a range of other drugs.[24] Police oversight initiatives were also popular with state and local voters.[25]

At the national level, politicians on both sides of the aisle are "keeping criminal justice reform on the table."[26] Republican leaders have touted criminal justice reform as an issue for which they are best suited,[27] and criminal justice reform was a prominent part of the Democrats' national platform for 2020.[28]

As the contributors demonstrate, however, plans to reform policy and practice are the just the beginning of a movement for evidence-based reform. For these new initiatives to succeed, politicians, practitioners, and the communities they serve must insist upon the rigorous and reliable investigation of reforms. Anecdotal reports and personal instincts about "what works" are no substitute for empirical evidence. The success of any big idea for reimaging criminal justice depends upon an equally large reliance on research as a road map for reform.

NOTES

1 Spohn, Verhagen, and Walker, chapter 5.
2 Pizarro, Pelletier, Zeoli and Corbin, chapter 8.
3 Ibid.
4 Donald Rumsfeld—then US secretary of defense—was famously mocked for defending (often) flawed evidence in intelligence reports with a "known unknown" taxonomy: "There are known knowns. There are things we know we know. We also know there are known unknowns. That is to say, we know there are some things we do not know. But there are also unknown unknowns, the ones we don't know we don't know." Shermer, "Rumsfeld's Wisdom." Whatever the relevance of that paradigm to foreign policy, Rumsfeld's clumsy phrasing points to an important distinction between the assessment of existing evidence and the absence of evidence, including the absence of an identified body of evidence that should be examined.
5 Armbrust, chapter 12.
6 Ibid.
7 Ibid.
8 Ibid.
9 Liao, Bryman, and Lewis-Beck, *The Sage Encyclopedia of Social Science Research Methods*, 892.
10 Ibid., 1142.
11 White and Malm, chapter 1.
12 Jayadev, Moore, and Sandy, chapter 3.
13 Corasaniti and Rutenberg, "Republicans Pushed to Restrict Voting."
14 Smith, Zhou, and Wu, "Map: Turnout Surged in 2020."
15 Schaul, Rabinowitz, and Mellnik, "2020 Voter Turnout Set to Break Record from 1960."
16 Holbrook and Weinschenk, "Campaigns, Mobilization, and Turnout in Mayoral Elections."

17 Midkiff, "Voter Turnout on the Local Level is Plummeting."

18 Who Votes for Mayor? website.

19 Wright, "Beyond Prosecutor Elections," 600.

20 Lean, "Waltzing to Power."

21 Mintz, "How Criminal Justice Reform Fared in the 2020 Elections."

22 Morrison, "Ballot Results"; Mintz, "How Criminal Justice Reform Fared in the 2020 Elections."

23 Mintz, "How Criminal Justice Reform Fared in the 2020 Elections."

24 Ibid.

25 Ibid.

26 Dewan, "Here's One Issue That Could Actually Break the Partisan Gridlock."

27 Ibid.

28 Democratic National Committee, "Protecting Communities and Building Trust by Reforming Our Criminal Justice System."

BIBLIOGRAPHY

Abrams, David S. "Is Pleading Really a Bargain?" *Journal of Empirical Legal Studies* 8, no. S1 (2011): 200–21.

Adelman, Lynn. "The Adverse Impact of Truth in Sentencing on Wisconsin's Efforts to Deal with Low Level Drug Offenders." *Valparaiso University Law Review* 43 (2013): 1–19.

Agbo, Nwamaka. "What Is Restorative Economics?" NwamakaAgbo.com. N.d. www.nwamakaagbo.com.

Alabama State Bar. "Ethics Opinion: Part-Time Judges; Part-Time Assistant District Attorneys and Imputed Disqualification." November 19, 2008. www.alabar.org.

Albert Cobarrubias Justice Project. "Mercury News: District Attorney's Office Charging Gang Enhancements for Graffiti." September 2, 2012. https://acjusticeproject.org.

———. "Santa Clara County Courts: Now Providing Legal Representation in Misdemeanor Court to Anyone Who Can't Afford Their Own." January 30, 2012. https://acjusticeproject.org.

———. Social Biography Videos. https://acjusticeproject.org.

———. "What It Was Like When My Child was Interrogated by Police." August 18, 2016. https://acjusticeproject.org.

Albiston, Catherine R., and Rebecca L. Sandefur. "Expanding the Empirical Study of Access to Justice." *Wisconsin Law Review* 2013, no. 1 (2013): 101–20.

Albonetti, Celesta. "Sentencing Under the Federal Sentencing Guidelines: Effects of Defendant Characteristics, Guilty Pleas, and Departures on Sentence Outcomes for Drug Offenses." *Law & Society Review* 31, no. 4 (1997): 789–822.

Alcorn, Ted. "Reporting for Work Where You Once Reported for Probation." *The Atlantic*, December 13, 2019.

Alexander, Michelle. *The New Jim Crow: Mass Incarceration in the Age of Color Blindness.* New York: New Press, 2010.

Ali, Safia Samee. "Did Illinois Get Bail Reform Right? Criminal Justice Advocates Are Optimistic." NBC News, February 15, 2021. www.nbcnews.com.

Alper, Mariel, Matthew R. Durose, and Joshua Markman. "2018 Update on Prisoner Recidivism: A 9-Year Follow-Up Period (2005–2014)." *Bureau of Justice Statistics Special Report.* May 2018.

American Bar Association Criminal Justice Section. *Conference Report: National Summit on Collateral Consequences.* Washington, DC: American Bar Association, 2015.

American Bar Association. "Criminal Justice Section Standards: Speedy Trial." 2004. www.americanbar.org.

———. *Criminal Justice Standards on Providing Defense Services.* 3rd ed. Washington, DC: American Bar Association, 2007.

———. *Standards Relating to Trial Courts, 1992 Edition.* Washington, DC: American Bar Association, 1992.

American Civil Liberties Union. "Primary Voter Turnout Signals Investment in Criminal Justice Reform." September 4, 2018. www.aclu.org.

American Council of Chief Defenders. "Policy Statement on Fair and Effective Pretrial Justice Practices." 2011. www.nlada.net.

American Friends Service Committee. "Join the Call to #Free Them All." www.afsc.org.

———. *Struggle for Justice: A Report on Crime and Punishment in America.* Boston: Little, Brown, 1971.

American Immigration Council. "Two Systems of Justice: How the Immigration System Falls Short of American Ideals of Justice." March 19, 2013. www.americanimmigrationcouncil.org.

Anderson, Chloe, Cindy Redcross, Erin Valentine, and Luke Miratrix. "Pretrial Justice Reform Study: Evaluation of Pretrial Justice System Reforms That Use the Public Safety Assessment: Effects of New Jersey's Criminal Justice Reform." MDRC, 2019. www.mdrc.org.

Anderson, James M., Maya Buenaventura, and Paul Heaton. "The Effects of Holistic Defense on Criminal Justice Outcomes." *Harvard Law Review* 132, no. 3 (2019): 819–93.

Anderson, James M., Jeffrey R. Kling, and Kate Stith. "Measuring Interjudge Sentencing Disparity: Before and After the Federal Sentencing Guidelines." *Journal of Law & Economics* 42, no. S1 (1999): 271–307.

Andrews, D. A., J. Bonta, and J. S. Wormith. "The Risk-Need-Responsivity (RNR) Model: Does Adding the Good Lives Model Contribute to Effective Crime Prevention?." 38 *Criminal Justice and Behavior* (2011): 735–55.

Andrilla, Holly, Davis Patterson, Lisa Garberson, Cynthia Coulthard, and Eric Larson. "Geographic Variation in the Supply of Selected Behavioral Health Providers." *American Journal of Preventive Medicine* 54, no. 6 (2018): S199–S207.

Angel, Arthur R., Eric D. Green, Henry R. Kaufman, and Eric E. Van Loon. "Preventive Detention: An Empirical Analysis." *Harvard Civil Rights–Civil Liberties Law Review* 6, no. 2 (1971): 300–96.

Anglemyer, Andrew, Tara Horvath, and George Rutherford. "The Accessibility of Firearms and Risk for Suicide And Homicide Victimization Among Household Members: A Systematic Review and Meta-Analysis." *Annals of Internal Medicine* 160, no. 2 (2014): 101–10.

Anthony, Sebastian. "New Holster Forces All Nearby Body Cams to Start Recording When Gun Is Pulled." Ars Technica, February 28, 2017. https://arstechnica.com.

Aposhian v. Garland, 21-159. 958 F.3d 969 (2020).

Appelbaum, Kenneth L. "American Psychiatry Should Join the Call to Abolish Solitary Confinement." *Journal of the American Academy of Psychiatry and the Law* 43, no. 4 (2015): 406–15.

Ariel, Barak. "Police Body Cameras in Large Police Departments." *Journal of Criminal Law & Criminology* 106, no. 4 (2016): 729–68.

Ariel, Barak, William A. Farrar, and Ariel Sutherland. "The Effect of Police Body-Worn Cameras on Use of Force and Citizens' Complaints Against the Police: A Randomized Controlled Trial." *Journal of Quantitative Criminology* 31, no. 3 (2015): 509–35.

———. "Report: Increases in Police Use of Force in the Presence of Body-Worn Cameras Are Driven by Officer Discretion: A Protocol-Based Subgroup Analysis of Ten Randomized Experiments." *Journal of Experimental Criminology* 12, no. 3 (2016): 453–63.

———. "Wearing Body Cameras Increases Assaults Against Officers and Does Not Reduce Police Use of Force: Results from a Global Multi-Site Experiment." *European Journal of Criminology* 13, no. 6 (2016): 744–55.

Ariel, Barak, Alex Sutherland, and Lawrence W. Sherman. "Preventing Treatment Spillover Contamination in Criminological Field Experiments: The Case for Body-Worn Police Cameras." *Journal of Experimental Criminology* 15, no. 4 (2019): 569–91.

Armacost, Barbara. "Police Shootings: Is Accountability the Enemy of Prevention?" *Ohio State Law Journal* 80, no. 1 (2019): 907–86.

Armour, Marilyn Peterson. "Journey of Family Members of Homicide Victims: A Qualitative Study of Their Posthomicide Experience." *American Journal of Orthopsychiatry* 72, no. 3 (2002): 372–82.

Arnold, David, Will Dobbie, and Crystal S. Lang. "Racial Bias in Bail Decisions." *Quarterly Journal of Economics* 133, no. 4 (2018): 1885–1932. https://doi.org/10.1093/qje/qjy012.

Ash, P., A. L. Kellermann, D. Fuqua-Whitley, and A. Johnson. "Gun Acquisition and Use by Juvenile Offenders." *JAMA* 275, no. 22 (1996): 1754–58.

Associated Press. "Lawsuit: 4,600 on Missouri Public Defender 'Wait Lists.'" *U.S. News & World Report*, February 27, 2020. www.usnews.com.

Austen, Ben. "In Philadelphia, a Progressive D.A. Tests the Power—and Learns the Limits—of His Office." *New York Times*, October 30, 2018. www.nytimes.com.

Austin, James, John Clark, Patricia Hardyman, and D. Alan Henry. *Three Strikes and You're Out: The Implementation and Impact of Strike Laws.* National Institute of Justice: Washington, DC, 2000. https://permanent.access.gpo.gov.

Austin, James, and John Irwin. *It's About Time: America's Imprisonment Binge.* 3rd ed. Belmont, CA: Wadsworth, 2001.

Austin, James, Barry Krisberg, and Paul Litsky. "The Effectiveness of Supervised Pretrial Release." *Crime & Delinquency* 34, no. 4 (1985): 519–37.

Azrael, Deborah, Anthony A. Braga, and Mallory O'Brien. *Developing the Capacity to Understand and Prevent Homicide: An Evaluation of the Milwaukee Homicide Review Commission.* Washington, DC: U.S. Department of Justice, 2013. www.ojp.gov.

Baćak, Valerio, Sarah E. Lageson, and Kathleen Powell. "'Fighting the Good Fight': Why Do Public Defenders Remain on the Job?" *Criminal Justice Policy Review* 31, no. 6 (2020): 939–61. http://doi.org.

Bach, Amy. *Ordinary Injustice: How America Holds Court.* New York: Macmillan, 2010.

Bachman, Ronet, Heather Zaykowski, Rachel Kallymer, Margarita Poteyeva, and Christina Lanier. "Violence Against American Indian and Alaska Native Women and the Criminal Justice Response: What Is Known." U.S. Department of Justice: Document 223691, 2008.

Ball, David, Robert Weisberg, and Kara Dansky. *The First 72 Hours of Re-Entry: Seizing the Moment of Release*. Stanford Executive Sessions on Sentencing and Corrections, 2008.

Bandes, Susan. "Patterns of Injustice: Police Brutality in the Courts." *Buffalo Law Review* 47, no. 2 (1999): 1275–1341.

Baradaran, Shima, and Frank L. McIntyre. "Predicting Violence." *Texas Law Review* 90, no. 3 (2012): 497–570.

Barry-Jester, Anna M., and Johnathon Kelso. fivethirtyeight.com. "Patterns of Death in the South Still Show the Outlines of Slavery." April 20, 2017. www.fivethirtyeight.com.

Barajas, Julia. "Here's the Latest on the Violence Against Women Act, Which Is Up for Reauthorization by Congress." *Los Angeles Times*, May 28, 2021. www.latimes.com.

Baszynski, Nikki Trautman. "States Should Give Temporary Guaranteed Income to People Exiting Incarceration." *The Appeal*, June 15, 2021.

Baumer, Eric P. "Reassessing and Redirecting Research on Race and Sentencing." *Justice Quarterly* 30, no. 2 (2013): 231–61.

Bazelon, Emily, and Miriam Krinsky. "There's a Wave of New Prosecutors. And They Mean Justice." *New York Times*, December 11, 2018. www.nytimes.com.

Bazelon, Lara. *Rectify: The Power of Restorative Justice After Wrongful Conviction*. Boston: Beacon Press, 2018.

Beam, Adam. "California Lawmakers Approve Nation's First State-Funded Guaranteed Income Plan." *Basic Income Today*. 2021. https://basicincometoday.com.

Bechtel, Kristin, Alexander M. Holsinger, Christopher T. Lowenkamp, and Madeline J. Warren. "A Meta-Analytic Review of Pretrial Research: Risk Assessment, Bond Type, and Interventions." *American Journal of Criminal Justice* 42, no. 2 (2017): 443–67.

Beck, Allen J. "Recidivism of Prisoners Released in 1983." *Bureau of Justice Statistics Bulletin*. April 2, 1990.

Beckett, Katherine. "The Politics, Promise, and Peril of Criminal Justice Reform in the Context of Mass Incarceration." *Annual Review of Criminology* 1, no. 1 (2018): 235–59.

Beckett, Katherine, Anna Reosti, and Emily Knaphus. "The End of an Era? Understanding the Contradictions of Criminal Justice Reform." *ANNALS of the American Academy of Political and Social Science* 664 (2016): 238–59.

Beckett, Katherine, and Theodore Sasson. *The Politics of Injustice*. Thousand Oaks, CA: Pine Forge Press, 2000.

Belenko, Steven, and Cassia Spohn. *Drugs, Crime and Justice*. Thousand Oaks, CA: Sage, 2014.

Bell v. Wolfish, 441 U.S. 520 (1979).

Bell, John. "Circuit Judges Become Scarce in Rural Counties." *Oregon Business*, June 30, 2008. www.oregonbusiness.com.

Bell, Monica C. "The Community in Criminal Justice: Subordination, Consumption, Resistance, and Transformation." *DuBois Review* 16, no. 1 (2019): 197–220.

———. "Police Reform and the Dismantling of Legal Estrangement." *Yale Law Journal* 126, no. 7 (2017): 2054–150.

Bellware, Kim. "Class, Race and Geography Emerge as Flashpoints in New York's Bail Reform Debate." *Washington Post*, February 15, 2020. www.washingtonpost.com.

Ben and Jerry's. "How Private Companies Are Profiting from Mass Incarceration." *Ben and Jerry's Report*. October 23, 2019.

Bender, Ruth. "Escape to the Country: Why City Living Is Losing Its Appeal During the Pandemic." *Wall Street Journal*, June 21, 2020. www.wsj.com.

Berg, Mark, and Janet Lauritsen. "Telling a Similar Story Twice? NCVS/UCR Convergence in Serious Violent Crime Rates in Rural, Suburban, and Urban Places (1973–2010)." *Journal of Quantitative Criminology* 32, no. 1 (2016): 61–87.

Bernal, Daniel. "Taking the Court to the People: Real-World Solutions for Nonappearance." *Arizona Law Review* 59, no. 2 (2017): 547–71.

Berry III, William W. "Life-with-Hope Sentencing." *Ohio State Law Journal* 76, no. 5 (2015): 1051–85.

Berwick, Donald. "Continuous Improvement as an Ideal in Healthcare." *New England Journal of Medicine* 320, no. 1 (1989): 53–56.

Besser, Terry, and Margaret Hanson. "The Development of Last Resort: The Impact of New State Prisons on Small Town Economies." Ames: Iowa State University, 2003. Paper presented at the Annual Meeting of the Rural Sociological Society, Montreal. www.realcostofprisons.org.

Bessette, Joseph M. "Prisoners in 1988." *Bureau of Justice Statistics Bulletin*. April 1989.

Bick, Joseph. "Infection Control in Jails and Prisons." *Clinical Infectious Diseases* 45, no. 8 (2007): 1047–55.

Big Valley News. "Lassen County Superior Court Mobile Access Center Visits Bieber." May 29, 2008. www.bigvalleynews.net.

Binnall, James. "Divided We Fall: Parole Supervision Conditions Prohibiting Inter-Offender Associations." *University of Pennsylvania Journal of Law and Social Change* 22, no. 1 (2019): 25–69.

Bittner, Egon. "Legality and Workmanship: Introduction to Control in the Police Organization." *Ethnographic Studies* no. 13 (2013) 247–53.

Black, Michele C., Kathleen C. Basile, Matthew J. Breiding, Sharon G. Smith, Mikel L. Walters, Melissa T. Merrick, Jieru Chen, and Mark R. Stevens. "The National Intimate Partner and Sexual Violence Survey (NISVS): 2010 Summary Report." Atlanta: National Center for Injury Prevention and Control, Centers for Disease Control and Prevention, 2011.

Blackstone, William. *Commentaries on the Laws of England*. https://avalon.law.yale.edu.

Blair, Dana W. "A Matter of Life and Death; Why Life Without Parole Should Be a Sentencing Option in Texas." *American Journal of Criminal Law* 22, no. 1 (1994): 191–214.

Blakinger, Keri. "'I Have No Teeth': Michigan Prisoners Say Long Wait to See Dentist Is Inhumane." *The Marshall Project*. July 2021. www.themarshallproject.org.

Bland, Scott. "George Soros' Quiet Overhaul of the U.S. Justice System." *Politico*, September 30, 2016. www.politico.com.

Blaylock, Dan. "I'm a Bail Bondsman Who's Tired of Being Demonized." *The Marshall Project*, June 1, 2017. www.themarshallproject.org.

Blenkinsopp, Alexander J. "Dangerousness and the Civil-Criminal Distinction: Another Reason to Rethink the Indefinite Detention of Sex Offenders." *Connecticut Law Review* 8, no. 5 (2012): 12.

Blumauer, Christine, Alessandra Brown, Mariella Castaldi, Seleeke Flingai, Phillip Hernandez, Stefanie Mavronis, Kalie Pierce, Tom Stanley-Becker, and Jordan Stockdale. "Advancing Bail Reform in Maryland: Progress and Possibilities." February 27, 2018. https://spia.princeton.edu.

Blumstein, Alfred, and Allen J. Beck. "Population Growth in U.S. Prisons, 1980–1996." *Crime and Justice: A Review of Research* 26 (1999): 17–61.

Bocanegra, Kathryn. "Community and Decarceration: Developing Localized Solutions." In *Smart Decarceration: Achieving Criminal Justice Transformation in the 21st Century*, edited by Matthew W. Epperson and Carrie Pettus-Davis, 115–33. New York: Oxford University Press, 2017.

Bobo, Lawrence P., and Johnson, Devon. "A Taste for Punishment: Black and White Americans Views on the Death Penalty and the War on Drugs." *Du Bois Review* 1, no. 1 (2004): 151–80.

Body-Worn Camera: Training and Technical Assistance. "About Us." www.bwctta.com.

Boerner, David. "Sentencing Guidelines and Prosecutorial Discretion." *Judicature* 78, no. 4 (1995): 196–200.

Bohn, Diane K. "Lifetime Physical and Sexual Abuse, Substance Abuse, Depression, and Suicide Attempts Among Native American Women." *Issues in Mental Health Nursing* 24, no. 3 (2003): 333–52.

Borchard, Edwin. *Convicting the Innocent*. New Haven: Yale University Press, 1932.

Bornstein, Brian, Alan J. Tomkins, and Elizabeth M. Neeley. "Reducing Courts' Failure to Appear Rate: A Procedural Justice Approach." May 2011. www.ncjrs.gov.

Bowman, John H., and Thomas J. Mowen."Building the Ties That Bind, Breaking the Ties That Don't." *Criminology & Public Policy* 16, no. 3 (2017): 753–74.

Braga, A. A., and D. M. Kennedy. "The Illicit Acquisition of Firearms by Youth and Juveniles." *Journal of Criminal Justice* 29, no. 5 (2001): 379–88.

Braga, A. A., G. J. Wintemute, G. L. Pierce, P. J. Cook, and G. Ridgeway. "Interpreting the Empirical Evidence on Illegal Gun Market Dynamics." *Journal of Urban Health* 89, no. 5 (2012): 779–93.

Braga, Anthony A., James R. Coldren, William Sousa, Denise Rodriguez, D., and Omer Alper. *The Benefits of Body-Worn Cameras: New Findings from a Randomized Controlled Trial at the Las Vegas Metropolitan Police Department*. NCJ-251416. Washington, DC: National Institute of Justice, September 2017.

Braga, Anthony A., William Sousa, James R. Coldren, and Denise Rodriguez. "The Effects of Body-Worn Cameras on Police Activity and Police-Citizen Encounters: A Randomized Controlled Trial." *Journal of Criminal Law & Criminology* 108, no. 3 (2018): 511–38.

Braithwaite, John. *Restorative Justice and Responsive Regulation.* Oxford: Oxford University Press, 2002.

Brants, Chrisje, "Wrongful Convictions and the Inquisitorial Process: The Case of the Netherlands." 80 *University of Cincinnati Law Review* 1069 (2013).

Breiding, Matthew J., Michele C. Black, and George W. Ryan. "Prevalence and Risk Factors of Intimate Partner Violence in Eighteen U.S. States/Territories, 2005." *American Journal of Preventive Medicine* 34, no. 1 (2008): 112–18.

Breiding, Matthew J., Sharon G. Smith, Kathleen C. Basile, Mikel L. Walters, Jieru Chen, Melissa T. Merrick, and the Division of Violence Prevention, National Center for Injury Prevention and Control. "Prevalence and Characteristics of Sexual Violence, Stalking, and Intimate Partner Violence Victimization—National Intimate Partner and Sexual Violence Survey, United States, 2011." *MMWR Surveillance Summaries* 63, no. 8 (2014): 1–18. Center for Surveillance, Epidemiology, and Laboratory Services, Centers for Disease Control and Prevention (CDC), U.S. Department of Health and Human Services.

Brennan Center for Justice. *Ending Mass Incarceration: Ideas from Today's Leaders.* May 16, 2019. www.brennancenter.org.

Breslau, Joshua, Grant Marshall, Harold Pincus, and Ryan Brown. "Are Mental Disorders More Common in Urban than Rural Areas of the United States?" *Journal of Psychiatric Research* 56, no. 1 (2014): 50–5.

Breyer, Stephen. 1988. "The Federal Sentencing Guidelines and the Key Compromises Upon Which They Rest." *Hofstra Law Review* 17, no. 1 (1988): 1–50.

Brito, Tonya L., David J. Pate Jr., and Jia-Hui Stefanie Wong. "'I Do for My Kids': Negotiating Race and Racial Inequality in Family Court." *Fordham Law Review* 83, no. 6 (2015): 3027–52.

Britt, Chester L. "Health Consequences of Criminal Victimization." *International Review of Victimology* 8, no. 1 (2001): 63–73.

Bronner, Ethan. "No Lawyer for Miles, So One Rural State Offers Pay." *New York Times*, April 8, 2013. www.nytimes.com.

Bryant, Erica. "Words Matter: Don't Call People Felons, Convicts, or Inmates." Blog of the Vera Institute of Justice. March 31, 2021. www.vera.org.

Bui, Lynh. "Reforms Intended to End Excessive Cash Bail in Md. Are Keeping More in Jail Longer, Report Says." *Washington Post*, July 2, 2018. www.washingtonpost.com.

Bureau of Justice Assistance. "Body-Worn Cameras (BWCS)." www.bja.gov.

———. "Body-Worn Camera Toolkit." www.bja.gov.

———. "Law Enforcement Implementation Checklist." www.bja.gov.

Bureau of Justice Statistics. "National Crime Victimization Survey, 2018." Washington, DC: U.S. Department of Justice, Office of Justice Programs, 2019.

————. "National Survey of Prosecutors." www.bjs.gov.

Burnette, Catherine E., and Clare Cannon. "'It Will Always Continue Unless We Can Change Something': Consequences of Intimate Partner Violence for Indigenous Women, Children, and Families." *European Journal of Psychotraumatology* 5, no. 1 (2014): 1–8.

Bushway, Shawn, Allison Redlich, and Robert Norris. "An Explicit Test of Plea Bargaining in the 'Shadow of the Trial.'" *Criminology* 52, no. 4 (2014): 723–54.

Buskey, Brandon, and Lauren S. Lucas. "Keeping *Gideon*'s Promise: Using Equal Protection to Address the Denial of Counsel in Misdemeanor Cases." *Fordham Law Review* 85, no. 5 (2017): 2299–339.

Butts, Jeffrey A., and Vincent Shiraldi. "Recidivism Reconsidered: Preserving the Community Justice Mission of Community Corrections." *Papers from the Executive Session on Community Corrections at Harvard Kennedy School*. Cambridge, MA: Harvard University, 2018.

Cahalan, Margaret Werner, and Lee Anne Parsons. "Historical Corrections Statistics in the United States, 1850–1984." *Bureau of Justice Statistics*. December 1986.

California Courts. "Evidence Based Practice." www.courts.ca.gov.

California Department of Corrections and Rehabilitation. *Offender Data Points: Offender Demographics for the 24-month Period Ending December 2018*. California Division of Correctional Policy Research and Internal Oversight, Office of Research, 2020. www.cdcr.ca.gov.

Campbell, Christopher, Janet Moore, Wesley Maier, and Mike Gaffney. "Unnoticed, Untapped, and Underappreciated: Clients' Perceptions of Their Public Defenders." *Behavioral Sciences & the Law* 33, no. 6 (2015): 751–70.

Campbell, Jacquelyn C. "Health Consequences of Intimate Partner Violence." *The Lancet* 359, no. 9314 (2002): 1331–36.

Campbell, Jacquelyn C., et al. "Risk Factors for Femicide in Abusive Relationships: Results from a Multisite Case Control Study." *American journal of public health* 93, no. 7 (2003): 1089–97.

Capaldi, Deborah M., Naomi B. Knoble, Joann Wu Shortt, and Hyoun K. Kim. "A Systematic Review of Risk Factors for Intimate Partner Violence." *Partner Abuse* 3, no. 2 (2012): 231–80.

Capers, I. Bennett. "Defending Life." In *Life Without Parole: America's New Death Penalty?*, edited by Charles J. Ogletree and Austin Sarat, 167–89. New York: New York University Press, 2012.

Carmichael, Dottie, Melissa Gibson, and Michael Voloudakis. *Evaluating the Impact of Direct Electronic Filing in Criminal Cases: Closing the Paper Trap*. Final Report, Office of Court Administration Task Force on Indigent Defense, 2006.

Carson, E. Ann. "Prisoners in 2018." *Bureau of Justice Statistics Bulletin*. April 2020.

Carson, E. Ann, and Daniela Golinelli. "Prisoners in 2012: Trends in Admissions and Releases, 1991–2012." *Bureau of Justice Statistics Bulletin*. Originally published December 2013, revised September 2014.

Caryl, Christopher. "Malpractice and Other Legal Issues Preventing the Development of Telemedicine." *Journal of Law & Health* 12, no. 1 (1998): 173–204. https://core.ac.uk.

Causey, Alexis. "Reviving the Carefully Limited Exception: From Jail to GPS Bail." *Faulkner Law Review* 5, no. 1 (2013–2014): 59–114.

Castillo-Carniglia, Alvaro, Rose MC Kagawa, Daniel W. Webster, Jon S. Vernick, Magdalena Cerdá, and Garen J. Wintemute. "Comprehensive Background Check Policy and Firearm Background Checks in Three US States." *Injury Prevention* 24, no. 6 (2018): 431–36.

Centers for Disease Control and Prevention (CDC). Web-based Injury Statistics Query and Reporting System (WISQARS). "Fatal Injury Reports." www.cdc.gov.

———, Web-based Injury Statistics Query and Reporting System (WISQARS). "Nonfatal Injury Reports." www.cdc.gov.

Center for Employment Opportunities. "Evaluating Outcomes." https://ceoworks.org.

———. "Returning Citizens Stimulus." https://ceoworks.org.

Champion, Ben. "New York City Plans Support Network for Defendants Freed Under New Bail Laws." *Wall Street Journal*, November 17, 2019. www.wsj.com.

Chan, Rosalie, and Belle Lin Jun. "The High Cost of Phone Calls in Prisons Generates $1.4 Billion a Year, Disproportionately Driving Women and People of Color into Debt." *Business Insider*. June 30, 2021.

Charney, Jonathan I. "The Need for Constitutional Protections for Defendants in Civil Penalty Cases." *Cornell Law Review* 59, no. 1 (1974): 491–506.

Chassin, Mark R., and Elise Becker. "The Wrong Patient." *Annals of Internal Medicine* 136, no. 11 (2002): 826–33.

Cheatwood, Derral. "The Life-Without-Parole Sanction: Its Current Status and a Research Agenda. *Crime & Delinquency* 34, no. 1 (1988): 43–59.

Cheesman, Fred, Matthew Kleiman, Cynthia Lee, and Kathryn Holt. "Ignition Interlock: An Investigation into Rural Arizona Judges' Perceptions." Department of Transportation, January 11, 2012. www.ajc.state.ak.us.

Chen, Elsa Y. "Impacts of 'Three Strikes and You're Out' on Crime Trends in California and Throughout the United States." *Journal of Contemporary Criminal Justice* 24, no. 4 (2008): 345–70.

———. "The Liberation Hypothesis and Racial and Ethnic Disparities in the Application of California's Three Strikes Law." *Journal of Ethnicity in Criminal Justice* 6, no. 2 (2008): 83–102.

Cherem, Alicia, and Carly Taylor. "Bail Reform Hasn't Led to Fewer Held in Jail, Court Records Show." MarylandReporter.com, Capital News Service, January 1, 2019. https://marylandreporter.com.

Chesnut, K. Y., M. Barragan, J. Gravel, N. A. Pifer, K. Reiter, N. Sherman, and G. E., Tita. "Not an 'Iron Pipeline,' but Many Capillaries: Regulating Passive Transactions in Los Angeles' Secondary, Illegal Gun Market." *Injury Prevention* 23, no. 4 (2017): 226–31.

Chettiar, Inimai, and Priya Raghavan, eds. *Ending Mass Incarceration: Ideas from Today's Leaders*. New York: Brennan Center for Justice, 2019.

Chettiar, Inimai, and Michael Waldman, eds. *Solutions: American Leaders Speak Out on Criminal Justice*. New York: Brennan Center for Justice, 2015.

Chief Justice Michael Cherry. "2017 State of the Judiciary Message." Nevada State Legislature. March 8, 2017.

Childress, Sarah. "Todd Clear: Why America's Mass Incarceration Experiment Failed." PBS: Frontline. April 29, 2014. www.pbs.org.

Chin, Gabriel J. "Collateral Consequences of Criminal Conviction." *Criminology, Criminal Justice, Law & Society* 18, no. 3 (2017): 1–17, 374–75, 383.

City of Tucson Police Department. "Critical Incident Review Board (CIRB)." www.tucsonaz.gov.

Clair, Matthew, and Alix S. Winter. "How Judges Think About Racial Disparities: Situational Decision Making in the Criminal Justice System." *Criminology* 54, no. 2 (2016): 332–54.

Clark, J. Morris. "Civil and Criminal Penalties and Forfeitures: A Framework for Constitutional Analysis." *Minnesota Law Review* 60, no. 1 (1976): 379.

Clark, LaToya Baldwin. "Education as Property." *Virginia Law Review* 105, no. 2 (2019): 408.

Clear, Todd. *Imprisoning Communities: How Mass Incarceration Makes Disadvantaged Neighborhoods Worse*. New York, Oxford University Press, 2007.

Clipper, Stephen J., Robert G. Morris, and Amanda Russell-Kaplan. "The Link Between Bond Forfeiture and Pretrial Release Mechanism: The Case of Dallas County, Texas." *Plos One* 12, no. 8 (August 2017): e0182772.

Cochran, Joshua, Daniel Mears, William Bales, and Eric Stewart. "Spatial Distance, Community Disadvantage, and Racial and Ethnic Variation in Prison Inmate Access to Social Ties." *Journal of Research in Crime and Delinquency* 53, no. 2 (2016): 220–54.

Cochrane, Emily, and Luke Broadwater. "Here Are the Differences Between the Senate and House Bills to Overhaul Policing." *New York Times*, June 17, 2020. www.nytimes.com.

Cockburn, Alexander. "Worse Than Death." *The Nation*, April 20, 2009.

Cohen, Thomas H., and Brian A. Reaves. "Pretrial Release of Felony Defendants in State Courts, 1990–2005." Washington, DC: U.S. Department of Justice, Bureau of Justice Statistics (November 2017). www.bjs.gov.

Cohen, Thomas H., and Tracey Kyckelhahn. *Felony Defendants in Large Urban Counties, 2006*. Washington, DC: Bureau of Justice Statistics, 2010. www.bjs.gov.

Cole, David D. *No Equal Justice: Race and Class in the American Criminal Justice System*. New York: New Press, 1999.

Colbert, Douglas. "Prosecution Without Representation." *Buffalo Law Review* 59, no. 1 (2011): 333–453. https://ssrn.com.

Colgan, Beth A. "Fines, Fees, and Forfeitures." *Criminology, Criminal Justice, Law & Society* 18, no. 3 (2017): 22–40.

Collins, Erin. "The Problem of Problem-Solving Courts." *UC Davis Law Review* 54, no. 3 (2021): 1573–1629. www.papers.ssrn.com.

Colombino, Ugo. "Is Unconditional Basic Income a Viable Alternative to Other Social Welfare Measures?" *IZA World of Labor*. 2015. https://wol.iza.org.

Colo. Rev. Stat. § 13-6-203(2) & 3(3).

Color of Change, and American Civil Liberties Union Campaign for Smart Justice. "Selling Off Our Freedom: How Insurance Corporations Have Taken over Our Bail System." May 2017. www.aclu.org.

Commission on Rural Courts. "Judicial Council of the State of Nevada." 2003.

Committee for Public Counsel Services & another v. Chief Justice of the Trial Court & others, 142 N.E.3d 525 (MA 2020).

Committee on Identifying the Needs of the Forensic Sciences Community. *Strengthening Forensic Science in the United States: A Path Forward*. National Research Council, 2009.

Committee to Review the Criminal Justice Act. "Report of the Ad Hoc Committee to Review the Criminal Justice Act." Washington, DC: Judicial Conference of the United States, 2017: xvii–xl. https://cjastudy.fd.org.

Community Defense of East Tennessee. "The Case of Reggie Wilson." May 26, 2020. www.facebook.com.

Community Resources for Justice. "Implementing Evidence-Based Policy and Practice in Community Corrections." 2009.

Community Works. Panel Discussion. Oakland, CA, 2021. www.youtube.com.

Community Works West. "Virtual Panel: Guaranteed Income for Reentry." June 20, 2021. www.youtube.com.

The Constitution Project National Right to Counsel Committee. *Justice Denied: America's Continuing Neglect of Our Constitutional Right to Counsel*. 2009. https://archive.constitutionproject.org.

Cooke, Brice, Binta Zahra Diop, Alissa Fishbane, Jonathan Hayes, Aurelie Ouss, and Anuj Shah. "Using Behavioral Science to Improve Criminal Justice Outcomes Preventing Failures to Appear in Court." January 2018. https://urbanlabs.uchicago.edu.

Cook, Philip, and Jens Ludwig. *Guns in America: Results of a Comprehensive National Survey on Firearms Ownership and Use*. Washington, DC: Police Foundation (2006).

Cook, Philip J., Jens Ludwig, Sudhir Venkatesh, and Anthony A. Braga. "Underground gun markets." *The Economic Journal* 117, no. 524 (2007): F588-F618.

Cook, Philip J., Stephanie Molliconi, and Thomas B. Cole. "Regulating gun markets." *Journal of Criminal Law & Criminology* 86, no. 1 (1995): 59–86.

Cook, P. J., S. T. Parker, and H. A. Pollack. "Sources of Guns to Dangerous People: What We Learn by Asking Them." *Preventive Medicine* 79, no. 1 (2015): 28–36.

Corasaniti, Nick, and Jim Rutenberg. "Republicans Pushed to Restrict Voting. Millions of Americans Pushed Back." *New York Times*, December 5, 2020. www.nytimes.org.

Core Civic. "CCA Announces Acquisition of Four Residential Re-Entry Facilities." August 31, 2015. http://ir.corecivic.com.

"Corrections and Reentry: Recidivism." Programs Review and Rating by *National Institute of Justice*. www.crimesolutions.gov.

COSCA Policy and Liaison Committee. "Courts Need to Enhance Access to Justice in Rural America." 2018. https://cosca.ncsc.org.

Cossyleon, Jennifer, John Orwat, Christine George, Don Stemen, and Whitney Key. "Deferring Felony Prosecution: A Process Evaluation of an Innovative Cook County State's Attorney's Office Program." *Journal of Criminological Research, Policy and Practice* 3, no. 4 (2017): 261–73.

Couloute, Lucius. "The Case for Temporary Guaranteed Income for Formerly Incarcerated People." *The Appeal*. June 9, 2021 https://theappeal.org.

———. "Organizing Reentry: How Racial Colorblindness Structures the Post-imprisonment Terrain." *Research in the Sociology of Organizations* 60 (2019): 89–109.

———. *Nowhere to Go: Homelessness Among Formerly Incarcerated People*. Prison Policy Initiative. August 2018.

Couloute, Lucius, and David Kopf. *Out of Prison & Out of Work: Unemployment Among Formerly Incarcerated People*. Prison Policy Initiative. (July 2018). www.prisonpolicy.org.

Covert, Bryce. "America Is Waking Up to the Injustice of Cash Bail." *The Nation*, October 17, 2017. www.thenation.com.

Craigie, Terry-Ann, Ames Grawert, and Cameron Kimble. *Conviction, Imprisonment, and Lost Earnings: How Involvement with the Criminal Justice System Deepens Inequality*. New York: Brennan Center for Justice at New York University School of Law, 2020. www.brennancenter.org.

Credible Messenger Justice Center. https://cmjcenter.org.

Cressey, Donald R. "Social Psychological Foundations for Using Criminals in the Rehabilitation of Criminals." *Journal of Research in Crime and Delinquency* 2, no. 2 (1965): 49–59.

———. "Changing Criminals: The Application of the Theory of Differential Association." *American Journal of Sociology* 61, no. 2 (1955): 116–20.

Crifasi, Cassandra K., Molly Merrill-Francis, Alex McCourt, Jon S. Vernick, Garen J. Wintemute, and Daniel W. Webster. "Association Between Firearm Laws and Homicide in Urban Counties." *Journal of Urban Health*, 95, no. 3 (2018): 383–90.

Crifasi, Cassandra K., John Speed Meyers, Jon S. Vernick, and Daniel W. Webster. "Effects of Changes in Permit-to-Purchase Handgun Laws in Connecticut and Missouri on Suicide Rates." *Preventive Medicine* 79, no. 1 (2015): 43–49.

Criminal Case Review Commission, https://ccrc.gov.uk.

"Criminal Nonsupport and Child Support." National Conference of State Legislatures, 2015.

Crow, Matthew S., Jamie A. Snyder, Vaughn J. Crichlow, and John Ortiz Smykla. "Community Perceptions of Police Body-Worn Cameras: The Impact of Views on Fairness, Fear, Performance, and Privacy." *Criminal Justice and Behavior* 44, no. 4 (2017): 589–610.

Cullen, Francis T. "The Twelve People Who Saved Rehabilitation: How the Science of Criminology Made a Difference." *Criminology: An Interdisciplinary Journal* 43, no. 1 (2005): 1–42.

Cullen, Francis T., Cheryl L. Jonson, and Daniel S. Nagin. "Prisons Do Not Reduce Recidivism: The High Cost of Ignoring Science." *Prison Journal* 91, no. 3 (2011): 48S–65S.

Cullen, Francis T., John P. Wright, Paul Gendreau, and Don A. Andrews. "What Correctional Treatment Can Tell Us about Criminological Theory: Implications for Social Learning Theory." *Social Learning Theory and the Explanation of Crime* 14, no. 1 (2003): 339–62.

Currie, Ab. "The Legal Problems of Everyday Life: The Nature, Extent and Consequences of Justiciable Problems Experienced by Canadians." Report. *The Department of Justice Canada* (2009): 24–25.

Curtis, Karise, and Andrew Davies. *Summary Report of the 2014 Survey of Town and Village Magistrates: Counsel at First Appearance.* Albany, NY: NY Office of Indigent Legal Services, 2014. (Unpublished report on file with the Deason Center).

D'Amico, Ronald, and Hui Kim. *Evaluation of Seven Second Chance Act Demonstration Programs: Impact Findings at 30 Months.* Oakland: Social Policy Research Associates, 2018.

Daniels, Jarrell. "What Prosecutors and Incarcerated People Can Learn From Each Other." Ted Talk. www.ted.com.

Daniels, Matt. "The Kim Foxx Effect: How Prosecutions Have Changed in Cook County." *The Marshall Project*, October 24, 2019. www.themarshallproject.org.

Davies, Andrew LB, and Alissa P. Worden. "State Politics and the Right to Counsel: A Comparative Analysis." *Law & Society Review* 43, no. 1 (2009): 187–220.

Davies, Andrew, and Alyssa Clark. "Access to Counsel in Local Courts in Rural New York State." *NYSBA Government Law & Policy Journal* 17, no. 1 (2018): 15. https://nysba.org.

———. "*Gideon* in the Desert: An Empirical Study of Providing Counsel to Criminal Defendants in Rural Places." *Maine Law Review* 71, no. 2 (2020): 245–72. https://digitalcommons.mainelaw.maine.edu.

Davies, Andrew LB, Giza Lopes, and Alyssa Clark. "Unique New York? Theorizing the Impact of Resources on the Quality of Defense Representation in a Deviant State." *Criminal Justice Policy Review* 31, no. 6 (2019): 962–86.

Davis, Angela J. "Prosecutorial Discretion: Power and Privilege." *Arbitrary Justice: The Power of the American Prosecutor*, 3–18. New York: Oxford University Press, 2007.

Davis, Kenneth Culp. *Discretionary Justice: A Preliminary Inquiry.* Baton Rouge: Louisiana State University Press, 1969.

De-Bug San José. "End Ice Presence in Santa Clara County." www.debugsanjose.org.

De Leon, George, and Human F. Unterrainer. "The Therapeutic Community: A Unique Social Psychological Approach to the Treatment of Addictions and Related Disorders." *Frontiers in Psychiatry* 11, no. 1 (2020): 786. https://doi.org/10.3389/fpsyt.2020.00786.

DeFrances, Carol. *State Court Prosecutors in Small Districts, 2001.* Washington, DC: Bureau of Justice Statistics. January 2003.

Dehghani-Tafti, Parisa. "Op-Ed: What I Believe in, by Parisa Dehghani-Tafti." *ARLnow* (Arlington, VA), November 1, 2019. www.arlnow.com.

Dekker, Sidney. "The Complexity of Failure: Implications of Complexity Theory for Safety Investigations." *Safety Science* 49, no. 6 (2011): 939–45.

———. *Drift Into Failure: From Hunting Broken Components to Understanding Complex Systems.* 1st ed. Boca Raton, FL: CRC Press, 2018.

———. *Safely Differently: Human Factors for a New Era.* 2nd ed. Boca Raton, FL: CRC Press, 2014.

———. *The Second Victim: Error, Guilt, Trauma and Resilience.* 1st ed. Boca Raton, FL: CRC Press, 2013.

Del. Code tit. 10 § 1302(b); tit. 11, § 5917.

della Cava, Marco. "New, More Progressive Prosecutors Are Angering Police, Who Warn Approach Will Lead to Chaos." *USA Today*, February 8, 2020. www.usatoday.com.

DeMichele, Matthew, Peter Baumgartner, Michael Wenger, Kelle Barrick, Megan Comfort, and Shilpi Misra. "The Public Safety Assessment: A Re-Validation and Assessment of Predictive Utility and Differential Prediction by Race and Gender in Kentucky." *SSRN Electronic Journal*, May 7, 2018.

Demir, Mustafa, Anthony A. Braga, and Robert Apel (2020). "Effects of Police Body-Worn Cameras on Citizen Compliance and Cooperation: Findings from a Quasi-Randomized Controlled Trial." *Criminology & Public Policy* 19, no. 3 (2020): 855–82.

Demuth, Stephen. "Racial and Ethnic Differences in Pretrial Release Decisions and Outcomes: A Comparison of Hispanic, Black, and White Felony Arrestees." *Criminology* 41, no. 3 (2003): 873–907.

Deloria Jr., Vine, and Clifford M. Lytle. *American Indians, American Justice.* Austin: University of Texas Press, 1983.

Democratic National Committee. "Protecting Communities and Building Trust by Reforming Our Criminal Justice System." 2020. www.democrats.org.

Dennis, Andrea L. "Criminal Law as Family Law." *Georgia State University Law Review* 33, no. 2 (2017): 207, 312.

Devine, Curt, Drew Griffin, Scott Bronstein, and Colleen Richards. "Minneapolis Police Are Rarely Disciplined for Complaints, Records Show." *CNN*, June 12, 2020. www.cnn.com.

deVuono-powell, Saneta, Chris Schweidler, Alicia Walters, and Azadeh Zohrabi. *Who Pays? The True Cost of Incarceration on Families.* Oakland, CA: Ella Baker Center, 2015. http://whopaysreport.org.

Dewan, Shaila. "Here's One Issue That Could Actually Break the Partisan Gridlock." *New York Times*, November 24, 2020. www.nytimes.com.

Dewees, Sarah, and Benjamin Marks. *Twice Invisible: Understanding Rural Native America.* Longmont CO: First Nations Development Institute, 2017. www.usetinc.org.

Diaz-Zuniga, Lauren. "New Bodycams Start Recording with the Draw of a Gun." CNN, July 21, 2017. www.cnn.com.

DiBenedetto, Rachel. "Reducing Recidivism or Misclassifying Offenders? How Implementing Risks and Needs Assessment In The Federal Prison System Will Perpetuate Racial Bias." *Journal of Law and Policy* 27, no. 2 (2018): 414–52.

Dickson, Megan, Nesa Wasarhaley, and Matthew Webster. "A Comparison of First-Time and Repeat Rural DUI Offenders" *Journal of Offender Rehabilitation* 52, no. 6 (2013): 421–37.

Díez, Carolina, et al. "State Intimate Partner Violence–Related Firearm Laws and Intimate Partner Homicide Rates in the United States, 1991 to 2015." *Annals of Internal Medicine* 167, no. 8 (2017): 536–43.

Digard, Léon, and Elizabeth Swavola. "Justice Denied: The Harmful and Lasting Effects of Pretrial Detention." Vera Institute of Justice, April 2019. www.vera.org.

District of Columbia v. Heller, 552 U.S. 1229 (2008).

Dobbie, Will, Jacob Goldin, and Crystal S. Yang. "The Effects of Pre-Trial Detention on Conviction, Future Crime, and Employment: Evidence from Randomly Assigned Judges." *American Economic Review* 108, no. 2 (2018): 201–40.

Doherty, Fiona. "Obey All Laws and Be Good: Probation and the Meaning of Recidivism." *Georgetown Law Journal* 104, no. 2 (2016): 291–354.

Dolovich, Sharon. "Creating the Permanent Prisoner." In *Life Without Parole: America's New Death Penalty?*, edited by Charles J. Ogletree and Austin Sarat, 96–137. New York: New York University Press, 2012.

Dolovich, Sharon, and Alexandra Natapoff, eds. *New Criminal Justice Thinking*. New York: New York University Press, 2017.

Domingo, Charisse. "How the Undeniable Force of Family Won Unprecedented Change in California's Justice System—from the Streets to the Courts." Silicon Valley De-Bug, October 3, 2018. https://siliconvalleydebug.org.

Dow, David R. "Life Without Parole: A Different Death Penalty." *The Nation*, October 26, 2012.

Doyle, Colin, Chiraag Bains, and Brook Hopkins. "Bail Reform: A Guide for State and Local Policymakers." Cambridge, MA: Harvard Law School Criminal Justice Policy Program (February 2019). http://cjpp.law.harvard.edu.

Doyle, James. "Learning from Error in American Criminal Justice." *Journal of Criminal Law & Criminology* 100, no. 1 (2010): 109–47.

———. "Orwell's Elephant and the Etiology of Wrongful Convictions." *Albany Law Review* 79, no. 3 (2016): 895–918.

———. "A Safety Model Perspective Can Aid Diagnosis, Treatment and Restoration After Criminal Justice Harms." *Santa Clara Law Review* 59, no. 1 (2019): 107–33.

Dripps, Donald A. "Criminal Procedure, Footnote Four, and the Theory of Public Choice: Or, Why Don't Legislatures Give a Damn About the Rights of the Accused?" *Syracuse Law Review* 44, no. 1 (1993): 1079–1101.

Ducker Worldwide. "2013–2014 Court Reporting Industry Outlook Report." https://cdn.ymaws.com.

DuClos, Danielle. "Continued Rise in Felony Caseload Cripples Missouri Public Defender System." *Columbia Missourian*, May 29, 2020. www.columbiamissourian.com.

Dudley, Earl C. Jr. "Getting Beyond the Civil/Criminal Distinction: A New Approach to the Regulation of Indirect Contempts." *Virginia Law Review* 79, no. 5 (1993); 1043, 1065.

Duker, William F. "The Right to Bail: A Historical Inquiry." *Albany Law Review* 42, no. 1 (1977): 33–120.

Dumont, Dora M., Brad Brockmann, Samuel Dickman, Nicole Alexander, and Josia D. Rich. "Public Health and the Epidemic of Incarceration." *Annual Review of Public Health* 33, no. 1 (2012): 325–39.

Duran, Bonnie, John Oetzel, Tassy Parker, Lorraine Halinka Malcoe, Julie E. Lucero, and Jiang Yizhou. "Intimate Partner Violence and Alcohol, Drug, and Mental Disorders among American Indian Women from Southwest Tribes in Primary Care." American Indian and Alaska Native Mental Health Research: *Journal of the National Center* 16, no. 2 (2009): 11–26.

Durose, Matthew R., Alexia D. Cooper, and Howard N. Snyder. *Recidivism of Prisoners Released in 30 States in 2005: Patterns from 2005 to 2010.* Washington, DC: U.S. Department of Justice, 2014.

Duwe, Grant. *Mass Murder in the United States: A History.* Jefferson, NC: McFarland, 2014.

Dyer, Owen. "Covid-19: Black People and Other Minorities are Hardest Hit in US." BMJ. April 2020. www.bmj.com.

Eason, John. "Mapping Prison Proliferation: Region, Rurality, Race and Disadvantage in Prison Placement." *Social Science Research* 39, no. 6 (2010): 1015–28.

———. "Prisons as Panacea or Pariah? The Countervailing Consequences of the Prison Boom on the Political Economy of Rural Towns." *Social Sciences* 6, no. 1 (2017): 7–30.

Eck, John E., Spencer Chainey, James G. Cameron, Michael Leitner, and Ronald E. Wilson. *Mapping Crime: Understanding Hot Spots.* Washington, DC: U.S. Department of Justice, 2005.

Edelman, Daniel Munczek. "Cash for Leaving Prison: A New Solution to Recidivism?" Blog entry, *Stanford Social Innovation Review*, August 15, 2017. https://ssir.org.

Editors, Law Review. "Bail Reform and Risk Assessment: The Cautionary Tale of Federal Sentencing." *Harvard Law Review* 131, no. 4 (2018): 1125–46.

———. "Civil Rico Is a Misnomer: The Need for Criminal Procedural Protections in Actions Under 18 U.S.C. § 1964." *Harvard Law Review* 100, no. 6 (1987): 1288.

Editors, Law Review. "Comments—The Concept of Punitive Legislation and the Sixth Amendment: A New Look at Kennedy v. Mendoza-Martinez." *University of Chicago Law Review* 32, no. 2 (1964): 290.

———. "The Concept of Punitive Legislation and the Sixth Amendment: A New Look at Kennedy v. Mendoza-Martinez." *University of Chicago Law Review* 32, no. 2 (1965): 290.

Edmonton Police Service. *Body Worn Video: Considering the Evidence—Final Report of the Edmonton Police Service Body Worn Video Pilot Project.* Edmonton, AB: Edmonton Police Service, 2015.

Edwards, Robert E. "Forfeitures—Civil or Criminal?" *Temple Law Quarterly* 191 (1970).

Einat, Tomer. "The Wounded Healer: Self-Rehabilitation of Prisoners Through Providing Care and Support to Physically and Mentally Challenged Inmates." *Journal of Crime and Justice* 40, no. 2 (2017): 204–21.

Eldred, Tigran W. "Prescriptions for Ethical Blindness: Improving Advocacy for Indigent Defendants in Criminal Cases." *Rutgers Law Review* 65, no. 2 (2012): 333–94.

Ellis, Tom, Craig Jenkins, and Paul Smith. *Evaluation of the Introduction of Personal Issue Body Worn Video Cameras (Operation Hyperion) on the Isle of Wight: Final Report to Hampshire Constabulary.* Portsmouth, UK: Institute of Criminal Justice Studies, University of Portsmouth, 2015.

Elms, Sarah. "Activists, Elected Officials Push for More Body Cameras for Police." *The Blade*, June 30, 2020. www.toledoblade.com.

Enns, Peter K., Youngmin Yi, Megan Comfort, Alyssa W. Goldman, and Christopher Hedwig Lee [Equal Employment Opportunity Commission]. *Enforcement Guidance on the Consideration of Arrest and Conviction Records in Employment Decisions Under Title VII.* Washington, DC: Equal Employment Opportunity Commission, 2012.

Epstein, Deborah. "Effective Intervention in Domestic Violence Cases: Rethinking the Roles of Prosecutors, Judges, and the Court System." *Yale Journal of Law and Feminism* 11, no. 1 (1999): 23–25.

Erickson, B. Second Amendment Federalism. *Stanford. Law Review* 73, no. 3 (2021): 727–75.

Estes, Andrea. "District Attorney Rollins Calls Public Defenders Too White and Privileged, Setting Off a Storm of Protest." *Boston Globe*, May 5, 2020.

Everett, Ronald S., and Roger A. Wojtkiewicz. "Difference, Disparity, and Race/Ethnic Bias in Federal Sentencing." *Journal of Quantitative Criminology* 18, no. 2 (2002): 189–211.

Ewing, Maura. "How Prisoners' Family Members Can Assist Overworked Public Defenders." *Atlantic Monthly*, July 5, 2017, www.theatlantic.com.

Fair and Just Prosecution. "Our Work and Vision." https://fairandjustprosecution.org.

Fairfax, Roger A. "From Overcriminalization to Smart on Crime: American Criminal Justice Reform Legacy and Prospects." *Journal of Law, Economics & Policy* 7, no. 3 (2011): 597–616.

———. "The 'Smart on Crime' Prosecutor." *Georgetown Journal of Legal Ethics* 25, no. 4 (2012): 905–12.

Fairfax, Roger Jr. "Delegation of the Criminal Prosecution Function to Private Actors." *UC Davis Law Review* 43, no. 1 (2009): 411–56. https://lawreview.law.ucdavis.edu.

Family Justice. "Enhancing Rural Reentry Through Housing Partnerships." 2009. www.appa-net.org.

Fan, Travis. "Conspiracy Theories, Criminal Investigations Plentiful in NC Bail Bonds World." WRAL.com, July 13, 2018. www.wral.com.

Farole, Donald, and Lynn Langton. *County-Based and Local Public Defender Offices, 2007.* Washington, DC: Bureau of Justice Statistics, 2010. www.bjs.gov.

Farrar, Tony. *Self-Awareness to Being Watched and Socially Desirable Behavior: A Field Experiment on the Effect of Body-Worn Cameras and Police Use of Force.* Washington, DC: Police Foundation, 2013.

Farrell, Jill. "Mandatory Minimum Firearm Penalties: A Source of Sentencing Disparity? *Justice Research and Policy* 5, no. 1 (2003): 95–115.

Farrigan, Tracey, and Amy Glasmeier. "The Economic Impacts of the Prison Development Boom in Persistently Poor Rural Places." *International Regional Science Review* 30, no. 3 (2007): 274–99.

Federal Bureau of Investigation. "2018 Crime in the United States." https://ucr.fbi.gov.

———. "Crime in the United States, 2018." https://ucr.fbi.gov.

Federal Bureau of Prisons. *Inmate Race.* 2021. www.bop.gov.

Federal Communications Commission. *2020 Broadband Deployment Report.* Washington, DC: Federal Communications Commission, April 24, 2020. www.fcc.gov.

Fellmeth, Aaron X. "Civil and Criminal Sanctions in the Constitution and Courts." *Georgetown Law Journal* 94, no. 1 (2005): 10.

Ferguson, Andrew. "'Defund the Police' Does Not Mean Defund the Police. Unless It Does." *The Atlantic*, June 14, 2020. www.theatlantic.com.

Ferri, Russell. "The Benefits of Live Court Date Reminder Phone Calls During Pretrial Case Processing." *Journal of Experimental Criminology* 18, no. 1 (2020): 149–69.

Fields, Alison, Kelly A. Holder, and Charlynn Burd. "Life Off the Highway: A Snapshot of Rural America." December 8, 2016. www.census.gov.

Flight, Sander. "Opening Up the Black Box: Understanding the Impact of Bodycams on Policing." *European Police Science and Research Bulletin*, 4, no. 1 (October 2018): 47–59. https://bulletin.cepol.europa.eu.

Follman, Mark, Jaeah Lee, Julia Lurie, and James West. "The True Cost of Gun Violence in America." *Mother Jones*, April 15, 2015. www.motherjones.com.

Foundations Recovery Network. "Alternatives to Prison." https://dualdiagnosis.org.

Forman, James Jr., 2018. *Locking Up Our Own: Crime and Punishment in Black America.* New York: Farrar, Straus and Giroux.

Formerly Incarcerated Convicted People and Families Movement. "Our History." https://ficpfm.org.

Fox, Aubrey, and Stephen Koppel. "Pretrial Release Without Money: New York City, 1987–2018: In 2018 There Were More Than Three Times as Many Releases Without Money Than Money Bails." New York: N.Y.C. Criminal Justice Agency Research Brief No. 44 (March 2019). www.nycja.org.

Fox, Kathleen A. "The Murder and Missing of Indigenous Women and Girls: New Policies on an Enduring Crisis." *Criminal Law Bulletin.* Forthcoming.

Fox, Kathleen A., Bonnie S. Fisher, and Scott H. Decker. "Identifying the Needs of American Indian Women Who Sought Shelter: A Practitioner-Researcher Partnership." *Journal of Family Violence* 33, no. 4 (2018): 251–56.

Fox, Kathleen A., Matt R. Nobles, and Bonnie S. Fisher. "Method to the Madness: An Examination of Stalking Measurements." *Aggression and Violent Behavior* 16, no. 1 (2011): 74–84.

Frakt, Austin. "A Sense of Alarm as Rural Hospitals Keep Closing." *New York Times*, October 29, 2018. www.nytimes.com.

Francis, Megan Ming. "The Price of Civil Rights: Black Lives, White Funding, and Movement Capture." *Law & Society Review* 53, no. 1 (2019): 275–309.

Frankel, Marvin. *Criminal Sentences: Law Without Order.* New York: Hall and Wang, 1972.

Frase, Richard. "Implementing Commission–Based Sentencing Guidelines: The Lessons of the First Ten Years in Minnesota." *Cornell Journal of Law and Public Policy* 2, no. 2 (1993): 279–337.

Frattaroli, Shannon, Emma E. McGinty, Amy Barnhorst, and Sheldon Greenberg. "Gun Violence Restraining Orders: Alternative or Adjunct to Mental Health–Based Restrictions on Firearms?" *Behavioral Sciences & the Law,* 33, no. 2–3 (2015): 290–307.

Frederick, Bruce, and Don Stemen. *Anatomy of Discretion: An Analysis of Prosecutorial Decision Making.* Summary Report to the National Institute of Justice. Vera Institute of Justice, 2012.

Free, Marvin. "Race and Presentencing Decisions in the United States: A Summary and Critique of the Research." *Criminal Justice Review* 27, no. 2 (2002): 203–32.

Freedman, Eric. "Earl Washington's Ordeal." 29 *Hofstra Law Review* 1089 (2001).

Freiberg, Arie, and W.G. Carson. "The Limits to Evidence-Based Policy: Evidence, Emotion, and Criminal Justice." *Australian Journal of Criminal Justice* 69, no. 2 (2010): 152–64.

Fritze, John. "Law Banning Handgun Sales to Americans Under 21 Violates Second Amendment, Court Rules." *USA Today,* July 13, 2021. www.usatoday.com.

Frizzell, William, and Joseph Chien. "Extreme Risk Protection Orders to Reduce Firearm Violence." *Psychiatric Services,* 70, no. 1 (2019): 75–77.

Galea, Sandro, Jennifer Ahern, Kenneth Tardiff, Andrew C. Leon, and David Vlahov. "Drugs and Firearm Deaths in New York City, 1990–98." *Journal of Urban Health* 79, no. 1 (2002): 70–86.

Gallup. "Black Americans Want Police to Retain Local Presence." 2020. https://news.gallup.com.

Garcia, Ivonne, Margaret Hennessy, Erin Jacobs Valentine, Jedediah Teres, and Rachel Sander. *Paving the Way Home: An Evaluation of the Returning Citizens Stimulus Program.* New York: MDRC, 2021. www.mdrc.org.

Garland, David. "Introduction: The Meaning of Mass Imprisonment." *Punishment & Society* 3, no. 1 (2001): 5–7.

Garrett, Brandon L. "Judging Innocence." 108 *Columbia Law Review* 94 (2008).

Gaub, Janne E., David E. Choate, Natalie Todak, Charles M. Katz, and Michael D. White. "Officer Perceptions of Body-Worn Cameras before and after Deployment: A Study of Three Departments." *Police Quarterly* 19, no. 3 (2016): 275–302.

Gaub, Janne E., Natalie Todak, and Michael D. White. "One Size Doesn't Fit All: The Deployment of Police Body-Worn Cameras to Specialty Units." *International Criminal Justice Review* 30, no. 2 (2020): 136–55.

Gehring, Thom. "Recidivism as a Measure of Correctional Education Program Success." *Journal of Clinical Ethics* 51, no. 2 (2000): 197–205.

"George Soros/Political Activity." Ballotpedia, n.d. www.ballotpedia.org.

George, Justin. "What Are Inmates Learning in Prison? Not Much." The Marshall Project. May 2017. www.themarshallproject.org.

George, Tracey E. "Court Fixing." *Arizona Law Review* 43, no. 1 (2001): 9–62.

Gershowitz, Adam M. "Justice on the Line: Prosecutorial Screening Before Arrest." *University of Illinois Law Review* (2019): 833–73.

Gershowitz, Adam M., and Laura R. Killinger. "The State Never Rests: How Excessive Prosecutorial Caseloads Harm Criminal Defendants." *Northwestern University Law Review* 105, no. 1 (2011): 261–302.

Gerstein v. Pugh, 420 U.S. 103 (1975).

Giffords Law Center to Prevent Gun Violence. "Categories of Prohibited People." https://lawcenter.giffords.org.

———. "Extreme Risk Protection Orders." https://lawcenter.giffords.org.

———. "Licensing." https://lawcenter.giffords.org.

———. "Universal Background Checks." https://lawcenter.giffords.org.

Gius, Mark. "Effects of Permit-to-Purchase Laws on State-Level Firearm Murder Rates." *Atlantic Economic Journal* 45, no. 1 (2017): 73–80.

Godsoe, Cynthia. "Participatory Defense: Humanizing the Accused and Ceding Control to the Client." *Mercer Law Review* 69, no. 3 (2018): 715–42.

Goldkamp, John S. "Questioning the Practice of Pretrial Detention: Some Empirical Evidence from Philadelphia." *Journal of Criminal Law & Criminology* 74, no. 4 (1983): 1556–88.

Goldman, Sheldon. "Should There Be Affirmative Action for the Judiciary?" *Judicature* 62, no. 10 (1979): 488–94.

Goldstick, Jason E., April Zeoli, Christina Mair, and Rebecca M. Cunningham. "US Firearm-Related Mortality: National, State, And Population Trends, 1999–2017." *Health Affairs* 38, no. 10 (2019): 1646–52.

Gonnerman, Jennifer. "Kalief Browder, 1993–2015." *The New Yorker*, June 7, 2015. www.newyorker.com.

Gonzalez Van Cleve, Nicole. *Crook County: Racism and Injustice in America's Largest Criminal Court*. Stanford: Stanford University Press, 2016.

Goodall, Martin. *Guidance for the Police Use of Body-Worn Video Devices*. London: Home Office, 2007. http://library.college.police.uk.

Goodfellow, Amelia, Jesus Ulloa, Patrick Dowling, Efrain Talamantes, Somil Chheda, Curtis Bone, and Gerardo Moreno. "Predictors of Primary Care Physician Practice Location in Underserved Urban and Rural Areas in the United States: A Systematic Literature Review." *Academic Medicine* 91, no. 9 (2016): 1313–21.

Goodison, Sean, and Tom Wilson. *Citizen Perceptions of Body-Worn Cameras: A Randomized Controlled Trial*. Washington, DC: Police Executive Research Forum, 2017. https://perf.memberclicks.net.

Goodman, Philip, Joshua Page, and Michelle Phelps. *Breaking the Pendulum: The Long Struggle Over Criminal Justice*. New York: Oxford University Press, 2017.

Goodwin, Michelle. "The Thirteenth Amendment: Modern slavery, capitalism, and mass incarceration." *Cornell Law Review* 104, no. 4 (2019): 899–990.

Gottfredson, Michael R., Chester L. Britt III, and John S. Goldkamp. "Evaluation of Arizona Pretrial Services Drug Testing Programs: Final Report." (January 1990). www.ncjrs.gov.

Gottschalk, Marie. *Caught: The Prison State and the Lockdown of American Politics.* Princeton, Princeton University Press, 2015.

Gould, Jon B. *The Innocence Commission: Preventing Wrongful Convictions and Restoring the Criminal Justice System.* New York: New York University Press, 2008.

———. "When Courts Refuse to Play by the Rules (of Law): The Failure of Public Administration Theory in Securing Constitutional Rights." *Journal of Chinese Governance* 4, no. 1 (2019): 34–51.

Gould, Jon B., Julia Carrano, Richard A. Leo, and Katie Hail-Jares. "Predicting Erroneous Convictions." *Iowa Law Review* 99, no. 2 (2014): 471–522.

Gould, Jon B., and Kenneth Sebastian Leon. "A Culture that is Hard to Defend: Extralegal Factors in Federal Death Penalty Cases." *Journal of Criminal Law & Criminology* 107, no. 4 (2016): 643–86.

Gouldin, Lauryn P. "Disentangling Flight Risk from Dangerousness." *Brigham Young University Law Review* 2016 (2016): 837–98.

———. "Defining Flight Risk." *University of Chicago Law Review* 85, no. 3 (2018): 677–742.

———. "New Perspectives on Pretrial Nonappearance." In *Handbook on Corrections and Sentencing: Pretrial Justice*, edited by Christine Scott-Hayward, Jennifer E. Copp, and Stephen Demuth, vol. 6. New York: Routledge, 2022. www.routledge. com.

Graham, Amanda, Hannah D. McManus, Francis T. Cullen, Velmer S. Burton, and Cheryl Lero Johnson. "Videos Don't Lie: African Americans' Support for Body-Worn Cameras." *Criminal Justice Review* 44, no. 3 (2019): 284–303.

Grant, Glenn A. "2018 Report to the Governor and the Legislature." Trenton: New Jersey Administrative Office of the Courts (2019). https://njcourts.gov.

Gray, Katti. "Friend in Court: The Growing Impact of "Participatory Defense." *The Crime Report*, CBS News, March 29, 2017. www.cbsnews.com.

Greater New Orleans Fair Housing Action Center. *Locked Out: Criminal Background Checks as a Tool for Discrimination.* 2015. https://storage.googleapis.com.

Greenberg, Greg A., and Robert A. Rosenheck. "Homelessness in the State and Federal Prison Population." *Criminal Behaviour and Mental Health* 18, no. 2 (2008): 88–103.

Greene, Judith, and Marc Mauer. *Downscaling Prisons: Lessons from Four States.* Washington, DC: The Sentencing Project, 2010.

Greene, Sara Sternberg. "Race, Class, and the Access to Civil Justice." *Iowa Law Review* 101, no. 4 (2016): 1289–90.

Greenwood, Elizabeth. "The Long Recovery After a Spouse Gets Out of Prison." *The Atlantic.* July 27, 2021.

Griffin, Hayden O. III, and Vanessa H. Woodward. *Routledge Handbook of Corrections in the United States*. New York: Routledge, 2018.

Griller, Gordon, Lee Suskin, David Sayles, and Erika Friess. "Reengineering Rural Justice in Minnesota's Eighth Judicial District—A Case Study: Improving Efficiencies, Reducing Costs, and Enhancing Operations in Rural Courts." Williamsburg, VA: National Center for State Courts. 2010. www.sji.gov.

Gross, John P. "Case Refusal: A Right for the Public Defender but Not a Remedy for the Defendant." *Washington University Law Review* 95, no. 1 (2017): 253–68.

———. "The Right to Counsel but Not the Presence of Counsel: A Survey of State Criminal Procedures for Pre-Trial Release." *Florida Law Review* 69, no. 3 (2018): 831–85.

Grossmith, Lynne, Catherine Owens, Will Finn, David Mann, Tom Davies, and Laura Baika. *Police, Camera, Evidence: London's Cluster Randomised Controlled Trial of Body Worn Video*. London: College of Policing and Mayor's Office for Policing and Crime, 2015.

Gust, Ted. "Civil Rights Advocates Say Risk Assessment May 'Worsen Racial Disparities' in Bail Decisions." *The Crime Report*, July 31, 2018. https://thecrimereport.org.

Guthrie, Peter G. *Purse Snatching as Robbery or Theft*, 42 A.L.R.3d 1381 (1972 & 2020 Supp.).

Haapanen, Rudy A. *Selective Incapacitation and the Serious Offender: A Longitudinal Study of Criminal Career Patterns*. New York: Springer-Verlag, 1990.

Hagan, John. "Extra-Legal Attributes and Criminal Sentencing: An Assessment of a Sociological Viewpoint." *Law & Society Review* 8, no. 3 (1974): 357–84.

Hager, Eli. "New York City's Bail Success Story." *The Marshall Project*, March 14, 2019. www.themarshallproject.org.

Hamedy, Saba, and Topher Gauk-Roger. "Los Angeles City Council Moves Forward with Plan to Replace Police Officers with Community-Based Responders for Non-violent Calls." *CNN*, June 30, 2020. www.cnn.com.

Hamilton, Keegan. "A Super-Spreader Jail Keeps Sparking COVID Outbreaks Across the U.S" *Vice News*. 2020. www.vice.com.

Hamilton, Keegan, and Keri Blakinger. "'Con Air' Is Spreading COVID-19 All Over the US Prison System." *Vice News*. August 13, 2020. www.vice.com.

Hamilton, Melissa. "Some Facts About Life: The Law, Theory, and Practice of Life Sentences. *Lewis & Clark Law Review* 20, no. 3 (2016): 803–55.

Hanora, Mallory. Email to Raj Jayadev, August 24, 2020 (on file with the authors).

Hansen, Andrew, and Gabrielle Lory. "Rural Victimization and Policing During the COVID-19 Pandemic." *American Journal of Criminal Justice* 45, no. 4 (2020): 731–42.

Hanzlick, Randy. "The Conversion of Coroner Systems to Medical Examiners in the US: A Lull in the Action." *American Journal of Forensic Medicine and Pathology* 28, no. 4 (2007): 279–83.

Harcourt, Bernard E. *Against Prediction: Profiling, Policing, and Punishing in an Actuarial Age*. Chicago: University of Chicago Press, 2007.

———. "Risk as a Proxy for Race: The Dangers of Risk Assessment." *Federal Sentencing Reporter* 27, no. 4 (2015): 237–43.

Harding, David J., Jeffrey D. Morenoff, and Claire W. Herbert. "Home Is Hard to Find: Neighborhoods, Institutions, and the Residential Trajectories of Returning Prisoners." *ANNALS of the American Academy of Political and Social Science* 647, no. 1 (2013): 214–36.

Harding, David J., Jeffrey D. Morenoff, and Jessica J.B. Wyse. *On the Outside: Prisoner Reentry and Reintegration.* Chicago, University of Chicago Press, 2019.

Harlow, Caroline Wolf. *Defense Counsel in Criminal Cases: Bureau of Justice Statistics Special Report.* Washington, DC: U.S. Department of Justice, Office of Justice Programs, 2000.

———. *Firearm Use by Offenders.* U.S. Department of Justice, Office of Justice Programs, Bureau of Justice Statistics, 2002. www.defesa.org.

Harmon, Mark G. "The Imprisonment Race: Unintended Consequences of 'Fixed' Sentencing on People of Color Over Time." *Journal of Ethnicity in Criminal Justice* 9, no. 2 (2011): 79–109.

Hasegawa, Raiden B., Dylan S. Small, and Daniel W. Webster. "Bracketing in the Comparative Interrupted Time-Series Design to Address Concerns about History Interacting with Group: Evaluating Missouri Handgun Purchaser Law." *Epidemiology* 30, no. 3 (2019):371–79.

Hatch v. Minnesota, 21-667. *State v. Hatch*, File No. A20-0176 (Minn. Sup. Ct. filed Aug. 4, 2021).

Hawton, Keith, Carolina Casañas i Comabella, Camilla Haw, and Kate Saunders. "Risk Factors for Suicide in Individuals with Depression: A Systematic Review." *Journal of Affective Disorders* 147, no. 1–3 (2013): 17–28.

Headley, A. M., and K. Blount-Hill. Race and Police Misconduct Cases. In Oxford Research Encyclopedia of Criminology and Criminal Justice. New York: Oxford University Press, 2021.

Headley, Andrea M., Rob T. Guerette, and Auzeen Shariati. "A Field Experiment of the Impact of Body-Worn Cameras (BWCs) on Police Officer Behavior and Perceptions." *Journal of Criminal Justice* 53 (November 2017): 102–109.

Heath, Sara. "Urban-Rural Divide Opens for COVID-19 Testing Sites, Access to Care." *Patient Engagement HIT.* May 21, 2020. https://patientengagementhit.com.

Heaton, Paul, Sandra Mayson, and Megan Stevenson. "The Downstream Consequences of Misdemeanor Pretrial Detention." *Stanford Law Review* 69, no. 3 (March 2017): 711–94.

Hedberg, Eric C., Charles M. Katz, and David E. Choate. "Body-Worn Cameras and Citizen Interactions with Police Officers: Estimating Plausible Effects Given Varying Compliance Levels." *Justice Quarterly* 34, no. 4 (2017): 627–51.

Heidemann, Gretchen, Julie A. Cederbaum, and Sidney Martinez. "Beyond Recidivism: How Formerly Incarcerated Women Define Success." *Affilia: Journal of Women and Social Work* 31, no. 1 (2016): 24–40.

———. "We Walk Through It Together: The Importance of Peer Support for Formerly Incarcerated Women's Success." *Journal of Offender Rehabilitation* 53, no. 7 (2014): 522–42.

Heidemann, Gretchen, Julia A. Cederbaum, Sidney Martinez, and Thomas P. LeBel. "Wounded healers: How Formerly Incarcerated Women Help Themselves by Helping Others." *Punishment & Society* 18, no. 1 (2016): 3–26.

Heiss, Jasmine, and Jack Norton. "The Hidden Scandal of US Criminal Justice? Rural Incarceration has Boomed." *The Guardian.* December 13, 2019. www.theguardian.com.

Helgesen, Elise. "Allotment of Justice: How US Policy in Indian Country Perpetuates the Victimization of American Indians." *University of Florida Journal of Law and Public Policy* 22, no. 3 (2011): 441–74.

Helland, Eric, and Alexander Tabarrok. "The Fugitive: Evidence on Public versus Private Law Enforcement from Bail Jumping." *Journal of Law & Economics* 47, no. 1 (April 2004): 93–122.

Hemenway, David. "Reducing Firearm Violence." *Crime and justice* 46, no. 1 (2017): 201–30.

Hemenway, David, Deborah Azrael, and Matthew Miller. "Whose Guns Are Stolen? The Epidemiology of Gun Theft Victims." *Injury Epidemiology* 4, no. 1 (2017): 1–5.

Henderson, Taja-Nia Y. "Note, New Frontiers in Fair Lending: Confronting Lending Discrimination Against Ex-Offenders." *New York University Law Review* 80, no. 4 (2005): 1237–71.

Henry, Jessica S." Death-in-Prison Sentences: Overutilized and Underscrutinized." In *Life Without Parole: America's New Death Penalty?*, edited by Charles J. Ogletree and Austin Sarat, 66–95. New York: New York University Press, 2012.

Henstock, Darren, and Barak Ariel. "Testing the Effects of Police Body-Worn Cameras on Use of Force during Arrests: A Randomised Controlled Trial in a Large British Police Force." *European Journal of Criminology* 14, no. 6 (2017): 720–50.

Heriot, Gail. "An Essay on the Civil-Criminal Distinction with Special Reference to Punitive Damages." *Journal of Contemporary Legal Issues* 77, no. 7 (1996).

Hess, Abigail Johnson. "Meet the Mayors Pushing for Guaranteed Income in 30 Cities Across the Country." CNBC. January 19, 2021. www.cnbc.com.

Higgens, Tucker. "Supreme Court Eyes More Gun Cases as Conservatives Signal Eagerness to Expand 2nd Amendment Protections." CNBC, May 17, 2020. www.cnbc.com.

Hilleary, Cecily. "COVID Spread May Put Native Americans at Increased Risk of Violence." VOA. U.S. Agency for Global Media, May 2020. www.voanews.com.

Hofer, Paul J., Kevin R. Blackwell, and R. Barry Ruback. "The Effect of the Federal Sentencing Guidelines on Inter-Judge Sentencing Disparity." *Journal of Criminal Law & Criminology* 90, no. 1 (1999): 239–321.

Hoffman, Peter B. *History of the Federal Parole System.* Washington, DC: U.S. Department of Justice, 2003. www.fedcure.org.

Holbrook, Thomas M., and Aaron C. Weinschenk. "Campaigns, Mobilization, and Turnout in Mayoral Elections." *Political Research Quarterly*, 67, no. 1, 2014.

Hollinshed, Denise. "Ferguson Police Are Using Body Cameras." *St. Louis Post-Dispatch*, August 31, 2014. www.stltoday.com.

Hollway, John, Calvin Lee, and Sean Smoot. "Root Cause Analysis: A Tool to Promote Officer Safety and Reduce Officer Involved Shootings Over Time." *Villanova Law Review* 62, no. 5 (2017): 883–924.

Hollway, John, and Ben Grunwald. "Applying Sentinel Event Reviews to Policing." *Criminology & Public Policy* 18 (July 21, 2019).

Hoover, Elizabeth. "Native Food Systems Impacted by COVID." *Agriculture and Human Values* (April 2020).

Hopwood, Shon. "The Effort to Reform the Federal Criminal Justice System." *Yale Law Journal Forum* (February 25, 2019): 791–817.

———. "The Not so Speedy Trial Act." *Washington Law Review* 89, no. 3 (2014): 709–46.

Horn, Abigail E. "Wrongful Collateral Consequences." *George Washington Law Review* 87, no. 2 (2019): 315.

Hoyman, Michelle, and Micah Weinberg. "The Process of Policy Innovation: Prison Sittings in Rural North Carolina." *Policy Studies Journal* 34, no. 1 (2006): 95–112.

Human Rights Watch. "Human Rights Watch Urges Governor Brown of California to Veto Senate Bill 10, the California Bail Reform Act: The New SB 10 Is Simply Not Bail Reform." August 24, 2018. www.hrw.org.

Hutton, Marie, and Dominique Moran, Editors. *The Palgrave Handbook of Prison and the Family*. London, Palgrave Macmillan, 2019.

Hyland, Shelley S. Body-Worn Cameras in Law Enforcement Agencies, 2016. NCJ 251775. United States Bureau of Justice Statistics. Washington, DC: Office of Justice Programs, U.S. Department of Justice, 2018.

Ikem, Chinelo Nkechi, and Matthew Ogbeifun. "Body Cameras Aren't Working. So What's Next?" *Huffington Post*, November 28, 2017. www.huffingtonpost.com.

Indiana Public Defender Commission. "Indiana Public Defense Overhead Costs: Statewide Survey Results & Findings." June 2020. www.in.gov.

Ingles, Jo. "New Ohio Bail Reform Plan Excludes Key Recommendation, Statehouse News Bureau." Ohio Statehouse News Bureau, January 21, 2020. www.statenews.org.

The Innocence Project. www.innocenceproject.org.

———. *Eyewitness Identification Reform*. www.innocenceproject.org.

———. *False Confessions & the Recording of Interrogations*. www.innocenceproject.org.

———. *Governor Signs Landmark Innocence Protection Law Against Unreliable Jailhouse Informants*. www.innocenceproject.org.

The Institute for Innovation in Prosecution at John Jay College. "Innovation in Criminal Justice." www.prosecution.org.

Internal Revenue Service. *Compliance Guide for 501(c)(3) Public Charities*. Washington, DC: Department of the U.S. Treasury, 2021.

———. *Self-Employment Tax (Social Security and Medicare Taxes)*. Washington, DC: Department of the U.S. Treasury, 2021.

International Association of Chiefs of Police. "Body-Worn Cameras: Model Policy." www.theiacp.org.

Iyengar, Radha. *I'd Rather Be Hanged for a Sheep Than a Lamb: The Unintended Consequences of 'Three-Strikes' Laws*. Cambridge, MA: National Bureau of Economic Research, 2008. www.nber.org.

Jacobs, David, and The Center Square. "'Public Defenders Are Paid to Lose': Louisiana Looking at Reforms to Legal Defense System." *New Orleans City Business*, November 15, 2019. https://neworleanscitybusiness.com.

James, Andrea, et al. Amicus Letter, Committee for Public Counsel Services and Massachusetts Association of Criminal Defense Lawyers v. Chief Justice of the Trial Court No. SJC-12926. March 27, 2020. www.mass.gov.

Jarecki, Andrew, dir. *The Jinx: The Life and Deaths of Robert Durst*. HBO. Aired February 8, 2015, through March 15, 2015. www.hbo.com.

Jauch v. Choctaw County, 874 F.3d 425 (2017).

Jayadev, Raj. "The Future of Pretrial Justice is Not Money Bail or System Supervision—It's Freedom and Community." Silicon Valley De-Bug, April 4, 2019. www.siliconvalleydebug.org.

———. "Tales from a Trial." *Metroactive*, January 16, 2008. www.metroactive.com.

———. "Why We Must Teach Law to Those Who Need It Most." *Time*, June 25, 2015. https://time.com.

Jennings, Wesley G., Lorie A. Fridell, and Matthew D. Lynch. "Cops and Cameras: Officer Perceptions of the Use of Body-Worn Cameras in Law Enforcement." *Journal of Criminal Justice* 42, no. 6 (2014): 549–56.

Jennings, Wesley G., Matthew D. Lynch, and Lorie A. Fridell. "Evaluating the Impact of Police Officer Body-Worn Cameras (BWCs) on Response-to-Resistance and Serious External Complaints: Evidence from the Orlando Police Department (OPD) Experience Utilizing a Randomized Controlled Experiment." *Journal of Criminal Justice* 43, no. 6 (2015): 480–86.

Jensen, Leif. "At the Razor's Edge: Building Hope for America's Rural Poor." *Rural Realities* 1, no. 1 (2006).

Johnson, Brian. "The Multilevel Context of Criminal Sentencing: Integrating Judge- and County-Level Influences." *Criminology* 44, no. 2 (2006): 259–98.

Johnson, Brian D., Cassia Spohn and Anat Kimchi. "Life Lessons: Examining Sources of Racial and Ethnic Disparity in Federal Life Without Parole Sentences." *Criminology* 59, no. 4 (2021).

Johnson, Lee Michael, Paul Elam, Susan M. Lebold, and Robert Burroughs. "Use of Research Evidence by Criminal Justice Professionals." *Justice Policy Journal* 16, no. 2 (2018): 1–23.

Johnson, Lydia D. "The Politics of the Bail System: What's the Price for Freedom?" *Scholar* 17, no. 2 (2015): 171–217.

Jones, Alexi. "Does Our County Really Need a Bigger Jail?: A Guide for Avoiding Unnecessary Jail Expansion." Prison Policy Initiative. May 2019. www.prisonpolicy.org.

Jones, Elaine R. "Failure of the 'Get Tough' Crime Policy." *University of Dayton Law Review* 20, no. 2 (1995): 803–08.

Jonson, Cheryl Lero, and Francis T. Cullen. *Prisoner Reentry Programs*. University of Chicago Press. Chicago, Illinois (2005).

Jouvenal, Justin. "In Texas District Attorney's Office, a Tattooed Tilt to the Left." *Seattle Times*, November 25, 2018. www.seattletimes.com.

Judicial Council of California/Administrative Office of the Courts. *Statewide Caseload Trends 2000–2001 Through 2009–2010*. San Francisco, CA, 2011.

Judicial Conference of the United States. *The 2017 Report of the Ad Hoc Committee to Review the Criminal Justice Act Program, Judicial Conference of the United States*. 2017.

Kaba, Miriame. "Yes, We Mean Literally Abolish the Police." *New York Times*, June 12, 2020. www.nytimes.com.

Kaeding, Danielle. "Some People are Considering Trading City Life for Rural Wisconsin Due to COVID-19 Pandemic." *Wisconsin Public Radio*. September 29, 2020. www.wpr.org.

Kagawa, Rose MC, Alvaro Castillo-Carniglia, Jon S. Vernick, Daniel Webster, Cassandra Crifasi, Kara E. Rudolph, Magdalena Cerdá, Aaron Shev, and Garen J. Wintemute. "Repeal of Comprehensive Background Check Policies and Firearm Homicide and Suicide." *Epidemiology* 29, no. 4 (2018): 494–502.

Kalb, Johanna. "Gideon Incarcerated: Access to Counsel in Pretrial Detention." *UC Irvine Law Review* 9, no. 1 (2018): 101–40.

Kang, Jerry, Judge Mark Bennett, Devon Carbado, Pam Casey, Nilanjana Dasgupta, David Faigman, Rachel Godsil, Arthur S. Greenwald, Justin Levinson, and Jennifer Mnookin. "Implicit Bias in the Courtroom." *UCLA Law Review* 59, no. 5 (2012): 1124–86.

Kang-Brown, Jacob, and Ram Subramanian. "Out of Sight: The Growth of Jails in Rural America." Vera Institute of Justice. June 2017.

Kanter, Rosabeth Moss. *Men and Women of the Corporation*. New York: Basic Books, 1977.

Karp, Aaron. *Estimating Global Civilian-Held Firearms Numbers*. Ginebra, Suiza: Small Arms Survey, 2018. www.club-caza.com.

Kashef, Ziba. "Barrier to Rural Opiod Treatment: Driving Distance to Methadone Clinics." *Yale News*, October 1, 2019. https://news.yale.edu.

Katz, Charles M., and Cassia C. Spohn. "The Effect of Race and Gender on Bail Outcomes: A Test of an Interactive Model." *American Journal of Criminal Justice* 19, no. 2 (1995): 161–84.

Katz, Charles M., David E. Choate, Justin R. Ready, and Lidia Nuño. *Evaluating the Impact of Officer Worn Body Cameras in the Phoenix Police Department*. Phoenix: Center for Violence Prevention and Community Safety, Arizona State University, 2014.

Katz, Charles M., Michael Kurtenbach, David W. Choate, and Michael D. White. *Phoenix, Arizona, Smart Policing Initiative: Evaluating the Impact of Police Officer Body-Worn Cameras*. Washington, DC: U.S. Department of Justice, Bureau of Justice Assistance, 2015.

Katz, Elizabeth D. "Criminal Law in a Civil Guise: The Evolution of Family Courts and Support Laws." *The University of Chicago Law Review* 86, no. 5 (2019): 1242, 1245, 1307.

Kaufman, Emma. "The Prisoner Trade." *Harvard Law Review* 133, no. 6 (2020): 1817–83.

Kaur, Harmeet. "There's a Renewed Call for Police Body Cameras. Here's Why That May Not Be the Right Solution." *CNN*, June 30, 2020. www.cnn.com.

Kaut, Paula, and Cassia Spohn. "Crack-ing Down on Black Drug Offenders? Testing for Interactions Among Offenders' Race, Drug Type, and Sentencing Strategy in Federal Drug Sentences." *Justice Quarterly* 19, no. 1 (2002): 1–35.

Kazemian, Lila, and Jeremy Travis. "Imperative for Inclusion of Long Termers and Lifers in Research and Policy. *Criminology & Public Policy* 14, no. 2 (2015): 355–96.

Keller, Josh, and Adam Pearce. "A Small Indiana County Sends More People to Prison Than San Francisco and Durham, N.C., Combined. Why?" *New York Times*, September 2, 2016. www.nytimes.com.

Kelly, Caroline. "Colorado Governor Signs Bill Mandating Police Body Cameras and Banning Chokeholds." *CNN*, June 19, 2020. www.cnn.com.

Kennedy, Randall. *Race, Crime and the Law*. New York: Vintage, 1998.

Kerrison, Erin, Jennifer Cobbina, and Kimberly. "Stop-Gaps, Lip Service, and the Perceived Futility of Body-Worn Police Officer Cameras in Baltimore City." *Journal of Ethnic & Cultural Diversity in Social Work* 27, no. 3 (2018): 271–88.

Keyes, Katherine M., Magdalena Cerda, Joanne E. Brady, Jennifer R. Havens, and Sandro Galea. "Understanding the Rural-Urban Differences in Nonmedical Prescription Opioid Use and Abuse in the United States." *American Journal of Public Health* 104, no. 2 (2014): 52–59.

Khurshid, Samar. "Should a Top Prosecutor Have Prior Prosecutorial Experience? 'Qualifications' Debate Rages in Queens District Attorney Race." *Gotham Gazette*, June 7, 2019. www.gothamgazette.com.

Kilborn, Peter T. "Rural Towns Turn to Prisons." *New York Times*, August 1, 2001. www.nytimes.com.

Kim, Byungbae, Cassia Spohn, and E.C. Hedberg. "Federal Sentencing as a Complex Collaborative Process: Judges, Prosecutors, Judge-Prosecutor Dyads, and Disparity in Sentencing." *Criminology* 53, no. 4 (2015): 597–623.

King, Nikki, Marcus Pigman, Sarah Huling, and Brian Hanson. "EMS Services in Rural America: Challenges and Opportunities." National Rural Health Association Policy Brief. May 2018. www.ruralhealthweb.org.

King, Ryan D. "Cumulative Impact: Why Prison Sentences Have Increased." *Criminology* 57, no. 1 (2019): 157–80.

King, Ryan D., Kecia R. Johnson, and Kelly McGeever. "Demography of the Legal Profession and Racial Disparities in Sentencing." *Law and Society Review* 44, no. 1 (2010): 1–32.

King, Ryan, Marc Mauer, and Tracy Huling. "Big Prisons, Small Towns: Prison Economics in Rural America." The Sentencing Project. February 2003. http://prison.ppjr.org.

Kirk, David S., and Sara Wakefield. "Collateral Consequences of Punishment: A Critical Review and Path Forward." *Annual Review of Criminology* 1 (January 2018): 171–94.

Kivisto, Aaron J., and Peter Lee Phalen. "Effects of Risk-Based Firearm Seizure Laws in Connecticut and Indiana on Suicide Rates, 1981–2015." *Psychiatric Services*, 69, no. 8 (2018): 855–62.

Klein, George C. "On the Death of Sandra Bland: A Case of Anger and Indifference." *SAGE Open* 8, no. 1 (2018): 215824401875493.

Klein, Susan R. "Redrawing the Criminal-Civil Boundary." *Buffalo Criminal Law Review* 2, no. 2 (1999): 679–80.

Kleinberg, Jon, Himabindu Lakkaraju, Jure Leskovec, Jens Ludwig, and Sendhil Mullainathan. "Human Decisions and Machine Predictions." *Quarterly Journal of Economics* 133 no. 1 (February 2018): 237–93.

Klinger, David. "Organizational Accidents and Deadly Officer Involved Shootings." *Annals of Political and Social Science* 688, no. 1 (2020): 28–48.

Knapp, Kay A. "What Sentencing Reform in Minnesota Has and Has Not Accomplished." *Judicature* 68, nos. 4-5 (1984): 181–89.

Kohn, Margaret, and Kavita Reddy. "Colonialism" *Stanford Encyclopedia of Philosophy* (Fall 2017 edition), Edward N. Zalta (ed.). https://plato.stanford.edu.

Kohn, Margaret, Kavita Reddy, and Edward N. Zalta (ed.). "Colonialism." *Stanford Encyclopedia of Philosophy* (Fall 2017 edition).

Koper, Christopher S. "Crime Gun Risk Factors: Buyer, Seller, Firearm, and Transaction Characteristics Associated with Gun Trafficking and Criminal Gun Use." *Journal of Quantitative Criminology* 30, no. 2 (2014): 285–315.

Koss, Mary P., W. Joy Woodruff, and Paul G. Koss. "Relation of Criminal Victimization to Health Perceptions Among Women Medical Patients." *Journal of Consulting and Clinical Psychology* 58, no. 2 (1990): 147–52.

Kovandzic, Tomislav V., John J. Sloan III, and Lynne M. Vieraitis. "Unintended Consequences of Politically Popular Sentencing Policy: The Homicide Promoting Effects of 'Three Strikes' in US Cities (1980–1999)." *Criminology & Public Policy* 1, no. 3 (2002): 399–424.

———. "'Striking Out' as Crime Reduction Policy: The Impact of 'Three Strikes' Laws on Crime Rates in US Cities." *Justice Quarterly* 21, no. 2 (2004): 207–39.

Kramer, Alice, Darcy Lorenzon, and George Mueller. "Prevalence of Intimate Partner Violence and Health Implication for Women Using Emergency Departments and Primary Care Clinics." *Women's Health Issues* 14, no. 1 (2004): 19–29.

Kramer, John H., Robin L. Lubitz, and Cynthia A. Kempinen. "Sentencing Guidelines: A Quantitative Comparison of Sentencing Policies in Minnesota, Pennsylvania, and Washington." *Justice Quarterly* 6 (1989): 565–87.

Kreager, Derek A., Jacob T.N. Young, Dana L. Haynie, Martin Bouchard, David R. Schaefer, and Gary Zajac. "Where 'Old Heads' Prevail: Inmate Hierarchy in a Men's Prison Unit." *American Sociological Review* 82, no. 4 (2017): 685–718.

Krouse, Peter. "Ohio Supreme Court Proposes Bail Reforms That Don't Include Risk Assessments." Cleveland.com, January 25, 2020. www.cleveland.com.

Kruger, Daniel J., Peter Hutchison, Matthew G. Monroe, Thomas Reischl, and Susan Morrel-Samuels. "Assault Injury Rates, Social Capital, and Fear of Neighborhood Crime." *Journal of Community Psychology* 35, no. 4 (2007): 483–98.

Kushner, Rachel. "Is Prison Necessary? Ruth Wilson Gilmore Might Change Your Mind." *New York Times Magazine*, April 17, 2019. www.nytimes.com.

Kusisto, Laura. "Criminal-Justice Changes Are Squeezing the Bail-Bond Industry." *Wall Street Journal*, February 21, 2020. www.wsj.com.

Kutateladze, Besiki, Nancy Andiloro, and Brian Johnson. "Opening Pandora's Box: How Does Defendant Race Influence Plea Bargaining?" *Justice Quarterly* 33, no. 3 (2016): 398–426.

Kutateladze, Besiki, Nancy Andiloro, Brian Johnson, and Cassia Spohn. "Cumulative Disadvantage: Examining Racial and Ethnic Disparity in Prosecution and Sentencing." *Criminology* 52, no. 3 (2014): 514–51.

La. Rev. Stat. § 33:441. La. Const. art. 6, § 24(A)(2).

Lacasse, Chantale, and A. Abigail Payne. "Federal Sentencing Guidelines and Mandatory Minimum Sentences: Do Defendants Bargain in the Shadow of the Judge?" *Journal of Law & Economics* 42, no. S1 (1999): 245–70.

LaFountain, Robert C., Richard Y. Schauffler, Shauna M. Strickland, Sarah A. Gibson, and Ashley N. Mason. *Examining the Work of State Courts: An Analysis of 2009 State Court Caseloads*. National Center for State Courts, 2011.

Lamber, Julia, and Mary Lee Luskin. "City and Town Courts: Mapping Their Dimensions." *Indiana Law Journal* 67, no. 1 (1991): 59–83. www.repository.law.indiana.edu.

Landenberger, Nana, and Mark Lipseym. "The Positive Effects of Cognitive-Behavior Programs for Offenders: A Meta-Analysis of Factors Associated with Effective Treatment." *Journal of Experimental Criminology* 1, no. 4 (2005): 451–76.

Landon, Jenny, and Alexi Jones. "Food Insecurity If Rising, and Incarceration Puts Families at Risk." Prison Policy Initiative. February 10, 2021. www.prisonpolicy.org.

Langford, Terri. "Schools, Courts Worry About New Truancy Law." *Texas Tribune*, July 12, 2015. www.texastribune.org.

Langton, Lynn, and Jennifer Truman. "Socio-Emotional Impact of Violent Crime." U.S. Department of Justice, Bureau of Justice Statistics, NCJ 247076, 2014.

Langwiesche, William. *Inside the Sky: A Meditation on Flight*. New York: Vintage, 2002.

LaPorte, Caroline. "National Workgroup on Safe Housing for American Indian and Alaska Native Survivors of Gender-Based Violence: Lessons Learned." National Indigenous Women's Resource Center, 2020.

Latessa, Edward J., Francis T. Cullen, and Paul Gendreau. "Beyond Correctional Quackery: Professionalism and the Possibility of Effective Treatment." *Federal Probation* 66, no. 2 (2002): 43–9.

Latessa, Edward J., Shelley J. Listwan and Deborah Koetzle. *What Works (and Doesn't) in Reducing Recidivism*. New York: Anderson Publishing, 2015.

Latessa, Edward J., Shelley L. Johnson, and Deborah Koetzle. *What Works (and Doesn't) in Reducing Recidivism*. New York, Routledge, 2013.

Lattimore, Pamela K., Susan Brumbaugh, Susan, Christy Visher, Christine Lindquist, Laura Winterfield, Meghan Salas, and Janine M. Zweig. "National Portrait of SVORI: Serious and Violent Offender Initiative." Urban Institute Research Report. July 1, 2004. www.urban.org.

Law, Victoria. 20201. *Prisons Make Us Safer, and 20 Other Myths About Mass Incarceration*. Boston: Beacon Press.

Lawrence, Daniel, Camille Gourdet, Duren Banks, Michael Planty, Dulani Woods, and Brian Jackson. "Prosecutor Priorities, Challenges, and Solutions." Santa Monica, CA: RAND Corp., 2019.

Lean, Raychel. "Waltzing to Power: Despite Elections, No One Challenges Hundreds of US Judges." *LAW.COM | dbr Daily Business Review*. October 26, 2020. www.law.com.

Leape, Lucien. "Error in Medicine." *Journal of the American Medical Association* 272, no. 23 (1994): 1851–57.

LeBel, Thomas P. "An Examination of the Impact of Formerly Incarcerated Persons Helping Others." *Journal of Offender Rehabilitation* 46, nos. 1–2 (2007): 1–24.

———. "Housing as the Tip of the Iceberg in Successfully Navigating Prisoner Reentry." *Criminology & Public Policy* 16, no. 3 (2017): 891–908.

LeBel, Thomas P., Matt Richie, and Shadd Maruna."Helping Others as a Response to Reconcile a Criminal Past." *Criminal Justice and Behavior* 42, no. 1 (2015): 108–20.

LeClair, Lewis. "Note—Enforcing Criminal Laws Through Civil Proceedings: Section 1964 of the Organized Crime Control Act of 1970." *Texas Law Review* 53, no. 5 (1975): 1055.

Lee, Hedwig, Tyler McCormick, Margaret T. Hicken and Christopher Wildeman. "Racial Inequalities in Connectedness to Imprisoned Individuals in the United States." *Du Bois Review: Social Science Research on Race* 12, no. 2 (2015): 269–82.

Lee, Lynette C., and Mary K. Stohr. "A Critique and Qualified Defense of 'Correctional Quackery.'" *Journal of Contemporary Criminal Justice* 28, no. 1 (2012): 96–112.

Lefstein, Norman. *Securing Reasonable Caseloads: Ethics and Law in Public Defense*. American Bar Association, 2011.

———. "Will We Ever Succeed in Fulfilling *Gideon's* Promise?" *Indiana Law Review* 51, no. 1 (2018): 39–58.

Legal Services Corporation. "Fact Sheet: Statutory Restrictions on LSC-funded Programs." January 2010. www.lsc.gov.

Legaspi, Aletha. "Attorney General Jeff Sessions Wants to Revive D.A.R.E. Program." *Rolling Stone*, July 12, 2017, www.rollingstone.com.

Leitman, Matthew F. "A Proposed Standard of Equal Protection Review for Classifications within the Criminal Justice System That Have a Racially Disparate Impact—A Case Study of the Federal Sentencing Guidelines' Classification between Crack and Powder Cocaine." *University of Toledo Law Review* 25 (1994): 215–50.

Lemke, Albert J. "Evaluation of the Pretrial Release Pilot Program in the Mesa Municipal Court." Williamsburg, VA: National Center for State Courts Institute for Court Management (May 2009). www.ncsc.org.

Leo, Richard A. "The Criminology of Wrongful Conviction: A Decade Later." *Journal of Contemporary Criminal Justice* 33, no. 1 (2016): 82–106.

Levenson, Jill S., and Richard Tewksbury. "Collateral Damage: Family Members of Registered Sex Offenders." *American Journal of Criminal Justice* 34, no. 1 (2009): 64–5.

Levenson, Michael, and Evan Allen. "Boston Police Union Challenges Body Camera Program." *Boston Globe*, August 26, 2016. www.bostonglobe.com.

Leverentz, Andrea, Elsa Y. Chen and Johnna Christian. *Beyond Recidivism: New Approaches to Research on Prisoner Reentry and Reintegration*. New York, New York University Press, 2020.

Levin, Marc, and Michael Haugen. "Open Roads and Overflowing Jails: Addressing High Rates of Rural Pretrial Incarceration." Texas Public Policy Foundation. May 2018. https://files.texaspolicy.com.

Levine, Kay L., and Ronald Wright. "Prosecutor Risk, Maturation, and Wrongful Conviction Practice." *Law & Social Inquiry* 42, no. 3 (2017): 648–76.

Levine, Ned. "CrimeState: A Spatial Statistics Program for the Analysis of Crime Incident Locations." National Institute of Justice. December 11, 2019. https://nij.ojp.gov.

Levine, Phillip B., and Robin McKnight. "Firearms and Accidental Deaths: Evidence from the Aftermath of the Sandy Hook School Shooting." *Science* 358, no. 6368 (2017): 1324–28.

Li, Weihua, and Humera Lodhi. "Which States Are Taking on Police Reform after George Floyd?" *The Marshall Project*, June 18, 2020. www.themarshallproject.org.

Liao, T. Futing, Alan E. Bryman, and Michael S. Lewis-Beck. *The SAGE Encyclopedia of Social Science Research Methods*. 1st ed. New York: SAGE Publications, 2003.

Lichter, Daniel. "Immigration and the New Racial Diversity in Rural America." *Rural Sociology* 77, no. 1 (2012): 3–35.

Liebling, Alison, Ben Laws, Elinor Lieber, Katherine Auty, Bethany E. Schmidt, Ben Crewe, Judith Gardom, Deborah Kant, and Martha Morey. "Are Hope and Possibility Achievable in Prison?" *Howard Journal of Crime and Justice* 58, no. 1 (2019): 104–26.

Link, Nathan W., and Caterina G. Roman. "Longitudinal Associations Among Child Support Debt, Employment, and Recidivism After Prison." *Sociological Quarterly* 58, no. 1 (2017): 140–60.

Lippke, Richard L. "Pretrial Detention Without Punishment." *Res Publica* 20 (May 2014): 111–27.

Liu, Patrick, Ryan Nunn, and Jay Shambaugh. "The Economics of Bail and Pretrial Detention." *The Brookings Institute Hamilton Project: Economic Analysis*, December 2018. www.brookings.edu.

Loeffler, Charles E., Jordan Hyatt, and Greg Ridgeway. *Measuring Self-Reported Wrongful Convictions Among Prisoners*. J. Quant. Criminology (April 2018).

Loeffler, Mike, and James Wanamaner. "The Ten Guiding Principles of DWI Courts." National Center for DWI Courts. www.dwicourts.org.

Loftin, Colin, and David McDowall. "The Deterrent Effect of the Florida Felony Fire-arm Law." *Journal of Criminal Law & Criminology* 75, no. 1 (1984): 250–59.

Logan, Wayne A. "Informal Collateral Consequences." *Washington Law Review* 88, no. 3 (2013): 1107–09, 1117.

Lollar, Cortney. "Criminalizing (Poor) Fatherhood." *Alabama Law Review* 70, no. 1 (2018): 125.

Long, Wei. "Does Longer Incarceration Deter or Incapacitate Crime? Evidence from Truth-in-Sentencing Reform." *Applied Economics* 50, no. 24 (2018): 2664–76.

Looney, Adam and Nicholas Turner. *Work and Opportunity Before and After Incarcera-tion.* Washington, DC: Brookings Institution, 2018.

Lopez, German. "The Failure of Police Body Cameras." *Vox*, July 21, 2017. www.vox.com.

Los Angeles Police Department. "Critical Incident Video Release Policy—Established." 2018. https://lapdonlinestrgeacc.blob.core.usgovcloudapi.net.

Love, Margaret Colgate, Jenny M. Roberts, and Cecelia Klingele. *Collateral Conse-quences of Criminal Convictions: Law, Policy and Practice.* Eagan, MN: Thomson West, 2016.

Lovins, Brian K., Francis T. Cullen, Edward J. Latessa, and Cheryl L. Jonson. "Proba-tion Officer as a Coach: Building a New Professional Identity." *Federal Probation* 82, no. 1 (2018): 13–19.

Lucas, Lauren Sudeall. "Deconstructing the Right to Counsel." *American Constitution Society* (July 2014). www.acslaw.org.

———. "Public Defense Litigation: An Overview." *Indiana Law Review* 51, no. 1 (2018): 89–109.

Lum, Cynthia, Megan Stoltz, Christopher S. Koper, and J. Amber Scherer. "Research on Body-Worn Cameras: What We Know, What We Need to Know." *Criminology & Public Policy* 18, no. 1 (2019): 93–118.

M4BL. "Vision for Black Lives." https://m4bl.org.

Macarthur Foundation. MacArthur Fellows Program. "Jonathan Rapping." September 17, 2014. www.macfound.org.

———. "Raj Jayadev." www.macfound.org.

MacDowell, Elizabeth L. "When Courts Collide: Integrated Domestic Violence Courts and Court Pluralism." *Texas Journal of Women and the Law* 20, no. 2 (2011): 95–130.

Maciag, Mike. "Addicted to Fines." September 2019. www.governing.com.

Macmillan, Ross. "Violence and the Life Course: The Consequences of Victimization for Personal and Social Development." *Annual Review of Sociology* 27, no. 1 (2001): 1–22.

Madej, Patricia. "Who Is Larry Krasner, Philadelphia's District Attorney-Elect, and Why Is His Win a Big Deal?" *Philadelphia Inquirer*, November 8, 2017. www.inquirer.com.

Mahoney, Barry, Bruce D. Beaudin, John A. Carver, III, Daniel B. Ryan, and Richard B. Hoffman. "Pretrial Service Programs: Responsibilities and Potential." Washington, DC: National Institute of Justice, U.S. Department of Justice, 2001. www.ncjrs.gov.

Makarios, Matthew, Benjamin Steiner, and Travis F. Lawrence. "Examining the Predictors of Recidivism Among Men and Women Released From Prison in Ohio." *Criminal Justice and Behavior* 37, no. 12 (2010): 1377–91.

Malcoe, Lorraine and Bonnie M. Duran. "Intimate Partner Violence and Injury in the Lives of Low-Income Native American Women." In *Violence Against Women and Family Violence: Developments in Research, Practice, and Policy Conference Proceedings. NIJ Report, NCJ 199701*, edited by Bonnie Fisher. Washington, DC: National Institute of Justice, U.S. Department of Justice, 2004.

Mann, Kenneth. "Punitive Civil Sanctions: The Middleground Between Criminal and Civil Law." *Yale Law Journal* 101, no. 8 (1992): 1795–1873.

Martinson, Robert. "What Works? Questions and Answers about Prison Reform." *The Public Interest* 35 (1974): 22–54.

Maruna, Shadd. *Making good: How Ex-Convicts Reform and Reclaim Their Lives.* Washington, DC: American Psychological Association, 2001.

Maruna, Shadd, and Thomas P. LeBel. "Strengths-Based Approaches to Reentry: Extra Mileage toward Reintegration and Destigmatization." *Japanese Journal of Sociological Criminology* 34 (2009): 58–80.

Maruschak, Laura M. "Medical Problems of Prisoners." *Bureau of Justice Statistics* (2008).

Maruschak, Laura M., and Jennifer Bronson. "HIV in Prison." *Bureau of Justice Statistics* (2017).

Mascharka, Christopher. 2000. "Mandatory Minimum Sentences: Exemplifying the Law of Unintended Consequences." *Florida State University Law Review* 28, no. 4 (2000): 935—977.

Maskaly, John, Christopher Donner, Wesley G. Jennings, Barak Ariel, and Alex Sutherland. "The Effects of Body-Worn Cameras (BWCs) on Police and Citizen Outcomes: A State-of-the-Art Review." *Policing: An International Journal of Police Strategies & Management* 40, no. 4 (2017): 672–88.

Masquelette v. State, 579 S.W.2d 478, 479–80 (Tex. Ct. Crim. App. 1979).

Massoglia, Michael. "Incarceration as Exposure: The Prison, Infectious Disease, and Other Stress-Related Illnesses." *Journal of Health and Social Behavior* 49, no. 1 (2008): 56–71.

———. "Incarceration, Health, and Racial Disparities in Health." *Law & Society Review* 42, no. 2 (2008): 275–306.

Massoglia, Michael, and Brianna Remster. "Linkages Between Incarceration and Health." *Public Health Reports* 134, no. 1S (2019): 8S–14S.

Mauer, Marc. "The Causes and Consequences of Prison Growth in the USA." *Punishment & Society* 3, no. 1 (2001): 9–20.

Mauer, Marc, and Meda Chesney-Lind. *Invisible Punishment: The Collateral Consequences of Mass Imprisonment.* New York: New Press, 2002.

Mauer, Marc, and Ashley Nellis. *The Meaning of Life: The Case for Abolishing Life Sentences.* New York: The New Press, 2018.

Maxfield, Michael G., and Terry L. Baumer. "Final Report: Evaluation of Pretrial Home Detention with Electronic Monitoring." Washington, DC: U.S. Department of Justice (August 1991). www.ncjrs.gov.

Mayeux, Sara. *Free Justice: A History of the Public Defender in Twentieth-Century America.* Chapel Hill: University of North Carolina Press, 2020.

Mayors for a Guaranteed Income. www.mayorsforagi.org.

Mayson, Sandra G. "Bias In, Bias Out." *Yale Law Journal* 128, no. 8 (2019): 2218–300.

———. "Dangerous Defendants." *Yale Law Journal* 127 no. 3 (January 2018): 490–568. www.yalelawjournal.org.

McAfee, Leonna, and Rodrikca Taylor. "Illinois Criminal Justice Reform Law Eliminates Bail, but Doesn't Erase Bias in 'Risk Assessment' for Pretrial Imprisonment." Medill Reports Chicago, April 19, 2021. https://news.medill.northwestern.edu.

McClure, Dave, Nancy La Vigne, Mathew Lynch, Laura Golian, Daniel Lawrence, and Aili Malm. *How Body Cameras Affect Community Members' Perceptions of Police: Results from a Randomized Controlled Trial of One Agency's Pilot.* Washington, DC: Urban Institute, 2017.

McCluskey John D., Craig D. Uchida, Shellie E. Solomon, Alese Wooditch, Christine Connor, and Lauren Revier. "Assessing the Effects of Body-Worn Cameras on Procedural Justice in the Los Angeles Police Department." *Criminology* 57, no. 2 (2019): 208–36.

McCoy, William. "What Identification Do I Need for a Motel Room?" *USA Today*, August 29, 2021.

McGrath, Michael P. "Making 'What Works' Work for Rural Districts." *Federal Probation* 72, no. 2 (2008). www.uscourts.gov.

McKeon, Hon. John, and Hon. David G. Rice. "Administering Justice in Montana's Rural Courts." *Montana Law Review* 70, no. 2 (2009): 202–5. https://core.ac.uk.

McNeill, Fergus, Steve Farrall, Claire Lightowler, and Shadd Maruna. "Reexamining Evidence-Based Practice in Community Corrections: Beyond 'A Confined View' of What Works." *Justice Research and Policy* 14, no. 1, (2012): 35–60.

Meagher, Tom, and Christie Thompson. "So You Think a New Prison Will Save Your Town?" The Marshall Project, June 14, 2016.

Meares, Tracey L. "Three Objections to the Use of Empiricism in Criminal Law and Procedure—And Three Answers." *University of Illinois Law Review* 2002, no. 4 (2002): 851–73.

Medina, Daniel A. "The Progressive Prosecutors Blazing a New Path for the US Justice System." *The Guardian*, July 23, 2019. www.theguardian.com.

Medwed, Daniel S. *Prosecution Complex: America's Race to Convict and Its Impacts on the Innocent.* New York: New York University Press, 2012.

Meeker, Katherine A., Eryn Nicole O'Neal, and Brittany E. Hayes. "Policing and Prosecuting Sexual Assault: An Examination of Arrest and Initial Filing Decisions in Cases Involving Adolescent Complainants." *Justice Quarterly*, 38, no. 5 (2019): 1–22.

"In Memoriam: Kenneth P. Thompson 1966–2016." *Justice News: The Brooklyn District Attorney's Office Newsletter*, October 2016.

Menefee, Michael R. "The Role of Bail and Pretrial Detention in the Reproduction of Racial Inequalities." *Sociology Compass* 12, no. 5 (2018): e12576.

Menendez, Matthew, Michael Crowley, Lauren-Brooke Eisen, and Noah Atchison. "The Steep Costs of Criminal Justice Fees and Fines." Brennan Center for Justice, November 21, 2019. www.brennancenter.org.

Merritt, Nancy, Tony Fain, and Susan Turner. "Oregon's Get Tough Sentencing Reform: A Lesson in Justice System Adaptation." *Criminology & Public Policy* 5, no. 1 (2006): 5–36.

Mesa Police Department. *On-Officer Body Camera System: Program Evaluation and Recommendations.* Mesa, AZ: Mesa Police Department, 2015.

Messenger, Tony. "*Gardner*'s New Conviction Integrity Unit Alleges Perjury and Misconduct in 1994 Murder Case." *St. Louis Post-Dispatch*, July 24, 2019.

Metcalfe, Christi, and Ted Chiricos. "Race, Plea, and Charge Reduction: An Assessment of Racial Disparities in the Plea Process." *Justice Quarterly* 35, no. 2 (2018): 223–53.

Metraux, Stephen, and Dennis P. Culhane. "Homeless Shelter Use and Reincarceration Following Prison Release." *Criminology & Public Policy* 3, no. 2 (2004): 139–60.

Metzger, Pamela. "Why Rural Americans Struggle for Equal Justice." *Dallas Morning News*, November 24, 2019. www.dallasnews.com.

———. "Rural Justice System Low on Pretrial Resources Leave Some to Languish, Die." *USA Today*, December 13, 2019. www.usatoday.com.

Metzger, Pamela, and Gregory Guggenmos, "COVID-19 and the Ruralization of U.S. Criminal Court Systems." *University of Chicago Law Review Online* (Nov. 16, 2020). https://lawreviewblog.uchicago.edu.

Metzger, Pamela, and Janet Hoeffel. "Criminal (Dis)Appearance." *George Washington Law Review* 88, no. 2 (2020): 392.

Meyn, Ion. "Constructing Separate and Unequal Courtooms." July 27, 2020: 1–50. https://papers.ssrn.com.

Midkiff, Sarah. "Voter Turnout On The Local Level Is Plummeting. It's Time To Change That." *Refinery29*. June 19, 2020. www.refinery29.com.

Miethe, Terence D. "Charging and Plea Bargaining Practices Under Determinate Sentencing: An Investigation of the Hydraulic Displacement of Discretion." *Journal of Criminal Law & Criminology* 78, no. 1 (1987): 155–76.

Miethe, Terence D., and Charles A. Moore. *Sentencing Guidelines: Their Effect in Minnesota.* Washington, DC: National Institute of Justice, 1989.

Miles-Thrope, Stacy. "Trauma for the Tough-Minded Prosecutor." *Texas Prosecutor Journal* (July–August 2016): 34–39.

Miller, Anna M. "People Are Fleeing Coronavirus Hotspots for Rural Areas that Don't Want Them to Come. Experts Say it's a Natural 'Fight or Flight' Response." *Business Insider*. March 26, 2020. www.businessinsider.com.

Miller, Cassie. "The Two-Tiered Justice System: Money Bail in Historical Perspective." Southern Poverty Law Center, June 6, 2017. www.splcenter.org.

Miller, Frederick. "Rural Courts are Fertile Ground for Caseload Management: The Case Processing and Delay Reduction in Rural Courts Project." National Center for State Courts, 1991. https://cdm16501.contentdm.oclc.org.

Miller, Joel, and Vijay F. Chillar. "Do Police Body Worn Cameras Reduce Citizen Fatalities? Results of a Country Wide Natural Experiment." *Journal of Quantitative Criminology* (2021): 1–32. https://doi.org/10.1007/s10940-021-09513-w.

Miller, Justin. "The New Reformer DAs." *American Prospect*, January 2, 2018. https://prospect.org.

Miller, Larry S., and Michael C. Brawell. "Teaching Criminal Justice Research: An Experiential Model." *American Journal of Criminal Justice* 13, no. 1 (1988): 26–39.

Miller, Lindsay, Jessica Toliver, and Police Executive Research Forum. *Implementing a Body-Worn Camera Program: Recommendations and Lessons Learned*. Washington, DC: Office of Community Oriented Policing Services, 2014.

Miller, Lisa L. *The Myth of Mob Rule: Violent Crime & Democratic Politics*. New York: Oxford University Press, 2016.

Miller, Marc, and Ronald Wright. "The Black Box." *Iowa Law Review* 94, no. 1 (2008): 125–96.

Miller, Matthew, Deborah Azrael, and David Hemenway. "Firearm Availability and Unintentional Firearm Deaths." *Accident Analysis & Prevention* 33, no. 4 (2001): 477–84.

Miller, Matthew, Lisa Hepburn, and Deborah Azrael. "Firearm Acquisition Without Background Checks: Results of a National Survey." *Annals of Internal Medicine* 166, no. 4 (2017): 233–39.

Minnesota Judicial Branch. "Access and Service Delivery 2 Committee: Report to Judicial Council." December 14, 2009. www.mncourts.gov.

Minton, Todd D., and Zhen Zeng. "Jail Inmates in 2020—Statistical Tables." Washington, DC: U.S. Department of Justice, Bureau of Justice Statistics, 2021.

Mintz, Evan. "How Criminal Justice Reform Fared in the 2020 Elections." *Arnold Ventures*. November 5, 2020. www.arnoldventures.org.

Missouri v. Johnson, Opinion of the Court, Missouri Sup. Ct. No. SC98393 (2021).

Missouri v. Johnson, Respondent's Substitute Brief, Missouri Sup. Ct. No. SC98393, 7 (2003).

Mitchell, Kelly Lyn. "State Sentencing Guidelines: A Garden Full of Variety." *Federal Probation* 81, no. 2 (2017): 21–36.

Mitchell, Ojmarrh. "A Meta-Analysis of Race and Sentencing Research: Explaining the Inconsistencies." *Journal of Quantitative Criminology* 21, no. 4 (2005): 439–66.

Monuteaux, Michael C., Lois K. Lee, David Hemenway, Rebekah Mannix, and Eric W. Fleegler. "Firearm Ownership and Violent Crime in the US: An Ecologic Study." *American Journal of Preventive Medicine* 49, no. 2 (2015): 207–14.

Moody's Investor Service. "Moody's: Rural America Faces Growing Economic and Demographic Troubles." July 19, 2018. www.moodys.com.

Moore, Charles A., and Terance D. Miethe. "Regulated and Unregulated Sentencing Decisions: An Analysis of First-Year Practices under Minnesota's Felony Sentencing Guidelines." *Law and Society Review* 20, no. 2 (1986): 253–78.

Moore, Janet. "The Antidemocratic Sixth Amendment." *Washington Law Review* 91, no. 4 (2016): 1705–67.

———. "Isonomy, Austerity, and the Right to Choose Counsel." *Indiana Law Review* 51, no. 1 (2018): 167–209.

———. "Reviving *Escobedo*." *Loyola Law Review* 50, no. 4 (2019): 1015–49.

Moore, Janet, and Andrew LB Davies. "Knowing Defense." *Ohio State Journal of Criminal Law* 14, no. 2 (2017): 345–71.

Moore, Janet, Raj Jayadev, and Marla Sandys. "Make Them Hear You: Participatory Defense and the Struggle for Criminal Justice Reform." *Albany Law Review* 78, no. 3 (2015): 1281–1316.

Moore, Janet, Vicki L. Plano Clark, Lori A. Foote, and Jacinda K. Dariotis. "Attorney–Client Communication in Public Defense: A Qualitative Examination." *Criminal Justice Policy Review* 31, no. 6 (2020): 908–38.

Morenoff, Jeffrey D., and David J. Harding. *Final Technical Report: Neighborhoods, Recidivism, and Employment Among Returning Prisoners*. National Criminal Justice Reference Service, 2011. www.ncjrs.gov.

Moriarty, Laura. *Criminal Justice Technology in the 21st Century: Third Edition*. Charles C. Thomas Pub. Ltd, 2017.

Morrison, Aaron. "Ballot Results: Groundswell Support for Criminal Justice Reform." *Christian Science Monitor*. November 23, 2020. www.csmonitor.com.

Morrow, Weston J., Charles M. Katz, and David E. Choate. "Assessing the Impact of Police Body-Worn Cameras on Arresting, Prosecuting, and Convicting Suspects of Intimate Partner Violence." *Police Quarterly* 19, no. 3 (2016): 303–25.

Mościcki, Eve K. "Epidemiology of Completed and Attempted Suicide: Toward a Framework for Prevention." *Clinical Neuroscience Research* 1, no. 5 (2001): 310–23.

Moran, Judith D. "Fragmented Courts and Child Protection Cases." *Family Court Review* 40, no. 4 (2002): 488, 492.

Morgan, Rachel E., and Barbara A. Oudekerk. "Criminal Victimization, 2018." U.S. Department of Justice, Bureau of Justice Statistics, NCJ 253043, 2019.

Mothers in Charge (@phillymic). July 20, 2020. https://twitter.com.

Mowen, Thomas J. "The Collateral Consequences of 'Criminalized' School Punishment on Disadvantaged Parents and Families." *Urban Review* 49, no. 5 (2017): 840–48.

Muller, Sara Wakefield, Emily A. Wang, and Christopher Wildeman. "What Percentage of Americans Have Ever Had a Family Member Incarcerated?: Evidence from the Family History of Incarceration Survey (FamHIS)." *Socius: Sociological Research for a Dynamic World Volume* 49, no. 5 (2019): 1–45.

Mumola, Christopher. *Incarcerated Parents and their Children*. Washington DC: Bureau of Justice Statistics, 2000. https://files.eric.ed.gov.

Murray, Brian M. "Are Collateral Consequences Deserved?" *Notre Dame Law Review* 94, no. 3 (2020): 1031, 1034.

Mustard, David B. "Racial, Ethnic, and Gender Disparities in Sentencing: Evidence from the US Federal Courts." *Journal of Law & Economics* 44, no. 1 (2001): 285–314.

Myers, Nicole Marie. "Eroding the Presumption of Innocence: Pretrial Detention and the Use of Conditional Release on Bail." *British Journal of Criminology* 57, no. 3 (May 2017): 664–83.

Nagel, Ilene H., and Stephen J. Schulhofer. "A Tale of Three Cities: An Empirical Study of Charging and Bargaining Practices under the Federal Sentencing Guidelines." *Southern California Law Review* 66, no. 1 (1992): 501–66.

Najmabadi, Shannon and Jay Root. "New Texas Law Protects Rent-to-Own Customers Against Criminal Prosecution." *Texas Tribune*, June 21, 2019. www.texastribune.org.

Natapoff, Alexandra. "Speechless: The Silencing of Criminal Defendants." *New York University Law Review* 80, no. 5 (2005): 1449–1504.

National Association for Public Defense. "Statement of Purpose." www.publicdefenders.us.

National Association of Counties. "The Stepping Up Initiative: Reducing Mental Illness in Rural Jails." www.naco.org.

National Association of Criminal Defense Lawyers. "Resolution Concerning Pretrial Release and Limited Use of Financial Bond." July 28, 2012. www.nacdl.org.

National Basketball Association. "Milwaukee Bucks Players' Statement Following Boycott of Game 5." August 26, 2020, www.nba.com.

National Basketball Players Association. "Joint NBA and NBPA Statement." August 28, 2020, https://nbpa.com.

National Center for State Courts. *Implementation of a Criminal Caseflow Management Plan: A Report to the North Carolina Commission on the Administration of Law and Justice.* August 17, 2016. www.nccourts.gov.

National Conference of State Legislatures. "Pretrial Release Violations and Bail Forfeiture." June 28, 2018. www.ncsl.org.

National Congress of American Indians. *VAWA 2013's Special Domestic Violence Criminal Jurisdiction (SDVCJ) Five-Year Report.* 2018.

National Congress of American Indians. *Policy Update: 2019 Annual Convention and Marketplace.* 2019.

National Health Service Corps. "About Us." https://nhsc.hrsa.gov.

National Indian Child Welfare Association. March 2020. *Child and Family Policy Update.* www.nicwa.org.

National Inquiry into Missing and Murdered Indigenous Women and Girls. "Reclaiming Power and Place: The Final Report of the National Inquiry into Missing and Murdered Indigenous Women and Girls Volume 1a." 2019.

National Institute of Corrections. "Measuring What Matters: Outcome and Performance Measures for the Pretrial Services Field." Washington, DC: U.S. Department of Justice (August 2011). https://s3.amazonaws.com/static.nicic.gov.

National Institute of Justice. "Crime Solutions." https://crimesolutions.ojp.gov.

National Registry of Exonerations. "Race and Wrongful Convictions in the United States." March 7, 2017. www.law.umich.edu.

National Research Council. *The Growth of Incarceration in the United States: Exploring Causes and Consequences.* Washington, DC: National Academies Press, 2014.

Neath, Scarlet. "Understanding Jail Growth in Rural America." Vera Institute of Justice. June 16, 2017. www.vera.org.

Nellis, Ashley. "Tinkering with Life: A Look at the Inappropriateness of Life Without Parole as an Alternative to the Death Penalty." *University of Miami Law Review* 67, no. 2 (2012): 439–57.

———. *Still Life: America's Increasing Use of Life and Long-Term Sentences*. Washington, DC: The Sentencing Project, 2017. www.sentencingproject.org.

Nellis, Ashley, and Ryan S. King. *No Exit: The Expanding Use of Life Sentences in America*. Washington, DC: The Sentencing Project, 2009. www.prisonpolicy.org.

Neubauer, David W., and Henry F. Fradella. *Americas Courts and the Criminal Justice System*. 13th ed. Boston: Cengage, 2019.

Nev. Rev. Stat. §§ 4.010(2) and (3).

New Jersey Commission of Investigation. "Inside Out: Questionable and Abusive Practices in New Jersey's Bail-Bond Industry." May 2014. https://dspace.njstatelib.org.

"New Text Message Reminders for Summons Recipients Improves Attendance in Court and Dramatically Cuts Warrants." The Official Website of the City of New York, January 24, 2018. www1.nyc.gov.

N.H. Rev. Stat. § 599:1.

N.J. CONST. art I. § II.

N.J. REV. STAT. § 2A:162–15 et. seq. (2018).

N.M. Stat. §§ 35-2-1(D), 35-3-4(A), § 35-14-2(A), 35-14-3.

N.Y. State Rifle & Pistol Ass'n, Inc. v. Beach, 19-156-cv (2nd Cir. Aug. 26, 2020).

New York v. Boone, Brief of Amicus Curiae National Association of Criminal Defense & Educational Fund, Inc., N.Y. Court of Appeals No. APL-2016-00015 (2017).

Noble, Gail. "Standing Up to the Court." Albert Cobarrubias Justice Project, July 16, 2011. https://acjusticeproject.org.

Noonan, Margaret. "Mortality in Local Jails, 2000–2014—Statistical Tables." Washington, DC: U.S. Department of Justice, Bureau of Justice Statistics (December 2016). www.bjs.gov.

North Carolina Actual Innocence Inquiry Commission. "About." http://innocencecommission-nc.gov.

North Carolina Judicial Branch. "North Carolina Commission on the Administration of Law and Justice." 2017. https://nccalj.org.

Norwood, Candice. "Body Cameras Are Seen as Key to Police Reform. But Do They Increase Accountability?" PBS NewsHour, June 25, 2020. www.pbs.org.

Nugent-Borakove, E., B. Mahoney, and D. Witcomb. "Strengthening Rural Courts: Challenges and Progress." *Future Trends in State Courts*. 2011. www.jmijustice.org.

Obama, Barack. "The President's Role in Advancing Criminal Justice Reform." *Harvard Law Review* 130, no. 3 (2017): 813–66.

ODS Consulting. *Body Worn Video Projects in Paisley and Aberdeen, Self Evaluation*. 2011. Glasgow: ODS Consulting.

The Office of the Attorney General. "Memorandum to The United States Attorneys and Assistant Attorney General for the Criminal Division." August 12, 2013. www.justice.gov.

Office of the Legislative Auditor General, State of Utah. *A Performance Audit of the Operating Efficiency of the Utah State Court System*. Report to the Utah Legislature No. 2011–11. Salt Lake City, UT, 2011.

———. *A Performance Audit of Utah's Monetary Bail System: A Report to the Utah Legislature*. January 2017. https://le.utah.gov.

Office of Press Secretary. *Executive Order on Establishing a Task Force on Missing and Murdered American Indians and Alaskan Natives*. November 26, 2019.

Office of Public Affairs. "Attorney General William P. Barr Launces National Strategy to Address Missing and Murdered Indigenous Persons." U.S. Department of Justice. November 2019. www.justice.gov.

Ogletree, Charles J., and Austin Sarat, eds. *Life Without Parole: America's New Death Penalty?* New York: New York University Press, 2012.

Oleson, James C., Scott W. VanBenschoten, Charles R. Robinson, and Christopher T. Lowenkamp. "Training to See Risk: Measuring the Accuracy of Clinical and Actuarial Risk Assessments Among Federal Probation Officers." *Federal Probation* 75, no. 2 (2011): 52–56. www.uscourts.gov.

Olson, Erik J., Mark Hoofnagle, Elinore J. Kaufman, Charles William Schwab, Patrick M. Reilly, and Mark J. Seamon. "American Firearm Homicides: The Impact of Your Neighbors." *Journal of Trauma and Acute Care Surgery* 86, no. 5 (2019): 797–802.

Olver, Mark E., Keira C. Stockdale, and J. Stephen Wormith. "A Meta-Analysis of Predictors of Offender Treatment Attrition and Its Relationship to Recidivism." *Journal of Consulting and Clinical Psychology* 79, no. 1 (2011): 6–21.

Onwuachi-Willig, Angela, and Ifeoma Ajunwa. "Combating Discrimination Against the Formerly Incarcerated in the Labor Market." *Northwestern University Law Review* 112, no. 6 (2018): 1385–1416.

Oppel, Richard. "Sentencing Shift Gives New Leverage to Prosecutor." *New York Times*, September 25, 2015. www.nytimes.com.

Or. Rev. Stat. §§ 3.050, 51.050, § 51.240(1)(e)(B) and (C), 221.339(2).

Orchowsky, Stan. "An Introduction to Evidence-Based Practices." 2014. www.ncjrs.gov.

Oregon State Bar. *Task Force on Access to State Courts for Persons with Disabilities*. Oregon Judicial Department, 2006. www.osbar.org.

Orians, Kelly E. "'I'll Say I'm Home, I Won't Say I'm Free': Persistent Barriers to Housing, Employment, and Financial Security for Formerly Incarcerated People in Low-Income Communities of Color." *National Black Law Journal* 25, no. 1 (2016): 24–57.

Orians, Kelly and Thomas Frampton. "In Defense of Reentry: A Response to Shreya Subramani's Productive Separations." *Fordham Urban Law Journal* 47, no. 4 (2020): 993–1008.

Orrell, Brent. Ed. *Rethinking Reentry*. Washington, DC: American Enterprise Institute, 2020.

Ortiz, Hankie P. *Tiwahe Initiative: Building Tribal Programs That Invest in Children, Youth and Families While Preserving Tribal Cultural Values and Traditions*. Washington, DC: U.S. Department of the Interior, Bureau of Indian Affairs, 2015.

Ostrom, Brian, and Roger Hanson. *Efficiency, Timeliness, and Quality: A New Perspective from Nine State Criminal Trial Courts*. Research Brief. National Institute of Justice, 2000.

Otterbein, Holly. "In the Trump Era, Voter Turnout Skyrockets in Philly's District Attorney Race." *Philadelphia*. (Philadelphia: PA), November 8, 2017. www.phillymag. com.

Owens, Catherine, David Mann, and Rory McKenna. *The Essex Body Worn Video Trial: The Impact of Body Worn Video on Criminal Justice Outcomes of Domestic Abuse Incidents*. London: College of Policing, 2014.

P.Z. v. New Jersey, 21-175. [J.S.] v. [P.Z.], No. FV-03-001864-18, Superior Court of New Jersey. Judgments entered May 25, 2018, June 1, 2018, and June 5, 2018.

Paceley, Rebecca. "The Power of Participatory Defense." *Gainesville Iguana*, November 13, 2018. https://gainesvilleiguana.org.

Page, Joshua, Victoria Piehowski, and Joe Soss. "A Debt of Care: Commercial Bail and the Gendered Logic of Criminal Justice Predation." *RSF: The Russell Sage Foundation Journal of the Social Sciences* 5, no. 1 (February 2019): 150–72.

Pager, Devah. "The Mark of a Criminal Record." Chicago: University of Chicago. 2003. https://scholar.harvard.edu.

———. *Marked: Race, Crime, and Finding Work in An Era of Mass Incarceration*. Chicago, University of Chicago Press, 2008.

Paquette, Danielle. "8,500 Residents, 12 Attorneys: America's Rural Lawyer Shortage." *Washington Post*, August 25, 2014. www.washingtonpost.com.

Parent, Dale, Terence Dunworth, Douglas McDonald, and William Rhodes. *Mandatory Sentencing*. Washington, DC: U.S. Department of Justice, 1997. www.ncjrs.gov.

Parker, Kim, Juliana Horowitz, Anna Brown, Richard Fry, D'Vera Cohn, and Ruth Igielnik. "What Unites and Divides Urban, Suburban and Rural Communities: Demographic and Economic Trends in Urban, Suburban and Rural Communities." Pew Research Center. May 2018. www.pewsocialtrends.org.

Participatory Defense Network. "Hubs." www.participatorydefense.org.

———. "Time Saved." www.participatorydefense.org.

Pearlin, Leonard I. "The Sociological Study of Stress." *Journal of Health and Social Behavior* 30, no. 3 (1989): 241–56.

Peerally, Mohammed, Susan Carr, Justin Waring, and Mary Dixon-Woods. "The Problem with Root Cause Analysis." *BMJ Quality & Safety* (2017): 417–22.

Pelfrey, William V. Jr., and Steven Keener. "Police Body Worn Cameras: A Mixed Method Approach Assessing Perceptions of Efficacy." *Policing: An International Journal of Police Strategies & Management* 39, no. 3 (2016): 491–506.

Pennington, Liana. "An Empirical Study of One Participatory Defense Program Facilitated by Public Defender Office." *Ohio State Journal of Criminal Law* 14, no. 2 (2017): 603–27.

People, Julie. "Do Some Types of Legal Problems Trigger Other Legal Problems?" *Updating Justice*, no. 37 (2014). www.lawfoundation.net.au.

Perrow, Charles. *Normal Accidents: Living with High Risk Technologies*. Princeton: Princeton University Press, 2000.

Perry, Barbara. "From Ethnocide to Ethnoviolence: Layers of Native American Victimization." *Contemporary Justice Review* 5, no. 3 (2002): 231–47.

———. "Nobody Trusts Them! Under- and Over-Policing Native American Communities." *Critical Criminology* 14, no. 4 (2006): 411–44.

———. "Impacts of Disparate Policing in Indian Country." *Policing & Society* 19, no. 3 (2009): 263–81.

Perry, Steven W., and Duren Banks. *Prosecutors in State Courts, 2007—Statistical Tables*. Bureau of Justice Statistics, 2011. www.bjs.gov.

Petersen, Nick. "Low-Level, but High-Speed: Assessing Pretrial Detention Effects on the Timing and Content of Misdemeanor versus Felony Guilty Pleas." *Justice Quarterly* 36, no. 7 (2019): 1314–35.

Petersilia, etersilia, Joan R. *The Influence of Criminal Justice Research*, Santa Monica, CA: RAND Corporation, 1987.

———. *When Prisoners Come Home: Parole and Prisoner Reentry*. New York: Oxford University Pres, 2003.

Pew Research Center, "5 Facts About Crime in the U.S." October 17, 2019. www.pewresearch.org.

Pfaff, John F. *Locked In: The True Causes of Mass Incarceration—and How to Achieve Real Reform*. New York: Basic Books, 2017.

Philadelphia Review Team. *Report of the Philadelphia Event Review Team on the Lex Street Massacre*. Philadelphia: Quattrone Center for the Fair Administration of Justice, 2015.

Philip, Meghna. "Where Criminal Defense Meets Civil Action: An Interview with Runa Rajagopal." *New York University Review of Law & Social Change* 40 (2015): 1–81.

Phillips, Mary T. "A Decade of Bail Research in New York City, Final Report." New York City Criminal Justice Agency, August 2012. www.prisonpolicy.org.

Phillips, Scott W. "Eyes Are Not Cameras: The Importance of Integrating Perceptual Distortions, Misinformation, and False Memories into the Police Body Camera Debate." *Policing: A Journal of Policy and Practice* 12, no. 1 (2016): 91–99.

Piehl, Anne, and Shawn Bushway. "Measuring and Explaining Charge Bargaining." *Journal of Quantitative Criminology* 23, no. 2 (2007): 105–25.

Pinard, Michael. "Broadening the Holistic Mindset: Incorporating Collateral Consequences and Reentry into Criminal Defense Lawyering." *Fordham Urban Law Journal* 31, no. 4 (2004): 1067–95.

———. "Reflections and Perspectives on Reentry and Collateral Consequences." *Journal of Criminal Law & Criminology* 100, no. 3 (2010): 1213–24.

Pinto, Nick. "The Bail Trap." *New York Times*, August 13, 2014. www.nytimes.com.

Pishko, Jessica. "The Shocking Lack of Lawyers in Rural America." *The Atlantic*, July 18, 2019, www.theatlantic.com.

Pizarro, Jesenia M., William Terrill, and Charles A. LoFaso. "The Impact of Investigation Strategies and Tactics on Homicide Clearance." *Homicide Studies* 24, no. 1 (2020): 3–24.

Pleasance, P., Nigel Balmer, Alexy Buck, M. Smith, and Ash Patel. "Mounting Problems: Further Evidence of the Social, Economic and Health Consequences of Civil Justice Problems." (2007): 67–68. www.researchgate.net.

Politico. "5 New Policy Ideas for Fixing Life After Prison." 2020. *Politico.* December 20, 2020. www.politico.com.

Politico Staff. "Biden vs. Trump: Who's the Actual Criminal Justice Reformer?" April 23, 2020, www.politico.com.

Pompoco, Amanda, John Wooldredge, Melissa Lugo, Carrie Sullivan, and Edward J. Latessa. "Reducing Inmate Misconduct and Prison Returns with Facility Education Programs." *Criminology & Public Policy* 16, no. 2 (2017): 515–47.

Pope, Leah, and Ayesha Delaney-Brumsey. *Creating a Culture of Safety: Sentinel Event Review of Suicide and Self-Harm in Correctional Facilities.* New York: Vera Institute, 2016.

Porter, Eduardo. "The Hard Truths of Trying to 'Save' the Rural Economy." *New York Times*, December 14, 2018. www.nytimes.com.

Portland State University. "Too Few People Choose Our Local Leaders." 2016. www. whovotesformayor.org.

Positive Youth Justice Initiative Brief. "Community Victories: Summary of Policy Achievements." December 2019: 3–4. www.nccdglobal.org.

Pound, Roscoe. "The Place of the Family Court in the Judicial System." *Journal of the American Institute of Criminal Law and Criminology* 24, no. 6 (1959): 1014–18.

Pratt, Travis C., and Francis T. Cullen. "Assessing Macro-Level Predictors and Theories of Crime: A Meta-Analysis." *Crime and Justice* 32 (2005): 373–450.

President's Task Force on 21st Century Policing. *Final Report of the President's Task Force on 21st Century Policing.* Washington, DC: Office of Community Oriented Policing Services, 2015.

Pretrial Justice Center for Courts. "Pretrial Services & Supervision." www.ncsc.org.

Pretrial Justice Institute. "How to Fix Pretrial Justice." 2018. www.pretrial.org.

———. "Updated Position on Pretrial Risk Assessment Tools." February 7, 2020. www. pretrial.org.

———. "Using Technology to Enhance Pretrial Services: Current Applications and Future Possibilities." 2012. http://thecrimereport.s3.amazonaws.com.

Primus, Eve Brensike. "Culture as a Structural Problem in Indigent Defense." *Minnesota Law Review* 100, no. 5 (2016): 1769 - 1821. https://repository.law.umich.edu.

———. "Defense Counsel and Public Defense." In *Reforming Criminal Justice*: *Pretrial and Trial Processes*, edited by Erik Luna, vol. 3, 121–45. Phoenix: Arizona State University, 2017.

———. "Disaggregating Ineffective Assistance of Counsel Doctrine: Four Forms of Constitutional Ineffectiveness." *Stanford Law Review* 72, no. 6 (2020): 1581–1653.

Prison Policy Initiative. "Detaining the Poor." 2016. www.prisonpolicy.org.

Prosecutors' Center for Excellence. "Who We Are." www.pceinc.org.

Pruitt, Lisa, Amanda Kool, Lauren Sudeall, Michele Statz, Danielle Conway, and Hannah Haksgaard. "Legal Deserts: A Multi-State Perspective on Rural Access to Justice." *Harvard Law and Policy Review* 13, no. 1 (2018): 15–156. https://harvardlpr.com.

Pullen, Erin, and Carrie Oser. "Barriers to Substance Abuse Treatment in Rural and Urban Communities: A Counselor Perspective." *Substance Abuse and Misuse* 49, no. 7 (2014): 891–901.

Pupilidy, Ivan, and Crista Vessel. "The Learning Review: Adding to the Accident Investigation Toolbox." *European Commission Joint Research Center.* November 2017.

Quandt, Katie Rose, and Alexi Jones. "Research Roundup: Incarceration Can Cause Lasting Damage to Mental Health Incarceration Can Trigger and Worsen Symptoms of Mental Illness—And Those Effects Can Last Long After Someone Leaves the Prison Gates." Blog of the Prison Policy Institute. May 13, 2021.

Rabuy, Bernadette, and Daniel Kopf. *Prisons of Poverty: Uncovering the Pre-Incarceration Incomes of the Imprisoned.* Prison Policy Institute. 2015. www.prisonpolicy.org.

Rad, Abdul, Wenshu Yang, and Frankie Wunschel. "The Arrest-Jail Admission Gap." Vera Institute of Justice. January 10, 2020. www.vera.org.

Radelet, M. L., H. A. Bedau, and C. E. Putnam. *In Spite of Innocence.* Boston: Northeastern University Press, 1992.

Rankin, Susan. "Punishing Homelessness." New Criminal Law Review, 22, no. 1 (2019): 99–135.

Raper, Stephen E., Lee A. Fleisher, David L. Mayer, Risa V. Ferman, and Kevin Steele. "Using Root Cause Analysis to Study Prosecutorial Error: A Collaboration between the Montgomery County (Pennsylvania) District Attorney's Office and the Quattrone Center for the Fair Administration of Justice." *Villanova Law Review* 62, no. 6 (2018): 13–28.

Rahman, Insha. "Highlights of the 2019 Bail Reform Law." Vera Institute of Justice, July 2019. www.vera.org.

Ramirez, Juan R., and William D. Crano. "Deterrence and Incapacitation: An Interrupted Time-Series Analysis of California's Three-Strikes Law." *Journal of Applied Social Psychology* 33, no. 1 (2003): 110–144.

Ramirez, Lee. "Santa Clara County Upholds Sanctuary Policy; No Cooperation With ICE." KPIX5 CBS, June 4, 2019. https://sanfrancisco.cbslocal.com.

Raphael, Steven, and Michael A. Stoll. *Why Are So Many Americans in Prison?* New York: Russell Sage Foundation, 2013.

Raphling, John. "Plead Guilty, Go Home. Plead Not Guilty, Stay in Jail." *Los Angeles Times,* May 17, 2017. www.latimes.com.

Rapping, Jonathan. *Gideon's Promise: A Public Defender Movement to Transform Criminal Justice.* Boston: Beacon Press, 2020.

Ray, Rashawn. "What Does Defund the Police Mean and Does It Have Merit?" June 19, 2020, www.brookings.edu.

Ray, Rashawn, Kris Marsh, and Connor Powelson. "Can Cameras Stop the Killings? Racial Differences in Perceptions of the Effectiveness of Body-Worn Cameras in Police Encounters." *Sociological Forum* 32, no. S1 (2017): 1032–50.

Reason, James. *Human Error*. Cambridge: Cambridge University Press, 1990.

Reaves, Brian A. *Felony Defendants in Large Urban Counties, 2009*. Bureau of Justice Statistics, 2013. www.bjs.gov.

———. "State Court Processing Statistics: Felony Defendants in Large Urban Counties, 2009-Statistical Tables." Washington, DC: U.S. Department of Justice, Bureau of Justice Statistics (December 2013). www.bjs.gov.

Reed, Tom, and John Chisholm. *From Funnels to Large-Scale Irrigation: Changing the Criminal Justice System Paradigm to Improve Public Health and Safety*. Cambridge, MA: Malcolm Weiner Center for Social Policy, 2019.

Reiman, Jeffrey and Paul Leighton. *The Rich Get Richer and the Poor Get Prison: Thinking Critically About Class and Criminal Justice*. 12th ed. New York: Routledge, 2020.

Riessman, Frank. "The 'Helper' Therapy Principle." *Social Work*, 10, no. 2 (1965): 27–32.

Reno, Janet. "Remarks of The Honorable Janet Reno Attorney General of the United States on Reentry Court Initiative." John Jay College of Criminal Justice. February 10, 2000.

Renshaw, Benjamin H. "Prisoners in 1980." *Bureau of Justice Statistics Bulletin*. May 1981.

Rhim, Ji Hyun. "Left at the Gate: How Gate Money Could Help Prisoners Reintegrate Upon Release." *Cornell Law Review* 106, no. 3 (2021): 783–814.

Rhodes, William, Gerald Gaes, Jeremy Luallen, Ryan King, Tom Rich, and Michael Shively. "Following Incarceration, Most Released Offenders Never Return to Prison." *Crime & Delinquency* 64, no. 7 (2016): 1003–25.

Ritter, Nancy. "Testing a Concept and Beyond: Can the Criminal Justice System Adopt a Non-Blaming Practice?" *National Institute of Justice Journal* (2015). www.nij.gov.

Rivas, Rebecca. "Pending Law to Correct Wrongful Convictions Could Depend on Missouri Attorney General." *Missouri Independent* (June 1, 2021).

Robbennolt, Jennifer. "Apologies and Medical Error." *Clinical Orthopedics and Related Research* (Feb. 2008). www.ncbi.nlm.nih.gov.

Roberts, Dorothy E. "Abolition Constitutionalism." *Harvard Law Review* 133, no. 1 (2019): 1–122.

Roberts, Jenny. "*Gundy* and the Civil-Criminal Divide." *Ohio State Journal of Criminal Law* 17, no. 1 (2019): 207–26.

Robinson, Paul H. "Life Without Parole Under Modern Theories of Punishment." In *Life Without Parole: America's New Death Penalty?*, edited by Charles J. Ogletree and Austin Sarat, 138–66. New York: New York University Press, 2012.

———. "The Criminal-Civil Distinction and the Utility of Desert." *Boston University Law Review* 76, nos. 1–2 (1996): 201–14.

Roman, Caterina G., and Jeremy Travis. "Where Will I Sleep Tomorrow? Housing, Homelessness, and the Returning Prisoner." *Housing Policy Debate* 17, no. 2 (2006): 389–418.

Romero, Maybell. "Profit-Driven Prosecution and the Competitive Bidding Process." *Journal of Criminal Law & Criminology* 107, no. 2 (2017): 161–212.

Roosevelt, Franklin Delano. "Address of the President Delivered to the National Parole Conference. East Room of the Whitehouse." (April 17, 1939).

Rosay, André B. "Violence Against American Indian and Alaska Native Women and Men." National Institute of Justice (2016).

Roskam, Kelly, and Vicka Chaplin. "The Gun Violence Restraining Order: An Opportunity for Common Ground in the Gun Violence Debate." *Dev. Mental Health L.* 36, no. 1 (2017): 1–22.

Ross, Catherine J. "The Failure of Fragmentation: The Promise of a System of Unified Family Courts." *Family Law Quarterly* 32, no. 1 (1998): 7–8.

Rossmo, Kim, and Jocelyn Pollack. "Confirmation Bias and Other Systemic Causes of Wrongful Convictions: A Sentinel Events Perspective." *Northeastern Law Review* 11 (2019): 791–834.

Rothman, David J. *The Discovery of the Asylum: Social Order and Disorder in the New Republic.* New York: New York University Press, 1971.

Rudolph, Kara E., Elizabeth A. Stuart, Jon S. Vernick, and Daniel W. Webster. "Association Between Connecticut's Permit-to-Purchase Handgun Law and Homicides." *American Journal of Public Health* 105, no. 8 (2015): e49–e54.

Russonello, Giovanni, "Why Most Americans Support the Protests." *New York Times*, June 5, 2020. www.nytimes.com.

Ryan, Richard M., and Edward L. Deci. "Self-Determination Theory and the Facilitation of Intrinsic Motivation, Social Development, and Well-Being." *American Psychologist* 55, no. 1 (2000): 68–78.

Sabbeth, Kathryn A. "The Prioritization of Criminal Over Civil Counsel and the Discounted Damages of Private Power." *Florida State University Law Review* 42, no. 4 (2017): 889–936.

Safety and Justice Challenge. "Advancing Prosecutorial Effectiveness and Fairness through Data and Innovation." https://caj.fiu.edu.

Sakiberm, Brendan, Kalind Parish, Julia Ward, Grace DiLaura, and Sharon Dolovich. "COVID-19 Cases and Deaths in Federal and State Prisons." *Journal of the American Medical Association* 324, no. 6 (2020): E1-E2.

Salter, Jim. "St. Louis County Adopts Waiting List for Public Defenders." *Columbia Daily Tribune*, January 10, 2020, www.columbiatribune.com.

Sampson, Robert J. *Great American City: Chicago and the Enduring Neighborhood Effect.* Chicago, University of Chicago Press, 2012.

Sampson, Robert J., and Charles Loeffler. "Punishment's Place: The Local Concentration of Mass Incarceration." *Daedalus* 139, no. 3 (2010): 20–31.

Sanders, Douglas E. "Indigenous Peoples: Issues of Definition." *International Journal of Cultural Property* 8, no. 1 (1999): 4–13.

Sandys, Marla, and Heather Pruss. "Correlates of Satisfaction Among Clients of a Public Defender Agency." *Ohio State Journal of Criminal Law* 14, no. 2 (2017): 431–61.

Sangero, Boaz. *Safety from False Convictions.* Jerusalem, Israel: Boaz Sangero, 2016.

Saunders, Jessica, Meagan Cahill, and Jirka Taylor. *Feasibility of a Survey Panel of Criminal Justice Agencies in Small, Rural, Tribal, and Border Areas.* Santa Monica, CA: RAND Corporation, 2017. www.rand.org.

Sawyer, Kathy. "Study of State Prisons Finds Recidivism Rates High in 1979." *Washington Post*, March 4, 1985.

Sawyer, Wendy, and Peter Wagner. *Mass Incarceration: The Whole Pie 2020.* Prison Policy Initiative, March 24, 2020. www.prisonpolicy.org.

Schaul, Kevin, Kate Rabinowitz and Ted Mellnik. "Elections: 2020 Turnout Is the Highest in Over a Century." *Washington Post*, November 5, 2020. www.washingtonpost.com.

Schilbach, Frank, Heather Schofield, and Sendhil Mullainathan. "The Psychological Lives of the Poor." *American Economic Review: Papers & Proceedings* 106, no. 5 (2016): 435–40.

Schlanger, Margo. "The Constitutional Law of Incarceration, Reconfigured." *Cornell Law Review*, 103, no. 2 (2018): 357–436.

Schlesinger, Tracy. "Racial and Ethnic Disparity in Pretrial Criminal Processing." *Justice Quarterly* 22, no. 2 (2005): 170–92.

Schnacke, Timothy R., Michael R. Jones, and Dorian M. Wilderman. "Increasing Court-Appearance Rates and Other Benefits of Live-Caller Telephone Court-Date Reminders: The Jefferson County, Colorado, FTA Pilot Project and Resulting Court Date Notification Program." *Court Review: The Journal of the American Judges Association* 48 (2012): 86–95. https://digitalcommons.unl.edu.

Schulhofer, Stephen J. "Rethinking Mandatory Minimums." *Wake Forest Law Review* 28, no. 2 (1993): 199–222.

Schwall, Benjamin. "More Bang for Your Buck: How to Improve the Incentive Structure for Indigent Defense Counsel." *Ohio State Journal of Criminal Law* 14, no. 2 (2017): 553–78.

Schwartz, Joanna. "Systems Failures in Policing." *Suffolk Law Review* 51 (2018): 536–63.

Scientific Working Group of Medicolegal Death Investigation. "Increasing the Supply of Forensic Pathologists in the United States." December 5, 2012. www.nist.gov.

Scott-Hayward, Christine S., and Henry F. Fradella. *Punishing Poverty: How Bail and Pretrial Detention Fuel Inequalities in the Criminal Justice System.* Berkeley, CA: University of California Press, 2019.

———. "The Bail Industry Blocks Reform—Again." UC Press Blog, February 7, 2019. www.ucpress.edu.

Scott-Hayward, Christine S., and Sarah Ottone. "Punishing Poverty: California's Unconstitutional Bail System." *Stanford Law Review Online* 70 (April 2018): 167–78.

Seamone, Evan R. "Sex Crimes Litigation as Hazardous Duty: Practical Tools for Trauma Exposed Prosecutors, Defense Counsel, and Paralegals." *Ohio State Journal of Criminal Law* 11, no. 2 (2014): 487–578.

Selvanathan, Hema Preya, and Jolanda Jetten. "From Marches to Movements: Building and Sustaining a Social Movement Following Collective Action." *Current Opinion in Psychology* 35 (2020): 81–85.

Shackford, Scott. "Is Criminal Justice Reform Leaving Small and Rural Communities Behind?" *Reason*, June 14, 2018. https://reason.com.

Shafir, Eldar, and Sendhil Mullainathan. *Scarcity: Why Having Too Little Means So Much*. New York: Henry Holt, 2013.

Shane, Jon. *Learning from Error in Policing: A Case Study in Organizational Accident Theory*. New York: Springer, 2013.

Sharpe, Virginia. "Promoting Patient Safety: An Ethical Basis for Policy Deliberation." *Hastings Center Reports* (2003): S8, S10.

Sheley, Joseph F., and James D. Wright. "Motivations for Gun Possession and Carrying Among Serious Juvenile Offenders." *Behavioral Sciences & the Law* 11, no. 4 (1993): 375–88.

Shen, Caroline. "A Triggered Nation: An Argument for Extreme Risk Protection Orders." *Hastings Constitutional Law Quarterly*, 46, no. 3 (2018): 683–712.

Shepherd, Joanna M. "Fear of the First Strike: The Full Deterrent Effect of California's Two-and-Three-Strikes Legislation. *Journal of Legal Studies* 31, no. 1 (2002): 159–201.

Sheppard, Samantha. "A Radically Different Way to Look at Incarceration." *The Atlantic*. October 17, 2020.

Sherman, Lawrence W. "Reducing Fatal Police Shootings as Systems Crashes: Research, Theory, and Practice." *Annual Review of Criminology* 1 (2018): 421–49.

Sherman, Lawrence W., Denise C. Gottfredson, Doris L. MacKenzie, John Eck, Peter Reuter, and Shawn D. Bushway. *Preventing Crime: What Works, What Doesn't, What's Promising*. NCJ-171676. National Institute of Justice. Washington, DC: U.S. Government Printing Office, 1998.

Shermer, Lauren, and Brian Johnson. "Criminal Prosecutions: Examining Prosecutorial Discretion and Charge Reductions in U.S. Federal District Courts." *Justice Quarterly* 27, no. 3 (2010): 394–430.

Shermer, Michael. "Rumsfeld's Wisdom: Where the Known Meets the Unknown Is Where Science Begins." *Scientific American* 293, no. 3 (2005):38.

Sigal, Samuel. "Everywhere Basic Income Has Been Tried, in One Map." Vox. October 20, 2020. www.vox.com.

Silverman, Hollie, Konstantin Toropin, and Sara Snider. "Navajo Nation Surpasses New York State for the Highest Covid-19 Infection Rate in the U.S." CNN. May 2020. www.cnn.com.

Simon, Jonathan. "Criminology and the Recidivist." In *Three Strikes and You're Out: Vengeance as Public Policy*, edited by David Shichor and Dale K. Sechrest, 24–52. Thousand Oaks, CA: Sage, 1996.

Simonson, Jocelyn. "The Criminal Court Audience in a Post-Trial World." *Harvard Law Review* 127, no. 8 (2014): 2173–2232.

———. "Democratizing Criminal Justice Through Contestation and Resistance." *Northwestern University Law Review* 111, no. 6 (2017): 1609–24.

———. "Police Reform through a Power Lens." *Yale Law Journal* 130, no. 4 (2021): 778–860.

Singleton, David A. "What is Punishment?: The Case for Conidering Public Opinion Under Mendoza-Martinez." *Seton Hall Law Review* 45, no. 435 (2015): 439.

Sixth Amendment Center. "Maine Report." April 2019. https://sixthamendment.org.

———. "The Right to Counsel in Indiana: Evaluation of Trial Level Indigent Defense Services." 2016.

———. "The Right to Counsel in Rural Nevada: Evaluation of Indigent Defense Services." 2018.

———. "The Right to Counsel in Texas." 2019. https://sixthamendment.org.

———. "Wisconsin: How the Right To Counsel is Administered and Structured." 2013. https://sixthamendment.org.

Skene, Lea and Jacqueline DeRoberts. "State Corrections overdetention woes, known since 2012, cost state millions, lawyer alleges." *The Advocate.* February 6, 2020.

Sklansky, David A. "Cocaine, Race, and Equal Protection." *Stanford Law Review* 47, no. 6 (1995): 1283–1322.

Slakoff, Danielle C., and Henry F. Fradella. "Media Messages Surrounding Missing Women and Girls: The 'Missing White Woman Syndrome' and Other Factors that Influence Newsworthiness." *Criminology, Criminal Justice, Law & Society* 20, no. 3 (2019): 80–102.

Slep, Amy M. Smith, Heather M. Foran, Richard E. Heyman, Jeffery D. Snarr, and the USAF Family Advocacy Research Program. "Identifying Unique and Shared Risk Factors for Physical Intimate Partner Violence and Clinically-Significant Physical Intimate Partner Violence." *Aggressive Behavior* 41, no. 3 (2015): 227–41.

Smith, Allan, Naitian Zhou and Jiachuan Wu. "Map: Turnout surged in 2020. See the numbers where you live." *NBC News*, December 2, 2020. www.nbcnews.com.

Smith, Alyssa, and Sean Madden. "Three-Minute Justice: Haste and Waste in Florida's Misdemeanor Courts." Washington, DC: National Association of Criminal Defense Lawyers, July 2011. www.nacdl.org.

Smith, Andrea. "The Moral Limits of the Law: Settler Colonialism and the Anti-Violence Movement." *Settler Colonial Studies* 2, no. 2 (2012): 69–88.

Smith, Clay J. *Emancipation: The Making of the Black Lawyer, 1844–1944.* Philadelphia: University of Pennsylvania Press, 1999.

Smith, Deneen. "While Defense Attorneys Await a Pay Increase, Fewer Willing to Take Public Defender Cases." *Kenosha News*, Sept. 23, 2019.

Smith, Jordan. "Missouri's Attorney General Is Fighting for the Right to Keep an Innocent Man in Prison." *The Intercept*, May 4, 2020. www.theintercept.com.

Smith, Linda Tuhiwai. *Decolonizing Methodologies: Research and Indigenous Peoples.* 2nd ed. New York: Zed Books, 2021.

Smith, Michael David. *Race Versus the Robe: The Dilemma of Black Judges.* Port Washington, NY: Associated Faculty Press, 1983.

Smith, Paula, and Myrinda Schweitzer. "The Therapeutic Prison." In *The American Prison: Imagining a Different Future.* Thousand Oaks, CA: Sage Publications, 2014.

Smith, Paula, Paul Gendreau, and Kristin Swartz. "Validating the Principles of Effective Intervention: A Systematic Review of the Contributions of Meta-Analysis in the Field of Corrections." *Victims & Offenders* 4, no. 2 (2009): 148–69.

Smith, Sharon G., Xinjian Zhang, Kathleen C. Basile, Melissa T. Merrick, Jing Wang, Marcie-Jo Kresnow, and Jieru Chen. "The National Intimate Partner and Sexual Violence Survey (NISVS): 2015 Data Brief—Updated Release." National Center for Injury Prevention and Control, Centers for Disease Control and Prevention, Atlanta, GA, 2018.

SMU Dedman School of Law. "Greening the Desert: Strategies to Recruit, Train, and Retain STAR Criminal Justice Practitioners." 2020. https://cpb-us-w2.wpmucdn.com.

Snook, Scott. *Friendly Fire: The Accidental Shoot Down of US Blackhawks Over Northern Iraq*. Princeton: Princeton University Press, 2000.

Society for Human Resource Management. "Top Organizations Join SHRM Initiative and Pledge to Change Hiring Practices for Those with Criminal Backgrounds." January 27, 2019. www.shrm.org.

Sommers, Samuel R. "On Racial Diversity and Group Decision Making: Identifying Multiple Effects of Racial Composition on Jury Deliberations." *Journal of Personality and Social Psychology* 90, no. 4 (2006): 597–612.

Sousa, William H., Terance D. Miethe, and Mari Sakiyama. "Inconsistencies in Public Opinion of Body-Worn Cameras on Police: Transparency, Trust, and Improved Police-Citizen Relationships." *Policing: A Journal of Policy and Practice* 12, no. 1 (2017): 100–08.

South Dakota Legal Self-Help. "Rural Attorney Recruitment Program." https://ujs-lawhelp.sd.gov.

South Dakota Unified Judicial System. "Rural Attorney Recruitment Program." https://ujs.sd.gov.

Southwest Indigenous Women's Coalition (SWIWC) *Resources*. (2020).

Spamer, B. J., Danielle Weiss, and Charles Heurich. "Solving the Missing Indigenous Person Data Crisis: NamUs 2.0." National Institute of Justice. July 2019. https://nij.ojp.gov.

The Special Commission on the Future of N.Y. State Courts. "Justice Most Local: The Future of Town and Village Courts in New York State." 2008. www.nycourtreform.org.

Spohn, Cassia. *How Do Judges Decide? The Search for Fairness and Justice in Punishment*. 2nd ed. Thousand Oaks, CA: Sage, 2009.

———. "The Sentencing Decisions of Black and White Judges: Expected and Unexpected Similarities." *Law & Society Review* 24, no. 5 (1990): 1197–1216.

———. "Thirty Years of Sentencing Reform: The Quest for a Racially Neutral Sentencing Process." In *Criminal Justice 2000: Policies, Process and Decisions of the Criminal Justice System*, 427–80. Washington, DC: U.S. Department of Justice, 2000.

Spohn, Cassia and David Holleran. "Prosecuting Sexual Assault: A Comparison of Charging Decisions in Sexual Assault Cases Involving Strangers, Acquaintances, and Intimate Partners." *Justice Quarterly* 18, no. 3 (2001): 651–88.

Stanley, Jay. *Police Body-Mounted Cameras: With Right Policies in Place, a Win for All*. New York: American Civil Liberties Union, 2015.

Stannard, David E. *American Holocaust: The Conquest of the New World*. Oxford University Press, 1993.

Stark, Christine and Eileen Hudon. "Colonization, Homelessness, and the Prostitution and Sex Trafficking of Native Women." National Resource Center on Domestic Violence, 2020.

Starr, Douglas. "A New Way to Reform the Justice System." *The New Yorker*, March 31, 2015.

Starr, Sonja B. "The New Profiling: Why Punishing Based on Poverty and Identity Is Unconstitutional and Wrong." *Federal Sentencing Reporter* 27, no. 4 (April 2015): 229–36. https://fsr.ucpress.edu.

Starr, Sonja B., and M. Marit Rehavi. "Mandatory Sentencing and Racial Disparity: Assessing the Role of Prosecutors and the Effects of *Booker*." *Yale Law Journal* 123, no. 1 (2013): 2–80.

———. "Racial Disparity in Federal Criminal Sentences." *University of Michigan Law School Scholarship Repository* 122, no. 6 (2014): 1320–54.

State of Illinois Sentencing Policy Advisory Council. *The High Cost of Recidivism*. Summer 2018. https://spac.icjia-api.cloud.

Statista. "Countries with the Most Prisoners per 100,000 Inhabitants as of June 2020." June 16, 2020, www.statista.com.

Steelman, David. "State and Local Trial Courts." *International Journal for Court Administration* 2, no. 2 (2010): 1–11. http://doi.org.

Steffensmeier, Darrell, and Chester L. Britt. "Judges' Race and Judicial Decision Making: Do Black Judges Sentence Differently?" *Social Science Quarterly* 82, no. 4 (2001): 749–64.

Steffensmeier, Darrell, and Stephen Demuth. "Ethnicity and Sentencing Outcomes in U.S. Federal Courts: Who Is Punished More Harshly?" *American Sociological Review* 65, no. 5 (2000): 705–29.

Steffensmeier, Darrell, Jeffery Ulmer, and John Kramer. "The Interaction of Race, Gender, and Age in Criminal Sentencing: The Punishment Cost of Being Young, Black, and Male." *Criminology* 36, no. 4 (1998): 763–98.

Steiner, Benjamin, Matthew Makarios, and Travis F. Lawrence. "Examining the Effects of Residential Situations and Residential Mobility on Offender Recidivism." *Crime & Delinquency* 61, no. 3 (2015): 375–401.

Steiner, Benjamin, and Benjamin Meade. "The Safe Prison." *The American Prison: Imagining a Different Future*. Thousand Oaks, CA: Sage Publications, 2014.

Steiker, Carol S. "Punishment and Procedure: Punishment Theory and the Criminal-Civil Procedural Divide." *The George Washington Law Journal* 85, no. 775 (1997): 224, 780–1, 793.

Stevenson, Bryan. *Just Mercy: A Story of Justice and Redemption*. New York: One World., 2015.

Stevenson, Megan T. "Distortion of Justice: How the Inability to Pay Bail Affects Case Outcomes." The Journal of Law, Economics, and Organization 34, no. 4 (November 2018): 511–42.

Stillman, Sarah. "'The Missing White Girl Syndrome': Disappeared Women and Media Activism." *Gender & Development* 15, no. 3 (2007): 491–502.

Stith Kate, and José A. Cabranes. *Fear of Judging*. Chicago: University of Chicago Press, 1998.

Stoever, Jane K. "Access to Safety and Justice: Service of Process in Domestic Violence Cases." *Washington Law Review* 94, no. 1 (2019): 351.

Stolzenberg, Lisa, and Steward J. D'Alessio. "Sentencing and Unwarranted Disparity: An Empirical Assessment of the Long-Term Impact of Sentencing Guidelines in Minnesota." *Criminology* 32, no. 2 (1194): 301–10.

Strom, Kevin. "Research on the Impact of Technology on Policing Strategy in the 21st Century, Final Report." NCJRS. September 2017. www.ncjrs.gov.

Strong, Suzanne M. "Special Report: State Administered Indigent Defense Systems, 2013." U.S. Department of Justice, Bureau of Justice Statistics. Rev. May 3, 2017. www.bjs.gov.

Strong, Suzanne, and Tracey Kyckelhahn. *Census of Problem-Solving Courts, 2012.* Washington, DC: Bureau of Justice Statistics, 2016. www.bjs.gov.

Sturm, Susan, and Haran Tae. *Leading with Conviction: The Transformative Role of Formerly Incarcerated Leaders in Reducing Mass Incarceration.* New York: Center for Institutional and Social Change, Columbia Law School, 2015.

Subramanian, Ram, and Ruth Delaney. *Playbook for Change? States Reconsider Mandatory Sentences.* New York: Vera Institute of Justice, 2014.

Subramanian, Ram, Ruth Delaney, Stephen Roberts, Nancy Fishman, and Peggy McGarry. "Incarceration's Front Door: The Misuse of Jail in America." Vera Institute of Justice, February 2015. www.safetyandjusticechallenge.org.

Subramanian, Ram, and Rebecka Moreno. *Drug War Détente: A Review of State-Level Drug Law Reform, 2009–2013.* 2014.

Subramanian, Ram, Kristine Riley, and Chris Mai. *Divided Justice: Trends in Black and White Jail Incarceration, 1990–2013.* New York, NY: Vera Institute of Justice, February 2018. www.vera.org.

Sukhatme, Neel U., and Jay Jenkins. "Pay to Play? Campaign Finance and the Incentive Gap in the Sixth Amendment's Right to Counsel." *Duke Law Journal* 70, no. 4 (2021): 775–845.

Sudeall, Lauren, and Ruth Richardson. "Unfamiliar Justice: Indigent Criminal Defendants' Experiences With Civil Legal Needs." *UC Davis Law Review* 52, no. 4 (2019): 2105–64.

Supreme Court of Arizona. "Justice for All: Report and Recommendations of the Task Force on Fair Justice for All: Court-Ordered Fines, Penalties, Fees, and Pretrial Release Policies." 2016. www.azcourts.gov.

Sutherland, Alex, Barak Ariel, William Farrar, and Randy De Anda. "Post-Experimental Follow-Ups—Fade-Out versus Persistence Effects: The Rialto Police Body-Worn Camera Experiment Four Years On." *Journal of Criminal Justice* 53 (2017): 110–16.

Sutton, John R. "Structural Bias in the Sentencing of Felony Defendants." *Social Science Research* 42, no. 5 (2013): 1207–21.

———. "Symbol and Substance: Effects of California's Three Strikes Law on Felony Sentencing." *Law & Society Review* 47, no. 1 (2013): 37–72.

Swanson, Jeffrey W. "Understanding the research on extreme risk protection orders: varying results, same message." *Psychiatric Services* 70, no. 10 (2019): 953–54.

Swanson, Jeffrey W., Michele M. Easter, Kelly Alanis-Hirsch, Charles M. Belden, Michael A. Norko, Allison G. Robertson, Linda K. Frisman, Hsiu-Ju Lin, Marvin S. Swartz, and George F. Parker. "Criminal Justice and Suicide Outcomes with Indiana's Risk-Based Gun Seizure Law." *Journal of the American Academy of Psychiatry and the Law* 47, no. 2 (2019): 188–97.

Swanson, Jeffrey W., Michael A. Norko, Hsiu-Ju Lin, Kelly Alanis-Hirsch, Linda K. Frisman, Madelon V. Baranoski, Michele M. Easter, Allison G. Robertson, Marvin S. Swartz, and Richard J. Bonnie. "Implementation and Effectiveness of Connecticut's Risk-Based Gun Removal Law: Does It Prevent Suicides?" *Law & Contemporary Problems* 80, no. 2 (2017): 179–208.

Tate, LaTonya and Barbara Jackson Interview with Lauren Johnson. 2020.

"Technical Flaws of Pretrial Risk Assessments Raise Grave Concerns." MIT, July 17, 2019.

Texas v. EEOC, 933 F.3rd 433 (5th Cir. 2019).

Thacher, David. "The Learning Model of Use of Force Reviews." *Law & Social Inquiry* 45, no. 3 (2020): 755–86.

The First 24 Project. "Your Loved One Just Got Arrested: What Do You Do Within the First 24 Hours?" www.thefirst24.org.

The Sentencing Project. *Report of The Sentencing Project to the United Nations Special Rapporteur on Contemporary Forms of Racism, Racial Discrimination, Xenophobia, and Related Intolerance.* Research and Advocacy for Reform, 2018.

Thomas, Wayne. *Bail Reform in America.* Berkeley: University of California Press, 1977.

Thompson, Robert S., Amy E. Bonomi, Melissa Anderson, Robert J. Reid, Jane A. Dimer, David Carrell, and Frederick P. Rivara. "Intimate Partner Violence: Prevalence, Types, and Chronicity in Adult Women." *American Journal of Preventive Medicine* 30, no. 6 (2006): 447–57.

Tippett, Elizabeth C. "The Legal Implications of the Metoo Movement." *University of Minnesota Law Review* 103, no. 1 (2018): 229–302.

Tjaden, P., and N. Thoennes. "Extent, Nature, and Consequences of Intimate Partner Violence." Report No. NCJ 181867. Washington, DC: Office of Justice Programs, 2000.

Tonry, Michael. *Malign Neglect: Race, Crime and Punishment in America.* New York: Oxford University Press, 1995.

———. "Remodeling American Sentencing: A Ten-Step Blueprint for Moving Past Mass Incarceration." *Criminology & Public Policy* 13, no. 4 (2014): 503–33.

———. *Sentencing Matters.* New York: Oxford University Press, 1996.

Tonry, Michael, and Matthew Melewski. "The Malign Effects of Drug and Crime Policies on Black Americans" *Crime and Justice: A Review of Research.* 37, no. 1 (2008): 1–44.

Toronto Police Service. Body-Worn Cameras: A Report on the Findings of the Pilot Project to Test the Value and Feasibility of Body-Worn Cameras for Police Officers in Toronto. Toronto, ON: Toronto Police Department Strategy Management—Strategic Planning Team, June 2016.

Totenberg, Nina. "Supreme Court to Take Up 1st Major Gun Rights Case in More Than a Decade." National Public Radio. 2021. www.npr.org.

Training and Technical Assistance Team. *BWC Cost and Storage Estimator*. https://bwctta.com.

Travis, Jeremy. *But They All Come Back: Facing the Challenges of Prisoner Reentry*. Washington, DC, Urban Institute Press, 2005.

Travis, Jeremy, and Michelle Waul. *Prisoners Once Removed: The Impact of Incarceration and Reentry on Children, Families, and Communities*. Washington, DC: Urban Institute Press, 2003.

Trenkner, Thomas. "Constitutional Restrictions on Non-Attorney Acting as Judge in Criminal Proceeding." *A.L.R.* 71 (2019): 562.

Trivedi, Somli, and Nicole Gonzalez Van Cleve, "To Serve and Protect Each Other: How Prosecutor-Police Codependence Enables Police Misconduct." *Boston University Law Review* 100, no. 3 (2020), 895–921.

Tucson Sentinel Events Review Board. *Report of the Tucson Sentinel Event Review Board (SERB) on the Deaths in Custody of Mr. Damien Alvarado and Mr. Adrian Ingram-Lopez*. September 18, 2020. www.tucsonaz.gov.

———. *Report of the Tucson Sentinel Event Review Board (SERB) on the Deaths in Custody of Mr. Damien Alvarado and Mr. Adrian Ingram-Lopez (6 months review)*. April 2021. www.tucsonaz.gov.

Tull, Dylan. "Proposition 57 Could Lead to Fewer Youth Serving Time in Adult Prison." *Peninsula Press*, November 7, 2016. http://peninsulapress.com.

Tulsa, Oklahoma, Family & Children's Services. "App Launches to Reduce Failure to Appears and Connect Defendant with Social Services." March 18, 2019. www.fcsok.org.

Turner, Franzetta D. "Reducing Failure to Appears Through Community Outreach." Williamsburg, VA: National Center for State Courts Institute for Court Management (May 2015). www.ncsc.org.

Turner, Michael G., Jody L. Sundt, Brandon K. Applegate, and Francis T. Cullen. "The Impact of Truth-in-Sentencing and Three Strikes Legislation: Prison Populations, State Budgets, and Crime Rates." *Stanford Law & Policy Review* 11, no. 1 (1999): 75–92.

Turner, Susan, Peter W. Greenwood, Elsa Chen, and Terry Fain. "The Impact of Truth-in-Sentencing and Three Strikes Legislation: Prison Populations, State Budgets, and Crime Rates." *Stanford Law & Policy Review* 11, no. 1 (1999): 75–83.

Tyler, Tom R. "Psychological Perspectives on Legitimacy and Legitimation." *Annual Review of Psychology* 57, no. 1 (2006): 375–400.

———. *Why People Obey the Law*. New Haven, CT: Yale University Press, 1990.

Tyler, Tom R., and Jeffrey Fagan. "Legitimacy and Cooperation: Why Do People Help the Police Fight Crime in Their Communities?" *Ohio State Journal of Criminal Law* 6 (2008): 230–67.

Tyler, Tom R., Phillip Atiba Goff, and Robert J. MacCoun. "The Impact of Psychological Science on Policing in the United States: Procedural Justice, Legitimacy, and Effective Law Enforcement." *Psychological Science in the Public Interest* 16, no. 3 (2015): 75–109.

Tyler, Tom R., and Yuen Huo. *Trust in the Law: Encouraging Public Cooperation with the Police and Courts*. New York: Russell Sage Foundation, 2002.

U.K. College of Policing. *What Is Evidence-Based Policing?* London: Author, 2017. whatworks.college.police.uk.

Uggen, Christopher, Sara Wakefield, and Bruce Western. "Work and Family Perspectives on Reentry." *Prisoner Reentry and Crime in America*. Cambridge, Cambridge University Press, 2005: 209–43.

Ulmer, Jeffery. *Social Worlds of Sentencing: Court Communities Under Sentencing Guidelines*. Albany: State University of New York Press, 1997.

Ulmer, Jeffery T., Megan C. Kurlycheck, and John H. Kramer. "Prosecutorial Discretion and the Imposition of Mandatory Minimum Sentences." *Journal of Research in Crime and Delinquency* 44, no. 4 (2007): 427–58.

United Nations News. "Coronavirus: Reshape the Urban World to Aid 'Ground Zero' Pandemic Cities." July 28, 2020. https://news.un.org.

United States v. Salerno, 481 U.S. 739 (1987).

United States Census. 2019. *Quick Facts*. 2019. www.census.gov.

United States Commission on Civil Rights. "Broken Promises: Continuing Federal Funding Shortfall for Native Americans." United States Department of Agriculture. *Rural America at a Glance*. Washington, DC: USDA, 2018. www.ers.usda.gov.

———. "A Quiet Crisis: Federal Funding and Unmet Needs In Indian Country." Washington, DC: U.S. Commission on Civil Rights, 2003.

———. *Rural Community Action Guide: Building Stronger, Healthy, Drug-Free Rural Communities*. Washington, DC: USDA, 2020. www.usda.gov.

———. "What Is Rural?" December 2019. www.nal.usda.gov.

United States Department of Agriculture Economic Research Service. "Highest Level of Education Attainment." February 28, 2019. https://data.ers.usda.gov.

United States Department of Commerce, Census Bureau. "New Census Data Show Differences Between Urban and Rural Populations." April 8, 2022. www.census.gov.

United States Department of Justice. *The Attorney General's Smart on Crime Initiative*. Washington, DC: U.S. Department of Justice.

———. "Attorney General William P. Barr Launches National Strategy to Address Missing and Murdered Indigenous Persons." November 22, 2019.

———. "Innovations in Community-Based Crime Reduction (CBCR)." 2020.

United States Department of Justice, and Scott Hertzberg, ed. "A Compiled Bibliography." 2020. https://nij.ojp.gov.

United States Department of Justice Archives. "The Attorney General's Smart on Crime Initiative." Last modified March 9, 2017. www.justice.gov.

United States Department of Justice, Bureau of Justice Assistance. *National Assessment of Structured Sentencing*. Washington, DC: U.S. Department of Justice, 1996.

———. *Prisoners in 1997*. Washington, DC: U.S. Department of Justice, 1999.

———. *Prisoners in 2017*. Washington, DC: U.S. Department of Justice, 2019.

United States Department of Justice, National Institute of Justice. *Mending Justice*. Washington, DC: National Institute of Justice, 2014.

———. "NIJ's Sentinel Events Initiative." www.nij.gov.

———. *Paving the Way*. Washington, DC: National Institute of Justice, 2016.

———. *Strategic Research and Implementation Plan*. Washington, DC: National Institute of Justice, 2017.

United States Department of Justice. N.d. *Public Safety Risk Assessment Clearing House*. Office of Justice Programs: Washington, DC. https://bja.ojp.gov.

United States Government Accountability Office. "Indian Country Criminal Justice: Departments of the Interior and Justice should Strengthen coordination to Support Tribal Courts." [GAO-11-252], 2011.

———. *Sexual Assault: Information on Training, Funding, and the Availability of Forensic Examiners*. Washington, DC: GAO, March 18, 2016. Retrieved from www.gao. gov.

United States Sentencing Commission (USSC). *The Federal Sentencing Guidelines: A Report on the Operation of the Guidelines System and Short-Term Impacts on Disparity in Sentencing, Use of Incarceration, and Prosecutorial Discretion and Plea Bargaining*. Washington, DC: USSC, 1991.

———. *Fifteen Years of Guideline Sentencing: An Assessment of How Well the Federal Criminal Justice System Is Achieving Its Goals of Sentencing Reform*. Washington, DC: USSC, 2004.

———. *Life Sentences in the Federal Criminal Justice System*. Washington, DC: USSC, 2015.

———. *Report to the Congress: Mandatory Minimum Penalties in the Federal Criminal Justice System*. Washington, DC: USSC, 2011.

———. *2018 Guidelines Manual*. www.ussc.gov.

University of Southern California. "Ensuring Financial Stability for Ex-Convicts Reduces Rates of Recidivism." University of Southern California, Suzanne Dworack Peck School of Social Work. October 2019. https://dworakpeck.usc.edu.

Urban Indian Health Institute (UIHI). "Missing and Murdered Indigenous Women and Girls: A Snapshot of Data From 71 Urban Cities in the United States." 2019. www.uihi.org.

Van Brunt, Alexa, and Locke E. Bowman. "Toward a Just Model of Pretrial Release: A History of Bail Reform and a Prescription for What's Next." *Journal of Criminal Law & Criminology* 108, no. 4 (2018): 701–74. https://scholarlycommons.law.northwestern.edu.

Van Cleve, Nicole G., and Lauren Mayes. "Criminal Justice Through 'Colorblind' Lenses: A Call to Examine the Mutual Constitution of Race and Criminal Justice." *Law & Social Inquiry* 40, no. 2 (February 2015): 406–32.

van den Haag, Ernest. *Punishing Criminals: Confronting a Very Old and Painful Question*. New York: Basic Books, 1975.

van Dorn, Aaron, Rebecca E. Cooney, and Miriam L. Sabin. "COVID-19 Exacerbating Inequalities in the US." *The Lancet* 395 (April 2020): 1243–44.

Van Duizend, Richard, David C Steelman, and Lee Suskin. *Model Time Standards for State Trial Courts*. National Center for State Courts, 2011.

VanNostrand, Marie. Kenneth J. Rose, and Kimberly Weibrecht. "State of the Science of Pretrial Release Recommendations and Supervision." National Center for State Courts, June 2011. www.ncsc.org.

Vaughan, Diane. *The Challenger Launch Decision: Risky Technology, Culture, and Deviance at NASA*. Chicago: University of Chicago Press, 1996.

Vaughn, Joshua. "Pleading Guilty to Get Out of Jail." *The Appeal*, June 6, 2019. https://theappeal.org.

Vera Institute of Justice. "The State of Justice Reform: The State of Jails: A Shifting Landscape." 2018. www.vera.org.

Verger, Rob. "Police Body Cameras were Supposed to Build Trust. So Far, They Haven't." *Popular Science*, June 10, 2020. www.popsci.com.

Vetter, Stephanie, and John Clark. "The Delivery of Pretrial Justice in Rural Areas." Pretrial Justice Institute & National Association of Counties. January 2013.

Vigdor, Elizabeth Richardson, and James A. Mercy. "Do Laws Restricting Access to Firearms by Domestic Violence Offenders Prevent Intimate Partner Homicide?" *Evaluation Review* 30, no. 3 (2006): 313–46.

Viguerie, Richard A. "A Conservative Case for Prison Reform." *New York Times*, June 9, 2013.

Virginia State Crime Commission. "Joint Report on Writ of Actual Innocence." 2013. http://vscc.virginia.gov.

Visher, Christy A. "Pretrial Drug Testing: Panacea or Pandoras Box?" *ANNALS of the American Academy of Political and Social Science* 521, no. 1 (1992): 112–31.

Visher, Christy A., and Jeremy Travis. "Transitions From Prison to Community: Understanding Individual Pathways." *Annual Review of Sociology* 29, no. 1 (2003): 89–113.

Visher, Christy A., Vera Kachnowski, Nancy G. La Vigne, and Jeremy Travis. "Baltimore Prisoners' Experiences Returning Home." *The Urban Institute* (2004): 1–16.

Vittes, Katherine A., Jon S. Vernick, and Daniel W. Webster. "Legal Status and Source of Offenders' Firearms in States with the Least Stringent Criteria for Gun Ownership." *Injury Prevention* 19, no. 1 (2013): 26–31.

Voice of the Experienced. "Our History." www.vote-nola.org.

von Hirsch, Andrew. *Doing Justice: The Choice of Punishments*. New York: Hill and Wang, 1976.

Waddell, Elizabeth Needham, Robin Baker, Daniel M. Hartung, Christi J. Hildebran, Thuan Nguyen, Deza'Rae M. Collins, Jessica E. Larsen, Erin Stack and the ROAR Protocol Development Team. "Reducing Overdose After Release from Incarceration (ROAR): Study Protocol for an Intervention to Reduce Risk of Fatal and Non-Fatal Opioid Overdose Among Women After Release from Prison." *Health and Justice* 8, no. 1 (2020): 18–37.

Wagner, Peter, and Bernadette Rabuy. "Following the Money of Mass Incarceration." *Prison Policy Initiative*, January 25, 2017. www.prisonpolicy.org.

Wahab, S., and L. Olson. "Intimate Partner Violence and Sexual Assault in Native American Communities." *Trauma, Violence & Abuse* 5 (2004): 353–66.

Wakefield, Sara, and Christopher Uggen. "Incarceration and Stratification." *Annual Review of Sociology* 36, nos. 23–24 (2010): 387–406.

Walker, Samuel. *Taming the System: The Control of Discretion in Criminal Justice, 1950–1990*. New York: Oxford University Press, 1993.

Wallace, Danielle, Michael D. White, Janne E. Gaub, and Natalie Todak. "Body-Worn Cameras as a Potential Source of De-policing: Testing for Camera-Induced Passivity." *Criminology* 56, no. 3 (2018): 481–509.

Wallerstedt, John F. "Returning to Prison." *Bureau of Justice Statistics Special Report.* (November 1984). https://bjs.ojp.gov.

Wang, Tricia. "Why Big Data Needs Thick Data." *Ethnography Matters* (May 13, 2013), https://medium.com.

Wanzo, Rebecca. "The Era of Lost (White) Girls: On Body and Event." *Differences* 19, no. 2 (2008): 99–126.

Ward, Geoff. "Race and the Justice Workforce: A System Perspective." In *The Many Colors of Crime: Inequalities of Race, Ethnicity, and Crime in America*, edited by Ruth D. Peterson, Lauren J. Krivo, and John Hagan. New York: New York University Press, 2006.

Ward, Geoff, Amy Farrell, and Danielle Rousseau. "Does Racial Balance in Workforce Representation Yield Equal Justice? Race Relations of Sentencing in Federal Court Organizations." *Law and Society Review* 43, no. 4 (2009): 757–806.

Ward, Tony, and Claire Stewart. "Criminogenic Needs and Human Needs: A Theoretic Model." *Psychology Crime and Law* 9, no. 2 (2003): 125–43.

Ward, Tony, Pamela M. Yates, and Gwenda M. Willis. "The Good Lives Model and the Risk Need Responsivity Model: A Critical Response to Andrews, Bonta, and Wormith (2011)." *Criminal Justice and Behavior* 39, no. 1 (2012): 94–110.

Ward, Tony, and Shadd Maruna. *Rehabilitation: Beyond the Risk Paradigm*. London, Routledge, 2007.

Wash. Rev. Code § 3.50.020; 3.50.040.

Washington Post. "The Federal Definition of 'Rural'—Times 15." *Washington Post*, n.d. www.washingtonpost.com.

Wears, Robert, and Tzion Karsh. "Thick v. Thin: Description and Classification in Learning from Case Reviews." *Annals of Emergency Medicine* 51, no. 3 (2008): 262–64.

Weaver, Hilary N. "Indigenous Identity: What Is It, and Who Really Has It?" *American Indian Quarterly* 25, no. 2 (2001): 240–55.

Webster, D., C. K. Crifasi, and J. S. Vernick. "Effects of the Repeal of Missouri's Handgun Purchaser Licensing Law on Homicides." *Journal of Urban Health* 91, no. 2 (2014): 293–302.

Webster, Daniel W., and Garen J. Wintemute. "Effects of Policies Designed to Keep Firearms from High-Risk Individuals." *Annual Review of Public Health* 36, no. 1 (2015): 21–37.

Weisner, L., H. D. Otto, S. Adams, and J. Reichert. *Criminal Justice System Utilization in Rural Areas*. Chicago: Illinois Criminal Justice Information Authority, 2020.

Welch, Susan, Michael Combs, and John Gruhl. "Do Black Judges Make a Difference?" *American Journal of Political Science* 32, no. 1 (1988): 126–36.

Welsh, James. "Welfare Reform: Born, Aug. 8, 1969; Died, Oct. 4, 1972—A Sad Case Study of the American Political Process." *New York Times*, January 7, 1973.

Western, Bruce. *Homeward: Life in the Year After Prison*. New York: Russell Sage Foundation, 2018.

———. *Punishment and Inequality in America*. New York, Russell Sage, 2006.

White, Michael D. *Police Officer Body-Worn Cameras: Assessing the Evidence*. Washington, DC: U.S. Department of Justice, Office of Justice Programs, 2014.

White, Michael D., and James Coldren. "Body-Worn Cameras: Separating Fact from Fiction." *PM Magazine*, February 12, 2017. https://icma.org.

White, Michael D., Michaela Flippin, and Aili Malm. *Key Trends in Body-Worn Camera Policy and Practice: A Four-Year Policy Analysis of US Department of Justice-Funded Law Enforcement Agencies*. Center for Violence Prevention and Community Safety, Arizona State University, 2019.

White, Michael D., Janne E. Gaub, and Kathleen E. Padilla. "Impacts of BWCs on Citizen Complaints: Directory of Outcomes." United States Bureau of Justice Assistance, Body-Worn Camera Training and Technical Assistance. www.bwctta.com.

———. "Impacts of BWCs on Use of Force: Directory of Outcomes." United States Bureau of Justice Assistance, Body-Worn Camera Training and Technical Assistance. www.bwctta.com.

White, Michael D., Janne E. Gaub, and Natalie Todak, "Exploring the Potential for Body-Worn Cameras to Reduce Violence in Police-Citizen Encounters." *Policing: A Journal of Policy and Practice* 12, no. 1 (2018): 66–76.

White, Michael D., and Aili Malm. *Cops, Cameras, and Crisis: The Potential and the Perils of Police Body-Worn Cameras*. New York: New York University Press, 2020.

White, Michael D., Natalie Todak, and Janne E. Gaub. "Assessing Citizen Perceptions of Body-Worn Cameras after Encounters with Police." *Policing: An International Journal of Police Strategies & Management* 40, no. 4 (2017): 689–703.

———. "Examining Body-Worn Camera Integration and Acceptance among Police Officers, Citizens, and External Stakeholders." *Criminology & Public Policy* 17, no. 3 (2018): 649–77.

Whitelemons, Carson, Ashley Thomas and Sarah Couture. "Driving on EMPTY: Florida's Counterproductive and Costly Driver's License Suspension Practices." (Florida: Fines and Fees Justice Center, 2019) 5, 15.

Wilson, James Q. *Thinking About Crime*. New York: Basic Books, 1975.

The White House. "Fact Sheet: President Bush Signs H.R. 1593, the Second Chance Act of 2007." Washington, DC, April 9, 2008. https://georgewbush-whitehouse.archives.gov.

———. "Fact Sheet: President Obama Announces New Actions to Reduce Recidivism and Promote Reintegration of Formerly Incarcerated Individuals." Washington, DC, June 24, 2016. https://obamawhitehouse.archives.gov.

Who Votes for Mayor? www.whovotesformayor.org.

Wilkins, Tracee. "Activists Demand All Prince George's Officers Wear Body Cams." *NBC Washington*, October 9, 2019. www.nbcwashington.com.

Williams Morgan C. Jr., Weil, Nathan, Rasich, Elizabeth A., Ludwig, Jules, Chang, Hye and Egrari, Sophia (2021). "Body-Worn Cameras in Policing: Benefits and Costs." National Bureau of Economic Research (NBER), NBER Working Paper No. 28622.

Wilson, William J. *The Truly Disadvantaged: The Inner City, the Underclass, and Public Policy*. Chicago: University of Chicago Press, 1990.

Wimberly, Morris, and Donald Woolley. *The Black Belt Databook*. Knoxville, TN: TVA Rural Studies, 2001.

Wintemute, Garen J. "Alcohol Misuse, Firearm Violence Perpetration, and Public Policy in the United States." *Preventive Medicine* 79 (2015): 15–21.

———. "Frequency of and Responses to Illegal Activity Related to Commerce in Firearms: Findings from the Firearms Licensee Survey." *Injury Prevention* 19, no. 6 (2013): 412–20.

———. "Where the Guns Come From: The Gun Industry and Gun Commerce." *The Future of Children* 12, no. 2 (2002): 55–71.

Wintemute, Garen J., Christiana M. Drake, James J. Beaumont, Mona A. Wright, and Carrie A. Parham. "Prior Misdemeanor Convictions as a Risk Factor for Later Violent and Firearm-Related Criminal Activity Among Authorized Purchasers of Handguns." *JAMA* 280, no. 24 (1998): 2083–87.

Wintemute, G. J., V. A. Pear, J. P. Schleimer, R. Pallin, S. Sohl, N. Kravitz-Wirtz, and E. A. Tomsich. "Extreme Risk Protection Orders Intended to Prevent Mass Shootings: A Case Series." *Annals of Internal Medicine* 171, no. 9 (2019): 655–58.

Wintemute, Garen J., Shannon Frattaroli, Barbara E. Claire, Katherine A. Vittes, and Daniel W. Webster. "Identifying Armed Respondents to Domestic Violence Re-straining Orders and Recovering Their Firearms: Process Evaluation of an Initiative in California." *American Journal of Public Health* 104, no. 2 (2014): e113–e18.

Winton, Richard. "2 Rialto Police Officers Resign, 4 Disciplined amid Sex Scandal Inves-tigation." *Los Angeles Times Blog*, November 19, 2010. http://latimesblogs.latimes.com.

Wodahl, Eric. "The Challenges of Prisoner Reentry from a Rural Perspective." *Western Criminology Review* 7, no. 2 (2006): 42. www.westerncriminology.org.

Woessner, Paula. "Mobile Courtroom Provides Justice on Wheels for the Cheyenne River Sioux Tribe." Federal Reserve Bank of Minneapolis. November 10, 2015. www.minneapolisfed.org.

Wolfe, Patrick. "Settler Colonialism and the Elimination of the Native." *Journal of Genocide Research* 8, no. 4 (2006): 387–409.

Wood, Peter B., and R. Gregory Dunaway. "Consequences of Truth-in-Sentencing: The Mississippi Case." *Punishment & Society* 5 (2003): 139–54.

Woods, David D. "Conflicts Between Learning and Accountability in Patient Safety." *DePaul Law Review* 54, no. 2 (2005): 485–502.

———. "Essentials of Resiliency, Revisited." *Handbook on Resilience in Socio-Technical Systems*, 52–65. Northampton, Massachusetts: Edward Elgar, 2019.

Wooten, Melissa E. *Race, Organizations, and the Organizing Process*. Bingley, England: Emerald Publishing, 2019.

Worrall, John L. 2004. "The Effect of Three-Strikes Legislation on Serious Crime in California." *Journal of Criminal Justice* 32, no. 4 (2004): 283–96.

Wright, J. E., and A. M. Headley. Can Technology Work for Policing? Citizen Perceptions of Police-Body Worn Cameras. *American Review of Public Administration* 51, no. 4 (2020): 1–11.

Wright, Benjamin J., Sheldon X. Zhang, David Farabee, and Rick Braatz. "Prisoner Reentry Research From 2000 to 2010: Results of a Narrative Review." *Criminal Justice Review* 39, no. 1 (2014): 37–57.

Wright, Kevin A. "Time Well Spent: Misery, Meaning and the Opportunity of Incarceration." *Howard Journal of Crime and Justice* 59, no. 1(2020): 44–64.

Wright, Kevin A., and Gabriel T. Cesar. "Toward a More Complete Model of Offender Reintegration: Linking the Individual-, Community-, and System-Level Components of Recidivism." *Victims & Offenders* 8, no. 4 (2013): 373–98.

Wright, Kevin A., and Natasha Khade. "Offender Recidivism." *Routledge Handbook of Corrections in the United States* 45 (2018): 494–502.

Wright, Ronald F. "Beyond Prosecutor Elections." *SMU Law Review* 67, no. 3 (2014): 593–616.

———. "The Civil and Criminal Methodologies of the Fourth Amendment." *Yale Law Journal* 93, no. 6 (1984): 1127–46.

W. Va. Code § 50-2-3, §§ 50-1-4, 8-10-2(c).

Wyo. Stat. § 5-9-208(c)(xviii)).

Xiong, Chao. "In Hennepin County, Text and Email Reminders of Court Dates Reduce Number of Warrants." *Star Tribune*, October 4, 2019. www.startribune.com.

Yan, Shi, and Shawn Bushway. "Plea Discounts or Trial Penalties? Making Sense of the Trial-Plea Sentence Disparities." *Justice Quarterly* 35, no. 7 (2018): 1226–49.

Yang, Andrew. "The Freedom Dividend." 2020. https://2020.yang2020.com.

Yang, Crystal S. "Toward an Optimal Bail System." *New York University Law Review* 92, no. 5 (2017): 1399–1493.

Yellow Bird, Michael. "What We Want to be Called: Indigenous Peoples' Perspectives on Racial and Ethnic Identity Labels." *American Indian Quarterly* 23, no. 2 (1999): 1–21.

Yellow Horse Brave Heart, Maria. "The Return to the Sacred Path: Healing the Historical Trauma Response Among the Lakota." *Smith College Studies in Social Work* 68, no. 3 (1998): 287–305.

Yokum, David, Anita Ravishankar, and Alexander Coppock. *Evaluating the Effects of Police Body-Worn Cameras: A Randomized Controlled Trial*. Washington, DC: The Lab @ DC, Office of the City Administrator, Executive Office of the Mayor, 2017.

Yoon, Hayne, Logan Schmidt, and Micah Haskell-Hoehel. "The Party Platforms Must Address the Urgent Need to Transform American Criminal Justice." Vera Institute of Justice. June 17, 2020. www.vera.org.

Young v. Hawaii, 20-1639. 915 F.3d 681 (2019).

Young, Jacob T. N., and Justin T. Ready. "Diffusion of Policing Technology: The Role of Networks in Influencing the Endorsement and Use of On-Officer Cameras." *Journal of Contemporary Criminal Justice* 31, no. 3 (2015): 243–61.

———. "A Longitudinal Analysis of the Relationship between Administrative Policy, Technological Preferences, and Body-Worn Camera Activation Among Police Officers." *Policing: A Journal of Policy and Practice* 12, no. 1 (2018): 27–42.

Young, Simon N. M. "Enforcing Criminal Law Through Civil Processes: How Does Human Rights Law Treat 'Civil for Criminal Processes'?" *Journal of International and Comparative Law* 4, no. 2 (2017): 133–70.

Yuan, Nicole P., Mary Koss, Mona Polacca, and David Goldman. "Risk Factors for Physical Assault and Rape among Six Native American Tribes." *Journal of Interpersonal Violence* 21, no. 12 (2006): 1566–90.

Yuko, Elizabeth. "Robert Durst Murder Trial Begins in Los Angeles." *Rolling Stone*, February 11, 2020. www.rollingstone.com.

Zalman, Marvin, and Matthew Larson. "Elephants in the Station House: Serial Crimes, Wrongful Convictions and Expanding Wrongful Conviction Analysis to Include Police Investigation." *Albany Law Review* 79, no. 3 (2016): 941–1044.

Zeller, Erika, and Andrew Coburn. "Health Equity Challenges in Rural America." American Bar Association. November 20, 2018. www.americanbar.org.

Zeng, Zhen. "Jail Inmates in 2019." Washington, DC: U.S. Department of Justice, Bureau of Justice Statistics (March 2021). https://bjs.ojp.gov.

———. "Jail Inmates in 2016." Washington, DC: U.S. Department of Justice, Bureau of Justice Statistics (February 2018). www.bjs.gov.

Zeoli, April M., Shannon Frattaroli, Kelly Roskam, and Anastasia K. Herrera. "Removing Firearms from Those Prohibited from Possession by Domestic Violence Restraining Orders: A Survey and Analysis of State Laws." *Trauma, Violence & Abuse*, 20, no. 1 (2019): 114–25.

Zeoli, April M., Alexander McCourt, Shani Buggs, Shannon Frattaroli, David Lilley, and Daniel W. Webster. "Retracted: Analysis of the Strength of Legal Firearms Restrictions for Perpetrators of Domestic Violence and Their Associations with Intimate Partner Homicide." *American Journal of Epidemiology* 187, no. 7 (2018): 1449–55.

Zeoli, April M., and Daniel W. Webster. "Effects of Domestic Violence Policies, Alcohol Taxes and Police Staffing Levels on Intimate Partner Homicide in Large US Cities." *Injury Prevention*, 16, no. 2 (2010): 90–95.

Zimring, Frank R. "Imprisonment Rates and the New Politics of Criminal Punishment." *Punishment & Society* 3, no. 1 (2001); 161–66.

Zokovitch, Grace. "Lamar Johnson's Decades-Old Wrongful Conviction Case on Potential Path to Trial." *St. Louis Post-Dispatch*, January 11, 2022. www.stltoday.com.

Zoukis, Christopher. "Nearly Half of Prisoners Lack Access to Vocational Training." Huffington Post, March 2017. www.huffpost.com.

ABOUT THE CONTRIBUTORS

SHAWN ARMBRUST is Executive Director of the Mid-Atlantic Innocence Project, a position she has held since 2005. In that capacity, she works to prevent and correct wrongful convictions in the District of Columbia, Maryland, and Virginia. She is on the Executive Board of the Innocence Network and is a member of the National Committee on the Right to Counsel.

RACHEL BOWMAN is a doctoral student in the School of Criminology and Criminal Justice at Arizona State University. Her research addresses prosecutorial discretion with a particular focus on racial and ethnic disparities in pretrial outcomes.

ANNE CORBIN is a JD–PhD who works at the intersection of state government, academe, and nonprofit organizations. She has held a variety of positions that support leadership development and healthy workplace climate along the lines of inclusivity, equity, and a strengths-based paradigm. Her research investigates role conflict among public servants, particularly juvenile defense attorneys.

TURQUOISE SKYE DEVEREAUX is a part of the Salish and Blackfeet tribes of Montana. She is the project coordinator for the Office of American Indian Projects within the School of Social Work at Arizona State University and the owner of Indigenous Skye, LLC. Turquoise works at the intersections of direct support to students, curriculum and program development, program evaluation, and training and facilitation on decolonizing strategies and Indigenous Social Justice.

JAMES DOYLE is a veteran indigent defense lawyer based in Boston. He was a Visiting Fellow at the National Institute of Justice and a Senior Consultant to its Sentinel Events Initiative.

KATHLEEN A. FOX is Professor in the School of Criminology & Criminal Justice at Arizona State University and director of the Research on Violent Victimization Laboratory. Her research focuses on crime victimization, particularly among underserved populations, including American Indian peoples.

HENRY F. FRADELLA is Professor in and Associate Director of the School of Criminology and Criminal Justice at Arizona State University, where he also holds an affiliate appointment as a professor of law. He researches substantive, procedural, and evidentiary criminal law; the dynamics of legal decision-making; and the consequences of changes in legal processes. He is the author or coauthor of numerous books and articles.

RAJ JAYADEV is Coordinator of Silicon Valley De-Bug, a community organizing, advocacy, and multimedia storytelling collaborative that is based in San José, California and is home to the Albert Cobarrubias Justice Project, the founding hub of the participatory defense movement. A MacArthur "Genius" award-winner, the collaborative is driven by the belief that people are stronger together, that collective action can challenge systems and institutions that oppress, and that modeling a world that embodies liberatory values can create such change.

BELÉN LOWREY-KINBERG is Assistant Professor in the Department of Sociology and Criminal Justice at St. Francis College in New York City. Her research focuses on prosecutor decision-making, wrongful convictions, and the application of linguistics to issues in the criminal justice system.

AILI MALM is Professor in the School of Criminology, Criminal Justice, and Emergency Management at California State University, Long Beach. Dr. Malm's primary research interests involve the assessment and evaluation of policing strategies and intelligence.

MAUREEN MCGOUGH is the Chief of Staff at the Policing Project at the New York University School of Law, where she oversees national initiatives to reimagine public safety, establish basic minimum standards for policing agencies, and advance women in policing. Prior to joining the Policing Project, she served as a senior policy adviser at the US Department of Justice, where she focused on evidence-based practice and systems-level criminal justice reform.

JANET MOORE is Professor of Law at the University of Cincinnati. A former public defender, her research focuses on empowering low-income people to reduce the scope and harmful impacts of the carceral state. She is the co-convener of the Indigent Defense Research Association.

STEPHANIE MORSE is a doctoral student in the School of Criminology and Criminal Justice at Arizona State University. Her work focuses on correctional rehabilitation and promoting resilience and positive outcomes with correctional populations.

KELLY ORIANS directs the Decarceration and Community Reentry Clinic at the University of Virginia School of Law. Previously, she was co–executive director of The First 72+ in New Orleans, Louisiana.

KARISSA R. PELLETIER is a postdoctoral scholar in the University of Michigan's Consortium of Firearm Safety Among Children and Teens (FACTS). Her research focuses on homicide and firearm violence with a specific focus on children and teen victims of firearm homicide.

JESENIA M. PIZARRO is Associate Professor in the School of Criminology and Criminal Justice at Arizona State University. Her research focuses on the situational dynamics that result in violence, particularly homicide. Her recent work focuses on intimate partner and youth violence

TROY RHODES, served nearly 20 years in prison, over two different periods. During the second time, he helped launch a reentry program based within the prison. Upon release, he first joined The First 72+ as a resident. Today, he serves as the Housing Services Program Coordinator for the organization.

CHRISTINE S. SCOTT-HAYWARD is Associate Professor in the School of Criminology, Criminal Justice, and Emergency Management at California State University, Long Beach. Her research emphasizes the practical implications of criminal laws and policies and currently focuses on bail and sentencing. She is the author or coauthor of numerous articles, published in both law reviews and social science journals. She and Henry Fradella are coauthors of the book *Punishing Poverty: How Bail and Pretrial Detention Fuel Inequalities in the Criminal Justice System.*

CHRISTOPHER SHARP is of the Mohave tribe, descendant of the Frog Clan (Bouh'th), and a citizen of the Colorado River Indian Tribes. He is a clinical assistant professor and director of the Office of American Indian Projects within the School of Social Work at Arizona State University. He has extensive experience working for and with American Indian and Alaska Native tribes and tribal populations in Arizona and throughout the United States.

CASSIA SPOHN is a Regents Professor in the School of Criminology and Criminal Justice at Arizona State University. Her research interests include prosecutorial and judicial decision-making, the intersections of race, ethnicity, gender, crime and justice, and sexual assault case processing decisions.

KAYLEIGH A. STANEK is a doctoral student in the School of Criminology and Criminal Justice at Arizona State University. Her research focuses on criminal justice responses to victims, particularly among college students, American Indian women, and underserved groups.

CONNOR STEWART is a doctoral student in the School of Criminology and Criminal Justice at Arizona State University. His primary research interests are terrorism and criminal social networks.

LAUREN SUDEALL is Associate Professor and the founding Faculty Director of the Center for Access to Justice at the Georgia State University College of Law. Her research focuses on access to the courts, both civil and criminal, and how lower-income individuals engage with the legal system. Previously, she clerked for Justice John Paul Stevens on the

Supreme Court of the United States and worked at the Southern Center for Human Rights, where she represented indigent capital clients and litigated civil claims regarding the right to counsel.

MADISON SUTTON earned her MS in Criminology and Criminal Justice at Arizona State University. She currently works as Program Coordinator in the ASU Office of Applied Innovation, helping to improve access to economic and education opportunities through application of the latest developments in policy, technology, and design.

MEGAN VERHAGEN is a doctoral student in the School of Criminology and Criminal Justice at Arizona State University.

JASON WALKER is a doctoral student in the School of Criminology and Criminal Justice at Arizona State University.

MICHAEL D. WHITE is a Professor in the School of Criminology and Criminal Justice at Arizona State University and is Associate Director of ASU's Center for Violence Prevention and Community Safety. He also is the Co-Director of Training and Technical Assistance for the US Department of Justice's Body-Worn Camera Policy and Implementation Program. Dr. White's primary research interests involve the police, including use of force, technology, and misconduct.

KEVIN WRIGHT is Associate Professor in the School of Criminology and Criminal Justice at Arizona State University. He founded and directs the ASU Center for Correctional Solutions, with a mission to enhance the lives of people living and working in our correctional system through research, education, and community engagement.

APRIL M. ZEOLI is Associate Professor in the School of Criminal Justice at Michigan State University. Her research focuses on the impact of state firearm laws on homicide and the implementation of those policies at the local level.

ABOUT THE EDITORS

JON B. GOULD is Dean of the School of Social Ecology at the University of California, Irvine, where he is a professor in the Department of Criminology, Law, and Society and affiliated with the School of Law. Previously, he was Foundation Professor and Director of the School of Criminology and Criminal Justice at Arizona State University. A sociolegal scholar, Gould has written on such subjects as wrongful convictions, hate speech, sexual harassment, higher education, the death penalty, indigent defense, and police conformance with the Constitution. His research has been supported by such funders as the National Science Foundation, the National Institute of Justice, the Administrative Office of the US Courts, the Canadian government, and various private foundations.

Gould has served in leadership positions at the intersection of academe, government, and nonprofit advocacy. He was appointed as a Senior Policy Adviser in the US Department of Justice during the Obama administration, was director for the Law and Social Sciences Program at the National Science Foundation, and served as a US Supreme Court Fellow, among other positions.

PAMELA R. METZGER is Professor of Law and Director of the Deason Criminal Justice Reform Center at Southern Methodist University. She came to academe after many years of experience as an Assistant Federal Defender and as a private criminal defense lawyer. From 2001–2017, she was a professor at Tulane University School of Law and directed the Tulane Criminal Litigation Clinic, where she became a leading voice in reforming the criminal justice system in New Orleans and throughout Louisiana. Metzger captured a national spotlight for her round-the-clock work to help 8,000 indigent defendants left incarcerated without legal representation after Hurricane Katrina devastated New Orleans. The civil rights attorney portrayed in the 2010–2013 HBO series *Treme* was a composite character based on Metzger and two of her colleagues.

Professor Metzger's scholarship has appeared in such publications as the *Yale Law Review*, *Vanderbilt Law Review*, *Southern California Law Review*, and *Northwestern University Law Review* and has been widely cited by leading authorities and by the US Supreme Court. Her work combines theory and practice in seeking improvements in criminal justice. Most recently, she has explored how a data-driven systems approach to high-risk practices can improve the implementation of public defense services.

INDEX

Page numbers in *italics* indicate Tables.

criminal justice and, 248–49, 251;
state experiments in reform of, 103–8;
status quo release conditions and, 114;
unconditional bail and, 10, 115
Pre-Trial Fairness Act, Illinois, 107
Pretrial Justice Institute (PJI), 113, 114
pretrial risk assessments, 111–13
pretrial supervision, 114–15
primary markets, for firearms, 226
prisons: failures of, 124; health in, 154;
rural criminal justice and construction
of, 249–50. *See also* correctional success; incarceration rate; mass incarceration; recidivism
Pritzker, J. B., 107
probable cause standard, 55
problem-oriented release conditions, 114
procedural justice, BWCs improving,
35–36
professionals, criminal justice, 21
progressive activism, for DA races, 50–51
prosecutors: accelerate time to charge for,
55–58, 65–66; attending to needs of,
60–62; BWCs assisting, 34–35; case
screening of, 54; charging reforms for,
8–9, 52–65; charging units for, 54–55,
65; competitive elections and, 50–51;
criminal history minimized for, 58–60,
66; daily jail review of, 53; defense experience of, 63–64; diversity of, 62–66;
early case screening prioritization for,
53–55; efficient communication for, 57;
emotional trauma of, 62, 66; excessive
caseloads of, 61; focal concerns perspective and, 59; ideology of, 64–65;
participatory defense and discretion
of, 89; plea bargaining and, 52; policing mistakes and, 61; power of, 48;
race of, 62–63; reform areas for, 48–49,
65–67; rural criminal justice shortages
of, 246–47; sentencing reform and,
131, 133; Smart on Crime Initiative and,
49–50; training for, 60–61; trends of,

49–52; victim cooperation with, 57–58,
69n46
PSA (Public Safety Assessment), Arnold
Ventures, 104, 111–12
PTPs (permit-to-purchase laws), 228–30,
234
PTSD (post-traumatic stress disorder),
204–5
public defense, 9; cost of, 71; crisis of,
75–78; independence of, ABA and, 77;
judges appointing, 77; mistrust with,
77–78; reform challenges of, 76–77;
right to, 75, 90; to-do list for improving, 91. *See also* participatory defense
Public Interest, 151
Public Law 280, 1953, 212
public safety: bail reform and concerns
with, 102–3, 111; civil-criminal divide
on, 281; mass incarceration and, 2–3;
recidivism reduction and, 156–57
Public Safety Assessment (PSA), Arnold
Ventures, 104, 111–12
punishment, civil-criminal divide on,
280–81
P.Z. v. New Jersey, 236

Quattrone Center for the Fair Administration of Justice, 330–31, 335–36

race: APRAIs and discrimination by,
112–13; civil-criminal divide and, 274;
criminal history and, 59, 193n67;
criminal justice system and, 6; erroneous convictions and racial bias,
296–97; incarceration rate and, 125–
26; indeterminate sentencing and, 129;
of judges, 69n62; life and LWOP sentences and, 141; mandatory minimum
sentences and, 135; mass incarceration
and, 164–65; "missing white woman
syndrome" and, 199; pretrial detention and, 102, 105–6; of prosecutors,
62–63; reentry burdens by, 179;

criminal divide and power of, 282; EBP and, 18; firearm legislation in, 223; life and LWOP sentences in, 141; MMIWG legislation in, 209–10; post-trial system variations in, 298; sentencing reform in, 126–27; three-strikes laws in, 137; truth-in-sentencing laws in, 139. *See also specific states*
status quo release conditions, 114
Steiker, Carol, 280, 281, 286, 292n85
Stepping Up Initiative, 256
stolen firearms, 227
Student Health Outreach for Wellness clinic, Arizona, 161
Substance Abuse and Mental Health Services Administration, 163
suicide: firearm, 225–26, 229–34; in jail, sentinel event reviews on, 327–28
supervision, pretrial, 114–15
Supreme Court: civil-criminal divide and, 277–79; firearms regulation and, 224–25, 234–37, 239n67
SVORI (Serious and Violent Offender Reentry Initiative), 176
SWIWC (Southwest Indigenous Women's Coalition), 215
systemic reviews, 350

Takano, Mark, 191n37
Taylor, Breonna, 25, 30, 198
technology: for court access, 116–17; training and assistance with, 41, 334; video, for remote court proceedings, 246, 259; video, police shootings captured and spread through, 352. *See also* body-worn cameras
Televerde, 160
temporary guaranteed income (TGI), 12; community involvement in, 187; concept of, 183; conditions for, 187–88; costs and benefits of, 185–86; drug abuse and, 188; implementing, 186–88; income taxes and, 187; legal identification and,

187–88; milestones for, 196n133; reentry improved with, 184–85; research on, 185, 188; as restorative economics, 186
Tenth Amendment, 235, 236
Texas, 18, 36; rent-to-own furniture laws in, 282–83; truancy laws in, 282
Texas State University, 327
Texas v. EEOC, 192n46
TGI. *See* temporary guaranteed income
Thomas, Clarence, 236
Thompson, Ken, 51
three-strikes laws, 10; historical development of, 136–37; impact of, 137; race and, 137–38; reforming, 138; in states, 137; "wobbler" cases and, 138. *See also* sentencing reform
Tice, Derek, 302–7, 320n25
TimeStat, 254
Tiwahe Initiative, 211–12
Tomlin, Tryone, 99
Toronto Police Service, 34
"tough on crime," 3, 134
training and technical assistance (TTA), 41, 334
transparency: BWCs for, 28, 30; in EBP, 20–21
truancy laws, in Texas, 282
Trump, Donald, 50, 212; First Step Act and, 1, 18, 190n21
truth-in-sentencing laws, 10, 128; historical development of, 138–39; purpose of, 139; reforming, 140; research on, 139–40; in states, 139. *See also* sentencing reform
TTA (training and technical assistance), 41, 334
Tubbs, Michael D., 183
Turkmenistan, 17, 22n30

UBI (universal basic income), 183. *See also* temporary guaranteed income
UCR (Uniform Crime Report), 225, 253
unconditional bail, 10, 115